The Targum of Canticles

THE ARAMAIC BIBLE

• THE TARGUMS •

PROJECT DIRECTOR
Martin McNamara, M.S.C.

EDITORS
Kevin Cathcart • Michael Maher, M.S.C.
Martin McNamara, M.S.C.

EDITORIAL CONSULTANTS
Daniel J. Harrington, S.J. • Bernard Grossfeld

The Aramaic Bible

Volume 17A

The Targum of Canticles

Translated, with a Critical Introduction, Apparatus, and Notes

BY

Philip S. Alexander

A Michael Glazier Book

THE LITURGICAL PRESS
Collegeville, Minnesota

www.litpress.org

About the Translator

Philip Alexander is Professor of Post-Biblical Jewish Literature in the University of Manchester, England, and Co-Director of the University's Centre for Jewish Studies. He is a former President of the Oxford Centre for Hebrew and Jewish Studies.

A Michael Glazier Book published by The Liturgical Press.

Logo design by Florence Bern.

Library of Congress Cataloging-in-Publication Data

Bible. O.T. Song of Solomon. English. Alexander. 2002.
The Targum of Canticles / translated, with a critical introduction, textual notes, and commentary by Philip S. Alexander.
p. cm. — (The Aramaic Bible ; v. 17A)
"A Michael Glazier book."
Includes bibliographical references and indexes.
ISBN 0-8146-5453-3 (alk. paper)
1. Bible. O.T. Song of Solomon. Aramaic—Translations into English. 2. Bible. O.T. Song of Solomon. Aramaic—Criticism, Textual. I. Alexander, Philip S. II. Title. III. Bible. O.T. English. Aramaic Bible. 1987 ; v. 17A.

BS709.2 .B5 1987 vol. 17A
[BS1483]
223'.9042—dc21 2002069509

In Memory of my Father

Robert Alexander
17 November 1910—14 March 2001

Lover of the Bible
Connoisseur of its Translations

And the scent of your ointments than all manner of spices.
Rabbi Samuel bar Nahman said:
"Just as oil of itself is odorless,
but gives off all kinds of scents when you mix with it spices,
so when you expound a verse,
you find in it all manner of excellent meanings."
(Canticles Rabba 4.10 §1)

CONTENTS

EDITORS' FOREWORD

While any translation of the Scriptures may in Hebrew be called a Targum, the word is used especially for a translation of a book of the Hebrew Bible into Aramaic. Before the Christian era Aramaic had in good part replaced Hebrew in Palestine as the vernacular of the Jews. It continued as their vernacular for centuries later and remained in part as the language of the schools after Aramaic itself had been replaced as the vernacular.

Rabbinic Judaism has transmitted Targums of all books of the Hebrew canon, with the exception of Daniel and Ezra-Nehemiah, which are themselves partly in Aramaic. We also have a translation of the Samaritan Pentateuch into the dialect of Samaritan Aramaic. From the Qumran library we have sections of a Targum of Job and fragments of a Targum of Leviticus, chapter 16, facts which indicate that the Bible was being translated into Aramaic in pre-Christian times.

Translations of books of the Hebrew Bible into Aramaic for liturgical purposes must have begun before the Christian era, even though none of the Targums transmitted to us by rabbinic Judaism can be shown to be that old and though some of them are demonstrably compositions from later centuries.

In recent decades there has been increasing interest among scholars and a larger public in these Targums. A noticeable lacuna, however, has been the absence of a modern English translation of this body of writing. It is in marked contrast with most other bodies of Jewish literature, for which there are good modern English translations, for instance the Apocrypha and Pseudepigrapha of the Old Testament, Josephus, Philo, the Mishnah, the Babylonian Talmud and Midrashic literature, and more recently the Tosefta and Palestinian Talmud.

It is hoped that this present series will provide some remedy for this state of affairs.

The aim of the series is to translate all the traditionally-known Targums, that is those transmitted by rabbinic Judaism, into modern English idiom, while at the same time respecting the particular and peculiar nature of what these Aramaic translations were originally intended to be. A translator's task is never an easy one. It is rendered doubly difficult when the text to be rendered is itself a translation which is at times governed by an entire set of principles.

All the translations in this series have been specially commissioned. The translators have made use of what they reckon as the best printed editions of the Aramaic Targum in question or have themselves directly consulted the manuscripts.

The translation aims at giving a faithful rendering of the Aramaic. The introduction to each Targum contains the necessary background information on the particular work. In general, each Targum translation is accompanied by an apparatus and notes. The former is concerned mainly with such items as the variant readings in the Aramaic texts, the relation of the English translation to the original, etc. The notes give what explanations the translator thinks necessary or useful for this series.

Not all the Targums here translated are of the same kind. Targums were translated at different times, and most probably for varying purposes, and have more than one interpretative approach to the Hebrew Bible. This diversity between the Targums themselves is reflected in the translation and in the manner in which the accompanying explanatory material is presented. However, a basic unity of presentation has been maintained. Targumic deviations from the Hebrew text, whether by interpretation or paraphrase, are indicated by italics.

A point that needs to be stressed with regard to this translation of the Targums is that by reason of the state of current targumic research, to a certain extent it must be regarded as a provisional one. Despite the progress made, especially in recent decades, much work still remains to be done in the field of targumic study. Not all the Targums are as yet available in critical editions. And with regard to those that have been critically edited from known manuscripts, in the case of the Targums of some books the variants between the manuscripts themselves are such as to give rise to the question whether they have all descended from a single common original.

Details regarding these points will be found in the various introductions and critical notes.

It is recognized that a series such as this will have a broad readership. The Targums constitute a valuable source of information for students of Jewish literature, particularly those concerned with the history of interpretation, and also for students of the New Testament, especially for those interested in its relationship to its Jewish origins. The Targums also concern members of the general public who have an interest in the Jewish interpretation of the Scriptures or in the Jewish background to the New Testament. For them the Targums should be both interesting and enlightening.

By their translations, introductions, and critical notes, the contributors to this series have rendered an immense service to the progress of targumic studies. It is hoped that the series, provisional though it may be, will bring significantly nearer the day when the definitive translation of the Targums can be made.

Kevin Cathcart Martin McNamara, M.S.C. Michael Maher, M.S.C.

PREFACE

The present volume in the Aramaic Bible series differs from its predecessors in a number of ways, because the Targum it translates is somewhat different from the other Targumim. Targum Canticles is clearly the work of a single author who has imposed a consistent and closely argued reading on the biblical text. He treats the text holistically: he has an overall exegetical schema which, once established in his mind, determines how he understands the detail of any individual verse. This contrasts with the generally atomistic approach of the Targumim and Midrashim. These tend, at most, to have a thematic unity. That is to say, they create coherence simply by discovering again and again in the biblical text a limited repertory of theological themes. Targum Canticles, as we shall see, also has a strong thematic unity, but it has more than that. It has an overarching structure that results from the Targumist seeing the biblical text as an orderly narrative from beginning to end, and not just as a series of discrete *theologoumena*. The Targum on the face of it is wildly exuberant. On closer inspection, however, it turns out to be derived with painstaking care from the Hebrew text. The Targumist has, paradoxically, treated the original with remarkable respect and reverence. Every single word of the Hebrew is represented in his Targum, and usually in the right order. And within the parameters of his presuppositions and methods there is a powerful exegetical logic to his interpretation. Targum Canticles is a work of surprising exegetical integrity.

One of the main aims of this edition is to lay bare the Targumist's reasoning. To do this it proved necessary to present a translation of the Hebrew text of Canticles. All the Targumim should be read in dialogue with the biblical text and not as free-standing translations, but this is particularly important in the case of Targum Canticles. Underlying our Targumist's allegory is a *peshat* reading of Canticles: this I have attempted to express in my rendering of the biblical text, which, though it differs sometimes sharply from the modern English versions, nonetheless can claim to be a "literal" translation of the Hebrew. With the aid of this translation I then try to clarify in the *Notes* how our Targumist has derived his Targum. The *Notes* also serve two other ends. They seek to explain the meaning of the Targum itself (and not just its relationship to the Hebrew), and they explore the Targum's relationship to the Midrashic tradition, particularly on Canticles. Since our Targumist detects in Canticles a hidden account of the history of Israel from the Exodus from Egypt to the Messianic Age he embraces, in effect, almost the whole of Aggadah. He is a formidable scholar, with a comprehensive knowledge of the Aggadah: his Targum is, in a sense, an Aggadic encyclopedia. Yet he is not a servile compiler: he cleverly molds the existing traditions to suit his own exegetical ends. The *Notes* seek to show how he uses tradition. At the same time they exploit the tradition to throw light on the Targum's darker places, since it is only in the context of the tradition that the Targum's meaning can be fully understood.

I have tended to quote the Midrashic parallels at length for two reasons. The first is practical. As Jacob Neusner is constantly reminding us, the study of Rabbinic literature is hampered by the fact that many classic texts do not have a satisfactory reference system. Using the standard references often directs the reader to several closely printed folios of Hebrew, and he or she, having painstakingly plowed through these, can still be left bemused as to what exactly the cross-reference is supposed to be. The problem is solved by quoting, wherever feasible, the precise words that constitute the parallel. But there is a further advantage: the actual wording of the parallel usually illuminates the Targum more brightly than any summary could do. These may well be the very words that our Targumist knew, and that he expected his readers to know. By juxtaposing them with his text we can often see what he meant, and how he has nuanced and finessed the tradition. Intertextuality plays a major role in Targum Canticles, but this can only be explored in the words of the tradition itself. There is no substitute for illuminating tradition by tradition.

The *Apparatus* serves two purposes. It gives a selection of variant readings from the manuscripts; basically any variant that would show up in translation has been recorded. And it indicates how I have solved the linguistic problems of the Aramaic. These are numerous. Though learned, our Targumist does not seem totally at home in Aramaic, and sometimes he does not express himself with complete clarity. The format of the present series does not lend itself to discussing these problems at length but I have tried to say enough for colleagues expert in these matters to see how I have resolved the linguistic and textual *cruces*. I hope to return to the text and language of Targum Canticles some time in the future.

The *Introduction* seeks to set Targum Canticles in its historical context, but once again the format of the series does not permit the expansiveness that may be required. Targum Canticles belongs to the apocalyptic revival in Palestinian Judaism in the seventh and eighth centuries of the current era. This early Gaonic era in Palestine is not well understood, despite the valiant labors of Jacob Mann, Moshe Gil, and others. The literature produced then needs to be isolated, studied in its own right (not simply as an appendix to the classic Talmudic period texts), and placed in a proper historical setting. It illuminates a troubled and turbulent world in transition from Byzantine to Islamic rule. I hope to return also to this subject in due course. Meanwhile I would offer this study of Targum Canticles as a window into that little-known world.

I have worked on this translation and commentary on and off over a long period of time. Many friends and colleagues helped me along the way. Dr. Carlos Alonso Fontela kindly supplied me with a copy of his edition largely of the western manuscripts of Targum Canticles. Professor M. J. Mulder donated a copy of his Dutch translation of the Targum—one of the most substantial contributions to the study of our Text in recent years. My student Judah Abel loaned me a copy of *Sefer Na'awah Qodesh,* which provides a good traditional commentary on the Targum. Shaul Yitzhaqi loaned me a fine copy of the Livorno 1926 edition of the Targum. Michael Klein answered with his usual kindness and erudition queries about the Cambridge Genizah fragments of the Targum. Raphael Loewe, who shares my passion for Targum Canticles, dispensed over the years his deep wisdom on this text. Colleagues in various countries and at various conferences offered constructive criticisms, too numerous to mention, on papers I presented on the Targum. Successive groups of M.A.

students at Manchester, with whom I read this text, constantly forced me to see it afresh. However, above all thanks are due to Father Martin McNamara, the editor of this series, who displayed the patience of a saint as this volume was delayed again and again. I have finally taken to heart his advice not to let the best become the enemy of the good, have drawn a line under the work and now submit it, with all its imperfections, to the judgment of the reader.

Philip S. Alexander
Centre for Jewish Studies
University of Manchester

ABBREVIATIONS

Arndt and Gingrich	W. F. Arndt and F. W. Gingrich, *A Greek-English Lexicon of the New Testament and Other Early Christian Literature* (Chicago: University of Chicago Press, 1957)
ARN	ʾAbot de Rabbi Natan
BDB	Francis Brown, S. R. Driver, and Charles A. Briggs, *A Hebrew and English Lexicon of the Old Testament* (Oxford: Clarendon Press, 1966)
Brockelmann	Carl Brockelmann, *Lexicon Syriacum* (2nd ed. Halle: Niemeyer, 1928)
CG	Cairo Genizah fragments of the Palestinian Targum
Charlesworth, *OTP*	James H. Charlesworth, ed., *The Old Testament Pseudepigrapha.* 2 vols. (New York and London: Doubleday, 1983)
CRINT	Compendia Rerum Iudaicarum ad Novum Testamentum
DDD	Karel van der Toorn, Bob Becking, and Pieter W. van der Horst, eds., *Dictionary of Deities and Demons in the Bible* (Leiden: Brill, 1995)
Eben-Shmuel, *MG*	Yehuda Eben-Shmuel, *Midreshei Geʾullah* (2nd ed. Jerusalem: Mosad Bialik, 1968)
EI^2	*Encyclopedia of Islam*, new edition. 9 vols. (Leiden: Brill, 1960–continuing)
Eisenstein, *OM*	J. D. Eisenstein, *Ozar Midrashim.* 2 vols. (New York: J. D. Eisenstein, 1915)
EJ	*Encyclopaedia Judaica.* 16 vols. (Jerusalem: Keter, 1972)
FT	Fragmentary Targum
Gaster, *ST*	Moses Gaster, *Studies and Texts.* 3 vols. (London: Maggs Bros., 1925–28)

Ginzberg, *Legends*	Louis Ginzberg, *The Legends of the Jews*. 7 vols. (Philadelphia: Jewish Publication Society, 1909–38)
HTR	*Harvard Theological Review*
HUCA	*Hebrew Union College Annual*
Jast.	Marcus Jastrow, *A Dictionary of the Targumim, the Talmud Babli and Yerushalmi, and the Midrashic Literature* (London: Luzac, 1903; repr. New York: Pardes, 2 vols., 1950)
JBL	*Journal of Biblical Literature*
JE	*Jewish Encyclopedia*. 12 vols. (New York and London: Funk and Wagnalls, 1901–06)
Jellinek, *BHM*	Adolf Jellinek, *Bet ha-Midrasch*. 6 vols. (Leipzig: F. Nies, 1878; 3rd ed. repr. Jerusalem: Wahrmann Books, 1967)
JJS	*Journal of Jewish Studies*
Jon.	Targum Jonathan to the Prophets
JPSV	The Jewish Publication Society Version = *The Holy Scriptures According to the Masoretic Text: A New Translation* (Philadelphia: Jewish Publication Society, 1955)
JQR	*Jewish Quarterly Review*
JSJ	*Journal for the Study of Judaism*
JSNT	*Journal for the Study of the New Testament*
JSP	*Journal for the Study of the Pseudepigrapha*
JTS	*Journal of Theological Studies*
KB	Ludwig Koehler and Walter Baumgartner, *The Hebrew and Aramaic Lexicon of the Old Testament*, translated and edited by M. E. J. Richardson. 5 vols. (Leiden: Brill, 1994–2000)
LAB	*Liber Antiquitatum Biblicarum*
Lag.	Paul de Lagarde, *Hagiographa Chaldaice* (Leipzig: Teubner, 1873; repr. Osnabrück: O. Zeller, 1967)
Levey, *Messiah*	Samson H. Levey, *The Messiah: An Aramaic Interpretation* (Cincinnati, New York, Los Angeles, and Jerusalem: Hebrew Union College/Jewish Institute of Religion, 1974)
LSJ	Henry G. Liddell and Robert Scott, *A Greek-English Lexicon*. 9th ed. revised by H. S. Jones (Oxford: Clarendon Press, 1961)
LXX	The Septuagint
Melamed	Raphael Hai Melamed, *The Targum to Canticles according to six Yemen MSS, compared with the "Textus Receptus" Ed. de Lagarde* (Philadelphia: Dropsie College, 1921)

MH	Mishnaic Hebrew
Miq.Ged.	*Miqraʾot Gedolot*
MT	Masoretic Text
Murphy	Roland E. Murphy, *The Song of Songs*. Hermeneia (Minneapolis: Fortress, 1990)
Neof.	Codex Neofiti 1
NRSV	New Revised Standard Version (1989) = *The Holy Bible containing the Old and New Testaments with the Apocryphal/Deuterocanonical Books* (New York and Oxford: Oxford University Press, 1989)
Onq.	Targum Onqelos
Payne Smith	Robert Payne Smith, *Thesaurus Syriacus* (Oxford: Clarendon Press, 1879–1901)
Pesiq. Rab.	Pesiqta Rabbati
Pesiq. Rab. Kah.	Pesiqta de Rab Kahana
Pirqei de R. El.	Pirqei de Rabbi Eliʿezer
Pope	Marvin H. Pope, *The Song of Songs*. AB 7C (Garden City, N. Y.: Doubleday, 1977)
Ps-J	Targum Pseudo-Jonathan
REJ	*Revue des Études Juives*
Schäfer, *Synopse*	Peter Schäfer, *Synopse zur Hekhalot Literatur* (Tübingen: Mohr, 1981)
Silber	Ephraim Silber, *Sedeh Jerusalem: Ein Kommentar zu Targum Chamesh Megiloth* (Chernovtsy: E. Haylpern, 1888)
Singer, *ADPB*	Simeon Singer, *The Authorized Daily Prayer Book*, Enlarged Centenary Edition (London: Singer's Prayer Book Publication Committee, 1992)
Sokoloff	Michael Sokoloff, *A Dictionary of Jewish-Palestinian Aramaic* (Ramat-Gan, Israel: Bar Ilan University Press, 1992)
Strack-Billerbeck	Hermann L. Strack and Paul Billerbeck, *Kommentar zum Neuen Testament aus Talmud und Midrasch*. vols 1–4 (Munich: C. H. Beck, 1926–28); vols 5–6, ed. Joachim Jeremias and Kurt Adolph (Munich: C. H. Beck, 1956–61)
TDNT	Gerhard Kittel and Gerhard Friedrich, eds., *Theological Dictionary of the New Testament*, translated and edited by Geoffrey W. Bromiley. 10 vols. (Grand Rapids: Eerdmans, 1964)
Tg.	Targum or Targumist

Tg. Tos.	Targumic Tosefta
Wertheimer, *BM*	Solomon A. Wertheimer, *Batei Midrashot*. 2 vols. (new ed. by Avraham Y. Wertheimer; Jerusalem: Mosad ha-Rav Kuk, 1951–54)
West.	The Western Recension of Targum Canticles = Mss A B C D E F G H I
Yem.	The Yemenite Recension of Targum Canticles = Mss J K L M N O
ZNW	*Zeitschrift für die neutestamentliche Wissenschaft*

INTRODUCTION

1. THE TEXT OF TARGUM CANTICLES

1.1. Manuscripts of Targum Canticles

The translation of Targum Canticles (= Tg. Cant.) offered below is based on the Paris ms., Bibliothèque Nationale, Héb. 110. This text has been compared with other manuscripts and with printed editions, and emended as indicated in the *Apparatus*. The *Apparatus*, however, does not list all the variants, but only those of use in establishing a more correct text, or in illuminating the textual transmission. The following manuscripts are cited, the readings being taken for the most part from the collations of Carlos Alonso Fontela, *El Targum de los Cantares* (1987: see *Intro.* 1.2(b)), and of Raphael Hai Melamed, *The Targum to Canticles according to Six Yemen MSS* (1920–21: see *Intro.* 1.2(b)):

A Paris, Bibliothèque Nationale, Héb. 110 (= Fontela 1: transcription).
B Vatican, Biblioteca Vaticana, Urb. Ebr. 1 (= Fontela 7). Facsimile: Levine; transcription: Díez Merino (*Intro.* 1.2(b)).
C Madrid, Biblioteca de la Universidad Complutense, 116-Z-40 (= Fontela 2). Transcription: Díez Merino (*Intro.* 1.2(b)).
D Nuremberg, Stadtbibliothek, Solger 1-7, 2° (= Fontela 3). Finishes at 8:6.
E New York, JTSA, L478 (= Fontela 4). Incomplete: begins at 1:13.
F Salamanca, Biblioteca Universitaria, M-2 (= Fontela 5).
G Parma, Biblioteca Palatina, 3218 (= Fontela 10).
H Parma, Biblioteca Palatina, 3231 (= Fontela 8).
I Copenhagen, Kongelige Bibliotek, Cod. Hebr. 11 (= Fontela 9).
J London, British Library, Or. 1302 (= Melamed A: transcription; Fontela 12).
K London, British Library, Or. 1476 (= Melamed F).
L London, British Library, Or. 2375 (= Melamed E; Fontela 11). Transcription: Sperber (*Intro.* 1.2(b)).
M Oxford, Bodleian, Opp. Add. 2333 (= Melamed B).
N New York, JTSA, L477 (= Melamed C). Missing 7:9-12 and 8:9-14.
O New York, JTSA, L476 (= Melamed D). 1:1–2:2; 7:9–8:2.

N.B.: H^1, H^2, etc. denote respectively the first and second writing in a ms., whether in the same or different hands. H^2 would normally be in the margin, but may sometimes be between the lines.

Tg. Cant. is one of the most popular texts in the history of Jewish religious literature and it survives in numerous manuscripts, printed editions (*Intro.* 1.2) and translations (*Intro.* 6.6) from northern Europe, Spain, Italy, North Africa, Egypt, the Levant, Persia, and the

Yemen. The following is a partial list of manuscripts not included in the editions of Fontela and Melamed:

Paris, Bibliothèque Nationale, Héb. 17
Rome, Biblioteca Angelica, N.72
Florence, Biblioteca Medicea Laurenziana, Plut. III.1
Milan, Biblioteca Ambrosiana, B. 35 inf.
Parma, Biblioteca Palatina, 2867, 3077, 3189, 3235
Turin, Biblioteca Nationale, A.II.8 [badly damaged in 1904]
Dresden, Sächsische Landesbibliothek, Dresd.A.46 [destroyed 1945]
Wrocław, Biblioteka Uniwersytecka, M 1106 [*olim* Stadtbibliothek No. 1]
London, British Library, Or. 9906, 9907 [*olim* Gaster 247, 517]; Harley 5709
Cambridge, University Library, T-S B 11.81 (Cant 2:7-16; 4:12–5:8) and T-S NS 312.3 (Cant 5:8–6:2). Probably from the same ms.[1]
Jerusalem, Ben Zvi Institute, Hebrew University, 1120, 1125, 1129, 1135, 1188, 1172, 3101, 3210
Jerusalem, Jewish National and University Library, Hebr. 8° 1066, 2413, 2636, 4025, 5215, 5344
New York, JTSA, L431, L472, L473, L474, L475
Cincinnati, Hebrew Union College Library, Ms. Acc. #66 (*Intro.* 1.2(b), no. 8)
Chicago, Spertus College of Judaica, Golb, *Catalogue*, Nos. A4, A7, A16, A17, A18, A19, A27, A28, A29[2]

1.2. Printed Editions

a. The *Textus Receptus*

The *editio princeps* of Tg. Cant., prepared by Felix Pratensis, was published by the printer Daniel Bomberg in his first Rabbinic Bible (Venice 1517 = Bomberg I). This text was reprinted with little change in Bomberg's second Rabbinic Bible (Venice 1525), edited by Jacob ben Ḥayyim (= Bomberg II). The close relationship between a number of Felix Pratensis' Targum texts and ms. Nuremberg (siglum D above) has been noted in a number of studies, and it is not impossible that this was the only manuscript that he used.[3] For Tg. Cant., Bomberg I and II give a good text of the Western type (*Intro.* 1.3).

The Complutensian Polyglot (Alcalá de Henares, 1514–17) does not provide Targumim for either the Prophets or the Writings. Its successor, the Biblia Regia (Antwerp, 1568–73), prepared for the press by Benito Arias Montano, rectified this omission. From the "Variae Lectiones et Annotationculae" to the Targumim published in volume VIII it emerges that the Bib-

[1] See Michael L. Klein, *Targumic Manuscripts in the Cambridge Genizah Collections* (Cambridge: Cambridge University Press, 1992) 23 (no. 286); 68 (no. 851). In a personal letter (June 29, 1992) Klein expressed the view that these fragments all "seem to be from the same manuscript" and to contain "consecutive text joined at Songs 5:8."

[2] See further Fontela, *El Targum al Cantar* 97–102; Albert van der Heide, *The Yemenite Tradition of the Targum of Lamentations* (Leiden: Brill, 1981) 16 (n. 41); David M. Stec, *The Text of the Targum of Job: An Introduction and Critical Edition* (Leiden: Brill, 1994) 53–66.

[3] Michael L. Klein, *The Fragment-Targums of the Pentateuch according to their Extant Sources* I (Rome: Biblical Institute Press, 1980) 26; Bernard Grossfeld, *The Two Targums of Esther* (Collegeville: The Liturgical Press, 1991) 6; Derek R. G. Beattie, "The Textual Tradition of Targum Ruth," in Derek R. G. Beattie and Martin J. McNamara, eds., *The Aramaic Bible: Targums in their Historical Context* (Sheffield: Sheffield Academic Press, 1994) 340–48.

lia Regia took its Targum to Canticles, which appears in volume III, from either Bomberg I or Bomberg II. However, the Bomberg text appears to have been collated with ms. Madrid, Biblioteca de la Universidad Complutense, 116-Z-40 (siglum C above).[4] This ms., and ms. Salamanca, Biblioteca Universitaria, M-2 (siglum F above), which is a copy of it, contain editions of the Targumim to the Writings, with Latin translations, prepared by Alfonso de Zamora for use in the Complutensian Polyglot but not printed in that work. Their textual basis is uncertain, but like the Bomberg Bibles they offer good Western texts of our Targum. Arias Montano edited his text quite heavily, correcting his textual authorities where he thought they were defective and excising passages he regarded as superfluous (see the list in volume VIII of "Loca ex chaldaica paraphrasi reiecta, quae supervacanea esse videbantur"). The Biblia Regia text of Tg. Cant. was reprinted without change in the Paris Polyglot (1629–45).

The influential *Biblia Rabbinica* of Johannes Buxtorf (Basle, 1618–19) appears to be a revision of Bomberg II, but it also contains a considerable number of changes. Some of these may be derived from the Biblia Regia, but the majority are editorial in character and do not point to any fresh collation of mss.[5] Buxtorf's text was reprinted by Brian Walton in the London Polyglot (1654–57). Like Buxtorf's *Biblia Rabbinica*, the traditional printed editions of the *Miqra'ot Gedolot* (e.g., Warsaw) are also ultimately derived from Bomberg, though probably in most cases at several removes. Bomberg also seems to lie behind the separate editions of Tg. Cant., which we find in works such as the *Sefer Na'awah Qodesh* (Livorno, 1875), and the *Sefer Shir ha-Shirim ʿim sharḥ ʿarabi* (Livorno, 1926).

Though there are numerous differences between these various printed texts of Tg. Cant., they are for the most part minor. What is noteworthy is the broad uniformity of the tradition: all these printed versions are basically divergent forms of the Western recension. Two points stand out: first, Bomberg I, the *editio princeps,* historically speaking was the single most important printed text. It influenced to greater or lesser degree Bomberg II, the *Biblia Regia,* Buxtorf, the London Polyglot and the standard Yeshibah *Miqra'ot Gedolot*. Its text prevailed for nearly five hundred years. It constitutes the *textus receptus* of our Targum. Second, it is astonishing how slender appears to be the ms. evidence behind this plethora of printed editions. It amounts possibly to no more than two manuscripts: ms. Nuremberg (siglum D), used by Felix Pratensis in Bomberg I, and ms. Madrid (siglum C), partially used by Arias Montano in the *Biblia Regia*. Any readings that cannot be traced to one or other of these mss. should probably be attributed to conjectural emendation by the various editors.

b. Modern Editions

The modern phase of editing Tg. Cant. is usually reckoned to begin with Paul de Lagarde's *Hagiographa Chaldaice* (Leipzig: Teubner, 1873) (= Lag. in the *Apparatus*). De Lagarde, however, did not go back to the mss. in Tg. Cant., but presented a modest revision of the *textus receptus.* As he himself tells us on p. XI of his introduction, he reprinted the text of Bomberg I (though, wisely, minus its vowels), with certain changes he lists on pp.

[4] Stec, *Targum of Job* 7–16 gives a detailed analysis of the Targum to Job in the *Biblia Regia*. He demonstrates conclusively how Arias Montano fused the Bomberg text with the Madrid manuscript. Indeed, from his analysis it would be hard to conclude which of these two was Arias Montano's base text. Stec seems inclined to think that it was actually the Madrid manuscript. The comment in the "Variae Lectiones et Annotationculae" in vol. VIII would seem, however, to decide the matter in the case of Tg. Cant. in favor of Bomberg.

[5] See Stec, *Targum of Job* 16–39 for a detailed analysis of Buxtorf's text of Targum Job.

XIV–XV. These changes seem to have been derived partly from other early printed texts (Bomberg II, the Antwerp Polyglot, and Buxtorf), and partly from conjectural emendation by de Lagarde himself. No fresh collation of mss. appears to have been involved, at least for Tg. Cant. It is remarkable, therefore, that de Lagarde's text, though its manuscript basis is totally obscure, remains, with the possible exception of Jerusalmi's edition (see no. 8 below), perhaps the best available eclectic text of our Targum.

It was not until 1921–22 that R. H. Melamed published the first modern edition of Tg. Cant. based on a fresh examination of mss.: *The Targum to Canticles according to six Yemen MSS, compared with the "Textus Receptus" (Ed. de Lagarde)* (Philadelphia: Dropsie College, 1921, reprinted from *JQR* n.s. 10 [1919–20] 377–410; 11 [1920–21] 1–20; 12 [1921–22] 57–117). The six Yemenite mss. selected by Melamed are sigla J–O above. He reproduced London, British Library, Or 1302 (siglum J), "the clearest and most accurate of the MSS," as a base text, and recorded the variants from the other mss. in the apparatus. The work is carefully done and marked in its day a real advance in the editing of the Targumim, but it gives only the Yemenite tradition, and as Melamed himself concedes, the Western recension's consonantal text is superior in most respects to that of the Yemenite mss. (p. 391). Consequently his edition, though pioneering in many ways, is of limited use for our present purposes, which are primarily concerned with the Targum's aggadic content.

In his doctorate submitted in 1986 to the Facultad de Filologia of the Universidad Complutense de Madrid, Carlos Alonso Fontela complemented Melamed's work with an edition of Tg. Cant. based mainly on mss. containing the Western recension: *El Targum al Cantar de los Cantares (Edición Crítica)*. Colección Tesis Doctorales, No. 92/87 (Madrid: Editorial de la Universidad Complutense de Madrid, 1987). He presents ms. Paris, Bibliothèque Nationale, Héb. 110 (siglum A above) as his base text, and gives the variants from the other manuscripts in the apparatus criticus (sigla B–J, L).

Other noteworthy modern texts of Tg. Cant. are as follows:

(1) Yosef Qafiḥ, *Ḥamesh Megillot . . . ʿim peirushim ʿattiqim* (Jerusalem, 1962): A text of Tg. Cant. in the Yemenite tradition.[6]

(2) Alexander Sperber, *The Bible in Aramaic*. Vol. 4A, *The Hagiographa* (Leiden: Brill, 1968) 127–41: A transcription of ms. London, British Library, Or 2375 (= siglum L above). Sperber inserts into this base ms. material taken from Bomberg II, which is distinguished by being printed without vowels. The result is a highly unsatisfactory hybrid text.

(3) S. Nagar, *Ḥamesh Megillot . . . Miqra, Targum, Tafsir ʿim peirushim* (n.p., 1970): A Yemenite text of Tg. Cant. different from that in Qafiḥ (no. 1 above).

(4) Ezra Zion Melamed, *Shir ha-Shirim: Targum ʾArami, Targum ʿIbri, Tafsir bi-leshon Yehudei Paras* (Jerusalem, 1971). The Judeo-Persian translation of Tg. Cant. is taken from a Persian ms. (completed in 1907) in the possession of the family of Rabbi Shelomoh ben David Katz, supplemented from another ms., the date and provenance of which are not given. The underlying text-type of the Judeo-Persian Tafsir is Western, as is the text of the Aramaic Targum that Melamed has added.

(5) Etan Levine, *The Targum to the Five Megillot: Ruth, Ecclesiastes, Canticles, Lamentations, Esther: Codex Urbinati 1* (Jerusalem: Makor, 1977) 71–74. A facsimile of ms. Vatican, Biblioteca Vaticana, Urb. Ebr. 1 (siglum B above).

[6] On the editions of Qafiḥ and Nagar see van der Heide, *Targum of Lamentations* 17–18.

(6) Luis Díez Merino, "El Targum al Cantar de los Cantares (Tradición Sefardi de Alfonso de Zamora)," *Estudios Biblicos* 38 (1979–80) 295–357. A transcription of ms. Madrid, Biblioteca de la Universidad Complutense, 116-Z-40 (= siglum C above). Díez Merino helpfully includes the Latin translation of the Tg. contained in this ms.

(7) Luis Díez Merino, "El Targum al Cantar de los Cantares (Texto arameo del Códice Urbinati 1 y su traducción)," *Anuario de Filología*, Facultad de Filología, Universidad de Barcelona (1981) 237–84. A transcription of ms. Vatican, Biblioteca Vaticana, Urb. Ebr. 1 (= siglum B above).

(8) Isaac Jerusalmi, *The Song of Songs in the Targumic Tradition: Vocalized Aramaic Text with Facing English Translation and La*<u>*d*</u>*ino Versions* (Cincinnati: La<u>d</u>ino Books, 1993). Jerusalmi offers several La<u>d</u>ino versions of Tg. Cant., including a new one of his own, together with the Aramaic text of the Targum. He presents a composite Aramaic text, with Tiberian *niqqud,* based on Melamed, Sperber, the Levine facsimile of Codex Urbinas 1, and the Yemenite ms. Acc. #66 in Hebrew Union College Library, Cincinnati. The resultant text has much to commend it.

Though there is no shortage of texts of Tg. Cant., we still lack a comprehensive edition that adequately represents both the Western and the Yemenite traditions and that tries to recover by text-critical and philological means the oldest form of the Targum that lies behind these traditions. By combining the work of Melamed (for the Yemenite recension), Fontela (for the Western recension), and de Lagarde or Jerusalmi (for a composite text) we can get some idea of how such an edition might look, but it has still to be created and its resultant text justified.[7]

1.3. The Textual History of Tg. Cant.

The numerous manuscripts and early printed editions of Tg. Cant. fall into two large groups: (1) the Western, comprising manuscripts mainly written in Spain, Northern Europe, Italy, and North Africa, and the early printed editions based on them (especially Bomberg I and the *Biblia Regia*), and (2) the Yemenite, comprising manuscripts of Yemenite provenance.

The existence of these two groups, which probably go back in each case to a single exemplar, is graphically illustrated at 5:14. There we can clearly distinguish two forms of the text—one Western (= West.) and the other Yemenite (= Yem.)—that offer two different lists of gems and enumerate the tribes of Israel in different ways. It is impossible to derive either of these forms of the text transcriptionally from the other or from a common archetype. They reflect conscious editorial intervention: someone deliberately rearranged the order of the tribal names and, probably at the same time, changed the names of the precious stones. The variants are recensional.

In this particular case it is hard to say which of the two recensions is older (see *Apparatus* to 5:14 and Appendix B). However, elsewhere in this Targum when the West. and Yem. witnesses diverge there can be little dispute that West. has usually the better text. This can be readily discovered by inspecting the *Apparatus* below and noting the cases where the

[7] See further Philip S. Alexander, "Textual Criticism and Rabbinic Literature: The Case of the Targum of the Song of Songs," in Philip S. Alexander and Alexander Samely, eds., *Artefact and Text: The Recreation of Jewish Literature in Medieval Hebrew Manuscripts* (= *Bulletin of the John Rylands University Library of Manchester* 75.3 [1993]) 159–74.

Yem. mss. (J K L M N O), in whole or in part, agree against West. in offering an inferior reading.[8] A typical case is found at 4:9:

HEBREW TEXT:
You have transfixed My heart, My Sister, My Bride;
You have transfixed My heart with one of your eyes,
With one bead of your necklace.

TG. CANT.: WESTERN TRADITION (REPRESENTED BY MS. A)
Fixed upon the tablet of My heart is love for you, O My Sister, Assembly of Israel, who is compared to a chaste bride. Fixed upon the tablet of My heart is as much affection for the least among you, if he is righteous, as for one of the leaders of the Sanhedrin, or for one of the kings of the House of Judah, on whose neck is placed the wreath of kingship.

TG. CANT.: YEMENITE TRADITION (REPRESENTED BY MS. J):
Fixed upon the tablet of my heart is love for the least of your leaders, if he is as one of the leaders of the Sanhedrin, and as one of the bride who is chaste. Fixed upon the kings of the House of Judah on whose [sg.!] neck is placed the wreath of kingship.

West. is totally coherent and displays careful analysis by the Targumist of all the elements of the original text in their proper sequence. Yem., however, is confused: we have attempted to render it above, but it is virtually untranslatable. Comparing the two texts, Melamed concluded: "The text of L[agarde = West.] . . . seems better preserved, although it is not beyond possibility that the shorter text of Y[emen] may have the original reading."[9] This is too cautious by half. It is surely obvious that West. is original and that the Yem. has arisen through a series of transcriptional accidents. The corruption probably began with parablepsis: further back in the Yemenite tradition a copyist's eye jumped from the first *qebiaʿ ʿal luaḥ libbi* ("fixed upon the tablet of my heart") to the second, resulting in the omission of the whole of the first sentence of the Targum. The copyist himself, or someone else, noted the omission and added some of the missing words in the margin. These were subsequently incorporated into the text at the wrong place, thus giving rise to our present garbled text. Ms. J contains a further simple corruption: *dbynyk* ("the least *among you*") as in Ms. A has been misread, by a common graphical confusion, as *rbnyk* ("the least of *your leaders*"). All the Yemenite mss. agree in error with J and all the Western mss. agree essentially with A.[10]

This is a particularly striking example of the superiority of West. over Yem., but it is by no means an isolated case. Time and again in Tg. Cant. West. is demonstrably better than Yem. It is closer to the original. It generally represents an earlier text-form than Yem., closer to the source from which the current Yem. text has evolved.

It should be carefully noted that the process by which the Yemenite text evolved at 4:9 is essentially mechanical, transcriptional, and accidental. This is the norm: the vast majority of the differences between the Western and Yemenite traditions are due to miscopying. There are some examples of recensional differences, but they are generally of a superficial,

[8] See Melamed's comprehensive comparison of the two recensions in *Targum to Canticles* 393–410; further Fontela, *El Targum al Cantar de los Cantares* 134–51. Parablepsis is surprisingly common in the Yem. mss.

[9] *Targum to Canticles* 394.

[10] See further *Apparatus* to 4:9. In the translation below I have not assumed the superiority of West.; rather, readings have been chosen on the grounds of intrinsic probability, but they consistently correlate with the Western text. There are some signs of secondary expansion in the Western tradition. For example, its penchant for more flowery, pious titles (Melamed, *Targum to Canticles* 398) is suspect.

stylistic nature and do not represent any serious attempt to rework the text. The one case of substantial recensional variation (at 5:14) is the exception that proves the rule. From this an important conclusion follows: the text of Tg. Cant. is, in fact, very stable: it is not an evolving tradition. Copyists, somewhat uncharacteristically for this genre of literature, were content to transcribe what was in front of them, and to resist the urge to improve and rework. The reason for this is not hard to find. Tg. Cant. offers a remarkably coherent, tightly-argued reading of Canticles (see *Intro. 3*). It applies its schema so systematically and skillfully that it left little room for "improvement." The indications are that we are dealing with a single-authored work that has been transmitted more or less unrevised in the mss.[11]

1.4. Tentative *Stemma Codicum*[12]

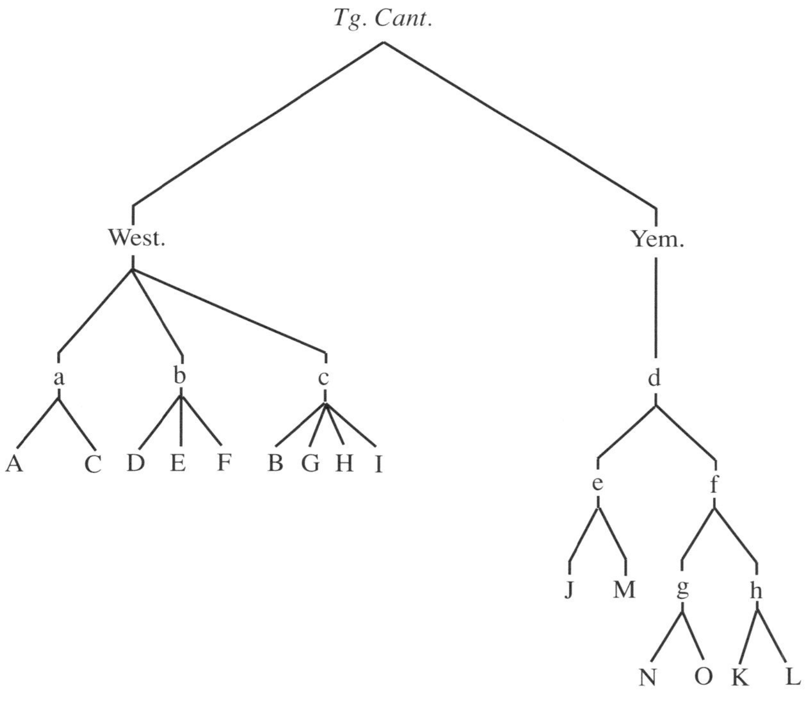

[11] In tracing the further history of the textual transmission of Tg. Cant. it would be interesting to see if any "non-aligned" mss. could be identified. The Cambridge Genizah fragments probably deserve a closer look.

[12] Cf. Melamed, *Targum to Canticles* 392; Fontela, *El Targum al Cantar de los Cantares* 150.

2. THE LANGUAGE OF TARGUM CANTICLES

2.1. The Origins of Tg. Cant.'s Dialect

A detailed analysis of the Aramaic of Tg. Cant. cannot be undertaken in the present context, and anything said here about the nature and origins of its dialect must be treated as very provisional. Three general points should be borne in mind.

First, the dialectal features of Tg. Cant. vary from manuscript to manuscript. It is difficult to distinguish the dialectal variants introduced by later copyists from the dialect of the original Targum.

Second, there is still no consensus about the evolution of the Jewish Aramaic dialects in late antiquity. For the purposes of the present discussion we may delineate three broad dialectal groups:[1]

(1) The western Aramaic dialect of the Palestinian Talmud and the Palestinian Targumim;

(2) The eastern Aramaic dialect of the Babylonian Talmud and the Jewish Aramaic incantation bowls;[2]

(3) The Aramaic dialect of the Onqelos and Jonathan Targumim.

Of these the status and origin of the Onq.-Jon. dialect are the most contentious. There is general agreement that Onq. and Jon. are basically in old Imperial Aramaic, a literary form of Aramaic more or less standardized for administrative purposes in the Persian empire. In other words, Onq.-Jon.'s Aramaic fundamentally predates the split in Jewish Aramaic literature into eastern and western dialect texts, a split first documented at a literary level post-200 C.E. Onq. and Jon., however, are not in "pure" Imperial Aramaic: they show modifications, and the question is whether these modifications suggest a western or an eastern provenance for the texts. In the extant manuscripts of both Targums both eastern and western dialectal features are found. According to one view the Onq.-Jon. dialect originated in Palestine, its eastern features being due to secondary scribal changes introduced when the texts were transmitted and copied in Babylonia.[3] According to another view these Targums originated in Babylonia, and this is supported by the fact that they have been transmitted in Jewish tradition as Babylonian.[4]

[1] These groups are not, of course, themselves uniform. The dialect of the Palestinian Talmud differs in significant ways from the dialect of Codex Neofiti 1 or of the Cairo Genizah fragments of the Palestinian Targum, and even within the Babylonian Talmud the dialect of Tractates Nedarim, Nazir, Keritot, Temurah, Meʿilah and Tamid is somewhat distinctive (Jacob N. Epstein, *Diqduq ʾaramit bablit* [Jerusalem: Magnes, 1960] 14). But for present purposes these three broad categories will suffice. For an authoritative overview of the Aramaic language see Stephen A. Kaufman, "Aramaic," in Robert Hetzron, ed., *The Semitic Languages* (London: Routledge, 1997) 114–30.

[2] The linguistic value of the Aramaic incantation bowls is disputed. See Hannu Juusola, *Linguistic Peculiarities in the Aramaic Magic Bowls*. Studia Orientalia 86 (Helsinki: Finnish Oriental Society, 1999).

[3] This view was advocated, with slightly different emphases, by Gustaf Dalman, *Grammatik des jüdisch-palästinischen Aramäisch* (Leipzig: J. C. Hinrich'sche Buchhandlung, 1905); Edward Y. Kutscher, "The Language of the Genesis Apocryphon: A Preliminary Study," in Chaim Rabin and Yigael Yadin, eds., *Aspects of the Dead Sea Scrolls*. Scripta Hierosolymitana 4 (Jerusalem: Magnes, 1957) 1–35; Abraham Tal, *The Language of the Targum of the Former Prophets and its Position within the Aramaic Dialects* (Tel Aviv: Tel-Aviv University, 1975 [Hebrew]); and Jonas C. Greenfield, "Aramaic and its Dialects. Jewish Languages: Theme and Variations," in Herbert Paper, ed., *Proceedings of Regional Conferences of the Association for Jewish Studies* (Cambridge, Mass.: Association for Jewish Studies, 1978) 29–43.

[4] The eastern origin of Onq. and Jon. has been championed by Paul Ernst Kahle, *The Cairo Geniza* (2nd ed. Oxford: Blackwell, 1959), and more recently by Klaus Beyer, *Die aramäischen Texte vom Toten Meer* (Göttingen: Vanderhoeck & Ruprecht, 1984) 45–48, 59–62, 70–71. If the Onq.-Jon. dialect is located in the east, then, as Epstein saw (*Diqduq ʾaramit bablit* 14), it is linguistically best placed not in the Gaonic era, but early, in the transition period between Imperial Aramaic and

There is a third aspect that must be borne in mind in any attempt to characterize and localize the dialect of Tg. Cant., viz., register. All our surviving Jewish Aramaic texts from late antiquity (including possibly even the incantation bowls) are in a literary register. This means that we must be cautious about drawing direct inferences from their dialects as to their place or time of origin. Dialectal variation tends to be stronger at the vernacular level and is only secondarily reflected in literature. In the case of the Yerushalmi and Babli Talmuds vernacular influence seems to be strong, and so their dialects do serve to localize these texts respectively to the Galilee and Babylonia. In the case of Onq. and Jon., however, the vernacular influence is more problematic, and this makes it more difficult to use this element to localize these texts. In other words, it could be argued that Onq. and Jon. are effectively in an artificial Targumic language that combines diverse linguistic elements and is not strongly rooted in any local vernacular. As such it could have been deployed by Jewish scholars almost anywhere and at almost any time, whatever their spoken language.

The most significant feature about the Aramaic of Tg. Cant. is its mixed character. It displays affinities to all three of the dialectal groups we distinguished above. The following brief examples will illustrate this phenomenon:

(1) One of the shibboleths differentiating western and eastern Aramaic is the verb "to see." In the eastern Aramaic of the Babylonian Talmud (and also in Onq. and Jon.) it is *ḥzy*. In western Aramaic (Palestinian Talmud and Palestinian Targums) it is *ḥmy*.[5] Tg. Cant. uses both verbs apparently indiscriminately. In fact, they are sometimes found side by side. Thus in ms. A *ḥzy* occurs at 2:9, 11, 12; 3:1; 6:9; 7:9, and *ḥmy* at 2:9; 6:11 (2x); 7:13; 8:5. The most revealing case is 2:9 where the two verbs appear in close proximity to each other in the same verse, with no difference in meaning, but apparently simply for the sake of stylistic variation.

(2) In western Aramaic texts (and, with minor exceptions, in Onq.-Jon.) the *status emphaticus* of the masculine plural noun ends in *-ayya'*, whereas in the eastern texts it ends in *-ei*. Tg. Cant. normally employs the western form, but occasionally the eastern is found. Thus at 3:8 and 8:3 we have *mazziqayya'*, but at 4:6 *mazziqei*, and there are no relevant textual variants (see *Apparatus ad loc.*).[6]

(3) In western Aramaic (Palestinian Talmud and Palestinian Targums) the conjunction "because, since" is *'rwm;* in Onq. and Jon., however, it is *'ry*. *'rwm* occurs in Tg. Cant. at 1:13; 2:5, 11, 14; 5:2, 5; 8:6. However, C G have *'ry*, inconsistently, at 1:13, and K L N at 5:5.

There are a number of possible explanations for this linguistic mixture. The first, and perhaps the most obvious, is that Tg. Cant. was originally composed in one of our three

---

the East Aramaic texts, in other words in the same period (roughly first to second centuries C.E.) to which Onq. and Jon. are normally assigned by the advocates of a western provenance. This reduces the linguistic issue to a very fine judgment as to whether the eastern features of the dialect are primary and the western secondary or vice versa. In general the latter view seems preferable, and it fits better with literary and aggadic studies of the Targumim and with the histories of the Jewish communities in Palestine and Babylonia. It should also be noted that although medieval Jewish scholars treated Onq. and Jon. as Babylonian, and contrasted them with the Palestinian Targumim that they knew, Talmudic tradition itself held that their authors, Onqelos/Aqilas and Jonathan, were Palestinians. See further Philip S. Alexander, "Jewish Aramaic Translations of Hebrew Scriptures," in Martin J. Mulder, ed., *Mikra*: *Text, Translation, Reading, and Interpretation of the Hebrew Bible in Ancient Judaism and Early Christianity*. CRINT II.1 (Assen: Van Gorcum; Minneapolis: Fortress, 1990) 217–53.

[5] Imperial Aramaic also uses *ḥzy*. It seems that eastern Aramaic preserved the old Imperial Aramaic verb whereas western Aramaic replaced it.

[6] This is a curious case: 3:8 and 4:6 contain similar lists of demons in which the demon names originally seem to have used the eastern form of the masculine plural *status emphaticus* in *-ei*. Perhaps the Targum has incorporated here unchanged a demon list of eastern origin.

dialects but in the process of copying by medieval scribes was contaminated by words and forms from the other dialects. The predominant character of the Aramaic of Tg. Cant. is western, and perhaps the more likely scenario would be that a western text was contaminated by eastern and by Onq.-Jon. elements, because the medieval copyists were better acquainted with the Babylonian Talmud and with Onq.-Jon., and regarded their Aramaic as in some sense normative. An examination of the mss. of Tg. Cant. suggests that such contamination has indeed taken place. Where one ms. has a western form, another has an eastern: the degree of dialectal admixture, as we noted above, varies from ms. to ms. But this cannot be the whole story. It is impossible to eliminate admixture from the extant mss. *All* known forms of the text are mixed, and there are many cases where *all* the numerous text-witnesses agree in presenting a western, and others where they *all* agree in presenting an eastern form. The phenomenon must go back to at least a very early stage in the transmission.

This might lead us to consider a slightly revised scenario, namely that a Targum composed in either the east or the west was taken at an early stage to the other linguistic domain and edited or copied there, and that all our extant medieval mss. descend from this contaminated text. Linguistically speaking the movement could either have been from east to west or vice versa, but since on other grounds it is reasonably certain that our Targum originated in Palestine a west to east movement is more likely. One could postulate, then, that a contaminated Babylonian exemplar of an original Palestinian Targum to Canticles lies behind all our extant medieval copies. But again this will not quite meet the case. The evidence suggests that the dialectal admixture is not simply early, but original: it goes all the way back to the author of our Targum. Here the example of 2:9 is instructive. Our Targumist adopts a consciously literary style and constantly varies his vocabulary and constructions to avoid monotony. The variation here, then, is in keeping with his stylistic predilections. He would have tried to avoid, if he could, writing *ḥzy . . . ḥzy* or *ḥmy . . . ḥmy.* It is very difficult to eliminate the admixture here: it must be original and not simply due to copying or editing.

If this is the case, then it suggests that the Aramaic of Tg. Cant. is a purely literary dialect. This dialect was created by someone who knew Jewish literature in both eastern and western dialects as well as in the Targumic Aramaic of Onq. and Jon., and was quite happy to combine for literary purposes elements drawn from all three of these dialectal groups. Literary analysis makes it abundantly clear that our Targumist did indeed know texts in a variety of dialects: he "quotes" from Onqelos *and* from the Palestinian Targumim, and there are grounds for thinking that he knew both the Babli and the Yerushalmi Talmuds as well.[7] Yet his language is no mere pastiche: it has a certain unity, and if we can resist for the moment the temptation to read Tg. Cant. with the eyes of the philologist we will be forced to admit that it is an effective piece of writing, as communicative and, in its way, as elegant as any well-written text in modern Hebrew, which is also, philologically speaking, a hybrid of forms, constructions, and vocabulary taken from a variety of dialectal sources. There are a number of other late Jewish Aramaic texts that show a similar admixture of eastern, western, and Onq.-Jon. Aramaic—the Pseudo-Jonathan Targum and the Targums to Chronicles, Psalms, and Job. The Aramaic of these texts is by no means identical. But this is hardly surprising, since we are not dealing here with a unified dialect grounded in a vernacular, but with an artificial literary language that was, to a degree, created anew by each author as he combined different elements from the Aramaic literary

[7] See Fontela, *El Targum al Cantar de los Cantares* 7–22; further *Notes* below.

sources that he knew. He could do this because his readership also knew those sources and so would have had no difficulty in understanding his language.

It is, of course, theoretically possible that the dialect of Tg. Cant. and its linguistically cognate texts could have arisen in a region, say somewhere in Syria, that, lying geographically between the homelands of eastern and western Aramaic, shared characteristics of both these dialectal systems.[8] On this hypothesis we might be able to defend the view that there *is* a coherent vernacular behind the language of our Targum, but this is unlikely. Linguistic evidence should not be divorced from other kinds of evidence and interpreted in isolation. Our Targum was almost certainly written in Palestine, in the heartlands of western Aramaic. Moreover, it is hard, given the historical context, to envisage where such a learned Rabbinic work as Tg. Cant., and all the other works linguistically like it, could have been composed, other than in either Palestine or Babylonia. At the time when they were probably written there was no Jewish cultural center geographically "in between" these regions that could plausibly have created such works, and even if there had been, it is surely improbable that our learned author would have used his local Aramaic vernacular for literary purposes. The very linguistic inconsistencies of this cluster of texts suggest that they have no vernacular basis, but are in a relatively fluid, artificial, literary language.

There is one further possible implication of this conclusion. It is that our Targumist was not an Aramaic speaker and so did not have a vernacular to guide him, consciously or unconsciously, in his choice of linguistic forms and vocabulary. There are hints that his vernacular may have been Arabic. His text contains Arabic loanwords and a few possible Arabisms.[9] Though E. Z. Melamed's claim that he commits schoolboy "howlers" in his Aramaic is exaggerated,[10] one does get the feeling that, for all his careful style and undoubted learning, he is not entirely at ease in Aramaic, which may indicate that he was not a native speaker. We do not know for certain when Jews in the Middle East gave up speaking Aramaic in favor of Arabic. The pace of the change probably differed from region to region, and of course some communities, such as the Jews of Kurdistan, managed to preserve their Aramaic vernacular down to modern times. But by the early tenth century Saʿadya felt it necessary to produce a translation of the Torah into Arabic for the benefit of his co-religionists. At roughly the same time the Christian Palestinian dialect of Arabic was emerging in the west. The transition to speaking Arabic among Jews had probably begun some considerable time earlier. Adoption of Arabic by Jews for literary purposes would have taken longer, and would have come on the back of the change in the spoken language. Even after the rise of the Judeo-Arabic vernacular, Jews continued to employ Aramaic for literary purposes,

[8] Certain aspects of Syriac place it "between" the eastern and western Aramaic dialects. It is the eastern dialect most closely related to Onq.-Jon.: see Tal, *The Language of the Targum of the Former Prophets* 133ff. Cf. Edward M. Cook's argument that the Onq.-Jon. dialect originated neither in Palestine nor in Babylonia but "in-between," in Upper Mesopotamia or Syria ("A New Perspective on the Language of Onqelos and Jonathan," in Derek R. G. Beattie and Martin McNamara, eds., *The Aramaic Bible: Targums in their Historical Context*. JSOT.S 166 [Sheffield: JSOT Press, 1994] 142–56). Intriguingly, Michael Weitzman places the origins of the Peshitta in the same region. Putting these two suggestions together, we might be tempted to postulate a "school" of Aramaic Bible translators in Upper Mesopotamia in the late second or third centuries C.E., but we would then surely expect a closer relationship between Onq.-Jon. on the one hand and the Peshitta on the other. See Michael P. Weitzman, *The Syriac Version of the Old Testament: An Introduction*. University of Cambridge Oriental Publications 56 (Cambridge: Cambridge University Press, 1999).

[9] See Appendix B. A possible "Arabism" occurs at 4:3 where Tg.'s unusual rendering of the Heb. *mi-baʿad* by *min bar* might be explained on the basis of his knowledge of the Arabic *baʿda* in the sense of "beside, aside from."

[10] Melamed, "Targum Canticles," 213.

though as time went by its use decreased and texts tended to be written in either Hebrew or Arabic.

If this account of the dialect of Tg. Cant. is correct, it suggests that it (along with the other works that share its mixed linguistic character) should be dated to around the eighth-ninth centuries C.E. A further, historical consideration supports this conclusion. The dialect of Tg. Cant. implies that its author, living in Palestine, would have known texts not only in western but in eastern Aramaic as well, and that he would have known Targums Onqelos and Jonathan. This would be consistent with the literary situation in the early Islamic period when the influence of the Babylonian Yeshibot was growing in Palestine, when the Babylonian Talmud was beginning to be studied there, and when the Targums of Onqelos and Jonathan, having probably originated long before in the west but in the meantime been supplanted there by the Palestinian Targumim, were re-imported to the region in a Babylonian form.

2.2. The Vocabulary of Tg. Cant.

Within the Hebrew Bible the language of Canticles is particularly rich and rare. It is full of *hapax legomena* and its vocabulary includes many names for plants, animals, and *realia*, as well as exotic places. It poses a serious challenge to any translator. Our Targumist's linguistic resources, on the whole, proved equal to his task. His style is carefully varied and, in fact, he introduces further plants and animals not found in the original Hebrew, as well as names of gemstones, which add yet more variety to his linguistic palette (see, e.g., 5:14). This richness is enhanced by his frequent use of loanwords. The largest group of these is Greek in origin (e.g., *ʾrkwn* = *archōn,* "ruler" [4:3]; *dwrwn* = *dōron,* "gift" [4:8]; *nymws* = *nomos,* "law" [1:6]; *pltyʾ* = *plateia,* "street" [3:2]; *sndlyn* = *sandalion,* "sandal" [7:2]; *ʾyṣtlʾ* = *stolē,* "cloak" [5:10]; *snhdryn* = *sunedrion,* "assembly" [4:1, 9; 5:12; 6:2; 7:5; 8:13]; *tyqs* = *taxis,* "battle array, order" [2:4; 5:10; 6:4, 10]; *nynpy* = *numphē,* "bride" [4:8, 9, 10, 11, 12; 5:1]); and it includes also Greek proper names (e.g., *ʾlksndrws* = Alexander; v.l., *ʾntwywkws* = Antiochus [6:8]). Many of these Greek loanwords had been part of the word-stock of Jewish Aramaic from an early period and tell us nothing about the date or provenance of our text. Some, however, are much rarer, and may betray the influence of later Greek. Perhaps most surprising are words like *nynpy.* Why use the Greek term when there is a perfectly good Aramaic word for "bride" *(kalletaʾ)* found in all Jewish Aramaic dialects as well as in Hebrew (it is actually the word used in Canticles!)—unless the intention is to add an exotic flavor to the language? There are a few Latin words, possibly mediated through Greek (e.g., *dux* [6:8] and *familia* [1:15]). There are also Persian loanwords, again mostly belonging to the older strata of the Aramaic lexicon (e.g., *pitgam* [2:5; 5:2, etc.]), though some of these may have come to our Targumist via Arabic (e.g., *zaʿafaran* [5:14]). Hebrew loanwords also occur, for ritual objects or technical religious terms (e.g., *mezuzah* [8:3]; *milah* [3:8]; *ʾaron* [1:14 (2x); 3:4, 10]; *nebuʾah* [1:1 (2x); 5:10; 7:1, 2]; *Mishnah* [1:2; 5:10]). The most significant collection of loanwords, however, is from Arabic. A cluster of Arabic terms is used for the precious stones at 5:14 in the western recension of the text. As we have noted in Appendix B there are variants in the mss. at this point and the textual history of the verse suggests that originally it was in two distinctive recensions, one of which called the gems by biblical names and the other by Arabic. It is probable, on balance, that the Arabic names are original. If this is the case, then it is surely a strong indication that our Targumist's vernacular was Arabic, as was that of his intended readership.

3. THE ARGUMENT AND STRUCTURE OF TARGUM CANTICLES

3.1. The Argument

The Targumist offers a strikingly coherent reading of Canticles that imposes on the book a consistent and well-reasoned interpretation from beginning to end. His holistic approach is possibly unique in classic Rabbinic Bible commentary which, at least in the case of aggadah, tends to proceed atomistically and to interpret each verse or even word or phrase without much reference to its immediate context, still less to the argument of the book as a whole. The Targumist detected two main voices in the Song: the voice of a male (the Beloved—the *Dod*) and the voice of a female (the Bride—the *Kallah*/*Raʿyah*). Following the broad outlines of Rabbinic exegesis, he identified the former as God and the latter as Israel, and interpreted the Song as an allegory of God's relationship with Israel. His distinctive contribution was to read the Song *systematically* as a cryptic *history* of that relationship, starting with the Exodus from Egypt and concluding with the Messianic Age. He detected in Canticles a rhythm in the relationship between the Beloved and the Bride of fellowship, estrangement, and reconciliation, and he saw that rhythm replicated in Israel's history, which moves through a cyclical pattern of communion with God, terminated by rebellion, sin, and exile, but leading ultimately to repentance and return.

He divides the long history of Israel into three great periods, each of which begins with an exile, leads to an exodus, and culminates in an occupation of the Land, the building of the Temple, the establishment of the monarchy, and the abiding of the Shekhinah in the midst of the people. The first era spans the exile in Egypt, the Exodus, the wilderness wanderings, the giving of the Torah on Sinai, and the entry into the Land, and climaxes with the building of the Temple under Solomon and the descent of the Shekhinah. The second covers the exile of Babylon, the exodus under Cyrus, the return to the Land, the rebuilding of the Temple, and the restoration of the Shekhinah. The climax of this period was the reestablishment of statehood under the Hasmoneans. The final era covers the exile of Edom (i.e., Rome/Christendom), the exodus under the Messiah, the return to the Land, the rebuilding of the Temple, and the restoration of the Shekhinah. Thus the history of Israel is seen as following the pattern of estrangement from God, reconciliation, and communion—three exiles (Egypt, Babylon, and Edom), three exoduses (under Moses, Cyrus, and the Messiah), culminating in three Jewish States (under Solomon, the Hasmoneans, and the Messiah). It is this pattern that our Targumist detects in the Song of Songs. The Song contains the inner history of Israel, its spiritual history, which lies behind and, in fact, determines the course of the outward events. To know this secret history is to understand what has happened to Israel in the past and what awaits her in the future. His correlations with history are not always very precise, and at times his chronology can seem a little willful: he tends to be suggestive rather than didactic. He is a scholar and knows his biblical history well: he expects his readers to have the same knowledge. A hint at times is all that he deems necessary: his learned audience can supply the rest.

3.2. The Structure

Close readers of Tg. Cant. have always detected a profound unity in the work, yet its overall structure has proved somewhat elusive. Richard Loring[1] analyzed it into an ingenious schema organized around the recurrent themes of God's choice of Israel, Israel's apostasy, and the means by which atonement was effected between God and Israel. Thus 1:4, the Exodus from Egypt, represents God's choice of Israel; 1:5, the episode of the Golden Calf, represents Israel's apostasy, which is followed immediately in the same verse by a reference to the construction of the Tabernacle, the instrument in this case by which Israel was reconciled to God. There can be no doubt, as we have already noted, that the Targumist detected a pattern of communion, estrangement, and reconciliation running through the history of Israel's relationship to God, and that this pattern consequently recurs fairly often in his text as he recounts Israel's history. But the pattern is not repeated with the regularity that Loring supposes. His detailed schema breaks down: sometimes the element asserting God's choice of Israel appears to be missing, or the means by which the atonement is achieved is not stated. And at several points he clearly forces the sense of the Targum to make it fit the pattern.

Larry Schneekloth,[2] following a proposal of Leon Liebreich,[3] attempted to show that the Targumist himself has actually indicated the structure of his work by his strategic placing of the rubrics "Solomon the prophet said" and "King Solomon said" (1:2; 1:17; 2:8; 7:2; 7:7; 8:5; 8:13). However, again the result is not entirely convincing: some of his sections extend over several chapters (Section III = 2:8–7:1), while others cover only a few verses (Section IV, A "Sermon" = 7:2-6).

A third attempt to clarify the structure of the Targum was offered by Raphael Loewe,[4] who suggested that it should be seen, "without incongruity," as having a "symphonic construction." He divides it into five movements, the first running from 1:2 to 3:6, the second from 3:7 to 5:1, the third from 5:2 to 6:1, the fourth from 6:2 to 7:11, and the fifth from 7:12 to 8:14. Loewe has more or less correctly clarified the structure of the Targum. His musical analogy is helpful in that it reminds us that our Targumist is an artist, and it allows us to play with his "flash-backs" (e.g., the reference to the division of the kingdom after Solomon's death in 8:11-12) and his "anticipations" or "flash-forwards" (e.g., the Messianic reference at 1:17) in aesthetic terms. But it rather falls down because he fails to demonstrate that his individual movements have any kind of inner musical structure, and consequently he fails to justify his division of the Targum as a whole into five "musical" sections.

No detailed, rigid schema can or should be imposed on the Targum for two reasons. First, for all its freedom, the interpretation of the Targumist is constrained by the underlying biblical text. There had to be a more or less plausible correlation between the text and the interpretation: the Targumist is fastidious in this regard (see *Intro.* 5). He was further limited by the fact that he imposed on his interpretation a broadly chronological framework. To a certain extent he had to get his correspondences between the text and history as best he could, and this may sometimes have forced him to take events somewhat out of sequence, or

[1] Richard T. Loring, *The Christian Historical Exegesis of the Song of Songs and its Possible Jewish Antecedents: A Chapter in the History of Interpretation.* Th.D. dissertation, General Theological Seminary, New York, 1967, ch. 2.

[2] Larry G. Schneekloth, *The Targum of the Song of Songs: A Study of Rabbinic Bible Interpretation.* Ph.D. dissertation, University of Wisconsin, Madison, 1977, 284–94.

[3] Leon J. Liebreich, "The Benedictory Formula in the Targum to the Song of Songs," *HUCA* 18 (1944) 182.

[4] Raphael Loewe, "Apologetic Motifs in the Targum of the Song of Songs," in Alexander Altmann, ed., *Biblical Motifs: Origins and Transformations* (Cambridge, Mass.: Harvard University Press, 1966) 169–73.

to omit elements that he might ideally have liked to include. But second, I doubt that the Targumist would have wanted to impose a rigid, repetitive schema on his work. He was too much of a poet to do so. The more predictable his text, the duller and less artistically pleasing it would have become. If we are to try and catch the elusive form of the Targum through a musical analogy, then I would suggest that the programmatic tone poem rather than the classical symphony would be the more appropriate comparison.[5] The unity of the work is essentially determined by the repetition of certain theological leitmotifs and themes rather than by a rigid, formal structure. Only when we identify those motifs and clarify the Targum's theological program are we able to discern its structure (see *Intro*. 4).

The broad structure of the Targum is, nonetheless, clear, and may be set out as follows:

A. 1:1-2, The Preamble

(1) 1:1 The Midrash of the Ten Songs

(2) 1:2 Opening benediction

B. 1:3–5:1, From the Exile of Egypt to King Solomon

(1) 1:3–3:4 The Egyptian oppression, the Exodus, and the Wilderness wanderings

(a) 1:3-8 First account

(b) 1:9–2:7 Second account

(c) 2:8–3:4 Third account

(2) 3:5-6 The Conquest of the Land

(3) 3:7–5:1 The glories of the Solomonic age

C. 5:2–7:11, From the Exile of Babylon to the Hasmoneans

(1) 5:2-7 The conquest of Jerusalem by the Babylonians

(2) 5:8–6:1 Israel in exile in Babylon

(3) 6:2-6 The return under Cyrus

(4) 6:7–7:11 The restoration of the ideal polity and the glories of the Hasmonean age

D. 7:12–8:12, From the Exile of Edom to the Coming of the King Messiah

(1) 7:12-14 The exile of Edom

(2) 8:1-12 The Messianic age

(a) 8:1-5 The ingathering of the exiles

(b) 8:6-12 The restoration of the Solomonic polity under the King Messiah

E. 8:13-14, The Peroration

(1) 8:13 Solomon's prophetic plea to Israel "at the end of days"

(2) 8:14 Concluding prayer

A. The Preamble (1:1-2)

The Midrash of the Ten Songs (1:1), which Tg. Cant. has adapted from elsewhere, ostensibly explains the opening words of Canticles, "The Song of Songs, which is Solomon's" (see *Notes* to 1:1 and Appendix A), but more obliquely it helps to indicate at the outset that the perspective of the exposition that follows will be historical. The Ten Songs cover the history

[5] The tone poem, also known as the symphonic poem, is a development of the classical symphony, in which the boundaries between the distinct movements have been dissolved, and the overall structure of the composition is looser and more impressionistic.

of humanity, from the creation to the consummation. The *Heilsgeschichte,* the subject of Canticles, runs from songs two to ten. Thus the history of Israel is set within the history of the world. The Targumist also uses the Midrash of the Ten Songs to strike at once a note of imminent eschatological hope, which will be heard again and again throughout the Targum: Solomon's song is the ninth song; the only song that remains to be sung is that which the exiles will sing when they are redeemed from captivity in the Messianic Age.

Canticles 1:1 is treated by the Targumist as a title: the Midrash of the Ten Songs therefore stands outside the narrative proper, which begins at 1:3. Canticles 1:2 is an opening benediction. It creates an *inclusio* with the concluding prayer at 8:14 and suggests that the Tg. was intended to have a liturgical function. It was probably meant by our Targumist to be recited publicly, like the Targumim to the Pentateuch (see *Intro.* 7).

B. From the Exile of Egypt to King Solomon (1:3–5:1)

The first major section falls into two subsections: 1:3–3:4 and 3:5–5:1, the former dealing with the Exodus and the Wilderness wanderings, the latter with the entry into the Promised Land and the establishment of the Solomonic state. The Exodus and Wilderness wanderings are covered three times: (1:3-8, 1:9–2:7 and 2:8–3:4). The reason for this is clear: Tg. saw the Exodus and the Wilderness as the period of Israel's formation, hardly surprisingly since it includes the giving of the Torah at Sinai and the constitution of Israel as a covenant people. In these brief forty years Israel played out her whole future history *in nuce*. They were marked by exile (Egypt), Exodus (the Red Sea), communion (Sinai), rebellion (the making of the Calf), and reconciliation (the building of the Tabernacle). The idea that Israel's Wilderness years encapsulate her future is pointedly expressed in the first account, which ends with Moses just before his death being given a vision of Solomon's Temple and more importantly of the Messianic Age (1:7-8). The Targumist frequently uses the device of "flash-forward" and "flash-back" to unify his work and to state his belief in the symmetry and cyclicality of the *Heilsgeschichte* (see *Intro.* 4). All the major themes of Tg. Cant. are contained in his account of the Wilderness wanderings (constant allusions to this period will be made in the rest of the Targum), and it is hardly surprising that he covers it three times, as a sort of theme and variations, in order to impress it upon his readers' minds.

In the second subsection (3:5–5:1), after a brief allusion to the entry into the Land (inspired by Song 3:6, "Who is this coming up from the Wilderness?"), the Targumist concentrates on the time of Solomon. The account of Solomon's "litter" and his "palanquin" made "from the wood of Lebanon" (3:7-11) is read as a cryptic description of the building and dedication of the Temple. This account of the Temple balances and echoes the account of the Tabernacle in the previous subsection of the Targum. The praises of the Bride in 4:1-15 are interpreted as an elaborate description of the ideal, theocratic polity of Israel, in which the Targumist depicts the king, the commoners, the priests, and the scholars as living in harmony under the rule of Torah. (Significantly, at 4:5 it includes a "flash-forward" to the Messiah son of David and the Messiah son of Ephraim.) This is, arguably, the pivot of the Targumist's reading of Canticles. For him Israel as a polity reached perfection in Solomon's reign. Echoes of the language he uses here can be traced earlier in his account of Israel under Moses in Tabernacle times, and later in the account of the Second Temple period and the Messianic Age. This section also marks the "real" time of the narrator, Solomon. What goes before for him is past history; what follows lies in the future and is foreseen through prophetic inspiration.

C. From the Exile of Babylon to the Hasmoneans (5:2–7:11)

Embedded in the account of the Babylonian attack on Jerusalem (5:2-7) is an important flash-back to the exile of the northern tribes (5:3-6). The Targumist's chronology is not at fault here: he is perfectly aware that the northern tribes were exiled before the southern. Rather he is obliquely making a theological point. He suggests that the exile of the northern tribes, imposed to punish them for the idolatry of "the molten calves" (5:4), was meant as a warning to the southern tribes, a warning they heeded too late, "because the Lord of the World had closed the doors of repentance in their face" (cf. 4:5). But of course the fate of the northern tribes was a burning issue for his readers: in the standard eschatological scenario their ingathering from beyond the River Sambation was to be one of the miracles of the Messianic Age, when once again all Israel would be united as in Solomon's reign. There is an implicit flash-forward here to the days of the Messiah, which is picked up at 8:11-12 in a striking flash-back to the division of the kingdom after the death of Solomon.

The account of the Babylonian exile (5:8–6:1) is cast as a dialogue between Israel and the exilic prophets, who successfully urge Israel to repent and return to the Torah. Israel in an ecstasy of love describes the "body" of her Beloved in 5:10-16, one of the key passages of the Song. The body of the Beloved turns out to signify much the same as the body of the Bride (4:1-15). The interpretation reinforces the importance of the study of Torah: God in heaven studies Torah and Talmud; so also should Israel on earth. But the idea of the *imitatio dei* passes easily over into the stronger idea of incarnation: Israel is God's embodiment on earth: his "legs" are the righteous, "the pillars of the world" (5:15). This section is deeply flattering to the Babylonians and may contain a hint as to the provenance of our Targum (see *Intro.* 8).

The account of the ingathering of the exiles from Babylon and the rebuilding of the Temple (6:2-6) climaxes in a lyrical description of the Hasmonean era (6:7–7:11). The beauties of the Bride in 6:4-7, and more importantly in 7:2-10, balance 4:1-15. The Targumist exploits the parallelism (note the verbal repetition of 4:1-2 at 6:5-6) to assert the reestablishment of the Solomonic polity in the post-exilic era. His positive evaluation of the Hasmonean state as one of the great peaks of the *Heilsgeschichte* stands in sharp contrast to the rather cool or even negative attitude toward the Hasmoneans in classic Rabbinic sources, and may contain an indication of the Targumist's date (see *Intro.* 8.1(5)).

D. From the Exile of Edom to the Coming of the King Messiah (7:12–8:12)

The exile of Edom (Rome and its successor Christendom) is introduced rather abruptly (7:12). No reference is made to when it starts, but presumably it is dated from the destruction of the Temple in 70 C.E. Our Targumist is frequently suggestive and seems to expect a considerable level of knowledge on the part of his readers. His treatment of the exile of Edom, which corresponds to his own time, is rather cursory. The role of the scholars is stressed: it is through their devotion to the study of Torah that the coming of the Messiah will be hastened (7:13-14)—a reprise of the part they played in helping to bring the Babylonian captivity to an end (cf. 6:2 and 5:12). But Israel is urged not to force the redemption: it will happen in God's good time (7:14; cf. 8:4)—just as she was exhorted at the time of the Exodus from Egypt not to go up prematurely to the Land (2:7: the verbal echo of 2:7 in 8:4 would have been seen as highly significant by the Targumist).

The ingathering of the exiles (8:1-5) will be in two phases: the living will be led up to Jerusalem by the King Messiah (8:1); then the righteous dead, buried outside the Land, will proceed by underground passages and surface in the Land from beneath the Mount of Anointing (8:5). There are allusions to the Exodus from Egypt, encouraged no doubt by the echo at 8:5 ("Who is this coming up from the Wilderness, leaning on her Beloved") of 3:6 ("Who is this going up from the Wilderness?"). The sign to the Destroyer at the eschatological Passover will not be the blood on the lintel and doorposts but the *mezuzah* and *tefillin* (8:3). There are references to the rebuilding of the Temple (8:2), to the Messianic banquet (the feast of Leviathan) (8:2), to the defeat of Gog and Magog (8:4, 7), and to other elements of the standard Rabbinic eschatological scenario. But once again the emphasis is on the importance of the study of the Torah: even in the Messianic Age Israel's security will depend not on her armies but on her Scribes and, in a delightful paradox, on "the merit of the Torah which the children study" (8:7-10).

The restoration of the ideal polity is alluded to at 8:11-12, in a flash-back to the division of the kingdom after the death of Solomon. As we noted earlier, our Targumist regarded the Solomonic state as the pinnacle of national perfection for Israel. The restoration after the Babylonian exile, for all its glories, was, in a sense, imperfect, since only the two tribes returned (cf. 5:4). By referring in the context of a Messianic scenario to the division of the kingdom, our Targumist obliquely reminds his readers of the promises that in the Messianic era the lost tribes too will be gathered in, and the perfection of Solomon's reign fully restored. The argument is oblique, but the implications would not have been missed by the Targumist's well-informed and pious audience.

E. The Peroration (8:13-14)

The peroration consists of two elements. The first (8:13) is an exhortation by "Solomon the prophet" addressed to Israel "at the end of days" yet again to sit in the House of Study and listen to the words of the Head of the College. The "end of days" is the period just before the coming of the Messiah; in other words, it is the Targumist's own time. Having Solomon speak directly to his audience is dramatically effective. But the second element (8:14) trumps it: Solomon, again under prophetic inspiration, confidently predicts that Israel "at that hour" *will* put her trust in God and pray: "Watch over us and observe our distress and affliction from the highest heavens, till such time as You are pleased with us and redeem us, and bring us up to the mountains of Jerusalem, where the priests will offer up before You incense of spices." Solomon himself, so to speak, provides the Targumist's generation with the wording of the prayer with which they can bring the liturgical performance of the Targum to a fitting close and pray for the coming of the Messiah. The phrase "at that hour" illustrates the Targumist's care to sustain his narrative perspective right to the end. At a cursory reading one might suppose that "at that hour" must refer to the Messianic Age, but it is clear from the rest of the verse that the Messianic Age has not yet dawned, and that "at that hour" refers to the Targumist's own day (it picks up "at the end of days" in v. 13). The Targumist could only describe his own day thus by adopting the viewpoint of Solomon looking forward in prophetic anticipation from the distant past.[6]

[6] On the argument and structure of Tg. Cant. see further Philip S. Alexander, "Tradition and Originality in the Targum of the Song of Songs," in Beattie and McNamara, eds., *The Aramaic Bible: Targums in their Historical Context,* 332–35; idem, "From Poetry to Historiography: The Image of the Hasmoneans in Targum Canticles and the Question of the Targum's Provenance and Date," *JSP* 19 (1999) 103–28.

4. THEOLOGICAL THEMES IN TARGUM CANTICLES

Though our Targumist is more of a poet than a theologian, his work is full of theological ideas. He keeps returning again and again to certain theological themes, which run through and unify his composition like *Leitmotifs* in a piece of music. Among the more significant of these are the following:

4.1. Exile

Our Targumist writes with an acute sense of the pain of exile and a deep longing for redemption. Exile and redemption for him are not personal but national: it is the condition of his people and his nation that concerns him. Exile for him means the loss of statehood and the absence of the divine presence, the Shekhinah; redemption means the return to the ancient homeland, the rebuilding of national institutions, especially the Temple, and the restoration of the Shekhinah to the Temple. He looks back with nostalgia to the period of Solomon as the time when Israel achieved full political maturity. Until the ideal Solomonic polity is restored in the Messianic Age she is forced to endure the decrees of the nations, which are as severe "as the scorching heat of the noonday sun at the summer solstice" (1:7). The cruel decrees Israel suffers "in exile among the provinces of the nations" are like the thorns that prick and tear the petals of the rose (2:2). The jealousy the nations bear toward her is as harsh as Gehinnom, the enmity they harbor against her like the coals of hell-fire (8:6).

The polar opposite to the experience of exile is the experience of the Shekhinah,[1] which involves every kind of blessedness. The Shekhinah nourishes and protects Israel (1:4; 2:1-2), ensures that she is fruitful and multiplies (1:16), and even banishes demons (2:6; 4:6). Israel enjoyed the Shekhinah during the Wilderness wanderings (1:4, 5, 16; 2:1, 6; 3:2-4), but this was a special case and one cannot generalize from it. Our Targumist seems to imply that the Shekhinah cannot be fully enjoyed outside the Land. Israel can attain full blessedness only in the Land: the proper abode of the Shekhinah on earth is the Tabernacle or the Temple (1:5; 3:4, 10; 5:1; 6:3; 8:14). And he confidently affirms, contrary to some traditions, that the Shekhinah was fully present even in the Second Temple (6:11). Sin has the effect of driving away the divine presence: God's response to it is to "take up" his Shekhinah to heaven (3:1; 5:3, 6; 6:1; 7:11). Since the destruction of the Second Temple it has resided in the highest heavens to avoid contamination from the polluted earth, and will only return in the Messianic Age (8:14).

If we put together the idea that the Shekhinah can be experienced fully only in the Land, when the Temple is rebuilt, with the idea that the Shekhinah protects Israel against demons, certain questions inevitably arise. Our Targumist lived at a time when the Temple was in ruins and most Jews lived outside the Land in the demonic realm of the *galut*. Is Israel, then, bereft of protection? His answer is "no." She has the words of Torah. Our Targumist has a very "magical" view of the world. Israel is engaged in constant spiritual warfare, and her principal weapon is the sword of Torah (2:17; 3:1, 8; 4:4, 6: see further *Intro.* 4.6). If she neglects the study of Torah she will find herself defenseless against the forces of

[1] On the Rabbinic doctrine of the Shekhinah see Joshua Abelson, *The Immanence of God in Rabbinical Literature* (London: Macmillan, 1912); Arnold M. Goldberg, *Untersuchungen über die Vorstellung von der Schechinah in der frühen rabbinischen Literatur—Talmud und Midrasch* (Berlin: De Gruyter, 1969).

darkness (3:1). m. ʾAbot 3:6 claims that the Shekhinah resides with those who study Torah. In many ways this doctrine would fit our Targumist's argument well, but he shies away from explicitly affirming it—and perhaps with good reason. To have universalized the experience of the Shekhinah would have been to downplay the importance of the Temple. However, study of the Torah comes close to the experience of the Shekhinah. It too protects against demons, and it hastens the coming of the Messiah and the restoration of the Temple. It is a foretaste of the Messianic Age.

It is worth noting in passing another technical term of Targumic theology that is common in Tg. Cant., viz., "Memra" (translated "Word" below). However, no developed Memra doctrine is evident in our text and our Targumist may have used the word largely because it is typical of Targumic style. Broadly speaking, for him the Memra is the agent or instrument through which God verbally communicated with Israel (2:12; 3:7; 4:8; 6:4, 12; 7:9), or with the angels in heaven (1:15). Behind this usage may lie the idea that speech on God's part can only be metaphorical: the basic intention is anti-anthropomorphic. Agency (perhaps angelic) rather than instrumentality[2] is suggested by the language at 5:8 and 7:10 ("the decree of the Word of the Lord"), at 7:1 ("the prophets who prophesy in the name of the Word of the Lord"), and possibly also at 2:12 ("I want to perform what I promised him through My Word"), and 2:17 ("the Covenant which He made through His Word with Abraham, Isaac and Jacob"). Memra also denotes the concrete utterance of God, what God actually says, and as such can effectively be equivalent to Torah: see 6:2, "the Levites have charge of His Holy Word;" 3:3, "the Guardians of the watch of the Word of the Lord in the Tent of Meeting"; and 5:15, "that transgress against His Word."[3]

4.2. Idolatry

The sin that seems to vex our Targumist most is idolatry. He dwells much on the making of the Golden Calf, and clearly regards it, as did many Jewish commentators,[4] as a particularly heinous act, committed as it was at the foot of Sinai (1:5, 12; 2:17), though he is careful to note that it was atoned for (2:17; 3:4). Idolatry ("the molten calves") was the cause of the exile of the northern tribes (5:4). Gehinnom was created specifically for idolaters (8:6). At 1:4 he has Israel pledge: "We will love your divinity and shun the idols of the nations" (cf. 8:6). But at 1:6 Israel says to the nations: "Do not despise me because I am darker than you, because I did what you did and bowed down to the sun and the moon. For it is the false prophets who have caused the fierceness of the Lord's anger to be visited upon me. They taught me to serve your idols and to walk in your laws, but the Lord of the World, who is my [own] God, have I not served, nor followed His laws, nor kept His commandments or His Torah."

It seems fairly obvious that "idolatry" carries a special meaning for our Targumist. It was probably for him a code-word for assimilation to the surrounding culture: he seems to have witnessed in his own milieu a loss of communal identity, a breaking down of the barriers between the Jewish community and the non-Jewish world, and perhaps widespread

[2] Contrast the language used of the *bat qol*, which is more instrumental (2:14; 4:1; cf. 2:5).

[3] On the vexed question of the Memra in the Targumim see Robert Hayward, *Divine Name and Presence: The Memra* (Totowa, N. J.: Allanheld, Osmun, 1981); Andrew Chester, *Divine Revelation and Divine Titles in the Pentateuchal Targumim* (Tübingen: J.C.B. Mohr [Paul Siebeck], 1986) 293–324.

[4] See Leivy Smolar and Moses Aberbach, "The Golden Calf Episode in Postbiblical Literature," *HUCA* 39 (1968) 91–116; Pier Cesare Bori, *The Golden Calf and the Origins of the Anti-Jewish Controversy* (Atlanta: Scholars, 1990).

apostasy. That he is not thinking of apostasy to crude paganism is clear from 1:7, where he accuses both Esau (Christendom) and Ishmael (Islam) of associating their idols with the one true God. His account of the Amalek incident is highly suggestive: "After they had crossed the sea they murmured for water, and wicked Amalek came against them, who bore a grudge against them on account of the birthright and the blessing which Jacob had taken from Esau. He came to wage war against Israel because they had ceased to observe the words of Torah. And wicked Amalek was stealing from beneath the wings of the clouds of glory souls from the tribe of Dan, and was killing them, because they had in their hands the idol of Micah" (2:15: see *Notes ad loc.*). Amalek here, the descendant of Esau, surely stands for Christianity, and what the Targumist fears is apostasy: note how Amalek steals souls from "beneath the wings of the clouds of glory," a reversal of the language of conversion to Judaism, by which proselytes are described as coming "under the wings of the Shekhinah." Significantly, the Targumist emphasizes that it was "the mixed multitude" who made the Golden Calf (1:9 and 1:12)—Israel had been corrupted by alien influences—and he praises the chasteness of the women of Israel in such a way as to suggest that he may be concerned about intermarriage (4:12).

4.3. The Merits of the Righteous

The doctrine of merits is central to the theology of the Targumist. It is the means by which he explains God's favor and beneficence toward his people, even when they have sinned. The merits of the righteous atone for the sins of Israel (2:17), provide for her sustenance, and protect her from harm in exile and in the Land (1:8; 4:5; 6:12; 8:9). They made possible the Exodus from Egypt (1:9) and the return from Babylon (7:9-10), and will in the end bring the Messiah (7:13-14). The righteous are "the pillars of the world" (5:15): if they did not exist in it, the world would have to be destroyed. All the righteous of every generation—even the schoolchildren who study Torah (8:9; cf. 1:8)—cast the cloak of their protecting merit over Israel, but certain great heroes of faith are singled out as having performed especially meritorious acts. Because of their great piety the merit of the Patriarchs, and interestingly of the Matriarchs (2:8), is especially efficacious, above all the merit of Abraham and Isaac, who showed supreme devotion and obedience to God on Mount Moriah (Genesis 22): the merit of the ʿAqedah "perfumes" Israel (3:6) and even turned back God's anger at the sin of the Calf (2:17). Also singled out are Daniel and the Three Hebrew Children, who refused to bow down to pagan idols and were prepared to sanctify the name of God in martyrdom. Their merit ensured the return from Babylon and brought about Ezekiel's temporary resurrection of the dead on the Plain of Dura (7:9-10). The example of Daniel and the Three Hebrew Children was doubtless particularly significant for our Targumist because they represented Jews who, like himself and his readers, lived in exile,[5] but who steadfastly resisted idolatry.

Tg. Cant. does not elaborate its doctrine of merit, but only alludes to it.[6] The "righteous" acquire merit, but it is not immediately obvious whether righteousness is attained by

[5] This would be true whether or not our Targumist lived in Babylonia or Israel. Even the Jewish community in Israel was, in a sense, "in exile."

[6] On the Rabbinic doctrine of merit see Solomon Schechter, *Aspects of Rabbinic Theology: Major Concepts of the Talmud* (1909; repr. New York: Schocken, 1965) 170–98; Efraim E. Urbach, *The Sages* (Jerusalem: Magnes, 1975; 4th printing Cambridge, Mass.: Harvard University Press, 1995) 496–508.

simply keeping the *miṣwot,* or by works of supererogation.[7] Certainly the great paradigms of merit, Abraham and Isaac, Daniel and the Three Hebrew Children, performed deeds of extraordinary piety: they were all willing to sanctify the name of God in martyrdom—a theme traditionally linked with the ʿAqedah[8] as well as with the story of Daniel and the Three Hebrew Children. On the other hand the Tg. stresses the meritorious nature of the study of Torah, and that is open to every Israelite, if not in person then vicariously through financial support for the schools (7:3; 8:7). The connection between righteousness and the study of the Torah is neatly expressed at 5:15 where "His legs are pillars of marble, set upon sockets of fine gold" is rendered "His righteous ones are the pillars of the world, set upon sockets of fine gold, that is [upon] the words of the Torah, which they study." It is Torah, in fact, "upon which the world is founded" (2:5), but Torah is only given "legs" when it is studied and put into practice. Not surprisingly the Scribes (= the Sages, 8:9), and above all Moses "the Great Scribe" (1:2; 4:5), the Sanhedrin (6:5), and the Head of the College (4:4; 7:3), all of whom devoted themselves to the study, teaching, and administration of Torah, are especially seen as earning merit for Israel.

4.4. The House of Study and the Sanhedrin

Our Targumist sees various institutions, such as the Temple (3:7-10) and the Synagogue (1:8; 2:14; 7:13), as central to the polity of Israel, but it is his treatment of the Sanhedrin that is most striking. Tg. Cant. is a paean of praise to the Rabbinical schools.[9] These schools are depicted as having both an educational function in teaching Torah (= House of Study) and a judicial function in deciding cases (= Sanhedrin) (5:12). Our Targumist claims that the Sanhedrin already existed in Babylonia during the exile (6:5), and in the time of Solomon: it forms a key element in his ideal Solomonic state (4:1, 4). Even in the Wilderness Israel studied Torah (2:5-6; 3:4): the Tabernacle has the characteristics of a Yeshibah (3:2; cf. 3:8 where the Priests and Levites behave like Torah-scholars), and the giving of the Torah at Sinai is described as a session of the House of Study (2:4-5). And when Israel returns to the Land in the Messianic era it will be to study Torah with the Messiah (8:1).

The relationship of the Sanhedrin to the Temple in our Targumist's thinking is somewhat problematic. The Temple is evidently important: it is the place where the Shekhinah manifested itself; it, like its predecessor the Tabernacle (3:4), made white the scarlet sins of Israel (4:3). A great deal of time is spent glorifying Temple worship, but in subtle ways the Targumist implies that the Sanhedrin is at least the Temple's equal in the divine scheme of things, and certainly it assumes the Temple's salvific functions when Israel is in exile. He assigns to it and its Head the sort of cosmic role that was traditionally assigned to the Temple and the High Priest, and the College, like the Temple, deserves the financial support of "tithes": "The Head of your College, through whose merit all the world is sustained,[10] just as the fetus is sustained through its navel in the belly of his mother, shines with [a knowledge of] the Torah like the disc of the moon, when he comes to pronounce pure and impure, innocent or guilty, and

[7] It is possible that for our Targumist the term *ṣaddiq,* like the term *ḥasid* in some Jewish ethical systems, denotes someone who goes beyond the norm.

[8] See Ronald E. Agus, *The Binding of Isaac and Messiah: Law, Martyrdom and Deliverance in Early Rabbinic Religiosity* (Albany: SUNY Press, 1988).

[9] On the historical background of his description of the schools see *Intro. 8.*

[10] Note how at 3:10 the ark of the Testimony is called "the pillar of the world."

the words of the Torah never fail [to flow] from his mouth, just as the waters of the great river which issues from Eden never fail. Seventy Sages surround him, like a round threshing-floor, and their treasuries are full of the holy tithes, votive and free-will offerings, which Ezra the priest, Zerubbabel, Jeshua, Nehemiah and Mordechai Bilshan, the Men of the Great Assembly, who are compared to roses, ordained for their benefit, so that they might be enabled to engage in the study of the Torah day and night" (7:3; see *Notes ad loc.*). The Sanhedrin is the one institution to which he gives the supreme validation of an *imitatio dei:* the Holy One himself studies Torah and Talmud "day and night" in the Celestial Yeshibah (5:10). The Terrestrial Yeshibah and above all its Head are his representatives *par excellence* on earth: just as God's face in heaven "shines like fire on account of the greatness of the wisdom and reasoning with which He discloses new meanings all day long" (5:10), so the Head of the College on earth "shines with [a knowledge of] the Torah like the disc of the moon,[11] when he comes to pronounce pure and impure, innocent or guilty" (7:3).[12]

4.5. Messianism

Like the early apocalyptists, our Targumist has a strong sense that history is both patterned and purposeful (and he sees this reflected in the repetitions of the Song of Songs). History for him is both cyclical and climactic. Certain patterns recur, but nevertheless history is moving forward purposefully toward an eschaton—the Messianic Age.[13] Tg. Cant. is an intensely Messianic document. Our Targumist believed that he was living at "the end of days" (8:13), i.e., in the period just preceding the Messianic Age, the time of "the ninth song" (1:1). He offered his Targum to his scattered and oppressed people to console them and to remind them of their imminent redemption. The concluding Messianic section, 7:13–8:14, which is strongly trailed at a number of points earlier in the work (1:1, 8, 17; 2:7; 3:5; 4:5; 7:3), has close links with the Midrashim of Redemption and other works of the apocalyptic revival in Judaism in the early Middle Ages (see *Intro.* 8).[14] It seems to have been composed against a background of Messianic speculation, shared by our Targumist and his audience. It is therefore allusive, and the chronology of events it envisages is not entirely clear. It contains the following elements:

(1) There will be not one but two Messiahs, the Messiah son of Ephraim and the Messiah son of David. Though this idea is well-trailed at 4:5 and 7:3, in fact in the Messianic section at the end of the Targum the emphasis is on only one Messiah, clearly the Messiah son of David. The reason for this is reasonably clear. The Messiah son of Ephraim is the Messiah anointed for war: in the traditional scenario he will fight and fall in battle against the nations who come to attack Israel in her Land. Our Targumist, however, consistently plays down the militaristic aspects of Messianism and may actually have held that the defeat of the nations in the last battle will be achieved by non-military means, a point to which we

[11] There is clearly some sort of intertextuality between 7:3 and 5:10. Is it too fanciful to see here the implication that the Head of the College reflects God's light just as the moon reflects the light of the sun?

[12] For other references to the Sanhedrin/College and the study of the Torah in the Targum see: 1:7-8, 10; 2:4-6; 3:4; 4:4, 9, 13-15; 5:10-13; 6:2, 5; 7:1; 8:7, 13.

[13] On apocalyptic as the "father" of Jewish historiography see Alexander, "From Poetry to Historiography," 103–28.

[14] For Jewish scenarios of the end see George Foote Moore, *Judaism* (Cambridge, Mass.: Harvard University Press, 1927–30) 2:323–95; Urbach, *The Sages* 649–90; G. W. Buchanan, *Revelation and Redemption: Jewish Documents of Deliverance from the Fall of Jerusalem to the Death of Nahmanides* (Dillsboro, N.C.: Western North Carolina Press, 1978)—a rich but chaotic collection of texts, rather poorly translated and presented; Emil Schürer, *The History of the Jewish People in the Age of Jesus Christ.* Revised ed. by Geza Vermes, Fergus Millar, and Matthew Black (Edinburgh: T & T Clark, 1979) 2:488–554.

shall return in a moment. Our Targumist is more interested in the Messiah son of David, consistently depicted not as a great military leader but as a Torah-scholar: note the reference at 8:1 to his participation in a great Talmudic *Shiʿur* in Jerusalem in the Messianic Age. The Messianic Age will be inaugurated by the "revelation" of the Messiah son David (8:1). The choice of verb is significant and indicates the preexistence of the Messiah either, as in the David Apocalypse in Heikhalot Rabbati (Schäfer, *Synopse*, §§122-26), in heaven (note 7:14, which may envisage him enthroned in heaven: "Arise now, and receive the kingdom that I have stored up for you"; see *Note* 62 *ad loc.*), or, as in Talmudic legend and the Book of Zerubbabel, living incognito on earth.

(2) The revelation of the Messiah, presumably in Jerusalem, will lead to the establishment of the Messianic kingdom (7:14). This will in turn provoke an attack by the nations, designated here as "Gog and Magog" (8:4). Gog is the king and Magog his people (8:7-8). It is clear that "Gog and Magog" do not represent the wild, barbarian tribes beyond the Caspian gates, as in Christian apocalyptic. Rather they designate the governments under which the exiles are now living. They are identical with "Edom" (Rome/Christendom) in 7:12. Though our Targumist probably lived after the Islamic conquest of the Middle East (note the reference to "Ishmael" as well as "Esau" in 1:7), he still, in keeping with standard Rabbinic eschatology, regarded Rome as the final enemy. Gog and Magog will be defeated in battle (8:4, 7, 8), but just how, our Targumist does not state.

(3) Only after the defeat of Gog and Magog will there be an ingathering of the exiles (8:4). The Messiah (son of David) will lead them up to Jerusalem (8:1-2; cf. 1:1, 8). The "flash-back" at 8:11-12 to the division of the kingdom after the death of Solomon hints that this ingathering will include the lost ten northern tribes, and that the Solomonic state will be reconstituted. The ingathering involves not only those living in exile but also the righteous who have died and been buried outside the Land. They will arrive by subterranean passages beneath the Mount of Olives (called here the "Mount of Anointing"), which will split open to facilitate their resurrection. Those, however, who have been buried in the Land will rise first. And so "at that hour Zion, which is the mother of Israel, will give birth to her sons [in the resurrection of the dead], and Jerusalem will receive her exiles [the living]" (8:5). At the same time as the resurrection of the righteous dead the Land will be purified of the polluting corpses of the wicked who have been buried there. These will be miraculously slung beyond her borders (8:5).

(4) The Temple will be rebuilt (though at precisely what point in the eschatological scenario is not entirely clear). This is trailed at 1:8 and 17, and a reference to the restoration of the offerings of incense closes the book (8:14). However, the Temple figures little in Tg. Cant.'s detailed Messianic scenario. Instead stress is placed on the continuing role of the House of Study in the days of the Messiah (8:1, 7, 9, 10). Even in the Messianic Age Israel's security will depend on the study of Torah (8:9-10). Israel will experience a new Sinai (8:5), but there will be no promulgation of a new Torah in the Messianic Age: rather the old Torah will reveal new depths and hidden meanings (8:1), meanings already disclosed to the heavenly Yeshibah, which God "will publish to His people on the great day" (5:10).

(5) The ingathered exiles will join in the Messianic banquet, the feast of Leviathan. This will take place in the Temple, which must, therefore, have been rebuilt earlier (8:2). Unlike some Jewish eschatological scenarios (which may have been influenced by Islamic models), Tg. Cant. does not dwell on the sensual pleasures of the Messianic Age but generally adopts a more "spiritual" outlook.

4.6. Pacifism

Our Targumist, though a fervent advocate of Messianism, realizes that it is fraught with dangers. People may try to calculate the end, and on the basis of these calculations take up arms to force the redemption. He will have none of this. While he holds that it is legitimate to search the Scroll of the Torah to discover whether the time of the redemption has arrived, he advises consulting the Sages on these matters (7:13). In the last analysis the redemption will only come at God's good pleasure, so the end is incalculable (7:14). And it is study of the Torah and the merits of the Sages and the Fathers that will bring it about, not rising in revolt against the enemies of Israel. "The King Messiah will say: 'I adjure you, O my people of the House of Israel, not to be stirred up against the nations of the world, in order to escape from exile, nor to rebel against the hosts of Gog and Magog. Wait yet a little till the nations that have come up to wage war against Jerusalem are destroyed, and after that the Lord of the World will remember for your sake the love of the righteous, and it will be the Lord's good pleasure to redeem you'" (8:4). The same point is trailed at 2:7 by the reference to the premature exodus of the Sons of Ephraim from Egypt: "Moses, the teacher of Israel, opened his mouth and thus said: 'I adjure you, Congregation of Israel . . . not to presume to go up to the Land of Canaan, until it should be the will of the Lord, and until all the generation of the men of war perish utterly from the midst of the camp—as your brothers, the sons of Ephraim presumed when they went out of Egypt thirty years before the [appointed] time had arrived, and they fell at the hands of the Philistines who dwelt in Gath, and they killed them. Rather wait out the period of forty years, and after that your sons will enter and possess it [the Land of Israel]'" (cf. 3:5). There is an urgency about these injunctions that suggests that the Targumist lived at a time when there was a real danger that zealots would take up arms against the nations in order to bring in the Messianic deliverance.[15]

Our Targumist is a pacifist, and he adopts this point of view because he believes that the decisive battles Israel has to fight are spiritual and not physical; her real defenses are prayer, study of Torah, and performance of the *miṣwot* rather than the "weapons of the warriors" (4:4). It is the words of Torah that form protective ramparts and towers around Israel. It is the scholars, and above all the Head of the College, who are the true "Guardians of the City" (cf. 8:9-10). Israel should rely upon divine aid: if necessary God will miraculously shield her against human foes as he did in Egypt, at the Red Sea, and in the Wilderness (1:3, 4, 9; 3:6; 5:15). Ranged against Israel are spiritual forces whom the Targumist seems to see as a greater threat to her survival than the nations of the world, and they can only be defeated by spiritual means. The clouds of glory that surrounded Israel in the Wilderness were primarily to protect her against the "evil eye" (2:6). The weapons Israel carried in the Wilderness were engraved with "the Great Name, expressed in seventy names" (2:17). In other words they were effective only because of magical incantation. It was by wielding "the curse of the Lord" that Joshua and the righteous men of Israel overcame the great magician Amalek (2:16). "So long as the people of the House of Israel were holding in their hands the instrument of their righteous fathers, malicious demons—[harmful] spirits that walk at night, in the morning, and at noon—were fleeing from them" (4:6). The Shekhinah is a sovereign remedy against these same malevolent beings (4:6). The Priestly Blessing, which puts God's Name on Israel, surrounds her "like a high and strong wall, and by it all the mighty

[15] For other messianic references in the Targum see 1:7-8; 4:5; 7:4; 8:2, 8, 12-13.

men of Israel prevail and prosper" (3:7). The mezuzah, the tefillin (8:3), and the seal of circumcision, by which Israel prevails "like a mighty man with a sword strapped upon his thigh" (3:8), protect against the Destroyer (2:9). Given this worldview, with which Paul and the Qumran Community would have had some sympathy, though the latter believed that they would also have to fight physically in the last days,[16] it is hardly surprising that our Targumist plays down the militarism that is inherent in some forms of Messianism.

[16] See Philip S. Alexander, "'Wrestling against Wickedness in High Places': Magic in the Worldview of the Qumran Community," in Stanley E. Porter and Craig A. Evans, eds., *The Scrolls and the Scriptures: Qumran Fifty Years After* (Sheffield: Sheffield Academic Press, 1997) 318–37. Interestingly, the Qumran community believed that the efficacy of their weapons was enhanced by magical inscriptions: see 1QM 6.2-3, and cf. Tg. Cant. 2:17.

5. THE EXEGETICAL APPROACH OF TARGUM CANTICLES

5.1. Tg. Cant.'s General Reading Strategy

The major problem that faces any exegete of Canticles is the fact that the work consists almost entirely of passages of unrubricated direct speech. It is made up of snippets of monologue and dialogue without any narrative framework. This speech has to be contextualized in some way: that is to say, the exegete has to deduce from a close examination of the text exactly who is speaking, to whom, and on what occasion. Canticles, in other words, presents a classic problem of pragmatics.[1] The Targumist solves this problem by creating a narrative framework, a co-text, based on a meticulous and reasoned analysis of the speech that gives his understanding of the setting the speech implies.

The Targumist, like other readers of Canticles, detected two dominant voices in the text—the male voice of the Beloved (the *Dod*) and the female voice of the Bride (the *Kallah*/*Ra'yah*). The action centers on a dialogue between these two actors, with occasional interventions of third parties such as the daughters of Jerusalem. He identified the Beloved as God and the Bride as Israel. There were a number of reasons for this basic exegetical move. First, for cultural reasons he could not accept the text at its face value: he could not believe that it could simply be expressing the carnal love between a man and a woman. It must be allegorical and have a religious meaning. Second, the identification of the Beloved as God and the Bride as Israel was traditional. It may, in fact, go back to the very beginnings of the religious use of the text in the Second Temple period (see *Intro.* 6). Though our Targumist, as we shall see, was no slave to the tradition, he was unlikely to challenge such a fundamental and long-standing premise of Rabbinic exegesis. But third, the identification had the sanction of Scripture. Canticles was part of the canon and had to be read in that setting. Elsewhere in Scripture, particularly in the Prophetic writings, the relationship between God and Israel is frequently pictured under the image of the relationship between a husband and a wife. The absolute fidelity that society demanded a wife should show her husband was seen as a fitting metaphor of the fidelity Israel owed to God. Israel was "married" to God at Sinai; worship of other gods was "adultery," and the prophets were prepared to describe it as such in very earthy terms (see, e.g., Exod 34:14-15; Hosea 1–4; Jer 2:1-2; Ezekiel 16; Isa 54:4-7; 62:4-5). As Gerson Cohen has persuasively argued, the identification of the Beloved as God and the Bride as Israel would have seemed totally natural to a Rabbinic reader of Canticles.[2]

Canticles thus becomes an allegory of God's relationship with Israel. Our Targumist's distinctive contribution, as we noted above (*Intro.* 3), was to see it as a *historical* allegory. He mapped the rhythm of communion, estrangement, and reconciliation that runs through Canticles onto the history of Israel as he knew it. This process of mapping was helped by

[1] There are other cases of unrubricated speech in the Bible, notably in the Psalms and in parts of the prophetic writings. The "headings" of the Psalms represent an early attempt to provide them with a context, and are broadly comparable to the contextualization attempted by our Targumist. On this phenomenon in the Targum see Alexander Samely, *The Interpretation of Speech in the Pentateuch Targums* (Tübingen: J.C.B. Mohr [Paul Siebeck], 1992), and Robert P. Gordon, *Studies in the Targums to the Twelve Prophets: From Nahum to Malachi* (Leiden and New York: Brill, 1994) 74–82. Similar problems, of course, arise in the staging of a play. The director and the actors have to create a living context in which the dialogue makes maximum sense, and they have to deduce this context largely from the direct speech.

[2] Gerson D. Cohen, "The Song of Songs and the Jewish Religious Mentality," in idem, *Studies in the Variety of Rabbinic Cultures* (Philadelphia: Jewish Publication Society, 1991) 3–17.

what he took to be a number of rather explicit historical allusions in the text. The most important of these was at 1:9, "To a mare in the chariots of Pharaoh have I compared you, O My Love." The Targumist saw here a reference to the chariots of Pharaoh pursuing the Israelites as they escaped from Egypt. The link was confirmed by the verbal echo in Canticles' *le-susati be-rikhebei far'oh* of *kol rekheb par'oh* in Exod 14:9. From this the Targumist deduced that this passage should be contextualized to the period of the Exodus from Egypt. A second time-note was detected at 3:6, "Who is this going up from the Wilderness." The Targumist naturally correlated this with the crossing of the Jordan and the entry of the Israelites into the Promised Land. He puts these words in the mouths of the peoples of the Land as they watch the Israelites approaching from the Wilderness. With the references to the "litter of Solomon" at 3:9 and the "palanquin of Solomon" at 3:7 he felt sure that he must be in the reign of Solomon: he identified both the litter and the palanquin with the Temple. Finally, he saw a time-note in 8:5, "Who is this coming up from the wilderness, leaning upon her Beloved?" The parallelism with 3:6 is obvious. The reference must be to Israel returning to the Land from exile, and the words must be spoken by the Gentiles. But the Targumist's schema suggested to him that here the allusion cannot be to the Exodus from Egypt, but rather to the return of the exiles in the Messianic Age.

There is a considerable amount of repetition in Canticles and our Targumist employs it to good effect. His schema allows him to avoid the problem of redundancy by applying these repetitions to different ages in Israel's history.[3] A case in point is the parallelism between 3:5 ("I adjure you, O Daughters of Jerusalem, by the gazelles, or by the hinds of the field, that you do not awaken or stir up love, till it please") and 8:4 ("I adjure you, O Daughters of Jerusalem, not to stir up or awaken love, till it please"). In both cases the Targumist sees an exhortation not to enter the Land prematurely, but in virtue of his schema he detects in the first instance the voice of Moses addressing the Israelites in the Wilderness, and in the second the voice of the Messiah addressing the Jews in the exile of Edom at the end of days. Thus he is able, cleverly, to satisfy a cardinal principle of Midrash, namely that there is no real redundancy in Scripture. The repetitions are nuanced and the potential of Scripture thus maximized. At the same time the repetition confirms him in his belief that the sacred history of Israel is cyclical. Once our Targumist has discovered a few key points where the inner spiritual history recorded in Canticles can be correlated with the outer political history recorded in the historical books of the Bible, he can begin to fill in the gaps. He does this by reading Canticles closely against the relevant historical narrative found in the rest of the Bible and seeking verbal echoes and allusions (for these see the detailed *Notes* below).

From this analysis of the Targumist's general reading strategy two important points emerge. First, his interpretation, contrary to first appearances, is not arbitrary or willful, but carefully reasoned and coherent. This impression will be confirmed by our analysis of the form and genre of his Targum (*Intro.* 5.2) and of his symbolic lexicon (*Intro.* 5.3). Second, as we hinted above (*Intro.* 3), our Targum is probably unique in Jewish Bible exegesis before the high Middle Ages in subjecting a book of the Bible to a holistic reading. Classic Midrash tends to be atomistic: it usually takes each verse or even each word or phrase on its own and explains it with little reference to its context, still less to any overall interpretative schema for the book.

[3] It is a common device in the Midrash to refer one element of a repetition to "this world" and another to "the world to come."

5.2. The Form and Genre of Tg. Cant.

Tg. Cant. is extremely paraphrastic: large quantities of interpretative material have been injected into the translation, so that it now runs to some five times the length of the original Hebrew. The paradox is that despite the expansions the Targumist has made a valiant effort to preserve the outward form of a translation. He could have presented his interpretation in a more straightforward way as a traditional commentary. He has chosen not to do so (for reasons we shall discuss in *Intro.* 7), but to create the fiction that what he is offering the reader is a translation. The form of his text broadly mirrors the form of the underlying Hebrew (though, as with all the Targumists, he fails to respect its poetic structure). Implicit in his work are certain notions about the nature of Targumic form. This fact comes out when we compare Tg. Cant. with classic Rabbinic Midrash. Midrash is argumentative in style. It cites different opinions introduced by formulae such as *dabar ʾaḥer* ("another interpretation"). It attributes these interpretations to named masters such as Rabbi Aqiba and Rabbi Ishmael. It quotes extensively from other parts of Scripture, introducing the quotations with citation formulae such as *she-neʾemar* ("as it is said"). It quotes "parables" *(meshalim)* introduced by one of the variants of the formula *mashal le-mah ha-dabar domeh.* And so forth. The Targumist avoids these standard features of Midrash. At a number of points he sails very close to Midrashic form, but he has a rather clear idea of the formal limits of the Targumic genre. He rather skillfully disguises what is his own material and what is biblical. If only his Targum were available it would be very difficult to decide in many cases what is Bible and what are the Targumist's additions. Only on one occasion, Cant 1:1, before the text proper begins, does he lapse into outright Midrash.[4]

The relationship between Tg. Cant. and the Hebrew is immensely complicated and sometimes hard to work out. Basically the Targumist employs three ways of representing the Hebrew in his paraphrase.

(1) In the first method the formula "X which is like Y" is used to link the Targum to the original, Y being an element in the biblical text and X its interpretative equivalent, e.g., Cant 2:11:

Hebrew Text:	Targum:
For lo, the winter is past,	For the time of servitude, which is likened to winter, has ended, and the years about which I spoke to Abraham between the pieces has been cut short,
The rain is over and gone.	and the tyranny of the Egyptians, which is compared to the [period of] incessant rain, has passed and gone. You shall not see them ever again.

[4] Alexander Sperber's classification of Tg. Cant., Tg. Lam., and Tg. Eccl. as "Translation and Midrash completely fused together" (*The Bible in Aramaic,* vol. 4A, *The Hagiographa* [Leiden: Brill, 1968]), Contents, is problematic. The problem lies with the term "Midrash." If he means by this "midrashic form," then this is not correct: the form of Tg. Cant. is pure Targum. If he means "midrashic method," then this is typical of *all* the Targumim. Even more problematic is his description of Tg. Esth. as "Targum, a misnomer for Midrash."

(2) In the second method the biblical text is more or less "dissolved" in a free-flowing paraphrase, in which the equivalents replace the original terms. However, the Targum never seems totally to replace the original terms: some of these always reappear unchanged in the paraphrase to act as points of reference in linking up the Targum to the Hebrew, e.g., Cant 4:3:

HEBREW TEXT:	TARGUM:
Your lips are like a thread of scarlet,	The lips of the High Priest were making intercession in prayer before the Lord on the Day of Atonement,
Your speech is fair;	and his words were turning back the sins of Israel, which are like a thread of scarlet, and making them white as clean wool.
Your brow is like a slice of pomegranate	And the King, who was their head, was as full of precepts as a pomegranate,
Behind your veil.	not to mention the Counselors and Magistrates who were close to the King, who were righteous, and in whom was no iniquity.

The basic equivalents here seem to be the following:

HEBREW TEXT:	TARGUM:
lips	lips
thread of scarlet	thread of scarlet
mouth (midbar)	words *(millin)*
fair (naʾweh)	clean *(neqeʾ)*
brow (raqqah)	head
slice (pelaḥ)	precepts *(piqqudayyaʾ)*
pomegranate	pomegranate
behind (mibbaʿad)	not to mention *(bar min)*
veil (ṣammah)	Counselors and Magistrates

(3) The third method of representing the biblical text involves translating it more or less literally. The element of interpretation consists of putting the words of the Bible into a certain dramatic setting, e.g., Cant 4:7:

HEBREW TEXT:	TARGUM:
	Whenever the people of the House of Israel do the will of the Lord of the World, He praises them in the heavens above, and thus says:
All of You is beautiful, My Love; *And there is no blemish in You.*	"All of You is beautiful, Assembly of Israel, and there is no defect in You."

The Targumim of the Pentateuch are almost entirely of the base-translation + detachable glosses type. Like Tg. Cant., they too may contain a sizable quantity of interpretative material, but this is carefully introduced in such a way that it can be bracketed out, leaving behind a freestanding, one-to-one rendering of the original. However, it is impossible to extract such a base translation from Tg. Cant. For short sections this might be achieved, but very rapidly we run into paraphrase and the base-translation vanishes. In the Middle Ages there were attempts to take some of the paraphrastic Targumim and scale them down into closer conformity with the original Hebrew. This movement probably led, for example, to the emergence of the Third Targum to Esther.[5] Significantly, no one seems to have tried to revise Tg. Cant. into closer conformity with the Bible.[6] It was clearly impossible. Tg. Cant., in fact, represents one of the most extreme cases of dissolved paraphrase in the whole of Targumic literature. Nevertheless, in a *tour de force*, our Targumist appears to have represented faithfully every single element of the Hebrew in his paraphrase and almost always in its correct biblical sequence.[7]

5.3. Tg. Cant.'s Symbolic Lexicon

In constructing his allegorical reading of Canticles the Targumist has worked with a sophisticated symbolic lexicon by which he decoded the terms in the original Hebrew. This lexicon is based on different sources. The Bible provided some of the equivalents. Thus "vine = Israel" (Tg. Cant. 7:13, with *Note* 52; cf. Ps 80:8; Isa 5:2; Jer 2:21; Ezek 17:6), "gold = Torah" (Tg. Cant. 3:10; 5:11, 15; cf. Pss 19:10; 119:27), and "waters = the nations" (Tg. Cant. 8:7, with *Note* 33; cf. Isa 17:12) can easily be justified from Scripture. Post-biblical tradition also contributed. A striking case of this is "Lebanon = the Temple." Though Scripture is quoted to support this very old equation (1 Kgs 7:2), it is not actually part of the Bible's own symbolic lexicon. The Targumist relies upon it at a number of critical junctures in his exposition (3:9, *Note* 25; 4:15). Other equivalents appear to be inventions of the Targumist himself. Some of these, such as "odor = repute" (1:3) would have seemed to him natural, and simply reflect the metaphorical use of language in everyday speech. Others, such as "breasts = redeemers" (4:5; 7:4), were dictated to him largely by the context in which he found them in Canticles and the exigencies of the interpretation. His lexicon is not always consistent. Sometimes the same symbol is decoded in different ways in different places. Doubtless he would have justified this variation on the grounds that the meaning of the symbol can change according to the context (in this case the period of the *Heilsgeschichte*) to which it applies.

Where the link between signifier and signified is already established in the Bible or in Rabbinic tradition, or can be regarded as natural and self-evident, it requires little justification. However, in certain cases some of the more extreme and manipulative techniques of aggadic midrash have had to be employed to justify the connection. Among these are the following:

[5] See Moshe H. Goshen-Gottstein, "The 'Third Targum' on Esther and MS. Neofiti 1," *Biblica* 56 (1975) 301–29.

[6] I do not count Arias Montano's rather halfhearted attempt to exclude "superfluous" material in the Antwerp Polyglot (see *Intro.* 1).

[7] On the genres of the Targumim see Philip S. Alexander, "Jewish Aramaic Translations of Hebrew Scriptures," in Martin J. Mulder, ed., *Mikra*. CRINT II.1 (Assen: Van Gorcum, 1988) 217–53.

(1) *ʾAl tiqrei,* i.e., changing the pointing of a word, or even the consonants, provided the new word is a reasonably close homophone of the old. In Midrash the full formula for this technique is "do not read X but Y." In the absence of the formula, which clearly could not be introduced in a translation, we cannot be sure of all the cases where our Targumist is invoking the principle. The category is flexible and somewhat ill-defined, but the following are probable examples: *ʿalamot* ("maidens") = *ʿolamot* ("worlds") (1:3); *kofer* ("henna") = *kippur* ("atonement") (1:14); *ʾimmo* ("his mother") = *ʿammo* ("his people"); *migdalot* ("towers") = *megaddelot* ("nurturers") (5:13); *shoshannim* ("roses") = *she-shonim* ("those who learn") (5:13); *saʿrekh* ("your hair") = *sheʾarekh* ("your remainder") (6:5).

(2) *Gematria,* i.e., computing the numerical value of the letters of the biblical word, e.g., *yayin* ("wine") = seventy (nations) (1:2, 4; 4:10); *bakh* ("in You") = twenty-two (letters of the Hebrew alphabet) (1:4). A similar device has been used to justify the equation "eye" = Sanhedrin: *ʿayin* ("eye") has been taken not only as the bodily organ but as the name for the sixteenth letter of the Hebrew alphabet, which stands numerically for 70, the number of members of the Sanhedrin (4:1, 9; 5:12; 6:5; 7:5).

(3) *Notarikon,* i.e., dividing a word so that it forms two or more separate words. *Notarikon* can often be seen simply as a form of *ʾal tiqrei.* Two possible examples are *she-galeshu* ("who streamed down") = *she-gal ʿasu* ("who made a heap/memorial") (4:1); and *Tarshish* (name) = *terei shesh* (2 [x] 6 = 12) (5:14).

(4) Etymologizing of proper names. *Shelomoh* ("Solomon") = "He to whom belongs peace," i.e., God (*she-shalom shelo:* 1:5); *Moriah* = "myrrh" (*mor:* 3:6); *Lebanon* = "white" (*laban:* 5:15); *Heshbon* = "calculation" (*ḥeshbon:* 7:5); *Bat-Rabbim* = "House of the Many," i.e., the Sanhedrin (*Beit Rabbim:* 7:5).

5.4. Tg. Cant. and the Oneirocritica

Tg. Cant.'s exegetical techniques stand foursquare within the tradition of mantological or oneirocritical exegesis in the ancient world. Our Targumist has treated Canticles as if it were like a dream and applied to it the technical procedures of the professional dream interpreters of his day. These treated the dream text as a collection of symbols that have to be individually decoded and then reassembled into a different story. Their method differs from dream interpretation found in literary and novelistic sources, and exemplified rather well by the dreams Joseph interprets in Genesis. In literary texts dreams tend to be rather straightforward allegories, and their relationship to the stories that decode them is reasonably direct. In the technical oneirocritica, however, the relationship is much more oblique, seemingly much more arbitrary. In fact, in the oneirocritica much of the dream content may be treated as of no significance; the meaning of the dream may turn totally on some key symbol in the text.[8] Our Targumist treats all the elements of the Hebrew text as significant (his doctrine of Scripture would not allow him to do otherwise), but he applies to them individually the procedures of the oneirocritica, and then links together the separately decoded symbols into a new narrative. Though his approach to the biblical book, as we have noted, is unusually holistic, his treatment of the individual verses tends to be atomistic. That is to say, he isolates the elements of the verse, in extreme cases ignores the links established between them in the

[8] On this distinction see Sigmund Freud, *Interpretation of Dreams*, trans. J. Strachey (Harmondsworth: Penguin, 1986) 170–72.

biblical narrative, decodes them separately, then reconnects them in a new narrative that establishes new and meaningful relationships between them.

An extreme case of this is found at 6:12, perhaps the most difficult verse in the whole of Canticles. The old JPS version translates: "Before I was aware, my soul set me upon the chariots of my princely people." Tg. simply breaks the verse down into its parts ("I did not know . . . My soul counseled me . . . Chariots . . . My people [is] noble"), interprets each part separately, and then reassembles the units of interpretation into a plausible story: "And when it was revealed before the Lord that they were righteous and were engaging in the study of the Torah, the Lord said through His Word: 'I will not again crush them, nor shall I make a total end of them, but I will take counsel with Myself to do them good and make them exalted in royal chariots, for the sake of the merits of the righteous of this generation, who resemble Abraham their forefather in their deeds'" (see *Notes ad loc.*).

Our Targumist could have been aware of the ancient oneirocritica. It was known in Rabbinic circles, both in Palestine and in Babylonia. In fact, *Babli Berakhot* contains one of the most important technical dream manuals to survive from antiquity.[9] But aspects of the oneirocritica had long since been absorbed into mainstream Jewish Bible interpretation, so our Targumist may not have been all that consciously applying oneirocritical methods. Borrowing by biblical exegetes from the techniques of the oneirocritica may have begun already in Second Temple times. It seems to have influenced the Qumran Pesharim. Significantly, the Qumran exegetes used *pesher,* a term derived from the oneirocritica, to designate this type of exegesis, which was applied only to prophetic texts, and not to legal.[10] And devices such as *gematria, notarikon,* and etymology had entered Rabbinic Midrash from the oneirocritica long before our Targumist's day. As an illustration of how parallel our Targumist's approach can be to the oneirocritica, compare his etymologizing of proper names with the etymologizing of the name "Cappadocia" as "ten beams" in Rabbi Ishmael's interpretation of a dream—a story that seems to have been used as a paradigm by the Rabbis of how a dream should be interpreted.[11] Note also how the symbolic lexicon of the Rabbinic dreambook in *Babli Berakhot* seems to be built up, like our Targumist's symbolic lexicon, partly on the basis of Scripture, partly on the basis of tradition, partly on the basis of natural linguistic usage, and partly on the basis of wordplays of various kinds.[12]

[9] On the Rabbinic dream book see Philip S. Alexander, "Bavli Berakhot 55a-57b: The Talmudic Dreambook in Context," *JJS* 46 (1995) 230–48.

[10] See Devora Dimant, "Qumran Sectarian Literature," in Michael E. Stone, ed., *Jewish Writings of the Second Temple Period.* CRINT II.2 (Assen: VanGorcum; Philadelphia: Fortress, 1984) 505–508; Michael A. Fishbane, "The Qumran-Pesher and Traits of Ancient Hermeneutics," *Proceedings of the Sixth World Congress of Jewish Studies* 6/1 (1977) 97–114. On mantological exegesis in general see Michael A. Fishbane, *Biblical Interpretation in Ancient Israel* (Oxford: Clarendon Press, 1986).

[11] y.MS IV, 55b; Lam.R. 1.1 §17; Gen.R. 67.12; b.Ber. 56b.

[12] See further Philip S. Alexander, "Quid Athenis et Hierosolymis? Rabbinic Midrash and Hermeneutics in the Graeco-Roman World," in Philip R. Davies and Richard T. White, eds., *A Tribute to Geza Vermes* (Sheffield: Sheffield Academic Press, 1990) 101–24. It has been argued that Canticles is actually intended as a sequence of dreams: see, e.g., Solomon B. Freehof, "The Song of Songs: A General Suggestion," *JQR* 39 (1948–49) 397–402. If this is the case, then the application of the oneirocritica is even more apt.

6. TARGUM CANTICLES AND THE HISTORY OF EXEGESIS

6.1. Allegory and the Canonization of Canticles

Within the tradition of Jewish Bible interpretation Canticles has probably engendered more exegesis in proportion to its size than any other book outside of the Pentateuch. This is a measure not only of its importance but of its intrinsic difficulty, since there is a fundamental law of Midrash that the more problematic the text, the more interpretation it requires.[1] The problems with Canticles are obvious. It contains no explicit mention of God (with the possible exception of 8:6), of Torah or Israel, or of any other of Rabbinic Judaism's great themes. It is full of explicit sexual imagery and appears to be talking simply about the carnal love of a man and a woman (see, e.g., 1:2, 13-14; 2:5-6; 4:9-15; 7:12-13). On the face of it, Canticles is a most improper and improbable book to find in Holy Writ. It is tempting to suppose that its explicit sexual language is religiously problematic only from the standpoint of our "repressed" modern age: earlier generations had a "healthier" attitude toward the body and sex. But this is not so. Sexuality was as much a problem in antiquity as it is today: Freud did not invent our sexual inhibitions; he merely chronicled them. *Our* surprise at finding such a text in Holy Writ is clearly mirrored in antiquity. Even when Canticles was accepted into the canon its study was hedged about with all sorts of safeguards that indicate that it was regarded as a dangerous text.

Yet canonized it was. The final canonization came late, itself an indication of unease. The crucial text is m.Yad. 3:5, which is concerned with the question of which books "render the hands unclean," that is to say, which were given under the inspiration of the holy spirit *(ruaḥ ha-qodesh)* or spirit of prophecy *(ruaḥ ha-nebu'ah)* (cf. t.Yad. 2:14), have the same status as a Torah scroll, and are, consequently, an integral part of Holy Scripture. This complex passage cannot be analyzed in depth here: suffice it to say that it has often been interpreted rather superficially. It is the source of the common claim that the canon of the Hebrew Bible was finally closed at the so-called Academy of Yabneh by the resolution of the status of the residually disputed books, Ecclesiastes and Song of Songs: "Rabbi Simeon ben Azzai said: I have heard a tradition from the seventy-two elders, 'On the day on which they seated Rabbi Eleazar ben Azariah in the Academy, [it was decided] that the Song of Songs and Ecclesiastes render the hands unclean.'" The enigmatic phrase "when they seated Rabbi Eleazar ben Azariah in the Academy" is commonly interpreted in the light of y.Ber. IV, 7d and b.Ber. 27b-27a as referring to the deposition of Rabban Gamaliel as head of the Academy at Yavneh, an event that, if it is historical, must have occurred around 100 C.E. But the link with y.Ber. IV, 7d and b.Ber. 27b-27a and, indeed, the historicity of Gamaliel's deposition are far from certain. Source analysis suggests that the phrase "on the day on which they seated Rabbi Eleazar ben Azariah in the Academy" is a secondary intrusion: what Simeon ben Azzai was originally reporting was a tradition from the pre-70 Sanhedrin. If around 100 C.E. there *was* a declaration in favor of the canonicity of Canticles it cannot have been very effective since, as the pericope also indicates, Rabbi Aqiba, possibly some thirty years later, still felt the need to issue his famous declaration: "God forbid! No man in Israel ever disputed about the Song of Songs [that he should say] that it does not defile the hands, for all

[1] This point can be made by analyzing "narrative time" against "midrashic time." Where midrashic time greatly exceeds narrative time it often indicates resistance in the text, "knots" that have to be untied.

the ages of Israel are not worth the day on which the Song of Songs was given to Israel; for all the Writings are holy, but the Song of Songs is the holy of holies." Nor did Aqiba's ringing endorsement end the matter (though, if historical, it would doubtless have been influential), for, as the pericope again shows, the status of Canticles was *still* being discussed in the time of Rabbi Judah, Rabbi Yosei and Rabbi Simeon in the generation after Aqiba. The pericope as it stands cannot have been edited before *c.*160 C.E. It was probably intended finally to resolve the issue of the status of Canticles and Ecclesiastes by summarizing the previous traditions on the question and coming down in favor of canonicity. Certainly from *c.*160 onward there is little evidence of any dispute over Canticles in the Rabbinic tradition.

Allegorization cannot have been the sole reason why Canticles was canonized (the text must already have achieved a certain currency and status before anyone would have bothered to attempt allegory), but presumably it finally stilled any doubts about Canticles' suitability as a part of Holy Writ.[2] ARN A.1 probably reflects accurately the role of exegesis in making Canticles acceptable: "Originally, it is said, Proverbs, Song of Songs, and Ecclesiastes were suppressed; for since they were held to be mere parables and not part of the Holy Writings, [the religious authorities] arose and suppressed them. [And so they remained] until the men of Hezekiah came and interpreted them (cf. Prov 25:1)."[3] The Rabbis did not invent the allegorical interpretation: it was probably already rather old in Aqiba's time. Copies of Canticles have been found among the Dead Sea Scrolls.[4] Given the nature of the Qumran community it is highly unlikely that they were reading the text literally, but just exactly how they interpreted it is unknown. Fourth Ezra 5:23-28 contains a series of allusions to Canticles that seem to involve identifying the Bride as Israel and the Bridegroom as God. Josephus, *C.Ap.* 1.40, implies that Canticles is "a hymn to God," which indicates some kind of non-literal reading. And if Rev 3:20 is an echo of Cant 5:2, then already in the first century the Church may have begun to appropriate the allegorical reading, identifying the Bridegroom with Christ and the Bride with the Church.

The acceptability of Canticles is shown by its frequent citation in the classic exoteric literature of Rabbinic Judaism—the Talmuds and the Midrashim. Three substantial commentaries on it have also survived intact. The largest of these is Canticles Rabba *(Midrash Ḥazita).* The date of this rich work, which displays considerable overlaps with Exodus Rabba, Numbers Rabba and the Mekhilta deRabbi Ishmael, is disputed. Moshe David Herr proposes a redaction around the middle of the sixth century. Samuel T. Lachs, however, suggests an original composition between 650 and 750, with a final redaction in the latter half of the eighth century.[5] In other words, Canticles Rabba dates very broadly from the time

[2] Daniel Boyarin, "Two Introductions to the Midrash on the Song of Songs," *Tarbiṣ* 56 (1986–87) 479–500 [Hebrew] argues that Tannaitic exposition of the Song of Songs is not allegorical, but his case is based on a rather precise and restrictive definition of allegory and does not affect our position here. The basic point remains that it was exegesis (however classified) that made the work acceptable.

[3] Cf. b.Hag. 13a: "That man must be remembered for a blessing, namely Ḥananiah ben Hezekiah; but for him, the Book of Ezekiel would have been withdrawn [from the canon], for its words contradict the words of the Torah. What did he do? Three hundred measures of oil were brought up to him and he sat in an upper room and expounded it."

[4] See Martin Abegg, Jr., Peter Flint, and Eugene Ulrich, *The Dead Sea Scrolls Bible* (San Francisco: HarperSanFrancisco, 1999) 611–18.

[5] M. D. Herr, *EJ* 15, cols. 152-54; Samuel T. Lachs, "Prolegomena to Canticles Rabba," *JQR* n.s. 55 (1964–65) 235–55. Further, Günter Stemberger, *Introduction to Talmud and Midrash.* Translated and edited by Markus Bockmuehl (2nd ed. Edinburgh: T & T Clark, 1996) 315–16. English translation: Maurice Simon in *Midrash Rabbah* 9 (London: Soncino, 1939). The quotations from Cant.R. below are based on the Simon's fine rendering, but I have throughout consulted the original Hebrew and made frequent changes.

when our Targum was composed, and may actually be later than it (*Intro.* 8). There is also *ʾAggadat Shir ha-Shirim.* Solomon Buber first published this work as *Midrash Zutaʾ to Canticles* from the Parma ms., De Rossi 541, in 1894. This edition was rather poorly done. Solomon Schechter's rather better transcription of the same manuscript appeared two years later under the title *ʾAggadat Shir ha-Shirim.* Subsequently a fragmentary copy of the same work was identified among the Genizah fragments in St. Petersburg and published by Zvi M. Rabinowitz in *Ginzé Midrash.*[6] Schechter proposed a date no "later than the middle of the tenth century" (*Agadath Shir Hashirim* 101), but this can be taken only as tentative: the work has been little studied. The third early Midrash on Canticles is *Midrash Shir ha-Shirim,* published by Eleazar Grünhut in 1897 from a Genizah manuscript (dated 1147) that can no longer be found. Moshe David Herr proposes an eleventh century date but, like *Aggadat Shir ha-Shirim,* the work has hardly been studied and the date must be treated as very provisional.[7] The Genizah has also yielded two further fragments, which appear to represent two further Midrashim on Canticles.[8] We should also mention here the great medieval compendium of Midrash, the *Yalqut Shimʿoni* (12th/13th century). This contains a rich anthology of midrashim on Canticles and, as elsewhere in the *Yalqut*, some of these appear to be derived from early sources no longer extant.[9] The literary interrelationships between these various Rabbinic texts have still to be worked out, but it is evident from even a cursory inspection that, along with our Targum, they display a broadly similar reading of Canticles, distinguished by two fundamental characteristics: first, they all identify the Bride as Israel; their reading is, consequently, nationalistic, not individualistic; and second, they all show a marked tendency to historicize (though only our Targum is *systematically* historical); that is to say, they contextualize elements of Canticles to moments in the history of Israel such as the giving of the Torah on Sinai or the crossing of the Red Sea. It is intriguing to note that in an interpretation of Cant 2:14, "Let me see your face," attributed to Rabbi Aqiba, the verse is contextualized to the giving of the Torah at Sinai. If the attribution is correct then it may suggest that Aqiba popularized this kind of reading.

6.2. Apologetic Elements in Tg. Cant.

Tg. Cant. stands firmly in the tradition of the "official," exoteric reading of Canticles, but two counter-readings of Canticles emerged in the Talmudic period, one within Judaism and the other within Christianity, and these could conceivably have been known to our Targumist. Raphael Loewe has advanced a learned and attractive case that our Targumist *was* aware of both of these, and that in his Targum he is waging a *Zweifrontenkrieg* against them.[10]

[6] Salomon Buber, *Midrasch Suta: Hagadische Abhandlungen über Schir ha-Schirim, Ruth, Echah und Koheleth* (Berlin: M'kize Nirdamim, 1894); Solomon Schechter, *Agadath Shir Hashirim, edited from a Parma Manuscript* (Cambridge: Deighton Bell & Co., 1896); Zvi Meir Rabinowitz, *Ginzé Midrash* (Tel Aviv: Chaim Rosenberg School of Jewish Studies, 1976) 250–95.

[7] Eleazar Grünhut, *Midrash Shir Ha-Shirim* (Jerusalem: 1897; reissued with introduction and notes by Joseph C. Wertheimer, Jerusalem: Ketav yad ve-sefer, 1971).

[8] Jacob Mann, "Some Midrashic Genizah Fragments," *HUCA* 14 (1939) 333–37; idem, *Texts and Studies* I (New York: Ktav, 1972) 322 n. 47a.

[9] See Stemberger, *Introduction to Talmud and Midrash* 351–52.

[10] Raphael Loewe, "Apologetic Motifs in the Targum to the Song of Songs," in: Alexander Altmann, ed., *Biblical Motifs: Origins and Transformations* (Cambridge, Mass.: Harvard University Press, 1966) 159–96.

Starting from a statement by Origen which he took as implying that Canticles was considered esoteric by Jews, Gershom Scholem argued that a distinctive reading of the book developed among the Heikhalot mystics of the Talmudic period. His claims were endorsed by Saul Lieberman, who tried to show that a mystical midrash on the description of the Body of the Beloved in Cant 5:10-16 circulated as an esoteric text in Heikhalot circles and is reflected in their literature, especially in the *Shiʿur Qomah* traditions.[11] The *Shiʿur Qomah* gives the dimensions of the Body of God, or rather the dimensions of the theophany (the Shekhinah or the Demiurge, the *Yoṣer Bereʾshit*) which the mystic sees seated on the Throne of Glory in the seventh celestial palace during his ascent to heaven. It functioned as a kind of mental *mandala,* an aid to mystical contemplation that gave the mystic something on which to focus at the climax of his ecstasy, and allowed him to prolong the moment of the mystical vision of God. The suggestion is that this bizarre notion was grounded in Scripture in a mystical interpretation of the description of the Body of the Beloved in Cant 5:10-16. The implications are rather obvious. The Heikhalot mystics had begun to develop a particularistic reading of Canticles as a cryptic account of the relationship not between Israel and God but between the individual mystic and God—a reading well attested later in both Jewish and Christian mysticism. Seen against this background Tg. Cant.'s treatment of the Body of the Beloved can appear very pointed. Our Targumist consistently avoids taking the limbs of the Beloved as direct descriptions of God's *own* body: rather he displaces them onto the Torah and the righteous, seen as dual manifestations or even incarnations of God on earth. The interpretation of the Body of the Beloved turns out to be little different in detail from the interpretation of the Body of the Bride.

But there are problems with this theory. In the first place Scholem's interpretation of Origen's statement is by no means the only one possible: what Origen seems actually to be talking about is allowing boys to study Canticles.[12] One does not need to invoke a mystical interpretation of the book to explain such a ban. Second, despite Lieberman's brilliant analysis, the idea that a mystical midrash on Cant 5:10-16 underlies the *Shiʿur Qomah* rests on shallow foundations. As Martin Cohen has pointed out, there is, in fact, scant reference to any text in Canticles in the *Shiʿur Qomah.*[13] Third, it is not at all obvious that Rabbis

[11] Gershom Scholem, *Jewish Gnosticism, Merkabah Mysticism, and Talmudic Tradition* (2nd ed. New York: Jewish Theological Seminary, 1965) 36–42; Saul Lieberman, "Mishnat Shir ha-Shirim," ibid. 118–26. In fact a link between *Shiʿur Qomah* and the Body of the Beloved in Canticles had previously been suggested by Adolf Jellinek, *Bet ha-Midrasch* 6 (Leipzig: Fridrikh Nies, 1878; 3rd ed. repr. Jerusalem: Wahrmann Books, 1967) xxxxii. On the *Shiʿur Qomah* see Martin S. Cohen, *The Shiʿur Qomah: Liturgy and Theurgy in Pre-Kabbalistic Jewish Mysticism* (Lanham, Md., New York, and London: University Press of America, 1983); idem, *The Shiʿur Qomah: Texts and Recensions* (Tübingen: J.C.B. Mohr [Paul Siebeck], 1985).

[12] *Commentary on Canticles*, Prol. 1.7: *"Aiunt enim observari etiam apud Hebraeos quod, nisi quis ad aetatem perfectam maturamque pervenerit, libellum hunc nec in manibus quidem tenere permittatur. Sed et illud ab iis accepimus custodiri, quoniamquidem moris est apud eos omnes scripturas a doctoribus et sapientibus tradi pueris, simul et eas quas* δευτερώσεις *appellant, ad ultimum quattuor ista reservari, id est principium Genesis, in quo mundi creatura describitur, et Ezechiel prophetae principia, in quibus de Cherubin refertur, et finem, in quo templi aedificatio continetur et hunc Cantici Canticorum librum."* See further David J. Halperin, *The Faces of the Chariot: Early Jewish Responses to Ezekiel's Vision* (Tübingen: J.C.B. Mohr [Paul Siebeck], 1988) 26–27.

[13] Cohen, *Liturgy and Theurgy* 19. One clear case, however, of a link between the *Shiʿur Qomah* and Cant 5:10-16 is *Heikhalot Rabbati* 12:1 (ed. Wertheimer, *BM* 1:87). This passage is sufficient to show that some mystics did read Cant 5:10-16 (perhaps secondarily), and by implication the whole of Canticles, as an account of the relationship of the individual mystic to God. (The reference to Canticles is not found in some mss.: see Peter Schäfer, *Synopse zur Hekhalot Literatur* [Tübingen: J.C.B. Mohr (Paul Siebeck), 1981] §167.) Note also the emphasis in the Heikhalot texts on the physical beauty of God (e.g., *Heikhalot Rabbati* 25:1-3, ed. Wertheimer, *BM* 1:105–106 [Schäfer, *Synopse* §§260-65], which has distant echoes of the language of Cant 5:10-16; further Cohen, *Liturgy and Theurgy* 7–8, 173–75).

before the Middle Ages would have been squeamish about the *Shiʿur Qomah*. The doctrine doubtless offends philosophical sensibilities,[14] but the Rabbinic attitude toward anthropomorphism is, to say the least, ambivalent. The Rabbis had little difficulty with anthropomorphic language about God in the Bible. Indeed, their own language is often much more vividly anthropomorphic than anything the biblical writers would have dared to use. The claim is frequently made that the Targumim avoid anthropomorphism, but the picture is so confused that it is probably better to classify certain circumlocutions more loosely as reverential language than as "anti-anthropomorphisms." Finally, the supposed allusions to mystical ideas in Tg. Cant. are nowhere near explicit enough to prove that our Targumist is consciously reading in contradiction to the mystical tradition.[15]

Similar problems beset the theory that the Targumist is consciously giving an anti-Christian reading. Possibly from as early as the book of Revelation (cf. Rev 3:20 with Cant 5:2) Christians appropriated Canticles by identifying the Beloved as Christ and the Bride as the Church. Origen, one of the most important of the early Christian commentators on Canticles, was certainly aware of Jewish tradition, and was, to a degree, consciously producing an anti-Jewish reading. It is interesting to note, for example, how his commentary opens with a "Midrash of the Seven Songs," just as our Targum opens with a Midrash of the Ten Songs (Appendix A).[16] But it is less easy to prove anti-Christian exegesis on the Rabbinic side. Tg. Cant. asserts some of the fundamental tenets of Rabbinic Judaism. These inevitably imply a rejection of Christianity, but whether in asserting them our Targumist had Christianity in his sights is far from certain. His deep interest in the story of the Golden Calf illustrates the problem. Christian apologists from as early as Acts (7:40-41) had used the making of the Calf to demonstrate the idolatrous tendencies of Israel, and to question her continuing election. Our Targumist's careful insistence that the Calf was atoned for by the merits of the ʿAqedah and by the offerings of the Tabernacle can be read as a direct counter to this claim. But does he have specifically Christian polemic in mind, or is he more vaguely reflecting earlier Rabbinic unease about this story? It is hard to say.[17] As with the supposed anti-mystical polemic, conclusive evidence of anti-Christian polemic is lacking. A more satisfactory way of understanding Tg. Cant.'s relationship to alternative readings may be in terms of the concept of "preemptive exegesis." Deeply conscious of the intrinsic difficulties of his biblical text, vaguely aware that it could be and had been given questionable interpretations, our Targumist set out to provide his community with an acceptable reading, which

[14] See Alexander Altmann, "Moses Narboni's 'Epistle on *Shiʿur Qoma*,'" in idem, ed., *Jewish Medieval and Renaissance Studies* (Cambridge, Mass.: Harvard University Press, 1967) 225–88; Moses Maimonides, *The Guide of the Perplexed*. Translated with an introduction and notes by Shlomo Pines (Chicago: University of Chicago Press, 1963).

[15] Loewe, "Apologetic Motifs," 186 makes great play of the "robe" of God in Tg. Cant. 5:10, but see *Note* 34 *ad loc*. Another case in point is the reference to the "chambers" of the king in Cant 1:4. The mystical interpretation of this phrase may be as old as t.Hag. 2:3, where Cant 1:4 is quoted in the context of the story of the Four who entered Pardes. Cant 1:4 is probably the origin of the Heikhalot term "the chambers of the Chariot" (Joseph Dan, "The Chambers of the Chariot," *Tarbiṣ* 47 [1977–78] 49–55 [Hebrew]). Against this background the Tg.'s identification of the "chambers" as Sinai, or possibly as the heavenly storehouses where the Torah was kept, may look rather pointed: see Tg. to 1:4, *Note* 26.

[16] See further Ephraim E. Urbach, "Rabbinic Exegesis and Origenes' Commentary on the Song of Songs, and Jewish-Christian Polemics," *Tarbiṣ* 30 (1960–61) 148–70 (Hebrew; English translation, "The Homiletical Interpretation of the Sages and the Expositions of Origen on Canticles, and the Jewish-Christian Disputation," *Scripta Hierosolymitana* 22 [1971] 247–75).

[17] Leivy Smolar and Moses Aberbach, "The Golden Calf Episode in Postbiblical Literature"; Pier Cesare Bori, *The Golden Calf, and the Origins of the Anti-Jewish Controversy*. Translated by David Ward (Atlanta: Scholars, 1990). Further *Intro*. 4.2.

entrenched the values of Rabbinic Judaism and so preemptively occupied the exegetical space of the text.[18]

6.3. The Problem of the "Sources" of Tg. Cant.

Tg. Cant. belongs to an old and rich exegetical tradition.[19] Its numerous links with that tradition will be systematically documented and discussed in the *Notes* below. However, some general remarks need to be made here on the nature of these links and what they show about the Targum's relationship to Rabbinic literature.

Where parallels exist between Targum and Midrash the tendency has been to assume that it is the Targum that depends on the Midrash. Much work on Tg. Cant., beginning already with John Gill in the eighteenth century, has been devoted to the search for parallels, and where a parallel has been found in a classic Rabbinic text it has usually been identified as the source of the Targum. Since by ransacking Rabbinic literature from end to end more or less convincing parallels can be found for over ninety per cent of our Targum, the Targum can be dissolved into a mere pastiche of Rabbinic tradition. This view is implicit especially in the work of Pinkhos Churgin and Ezra Z. Melamed. Churgin treats the parallels to *Targum Shir ha-Shirim* under the heading "Sources of the Aggadah of the Targum" *(Meqorot ha-Aggadah shel ha-Targum),*[20] while in Melamed's article the central section on "*Targum Shir ha-Shirim* and Talmudic Literature" begins with a discussion of the "use of the sources" *(shimmush ba-meqorot).*[21]

This position is questionable on a number of counts. First, as Joseph Heinemann rightly objected,[22] it presupposes a static model of Rabbinic tradition in which it is viewed essentially as a collection of finished literary works. This is problematic. Rabbinic tradition seems to have been in a very fluid state in late antiquity. Each of the classic documents of Rabbinic literature (even Mishnah and Talmud) is to a greater or lesser degree textually unstable, as an examination of the manuscripts will show. Even in the Middle Ages the revered texts of the Talmudic period were not simply copied but were, to an extent, *recreated.* Moreover, each of these works had *its* sources, so when we find a parallel between Tg. Cant. and, say, Canticles Rabba, how are we to decide whether the Targum is directly dependent on the Midrash or on the source of the Midrash? In many instances a given aggadah in Tg. Cant. can be paralleled from a number of different Midrashic and Talmudic texts. How, in such cases, are we to choose which is the "source" of the Targum? Rabbinic tradition in late antiquity was transmitted not only through written texts but also orally, through preaching in synagogue and through study and debate in the schools. This mixture of oral and written media complicates the problem of literary dependence and in many cases makes it insoluble. The complexities of the situation are too often ignored. In a few cases direct literary dependence may be satisfactorily established, but usually the best we can do is to collect the attestations of a given aggadah, compare and contrast them, and try to work out some sort of tradition history.

[18] For the concept of preemptive exegesis see Philip S. Alexander, "Pre-emptive Exegesis: Genesis Rabba's Reading of the Story of Creation," *JJS* 43 (1992) 230–45.

[19] Only two "sources" have been incorporated intact within Tg. Cant., viz., the "Midrash of the Ten Songs" at 1:1 and the list of gemstones at 5:14. On these see Appendices A and B.

[20] Pinkhos Churgin, *Targum Ketuvim* (New York: Horeb, 1945) 129.

[21] Ezra Z. Melamed, "Targum Canticles," *Tarbiṣ* 40 (1970–71) 208.

[22] Joseph Heinemann, "Targum Canticles and its Sources," *Tarbiṣ* 41 (1971–72) 126–29.

The parallels between Tg. Cant. and the other Rabbinic expositions of Canticles are of two broad kinds: (1) aggadic, and (2) translational. The aggadic group comprises parallels to the aggadic substance of the Targum; the translational comprises texts that parallel the way in which Tg. Cant. translates the biblical text, and that use the same Aramaic words to render the underlying Hebrew. Aggadic parallels are found mainly (though not exclusively) in the Midrashim; translational parallels are found in the other Targumim.

(1) Aggadic Parallels

In almost every case the aggadic parallels to the Targum turn out on closer examination to be inexact. They usually display small but significant differences. These differences are important since the Rabbis, unlike ourselves, did not lay great store by originality. Originality in their world was displayed by the subtle manipulation of tradition. The sort of nuancing to which I am alluding may be illustrated from Cant 5:1:

> Hebrew Text:
> *I have come into My garden, My Sister, Bride;*
> *I have gathered My myrrh with My spice;*
> *I have consumed My honeycomb with My honey;*
> *I have drunk My wine with My milk.*
> *Eat, friends, drink,*
> *Be drunk, lovers!*

> Targum: The Holy One, blessed be He, said to His people, the House of Israel: "I have come into My Temple, which you have built for Me, My Sister, Assembly of Israel, who is likened to a chaste bride. I have caused My Shekhinah to reside among you. I have received with favor the incense of your spices which you have offered for My name's sake. I have sent fire from heaven and it has consumed the burnt offerings and the sacrifices of holy things. The libations of red and white wine which the priests pour upon My altar have been received with favor before Me. Now come, priests, lovers of My precepts, eat what is left of the offerings, and enjoy the bounty that has been prepared for you!"

As a parallel to the Targum the commentators naturally cite Cant.R. 5.1 §1:

> *I have come into My garden.* R. Menahem, the son-in-law of R. Eleazar b. Abuna, said in the name of R. Simeon b. Yusna: It does not say here, "I have come into *the* garden," but "I have come into My garden *(ganni),*" as if to say, to my bridal-chamber *(ginnuni):* to the place which was My home originally; for was not the original home of the Shekhinah in the lower realm, as it says, *And they heard the voice of the Lord God walking in the garden* (Gen 3:8)? . . . When did the Shekhinah rest upon the earth? On the day when the Tabernacle was set up . . . *I have gathered My myrrh with My spice.* This refers to the incense of spices and the handful of frankincense. *I have consumed My honeycomb with My honey.* This refers to the parts of the burnt offerings and the sacrificial parts of the most holy things. *I have drunk My wine with My milk.* This refers to the drink offerings and the sacrificial parts of the lesser holy things. *Eat, friends.* These are Moses and Aaron. *Drink, be drunk, lovers.* These are Nadab and Abihu, who became drunk to their hurt.

Now there can be no dispute that both these texts reflect a broadly similar reading of the biblical verse, but it would be careless to ignore the differences. Cant.R. refers the verse to the Tabernacle, and so contextualizes it historically to the Wilderness period; the Targum sees a reference to the Temple and so contextualizes it to the reign of Solomon. For Cant.R. the "garden" is the world, and the word suggests an allusion to the Garden of Eden; for the Targum the "garden" is the Temple, an equation the Targumist uses elsewhere. For Cant.R. the "wine" suggests the libations and the "milk" *(ḥalab)* the fat-portions *(ḥalabim)* of the sacrificial victims; for the Targum *both* "wine" and "milk" suggest libations—the former *red* wine, the latter *white* wine. The Targum here, surely, has the exegetical edge, and provides the more coherent reading, since one can hardly "drink" the fat portions of the sacrificial animals. The Targum, by the way, is at variance here with b.B. Bat. 97b, which states that white wine was not used for libations. I am not, however, persuaded by Melamed's argument that this constitutes a misunderstanding of the Talmudic text and so demonstrates the reliance of the Targum on the Talmud.[23] Finally, note at the end how Cant.R. distinguishes the "friends" from the "lovers," and takes the drunkenness literally, whereas the Targum identifies both the "friends" and the "lovers" with the priests and takes drunkenness as a metaphor for enjoyment.

Most of the parallels are of this kind, as the detailed *Notes* below will show, so that even if we concede that the parallels *are* the sources of the Targum we must acknowledge that the Targumist does not take over the traditions unchanged, but finesses them in clever ways, in a number of instances providing a better-reasoned, more consistent reading of the biblical text.

(2) Translational Parallels

The translational category of parallels is rather different from the aggadic in that translational parallels, in principle at least, offer a better chance of establishing a close literary relationship between Tg. Cant. and other texts, and thus of identifying genuine sources for the Targum. For example, suppose we find that Tg. Cant. consistently translates certain distinctive Hebrew words and phrases in the same way as Onqelos; then we would be justified in suspecting that our Targumist knew Onqelos and has used him as a source. This argument will, of course, be strengthened if the Palestinian Targumim differ from Onqelos in their choice of vocabulary or idiom.

In applying this approach we should distinguish between primary and secondary translation. Primary translation is direct translation of the Hebrew text of Canticles that lay before the Targumist. Secondary translation is translation of *other* biblical texts embedded in the Targumist's paraphrase of Canticles. For a number of reasons the primary translations yield few results. There is little significant overlap of vocabulary between Canticles and the other biblical books. The contrast with Chronicles is instructive. There we have a historical narrative, large sections of which run parallel to the other historical books. Moreover, Tg. Cant. often gives an allegorical paraphrase of the Hebrew rather than a direct translation. However, the following examples illustrate how this mode of analysis works:

(a) It can hardly be accidental that Tg. Cant. agrees with the Pentateuchal Targumim in rendering *degel* (Cant 2:4, *we-diglo ʿalay ʾahabah*) by *teqas*. This equivalent is found in both Onqelos and the Palestinian Targumim (see, e.g., *ʾish ʿal diglo* in Num 2:2). Too much should not, perhaps, be made of the fact that Tg. Cant.'s spelling of the word (which is derived from the Greek *taxis*) agrees with Onqelos rather than with Neofiti *(takhs/tekhes)*.

[23] Melamed, "Targum Canticles," 211–12.

(b) Tg. Cant.'s rendering of *ʾerez* ("cedar") at Cant 1:7 by the recherché Persian loanword *gulmish* is noteworthy. The consistent equivalent in Onqelos, Jonathan, Neofiti, and the Cairo Geniza texts is *ʾerez*. However, at Num 19:6 Pseudo-Jonathan has *gulmish*. This striking agreement does not necessarily indicate the dependence of Tg. Cant. on Pseudo-Jonathan, since both Tg. Cant. and Pseudo-Jonathan may have derived the equivalent from b.Rosh Hash. 23a or b.Sanh. 108b.

(c) At Cant 2:1 the Targum renders *ḥabaṣṣelet* by *narqis,* "narcissus." *Ḥabaṣṣelet* occurs elsewhere only in Isa 35:1, and there Jonathan translates *shoshannah*. That translation is clearly out of the question at Cant 2:1, since *ḥabaṣṣelet* is there in parallelism with *shoshannah*. The well-known passage in b.Ber. 43b that distinguishes between the "garden narcissus" *(narqis de-gintaʾ)* and the "wild narcissus" *(narqis de-dabraʾ)* may be the source of the Targumic equivalent.

(d) At Cant 2:13 and 6:2 the Targum renders *shoshannah* by *wardaʾ*. (At 7:3 it treats *shoshannah* metaphorically.) In the only two occurrences of the word outside of Canticles, viz., Hos 14:6 and 2 Chr 4:5, the Targumic equivalent is *shoshannah*.

(e) The botanical identity of the biblical *tappuaḥ* is uncertain, as the diverse equivalents in the ancient versions show. Tg. Cant. renders at 2:3 *ʾetrogaʾ,* and at 2:5 and 7:9 *tappuḥaʾ de-gintaʾ de-ʿeden*. (At 8:5 *tappuaḥ* is treated as allegorical.) Since one strand of Jewish tradition identified the forbidden fruit of paradise as the ethrog, the "apple of the Garden of Eden" is almost certainly another name for the ethrog. So the Targum's rendering is consistent. In fact, Rabbenu Tam appears to have had a text of the Targum at Cant 7:9 that read *ʾetrogaʾ de-gan ʿeden* (see *Apparatus ad loc.*). *Tappuaḥ* occurs only in two other places outside of Canticles, viz., Joel 1:12 (Targum: *ḥarozaʾ*), and Prov 25:11, in the phrase *tappuḥei zahab* (Targum: *ḥizzurei de-dahabaʾ*).

(f) Since all these are examples of "literal" translation I shall conclude the discussion of this topic with an example of an "aggadic" rendering. At Cant 2:3 the Targum offers *malʾakhayyaʾ* as a translation of the Hebrew *ha-banim*. This surprising equivalent surely betrays a knowledge of the Old Palestinian Targum's translation of *benei ʾelohim* in Gen 6:2 by *malʾakhayyaʾ*. Cf. also Job 38:7, "All the sons of God shouted for joy"; Targum: "All the companies of the angels shouted for joy."

These few examples are not untypical. They indicate that no consistent pattern emerges from an analysis of the translation equivalents in the primary translation. The most that can be said is that our Targumist was eclectic in his choice of vocabulary and drew on a capacious knowledge of diverse traditions of translation.

Analysis of the secondary translations is more promising. To illustrate I will take the Targum's rendering of Cant 1:9:

> HEBREW TEXT:
> *To a mare in the chariots of Pharaoh*
> *Have I compared you, O My Love.*

> TARGUM: (1) <u>When Israel went out from Egypt, Pharaoh and his host pursued after them with chariots and horsemen,</u> and (2) <u>the way was barred to them</u> on their four sides. To the right and to the left were (3) <u>deserts full of fiery serpents</u>. Behind them was wicked Pharaoh and his hosts, and in front of them was the Red Sea. What did the Holy One, blessed be He, do? He revealed Himself in the power of His might by the sea and dried up the water, but the mud He did not dry up. The wicked, (4) <u>the mixed multitude and the strangers who were among them</u>, said:

"He is able (5) to dry up the water, but the mud He is not able to dry!" At that hour the wrath of the Lord waxed hot against them, and (6) He would have drowned them in the waters of the sea, just as Pharaoh and his mares, chariots and horsemen were drowned, had it not been for Moses the prophet (7) who spread out his hands in prayer before the Lord, and (8) turned back from them the wrath of the Lord. (9) He and the righteous of that generation opened their mouths, recited the song, and (10) passed through the midst of the sea on dry land, on account of the merit of Abraham, Isaac, and Jacob, the beloved of the Lord.

The Targumist, following his normal procedure, contextualizes the unrubricated speech of Canticles to a significant moment in the sacred history. Cant 1:9, he claims, was addressed by God to Israel at the time of the Exodus. This contextualization is not arbitrary, but is based on the fact, as we noted earlier (*Intro.* 5), that the Targumist detects at Cant 1:9 a clear verbal echo of Exod 14:9. His retelling of the story of the Exodus has, naturally, many echoes of the Pentateuchal narrative—the more obvious are marked by underlining in the translation—and these can be compared with the Pentateuchal Targumim.[24] Two examples will suffice to illustrate:

(a) No. 3: "deserts full of fiery serpents" *(madberayyaʾ de-malyan ḥiwayan qalan)* echoes Deut 8:15, *ha-molikhekha ba-midbar . . . naḥash saraf*. The rendering of *naḥash saraf* by *ḥiwayan qalan* is distinctive, and agrees with Onqelos. Neofiti, by way of contrast, has *ḥiwayan serafin,* taking over the *saraf* of the original Hebrew. We appear to have here an alignment of Tg. Cant. with Onqelos and against the Palestinian Targum. Pseudo-Jonathan, as so often, rather spoils the pattern, since it renders *de-dabberakh be-madbar . . . ʾatar ḥiwayan qalan*. Pseudo-Jonathan, however, is by no means a straightforward representative of the Palestinian Targum. It contains large elements of Onqelos, so its translation *ḥiwayan qalan* here may well be derived from Onqelos.

(b) No. 6: "He would have drowned them in the waters of the sea, just as Pharaoh and his mares, his chariots and his horsemen were drowned"—*u-beʿaʾ le-shannaqutehon be-moy de-yammaʾ hekhemaʾ de-ʾishtannaqu parʿoh we-susawatohi retikkohi u-farashohi*. This clearly echoes Exod 14:27-28: *wa-yenaʿer yhwh ʾet miṣrayim be-tokh ha-yam wa-yashubu ha-mayim wa-yekhassu ʾet ha-rekeb we-ʾet ha-parashim le-khol ḥel parʿoh*. Tg. Cant. represents the distinctive Hebrew verb *niʿer* by *shanneq*. This corresponds to Onqelos's rendering of Exod 14:27, *we-shanneq yyy miṣraʾei be-go yammaʾ*. The verb *shanneq* is also found in the Paris manuscript of the Fragmentary Targum *ad loc.*, and in the Targum to the parallel passage in Ps 136:15, *we-niʿer parʿoh we-ḥelo be-yam suf*. Neofiti to Exod 14:27 has *shebaq* ("abandoned"), which makes reasonable sense. However, there is a suspicion that this is a simple graphical corruption of *shanneq* (as Neofiti margin seems to imply). Pseudo-Jonathan, playing on *niʿer*/*naʿar,* offers the unique aggadic rendering *ʿallem* (possibly = "he

[24] The "quotations," apart from the two discussed below (nos. 3 and 6), are as follows: (1) = Exod 14:8-9, "Pharaoh pursued after the children of Israel; for the children of Israel went out with a high hand. And the Egyptians pursued after them, all the horses [*kol sus*] and chariots of Pharaoh, and his horsemen, and his host." (2) = Exod 14:3, "The desert shut them in [*sagar ʿaleihem*]." (4) = Num 11:14, "The mixed multitude [*ʾasafsuf*] that was among them"; Exod 12:28, "A mixed multitude [*ʿereb rab*] went up with them." (5) = Exod 14:21, "(The Lord) made the sea dry land [*ḥarabah*]"; Gen 8:13, "The face of the ground was dry [*ḥarebu*]"; cf. Ps 66:6, "He turned the sea into dry land [*hafakh yam le-yabbashah*]." (7) = Exod 9:33, "Moses spread out his hands unto the Lord." (8) = Exod 32:12, "Turn from your fierce wrath." (9) = Exod 15:1, "Then sang Moses and the Children of Israel this song." (10) = Exod 14:22, "The Children of Israel went into the midst of the sea upon the dry ground"; 14:29; 15:19, "The Children of Israel walked upon dry land in the midst of the sea;" Num 33:8, "They passed through [*wa-yaʿabru*] the midst of the sea."

made them young again," in order to prolong their death throes!).[25] Tg. Cant. must surely have known the rendering *shanneq* for *niʿer;* it could hardly have hit upon the same equivalent independently. However, since *shanneq* is the common Targumic rendering it does not serve to align our Targum exclusively with either the tradition of Onqelos or the Palestinian Targum.

There are a number of imponderables in this sort of analysis. We must take account of the Targumist's memory, since he may not have had the Pentateuchal text actually in front of him. Sometimes he fuses together parallel texts from the Torah; at other times he seems to recall the underlying Hebrew and translate it anew into Aramaic. However, after giving all these caveats their due weight the analysis I have illustrated yields some useful results. Despite its limited scope it suffices to show that the Targumist of Canticles knew and utilized already extant Targumim of the Pentateuch and, indeed, of the Prophets. Here, unquestionably, we have "sources" for his work. Some of his renderings reflect the common tradition of all the Targumim; others incline toward the so-called "Palestinian" tradition; still others incline toward Onqelos (these Onqelos alignments are seriously neglected by Melamed and Churgin). In a few cases he offers a distinctive translation unattested elsewhere. Sometimes (as I have already suggested) this may be due to his remembering and retranslating the original Hebrew. Sometimes, however, he appears to have preserved "lost" Targumim. The most striking example of this is his rendering of Isa 30:29, embedded in his paraphrase of Cant 1:1:[26]

> TG. CANT. 1:1: The tenth song will be recited by the children of the exile when they depart from their exiles, as is clearly written by Isaiah the prophet (Isa 30:29): "You shall have a song <of joy>, as on the night when the festival <of Passover> was sanctified, and [you shall have] gladness of heart, like the people who go <to appear before the Lord three times in the year (= Exod 23:17 etc.)> with all kinds of musical instruments <and [with] the sound of the pipe *[tablaʾ]*, [who go]> to ascend into the Mountain of the Lord, <and to worship> before the Mighty One of Israel."
>
> HEBREW TEXT ISA 30:29: You shall have a song, as on a night when a festival is sanctified, and [you shall have] gladness of heart, as one who goes with the pipe *[ḥalil]*, to come into the Mountain of the Lord, to the Rock of Israel.
>
> TARGUM JONATHAN ISA 30:29: You shall have [a song of] praise, as on the night when the festival was sanctified, and [you shall have] gladness of heart like those processing <with thanksgiving and> with the pipe *[ʾabbubaʾ]*, to ascend into the Mountain <of the Temple> of the Lord, <to appear> before the Mighty One of Israel.

It is very likely that our Targumist is quoting here from a lost "Palestinian" Targum of Isa 30:29.

It emerges from our analysis of both the aggadic and translational parallels to Tg. Cant. that our Targumist had a comprehensive knowledge of Rabbinic tradition and that his approach to that tradition was highly eclectic. He was, however, no mere compiler: his work is not a pastiche. His use of the tradition was controlled by a highly detailed and coherent reading of the Hebrew, and he chose only those elements of the tradition that were congruent

[25] Cf. Mekhilta de Rabbi Ishmael, *Beshallaḥ* 7 (Edited by Jacob Z. Lauterbach. 3 vols. [Philadelphia: Jewish Publication Society, 1933–35] 1:246): "*And the Lord rejuvenated (wa-yenaʿer) the Egyptians.* He put into them the strength of youth (*koaḥ naʿarut*) so that they could receive the punishment." See further Menahem M. Kasher, *Torah Shelemah* (Jerusalem: No'am Aharon, 1994) note to Exod 14:27 (no. 181).

[26] < > enclose explanatory additions in the Targum; [ ] enclose words added for the sake of the English sense, or equivalents in the original; ( ) enclose biblical references.

with, or could be adapted to that reading. He rigorously applied to the tradition the discipline of the biblical text. It is a failure to stress this point that mars Churgin's and Melamed's handling of the sources of the Targum. In their passion for parallels they have failed to respect the integrity of the text and to treat it in its own terms.

6.4. The Influence of Tg. Cant. on Later Exegesis

(1) Tg. Cant. and Jewish exegesis[27]

As we noted earlier (*Intro.* 1.1) the number of manuscripts of Tg. Cant. surviving from all over the Jewish world testify to its popularity. It is not surprising, therefore, that its influence on later Jewish exegesis was considerable. It was demonstrably consulted by commentators such as Tobias b. Eliezer in his *Midrash Leqaḥ Tob,* probably written in the Balkans in the late eleventh or early twelfth centuries (see *Notes* on 5:14 etc.).[28] Its greatest influence was exercised, however, not so much through its interpretation of individual verses or phrases as through its overall view of the book. It inaugurated in Jewish tradition the reading of Canticles as allegorical *history,* and this approach was soon taken up by others. It is found in the commentary on Canticles attributed to Saʿadya (882–942). The attribution is almost certainly incorrect, but the work is early and possibly dates to the tenth century. Pseudo-Saʿadya proposes a somewhat different historical schema from that in the Targum, but it is reasonable to postulate that he was inspired by the Targum's example.[29] The influence of the Targum on Rashi (1040–1105) is more clear-cut.[30] Rashi, as usual, is his own man and attempts to "improve" on the Targum, but at times he seems to be doing little more than summarizing or paraphrasing it, which surely indicates that he actually possessed a copy of the Targum and was not simply relying on a third-party report. What Rashi provides is not only a commentary on Canticles but, in a sense, a commentary on Tg. Cant. as well. He is an important and sensitive early reader of the Targum and throws some light on its darker places. He will, consequently, be cited regularly in the *Notes* below.[31] Rashi's

[27] For a survey of Jewish interpretation of Canticles see Christian D. Ginsburg, *The Song of Songs* (London: Longman, 1857) 20–102; Siegmund Salfeld, *Das Hohelied Salomo's bei den jüdischen Erklärern des Mittelalters* (Berlin: Julius Benzian, 1879); Marvin Pope, *The Song of Songs.* AB 7C (Garden City, N.Y.: Doubleday, 1977) 89–112, 153–79; Barry D. Walfish, "Annotated Bibliography of Medieval Jewish Commentaries on Song of Songs," in Sarah Yafet, ed., *Ha-Miqra be-re'i Mefarshav: Sefer Zikkaron le-Sarah Kamin* (Jerusalem: Magnes, 1994) 518–71 [Hebrew].

[28] Albert W. Greenup, *The Commentary of Rabbi Tobia ben Elieser on Canticles* (London [no publisher], 1909). The Pentateuch portions of *Leqaḥ Tob* were published by Salomon Buber and Moses Katzenellenbogen (1884).

[29] Judeo-Arabic text with Hebrew translation: Y. Qafiḥ, *Ḥamesh Megillot* (Jerusalem, 1962). The portion of Hebrew text given by Ginsburg (*Song of Songs* 36–37) from a copy of the original Constantinople edition in the British Museum differs considerably from that in Qafiḥ. Qafiḥ discusses the authorship of the work on pp. 9–11 of his introduction.

[30] See further Ivan G. Marcus, "The Song of Songs in German Hasidism and the School of Rashi: A Preliminary Comparison," in: Barry Walfish, ed., *The Frank Talmage Memorial Volume I* (Haifa: Haifa University Press; Hanover, N.H.: University Press of New England, 1994) 182–83. Abraham Berliner and others have denied that Rashi knew Tg. Cant., but the parallels are too close for such a view to be tenable. Nothing can be inferred from the fact that Rashi does not mention Targumim to the Writings in his comment on b.Meg. 3a, which seems to deny their existence. The Talmudic passage is not as straightforward as it looks. It is not necessarily denying that such Targumim exist, and even if it is, this is hardly surprising, since all the Targumim to the Writings are probably post-Talmudic.

[31] Edition: Judah Rosenthal, "Peirush Rashi ʿal Shir ha-Shirim," in: Simon Bernstein and Gershon A. Churgin, eds., *Samuel K. Mirsky Jubilee Volume* (New York: The Jubilee Committee, 1958) 130–88. A transcription of a JTS ms. (L778) of Rashi on Canticles is given in Sarah Kamin and Avrom Saltman, *Secundum Salomonem: A Thirteenth Century Latin Commentary on the Song of Solomon* (Ramat Gan: Bar-Ilan University Press, 1989) 81–99 (Hebrew section). The mss. differ considerably from one another.

younger contemporary, Abraham ibn Ezra (1089–1164), in his tripartite commentary on Canticles also adopts a historical schema. Although this differs from the Targum's and Rashi's, the influence of the Targum, either directly or indirectly, can again be plausibly postulated.[32]

The historicizing approach to Canticles adopted by the Talmud, Cant.R., and above all Tg. Cant. remained the norm in Jewish exegesis throughout the Middle Ages. However, it was challenged with increasing boldness by alternative readings. The mystical interpretation, present already in the Talmudic period (see *Intro.* 6.2), continued to develop. Canticles was understood by the mystics in a variety of ways. Some continued to see it as an allegory of the *via mystica* and of the soul's desire for union or communion with God. Others saw it as an allegory of the sacred marriage of God (the Bridegroom) and the Shekhinah (the Bride). The commentary of Ezra of Gerona (1169–1238) on Canticles was of particular importance in the development of the mystical interpretation and seems to have inspired the Zohar's expositions of Canticles, the most influential of the medieval Jewish mystical readings of the book. The philosophers also appropriated Canticles to their cause. Once philosophy took root in Judaism it was tempting to see the relationship between the two protagonists of Canticles as mirroring the relationship between the philosopher and Wisdom/Torah. The underlying story of Canticles can be regarded as an allegory of the search of the soul for knowledge and truth, with all its trials and triumphs. After all, there was a long philosophical tradition, going back to Plato's *Symposium,* of picturing the pursuit of truth in erotic terms. This particular reading is found in a commentary on Canticles by the great fifteenth-century Spanish scholar Don Isaac Abarbanel. However, it faces a major difficulty. On this reading it would be natural to identify the female voice in Canticles with Wisdom/Torah and the male with the philosopher or the soul. The reason for this is basically linguistic: "wisdom" *(hokhmah)* and "Torah" are feminine nouns in Hebrew. However, in the text of Canticles the female is surprisingly dominant. *She* does most of the running. She is surprisingly forward in her pursuit of the young man. This creates problems for this form of philosophical allegory, since one would expect that it would not be wisdom that pursues the soul, but the soul that pursues wisdom.

It may have been a perception of this difficulty that led to another, more technical philosophical interpretation of Canticles. The Bridegroom was identified with the Active Intellect and the Bride with the human intellect. The Active Intellect in medieval philosophy was the lowest of a series of emanations from God. The human intellect was the faculty in humankind that achieved knowledge through union with the Active, divine Intellect. That union could only be achieved through discipline and study, and through the suppression of the imagination and desires. This reading allowed the dominant masculine element to be identified with the divine, and the subordinate, seeking, feminine element to be identified with the human. The origins of this interpretation are obscure, but it is possible that it was introduced by Maimonides (1135–1204). Germs of it can be found in his law code, the *Mishneh Torah,* and in his philosophical masterpiece, *The Guide of the Perplexed.* This approach was certainly advocated by two of his disciples, Moses Ibn Tibbon (died *c.*1283) and Joseph Ibn Caspi (*c.*1280–*c.*1340), but its greatest exponent was the scientist and philosopher Levi ben Gershom (Gersonides, 1288–1344).[33]

[32] H. J. Mathews, *Commentary of Abraham ibn Ezra on the Canticles after the First Recension* (London: Trübner, 1874). See also the standard Rabbinic Bibles.

[33] In fact Levi ben Gershom detects two dialogues in Canticles, one "external" between the human intellect (the Bride) and the Active Intellect (the Bridegroom), the other "internal" between the faculties of the soul (the Bride) and the human in-

It is also interesting to note the first glimmerings of a naturalistic reading of Canticles among Jewish Bible exegetes, which took the book at its face value as a poem or series of poems about human love. This view was not, however, advocated on its own, but as a level of interpretation.[34] Thus we find it in the second level of Abraham ibn Ezra's tripartite exposition of Canticles, which forms the basis of his third, historical reading. It may also be found in the multi-layered commentaries of Joseph Ibn Aknin (1160–1226), Immanuel of Rome (1270–1330), and Isaac Arama (1420–1494). The allegorical interpretation had always implicitly acknowledged this sense but had simply denied that the text was to be taken as it stands. However, it is significant that some commentators now began to spell out and highlight this "literal" level of exegesis.

(2) Tg. Cant. and Christian exegesis of Canticles[35]

The historical reading of Canticles, proposed by the Targum and Rashi, is found also in Christian sources. Its most influential advocate was Nicholas de Lyra (*c.*1270–1349). In his *Postilla* Lyra follows standard Christian exegesis in taking Canticles as an allegory of the relationship between Christ and the Church, but he insists that it spans that relationship under the dispensations of both the Old and the New Covenants. He thus asserts the continuity of the Church with Israel.[36] The rhythm of communion, estrangement, repentance, and reconciliation between the Bride and the Bridegroom mirrors the actual historical vicissitudes of the Church's relationship to Christ from the beginning of time. The Church has, in fact, existed since the creation, but because it only became a Bride with the giving of the Law at Sinai, whereby God espoused Israel to himself, Solomon's account of God and Israel under the images of Bridegroom and Bride begins with the Exodus from Egypt, which led up to the solemnizing of the Sinai covenant. Canticles 1–6 relate to the period of the Old Testament: they correlate with the Exodus, the giving of the Law, the desert wanderings, the entry into the Land under Joshua, the establishment of the Davidic kingdom, the exile, the return, and the post-exilic era down to the time of the Maccabees. Canticles 7–8 allude to the period

---

tellect (the Bridegroom). The former is found in 1:1-11, the latter in 1:12 to the end. See his comment to 1:12 (Menachem Kellner, *Commentary on Song of Songs: Levi ben Gershom (Gersonides)* [New Haven and London: Yale University Press, 1998] 34). On the philosophical reading of Canticles see further Shalom Rosenberg, "Philosophical Hermeneutics on the Song of Songs: Introductory Remarks," *Tarbiṣ* 59 (1990) 133–51 [Hebrew].

[34] The "Anonymous Commentary on the Song of Songs" published by H. J. Mathews in *Festschrift zum achtzigsten Geburtstage Moritz Steinschneider's* (Leipzig: Otto Harrasowitz, 1896; repr. Jerusalem: Makor, 1970) seems to be exclusively literal, but I am not sure it was intended to be a free-standing and complete commentary.

[35] On Christian interpretation of Canticles see Friedrich Ohly, *Hohelied-Studien: Grundzüge einer Geschichte der Hoheliedauslegung des Abendlandes bis zum 1200* (Wiesbaden: Franz Steiner Verlag, 1958); Max Engammare, *Le Cantique des Cantiques à la renaissance: étude et bibliographie* (Geneva: Librairie Droz, 1993). See further Ginsburg, *Song of Songs* 20–102; Richard F. Littledale, *A Commentary on the Song of Songs from Ancient and Mediaeval Sources* (London: Joseph Masters, 1869) xxxii–xl; Helmut Riedlinger, *Die Makellosigkeit der Kirche in den lateinischen Hoheliedkommentaren des Mittelalters* (Münster: Aschendorff, 1958); Rosemarie Herde, *Das Hohelied in der lateinischen Literatur des Mittelalters bis zum 12. Jahrhundert.* Münchener Beiträge zur Mediävistik und Renaissance-Forschung 3 (Spoleto: Centro italiano di studi sull'alto medioevo, 1968); Pope, *Song of Songs* 89–229; Elizabeth A. Clark, "The Uses of the Song of Songs: Origen and the Later Latin Fathers," in eadem, *Ascetic Piety and Women's Faith: Essays on Late Ancient Christianity* (Lewiston, N.Y.: Edwin Mellen Press, 1986) 386–427; Ann W. Astell, *The Song of Songs in the Middle Ages* (Ithaca, N.Y.: Cornell University Press, 1990); E. Ann Matter, *The Voice of My Beloved: The Song of Songs in Western Mediaeval Christianity* (Philadelphia: University of Pennsylvania Press, 1990).

[36] Nicholas's positive attitude toward Israel and Judaism should not be overestimated. See Jeremy Cohen, *The Friars and the Jews: The Evolution of Medieval Anti-Judaism* (Ithaca, N.Y.: Cornell University Press, 1982) 170–98.

of the new covenant from the advent of Christ to the triumph of Christianity under Constantine, when the Church was finally freed from all persecution and the *pax Christiana* was established throughout the whole world.

Jewish sources undoubtedly played an important role in Lyra's reading of Canticles. His knowledge of Hebrew is well documented, as is his use of the commentaries of Rashi—the Rabbi Salomon quoted frequently in the *Postilla*. Lyra's debt to Rashi specifically in Canticles has been studied by Herman Hailperin and others.[37] The point, however, that has not been brought out with sufficient clarity is that his dependency in Canticles is uniquely deep. It is not simply a matter of discrete citations of Rashi to help elucidate the *hebraica veritas* or establish the *sensus litteralis*. The *total* hermeneutical schema of Lyra's reading of Canticles is based on Rashi. Needless to say, Rashi does not correlate any part of Canticles with the history of the Church in New Testament times, so Lyra's coverage of chapters 7–8 perforce diverges from his (a point he explicitly acknowledges), but elsewhere he follows Rashi's historical correlations very closely. Lyra also knew the Targum. This is evident from his gloss to Cant 8:1, where he introduces a quotation from the *translatio chaldaica* that we can still easily find in our mss. of the Targum. Since, as we have noted, Tg. Cant. and Rashi often coincide we cannot always be sure, where Lyra himself does not explicitly inform us, which of the two he is following.

The exegesis of Canticles as historical allegory is very rare in Christian circles before the time of Lyra. I can find only three significant examples of it.

(a) The first is in the *Compendium totius Biblie* of Lyra's slightly older contemporary, the Franciscan Petrus Aureoli (*c.*1280–1322).[38] This, astonishingly, gives a totally "Jewish" reading, without a single mention of Christ or the Church! It correlates Canticles with the history of God's relationship to Israel in the period running from the departure of Abraham from Ur to the establishment of the Temple cult on Mount Zion. In other words, in a curious anticipation of Joüon and Robert (see below), Petrus Aureoli gives a historicizing interpretation that, from the standpoint of the putative author, Solomon, relates totally to the past. There is no evidence that Lyra knew the *Compendium*. Petrus Aureoli was probably inspired by the same Jewish sources that influenced Lyra.

(b) Somewhat earlier is the *Expositio Hystorica Cantici Canticorum secundum Salomonem,* which survives in the unique Vatican manuscript, Vat. Lat. 1053. This correlates Canticles with the period from the Exodus to the end of Hasmonean independence and the conquest of Judea by the Romans, one hundred years before the beginning of Jesus' ministry. As Sarah Kamin and Avrom Saltman have demonstrated, the *Expositio Hystorica* is, in fact, an adaptation and christianization of Rashi's commentary on Canticles.[39] Once again the Jewish origin of a Christian historical reading of Canticles appears to be beyond reasonable doubt. Again, however, there is no evidence that Lyra knew or used the *Expositio Hystorica*. He consulted Rashi directly.

[37] Herman Hailperin, *Rashi and the Christian Scholars* (Pittsburgh: University of Pittsburgh Press, 1963) 137–246, especially 240ff.

[38] The *editio princeps* appeared at Strasbourg in 1476 under the title *Compendium literalis sensus totius Biblie seu divine Scripture*. There were reprints in 1508, 1514, and 1585. See Engammare, *Le Cantique des Cantiques* 42–43.

[39] Sarah Kamin and Avrom Saltman, *Secundum Salomonem*.

(c) The third example is Apponius' *In Canticum Canticorum Expositio.*[40] This states that the Song of Songs speaks of *quidquid ab initio mundi usque in finem in mysteriis egit acturusve erit Dei Sermo erga Ecclesiam.* This enigmatic commentary, in its full form, is large, and as a result its historical schema does not emerge all that clearly from the mass of detail. But that Apponius offers a historical schema cannot be denied. Thus Cant 1:1–2:6 covers Israel under the old dispensation; 2:7-15 refers to the Incarnation, and 2:16–3:11 speaks of the crucifixion, the resurrection, the conversion of the Church of Jerusalem, and the bringing in of the Gentiles by Paul. Chapters 4–6 rather lose the chronological thread, but they do speak of a time of persecution and martyrdom, and of a fall into heresy by the Church. The thread is picked up again strongly in 7:1-9, which is seen as referring to the conversion of Rome to Christianity. Cant 7:10–8:4 deals with the barbarian invasions of the Roman empire, which are looked upon in a rather positive light since they allowed the barbarians to be converted to Christ. This leaves only the conversion of the Jews outstanding, and Apponius anticipates this event in the exposition of Cant 8:5-14.

Apponius is a very shadowy figure. Bernard de Vregille and Louis Neyrand are inclined to accept Johannes Witte's view that he wrote his commentary on Canticles (his sole known work) in Rome between 405 and 415 C.E.[41] They are less certain that he was a converted Jew, and with good reason: there is little in his commentary to suggest a Jewish origin. His occasional sympathetic references to the Jews and his interest in Israel's place in the divine scheme of things prove little. The persistent suggestions that he drew on Jewish Bible exegesis, and perhaps even directly on the Targum of Canticles, are unsubstantiated.[42] E. Ann Matter notes that "his commentary on the Song of Songs seems to show knowledge of Jewish biblical interpretation," though she cautiously adds that "this may be secondary, as he is heavily dependent on Jerome." She suggests that "like Jerome, Apponius may be most accurately described as a Christian who lived and studied in Italy and/or Palestine, and perhaps had some connection with an intellectual center such as Caesarea, where many worlds—East and West, Christian and Jewish, Semitic, Greek and Latin—came together."[43] All this is highly speculative. One thing can, however, be stated with considerable confidence: Apponius and Tg. Cant. are totally unrelated. If Apponius' dates are correct, then he flourished about three hundred years before the Targum was composed. There is not a shred of evidence that the Targum's historical reading or, for that matter, any other systematic historical allegorizing of Canticles was current in Jewish circles as early as the time of

[40] Bernard de Vregille and Louis Neyrand, eds., *Apponii in Canticum Canticorum Expositionem* [sic]. Corpus Christianorum, Series Latina XIX (Turnhout: Brepols, 1986).

[41] See de Vregille and Neyrand, *Apponii in Canticum Canticorum Expositio* cvii. Johannes Witte, *Der Kommentar des Aponius zum Hohenliede.* Inaugural-Dissertation (Erlangen: K. b. Hof- und Univ.-Buchdruckerei von Junge & Sohn, 1903), remains the most important discussion of Apponius.

[42] So convinced was Ginsburg of the dependence of Apponius on the Targum that he dated him to the seventh century (he dated the Targum c. 550): "The influence of the Chaldee mode of interpretation seems now to become more apparent in the Christian Church. Aponius, who is quoted by the venerable Bede, and must therefore have lived in the seventh century . . . takes the book as a historico-prophetical description of the dealings of God with his people, only that the Chaldee takes the Jews as the object of the description, but Aponius substitutes the Gentile Church" (*Song of Songs* 67). See also Littledale, *Commentary on the Song of Songs* xxxiv (cf. his remarks on p. xxxii on the Targum as "first in order, though perhaps not in actual date of present condition"). The alternative would be to hold on to Witte's early fifth-century date for Apponius and argue that, despite appearances, some form of the Targum, or of the exegesis therein, must have been current in Jewish circles then. But the detailed convergence of the Targum and Apponius would have to be a lot stronger to make that suggestion plausible.

[43] Matter, *The Voice of My Beloved* 89–90. See pp. 90–91 for a summary of the evidence that Apponius used Jewish/Rabbinic tradition.

Apponius. Conversely it is highly unlikely that Apponius could have influenced the Targum. In fact, the detailed historical schemas of Apponius and the Targum do not coincide at any point. The conclusion seems unavoidable: both Apponius and the Targumist of Canticles hit quite independently on the device of reading the book as an allegorical history.

Lyra transmitted the historical reading of Canticles (and hence, indirectly, the influence of the Targum and Rashi) to later Christian exegetes. The heyday of the historical approach was the seventeenth century, when it enjoyed particular vogue among Protestant commentators. The key figure appears to have been Thomas Brightman. Brightman argued that Canticles is a prophetic history of the Church under both the old and the new dispensations from the time of King David till the Second Coming, and so detailed were the correlations he made between the text and history that he found allusions in it to events in Geneva in the time of Calvin![44]

Brightman's "Propheticall Exposition" of Canticles first appeared in English in 1644, but Brightman himself flourished in the Tudor period (he died in 1607), and the Latin version of his commentary was published (posthumously) in Basel in 1614.[45] He is the oldest of the group of seventeenth-century scholars who take this historical line, and his work, whether directly or indirectly, probably influenced the others. The group includes the Englishmen John Cotton,[46] Nathanael Homes,[47] John Davenport, and George Wither,[48] and the Germans Johannes Cocceius[49] and Caspar Heunisch.[50] Cocceius and Heunisch are noteworthy for the way in which they develop Brightman's suggestion of a parallelism between Canticles and Revelation by superimposing a detailed *apocalyptic* historical schema on the Song of Songs. Thus Cocceius divided the Song into seven periods corresponding to the seven seals and seven trumpets of Revelation, and Heunisch discovered in Canticles seven

[44] Brightman's *Commentary on the Canticles* appeared twice in English in 1644, once in Amsterdam as a separate volume and once in London as part of the volume of his collected works (pp. 971–1070), along with his commentary on Revelation. The historical school dominated Protestant exegesis of Revelation from the Reformation till the early nineteenth century (Richard J. Bauckham, *Tudor Apocalypse* [Abingdon and Oxford: The Sutton Courtenay Press, 1978]). The idea that Canticles is the Old Testament counterpart of the New Testament Apocalypse is found already in patristic and medieval commentators; see Ann Matter's observations on this point: "Besides his virtually complete elaboration of the Song of Songs as an allegory of the immediate tribulations of institutional Christianity, Gregory of Elvira also gives a hint of another development in Latin Song of Songs interpretation: the connection between the Song of Songs and the Apocalypse as related allegories of the Church. . . . The Song of Songs and the Apocalypse were . . . increasingly read together, as two accounts of the same divine plan; . . . an apocalyptic theme in Song of Songs exegesis is well developed by Honorius in the twelfth century" (*The Voice of My Beloved* 89, and *passim*). Linking the two texts may have been encouraged by the fact that the one more or less plausible quotation from Canticles in the New Testament is found in Rev 3:20, "Behold, I stand at the door and knock"; cf. Cant 5:2, "It is the voice of My Beloved that knocks."

[45] *Scholia in Canticum Canticorum* (Basel, 1614). Brightman's dates are given in the *Dictionary of National Bibliography* (2:1247) as 1562–1607.

[46] John Cotton, *A Brief Exposition of the whole Book of Canticles* (London: Printed for P. Nevil, 1642).

[47] Nathanael Homes, "Commentary on Canticles," in *The Works of Dr Nathanael Homes* (London: Printed [by J. Legate] for the Author, 1652).

[48] I have gleaned the information about Wither and Davenport from Christopher Hill's interesting discussion of seventeenth-century interpretations of the Song of Songs in *The English Bible and the Seventeenth-Century Revolution* (London: Penguin, 1994) 362–70: "John Davenport's unpublished sermons on Canticles . . . apparently shared Brightman's historical interpretation" (p. 367 n. 137; further p. 363). "George Wither regarded the song as a history of the church, 'from Abel to the last judgement,' when the 'blessed marriage' (of Christ and his church) shall be fully consummated" (pp. 365–66, with a reference to the Song of Songs in Wither's *Hymns and Songs of the Church* [London: J. R. Smith, 1856] 39).

[49] Johannes Cocceius, *Cogitationes de Cantico Canticorum* (Leiden, 1665).

[50] Caspar Heunisch, *In Canticum Canticorum commentarius apocalypticus* (Leipzig, 1688). The work is rare, but there is a copy in the British Library. See Ginsburg, *Song of Songs* 78–79 for a summary (though note that Ginsburg spells the name as "Hennischius").

successive ages reflecting the spiritual states of the Seven Churches of Asia in Revelation, the final age (that of Laodicea) beginning in the year 2060!

Reading the Song of Songs as allegorical history went out of fashion at the end of the seventeenth century. Heunisch's *Apocalyptic Commentary on the Song of Songs* (1688) was possibly its swan song. I can find no significant traces of the approach in the eighteenth and nineteenth centuries. Jacques Bossuet's elegant commentary on Canticles, published in 1693,[51] inaugurated a more naturalistic interpretation that was picked up by Lowth, Percy, and other leading biblical scholars in the following century. Bossuet, developing an earlier, minor strand of tradition, suggested that Canticles was nothing more than a celebration of the seven-day nuptials of Solomon and Pharaoh's daughter. Allegory by no means disappeared, but the allegory proposed was no longer a cryptic history of the Church. However, the twentieth century witnessed a curious late revival of historical allegory—and in an unexpected quarter—in the work of the distinguished French Catholic scholars Paul Joüon and André Robert.[52] But there was an important difference: though Joüon and (especially) Robert detected messianic elements in Canticles, both took Canticles essentially as a *backward* look over the history of Israel from the post-exilic standpoint of the author rather than as a detailed prophecy of the future.

6.5. Targums of the Tg. Cant.

Tg. Cant. played an important role more generally in Jewish religious life and piety. Its use in the liturgy is discussed in *Intro.* 7 below. Its influence was amplified by a number of popular renderings of the Aramaic text into Jewish vernaculars—Judeo-Arabic, Lad̲ino, Yiddish, Judeo-Persian, Neo-Aramaic, and even Judeo-Italian, Judeo-Turkish, and Hebrew. These translations are rather different from scholarly versions of the Aramaic into Latin, English, French, German, Modern Hebrew, or other modern languages. They were meant to edify the faithful and to assist them in their devotions. In the spirit of the Talmudic injunction to read the weekly *parashah* "twice in Scripture and once in the Targum," the custom seems to have arisen in some communities of reading the *Targum* of Canticles, both in Aramaic and in a vernacular translation. And in a number of cases these vernacular versions are not straightforward, but contain significant expansions in the spirit of the original Targum. They are Targums of the Targum. This is rather curious. We noted earlier that the manuscript tradition of Tg. Cant. is remarkably stable and shows that no serious attempt was made to rework the Targum in Aramaic. However, attempts were made to rework it in some of its vernacular versions. This suggests that the phenomenon of Targumism did not die out in the Middle Ages but simply transferred itself to other Jewish languages.

One might expect that the earliest of these Targums of the Targum would be the Judeo-Arabic. Of the various Jewish vernaculars that produced Targums of Tg. Cant., Judeo-Arabic

[51] *Libri Salomonis, Canticum Canticorum* (Paris, 1693). Littledale rightly notes that Bossuet marks a turning point in the history of Canticles exegesis: "With this author [Cocceius] closes the period formally embraced in the following commentary, which does not profess to deal with the exegesis of the eighteenth and nineteenth centuries, properly beginning with Bossuet's commentary in 1690" (*Commentary on the Song of Songs* xl).

[52] Paul Joüon, *Le Cantique des Cantiques: commentaire philologique et exégétique* (Paris: Beauchesne, 1909); André Robert, Raymond Tournay, and André Feuillet, *Le Cantique des Cantiques: traduction et commentaire.* Études Bibliques (Paris: Gabalda, 1963). Tournay and Feuillet were pupils of Robert who adopted their teacher's approach and completed his work. See the discussion by Pope, *Song of Songs* 179–83.

is the earliest attested and the earliest to create an extensive Jewish literature. However, I have been unable to find a Judeo-Arabic translation of Tg. Cant. before the late sixteenth century, the period when the Ladino and Yiddish versions also begin to appear. A preliminary investigation of these Targums of Tg. Cant. suggests that they fall into two broad groups: (a) the Ladino (in one of its forms), the Judeo-Arabic, the Judeo-Persian, and the Neo-Aramaic; (b) the Ladino (in another recension), the Yiddish, and the Judeo-Italian. The Judeo-Italian, in fact, appears to be a translation not from the Aramaic but from the Ladino. The pivotal tradition may well be the Ladino, which, originating in Spain in the late Middle Ages, traveled after the expulsion in 1492 eastward through Italy to Turkey where it came into contact with, or possibly even inspired, the eastern versions of Tg. Cant. The Ladino tradition also traveled northward to the Low Countries, where it may well have come into contact with, or inspired, the Yiddish version of Tg. Cant. These Targums of Tg. Cant. deserve a closer look. They are not only evidence of the popularity of the Targum and of its influence in Jewish life, but they may be of some importance in tracing the history of its Aramaic text.[53]

[53] See further my essay, "Notes on Some Targums of the Targum of the Song of Songs," in: Paul V. M. Flesher, ed., *Ernest Clarke Memorial Volume* (Leiden: Brill, forthcoming 2002).

7. TARGUM CANTICLES AND THE LITURGY

Although, as we have seen (*Intro.* 6.1), Canticles' place within the canon of Scripture was securely established from the late second century C.E. onward, and it is frequently referred to and interpreted in the Talmud and the classic Midrashim, it does not seem to have gained a role in the Synagogue liturgy till after the close of the Talmud. It came to be linked particularly with the festival of Pesaḥ. Massekhet Soferim 14:3 stipulates that it should be publicly read on Pesaḥ, preceded by a benediction. This seems to have been part of a more general liturgical development in Gaonic times to assign each of the Five Scrolls to five festivals: Ruth to Shabuʿot, Ecclesiastes to Sukkot, Esther to Purim, Lamentations to the 9th of Ab, and Canticles to Pesaḥ. Esther provided the model. It was inextricably linked to Purim, and its public reading from a separate scroll on the festival is explicitly enjoined within the text. This injunction had been observed in Rabbinic communities at least from Tannaitic times. Massekhet Soferim directs that the other four books should also be read publicly from separate scrolls on their respective festivals, and the benediction that precedes their reading should follow the form of words used for the Scroll of Esther: "Blessed are You, O Lord our God, King of the Universe, who has sanctified us by Your commandments and has given us the command to read the Holy Writings" (Massekhet Soferim 14:4).[1]

The injunction to read Canticles on Pesaḥ has been implemented somewhat differently in different communities. Massekhet Soferim 15:4 stipulates that it should be read on the last two nights of the festival, "half on the first night and half on the second,"[2]—a custom reflected in the Masoretic gloss to Cant 4:14, which notes that this is the middle verse of the book. The *Maḥzor Vitry* states that it is read on a Shabbat that falls in *Ḥol ha-Moʿed* of Pesaḥ, before the Torah Scroll is taken out of the Ark. However, if Pesaḥ begins on Shabbat, then it is read on that day in Israel and on the last day of the festival in the Diaspora.[3] Ezra Z. Melamed notes that the Persian custom was to read it between *Minḥah* and *ʿArbit* on the evenings of *Ḥol ha-Moʿed* of Pesaḥ, or on the evenings of Sabbaths between Pesaḥ and Shabuʿot.[4] Isaac Jerusalmi observes that Canticles was held in particularly high esteem among Sephardi Jews. "Its memorization from cover to cover has priority in the elementary education curriculum, not only in preparation for its formal chanting on Friday nights during the seven weeks between Passover and Shabuʿot, but also as background material for the reading of the Targum in La<u>d</u>ino and the preaching on *Pirké Avoth* which take place on those Saturday afternoons before the *Minha* service. That is how this writer, too, was taught and already knew the entire book by heart by the time he reached his seventh birthday."[5] The links between Pesaḥ and Canticles were further strengthened by the composition of *piyyutim*

[1] Cf. the benediction for Esther: "Blessed are You, O Lord our God, King of the Universe, who has sanctified us by Your commandments, and has given us the command to read the *Megillah*." The general practice now is to read only Esther from a separate scroll. The others are read from printed texts, and without a benediction.

[2] The text is problematic: see Abraham Cohen, ed., *Hebrew-English Edition of the Babylonian Talmud: Minor Tractates* (London: Soncino, 1984) n. 70 to Soferim 15:4.

[3] Simon Hurwitz, *Maḥsor Vitry* (2nd ed. Nuremberg: Bulka, 1923) 304.

[4] Melamed, *Shir ha-Shirim: Targum Arami, Targum ʿIbri, Tafsir bi-leshon Yehudei Paras* (Jerusalem, no publisher, 1971) 76.

[5] Isaac Jerusalmi, *The Song of Songs in the Targumic Tradition: Vocalized Aramaic Text with Facing English Translation and La<u>d</u>ino Versions* (Cincinnati: La<u>d</u>ino Books, 1993) xxxviii.

for the festival, such as the *Beraḥ Dodi,* which allude to Canticles and to its allegorical interpretation.

However, the liturgical associations of Canticles ultimately spread beyond the period of Pesaḥ. This seems to have been a very late development that resulted from imposing a Qabbalistic interpretation on the text. Under the influence of the Safed school of mystics in the sixteenth century many communities adopted the custom of reciting Canticles in Synagogue every *ʿEreb Shabbat* before the beginning of the evening service as part of the rituals for the reception of Shabbat *(Qabbalat Shabbat).*[6] Behind this practice lies the idea that Canticles is an account of the mystical union of God (the Bridegroom) and the Shekhinah (the Bride), which takes place on Shabbat. This idea is reflected in the great Shabbat hymn *Lekhah Dodi liqraʾt Kallah* ("Go, my Beloved, to meet the Bride"), composed by the Safed Qabbalist, Solomon Alkabetz, and incorporated into many prayerbooks.[7]

Tg. Cant. clearly exploits the link between Canticles and Pesaḥ. It is full of Passover imagery. It may not have been responsible for making Canticles a special reading for Pesaḥ (*Maḥzor Vitry* claims the crucial factor in forging this link was not the Targum but the Talmudic interpretation of Song 1:9 as referring to the Exodus), but it helped to reinforce the connection. Its liturgical function is clearly indicated by its opening benediction and by its Messianic close. It is not impossible that our Targumist intended his Targum to be used in the *public* reading of Canticles. It can certainly be recited verse-by-verse against the Hebrew. Massekhet Soferim 18:4 records the practice of publicly reading Lamentations with a Targum, and our Targumist may have envisaged a similar role for his work. However, Tg. Cant. seems in fact to have functioned more commonly as an aid to private devotion. The Talmud enjoined preparing for the public reading of the Torah in synagogue by going over the weekly *parashah* "twice in the Hebrew and once in the Targum" (b.Ber. 8a). Tg. Cant. seems to have been used in a similar fashion in private devotions at home before going to the Synagogue, or at public, but non-statutory, study sessions prior to the statutory prayers, and it was probably in this setting that the Jewish vernacular versions of the Targum arose (*Intro.* 6.6). Ḥananiah Katz, in the preface to Melamed's edition of a ms. of the Judeo-Persian rendering of Tg. Cant. that had belonged to his father Rabbi Shelomoh Katz, records that it was the custom in his home town of Yezd in Iran at the end of the nineteenth and beginning of the twentieth centuries to read Canticles during the seven days of Pesaḥ, "once in the Hebrew and once in the Persian *Tafsir*." The *Tafsir* was read at home and Canticles itself in the synagogue. And he recalls movingly how the special *niggun* used to chant both texts had lingered in his memory.[8]

[6] See, e.g., the "Pious Customs" of the Safed scholar Abraham Galante: No. 5, "On the intermediate days of the Festival of Passover, at midday, they assemble in the synagogues and recite the Song of Songs, translating it and commenting upon it each day." No. 28, "There are some who practice the custom of welcoming the Sabbath following the afternoon service dressed in Sabbath garments. They recite the Song of Songs followed by the hymn for the *Kabbalat Shabbat,* 'Come, my Beloved.'" *Safed Spirituality.* Translated by Lawrence Fine. Classics of Western Spirituality (Mahwah, N.J.: Paulist, 1984), 43 and 46. Note also Fine's remarks on p. 28: "A great many . . . Safed devotional practices found a prominent place in the religious life of subsequent generations, both among Near Eastern and European Jewry, especially from the middle of the seventeenth century forward. For example, *Kabbalat Shabbat* (Welcoming the Sabbath), the special service that ushers in the Sabbath, became a highly popular and enduring feature of Jewish ritual. Similarly, the practice of reciting the Song of Songs on Sabbath eve, as well as Proverbs 31:10-31 at the festive table, originated in Safed. Even today these customs are popular, although in many communities they have been shorn of their kabbalistic associations."

[7] See Fine, *Safed Spirituality* 33 and 38–40.

[8] Melamed, *Shir ha-Shirim* 7–8. On the liturgical use of Canticles see further Ismar Elbogen, *Jewish Liturgy: A Comprehensive History.* Translated by Raymond P. Scheindlin (Philadelphia: Jewish Publication Society, 1993) 115, 150, 292.

8. THE DATE AND PROVENANCE OF TARGUM CANTICLES

Tg. Cant. draws on traditions originating from very different periods, some of which (e.g., Lebanon = the Temple)[1] are probably as old as Second Temple times. However, it would be wrong to infer from this that it is a composite work that evolved over many generations. It is, in fact, remarkably unified in terms of its style, its exegetical method, its argument, and its theology, and this, coupled with the lack of substantial recensional variants in the numerous manuscripts,[2] points, unusually for the Targumim or Midrashim, to a single author. Our Targumist almost certainly attended one of the great Talmudic schools of his day and was clearly a learned scholar with a comprehensive knowledge of Rabbinic tradition. Where and when did he live?

8.1. The Date of Tg. Cant.

Tg. Cant. was probably composed in the seventh or eighth century C.E., the balance of probability being marginally in favor of the later date.

(1) The Aramaic of the Targum

In *Intro.* 2.1 we argued that Tg. Cant. is in a late literary dialect of Aramaic that lacks a unified vernacular base. Its language is learned and "artificial," combining elements from both eastern and western Aramaic literary sources (notably Onqelos, the Palestinian Targumim, and the Babylonian Talmud), which were known to our author and also, presumably, to his putative audience. Other late Aramaic texts in a similar mixed dialect are Targum Pseudo-Jonathan and the Targums to Chronicles, Psalms, and Job. Our author's style, though competent, is rather labored, and this, as well as his occasional Arabisms, suggests that he was not a native Aramaic speaker. The implication is that Tg. Cant. originated in the narrow linguistic "window" of the eighth to ninth centuries C.E. when most Jews had adopted Arabic for everyday speech but were not yet using Arabic for literary or religious purposes. Our author's choice of Aramaic for his text, even though he and his audience were Arabic speakers, would have been dictated by the fact that he was presenting a *Targum,* and Aramaic traditionally was the language of the Targums. It was not until the time of Saʿadya (882–942) that anyone of standing was prepared to offer a Targum in *Arabic* or to employ Arabic for religious texts.

(2) Tg. Cant. and Pesaḥ

As early as the third century C.E. Jewish exegetical tradition had contextualized certain verses in Canticles to the events surrounding the Exodus from Egypt, but our Targum's constant and insistent Exodus references are new. This interest in the Exodus is most obviously explained by supposing that the Targum has a particularly close connection with Passover, that it was intended to be read during that festival. Liturgical use during Pesaḥ provides an obvious *Sitz im Leben*. But, as we indicated in *Intro.* 7 above, Canticles seems to have

[1] See Tg. to 3:6 (*Note* 25); 3:9 (*Notes* 47-48); 4:8 (*Note* 34); 4:15 (*Note* 60). However, Lebanon is interpreted differently at 7:5 (*Note* 22). See further Geza Vermes, "The Symbolical Interpretation of Lebanon in the Targums," *JTS* n.s. 9 (1958) 1–12.

[2] See *Intro.* 1–5 above.

become a special reading for Pesaḥ only in the early Gaonic period. It is unlikely, therefore, that our Targum originated before then.

(3) Tg. Cant. and Jewish commentary on Canticles

Tg. Cant. is exegetically a very mature work behind which manifestly stands a long and rich tradition of interpreting Canticles, much of it known to our Targumist (*Intro.* 6.1, 6.4). He seems to have drawn on both the Palestinian Targumim and Onqelos. He was almost certainly at home in the Talmud and had access to a number of Midrashim both on Canticles and on other biblical books such as Exodus (e.g., he probably knew the Mekhilta deRabbi Ishmael). His exposition has particularly close affinities with Canticles Rabba, which dates from the sixth to eighth centuries C.E., though, as we noted above, direct dependence of the Targum on Canticles Rabba should not be assumed (*Intro.* 6.4). Tg. Cant.'s literary affinities suggest that it is a late, post-Talmudic composition, belonging to the early Gaonic period.

(4) Tg. Cant.'s Messianism

As we noted in *Intro.* 4.5, Tg. Cant. is a profoundly Messianic document. It is best seen as a product of the apocalyptic revival in Judaism during the seventh and eighth centuries C.E. As has often been noted, the Talmud is ambivalent about the Messiah. The Mishnah says remarkably little about him, given that the Rabbis almost certainly inherited strong Messianic beliefs from their Second Temple forebears. Messianic fervor had been greatly dampened by two disastrous Messianic wars against Rome, and from the mid-second century C.E. the Rabbis consciously played down Messianism and instead set about constructing a worldview that stressed the creation of a civil society here and now through obedience to the *miṣwot* and the teachings of the Sages. However, the Messianic inheritance could not be entirely suppressed. It lived on in popular piety and was constantly reinforced by prayers such as the ʿAmidah. In the late Talmudic period, probably under popular pressure, Messianism began to creep back into mainstream Rabbinic thought (see especially b.Sanh. 49a). The Rabbis tried to harness Messianism to their own ideals by arguing that if Israel were faithfully to keep the *miṣwot* it could hasten the coming of the Messiah (a point our Targumist also makes). In the post-Talmudic period, beginning probably in the late sixth or early seventh century C.E., there was an upsurge of Messianism in Judaism. It was accompanied by a rediscovery of the apocalyptic genre of writing and the recovery of "lost" Second-Temple-period apocalyptic traditions. Just how and why this happened it is hard now to say, but it is probably no accident that at the same period there was a flowering of apocalyptic in Christianity. This apocalyptic Messianic speculation was given powerful impetus by the rise of Islam, which provoked interest in the end of the world across the whole of the Middle East—in Christianity, in Judaism, in Zoroastrianism, and finally in Islam itself. To this apocalyptic revival in Judaism belong 3 Enoch, the Book of Zerubbabel, the Prayer of Simeon bar Yoḥai, Pirqei deRabbi Eliezer, and, I would suggest, Tg. Cant. Tg. Cant.'s scenario of the end is generally similar to the late eschatological scenarios put forward by Saʿadya and by Hai Gaon.[3]

[3] See further Philip S. Alexander, "The King Messiah in Rabbinic Judaism," in John Day, ed., *King and Messiah in Israel and the Ancient Near East* (Sheffield: Sheffield Academic Press, 1998) 456–73.

(5) Tg. Cant. and the Hasmoneans

The late dating of Tg. Cant. is further strengthened by a consideration of our Targumist's attitude toward the Hasmoneans, which, as we noted in *Intro.* 3.2, is very positive. For him the Hasmonean period represents one of the three peaks of the *Heilsgeschichte:* it matches the ideal polity Israel achieved in the time of Solomon and will again achieve in the days of the Messiah. But our Targumist's positive appraisal of the Hasmoneans contrasts strikingly with the generally lukewarm or negative attitude toward them in the Talmud and the classic Rabbinic sources. They are, in fact, not all that often mentioned there, but when they are it is generally in unflattering terms. Hand in hand with this neglect of the Hasmoneans went a general disregard of the festival of Hanukkah, which, of course, celebrated their achievements. In the post-Talmudic period, however, again for reasons that are not entirely clear, though they are probably linked to the recovery of Second Temple traditions and the rebirth of Messianism, a reappraisal of the Hasmoneans occurred, and with it a revival of the festival of Hanukkah. Tg. Cant. once again fits into these developments.[4]

(6) Historical allusions

A number of historical allusions suggest that Tg. Cant. is to be dated to the early Islamic period.

(a) Esau and Ishmael. At 1:7 Moses is represented as challenging God to tell him how in their future exile the Jews "will be provided for, and how they will settle down among the nations whose decrees are as harsh as the scorching heat of the noonday sun at the summer solstice, and why they should wander among the flocks of Esau and Ishmael who associate with You their idols as [Your] companions?" This seems to look out on a world divided between Christianity (Esau) and Islam (Ishmael). The charge of polytheism leveled here against Islam sounds a little odd but, as Raphael Loewe shrewdly remarks, it may imply "a *Sitz im Leben* in which Jewry had not yet come to appreciate the monotheistic insistence of Islam, and conversely one in which the Targum was as yet unlikely to come to the notice of Islam's own apologists and propagandists."[5] Tg. Cant. 6:8 envisages the armies of Esau and of Ishmael, led by "the wicked Alexander," attacking the Jews during the Hasmonean period. The picture is, of course, historically speaking, hopelessly confused. It probably reflects in part what the Targumist imagined was going to happen at the end of history. The political picture we have derived from 1:7 and 6:8 is not contradicted by 7:12, which designates the present period as the "exile of Edom," i.e., of Christianity. There are several ways in which the failure to mention Ishmael here can be explained. In the first place, the Targumist may be speaking historically. He is referring in context to the exile that occurred after the destruction of the Temple in 70 C.E. That was an exile caused by "Rome." It is also possible that, although living under Islam, he still saw Rome as Israel's principal foe. This would fit in with Talmudic tradition, and he may have lived in the early Islamic period when the memory of Rome's oppression of his community was still strong. It is also true that many Jewish apocalyptic scenarios of the post-Islamic period still saw Rome as the eschatological foe: Armillus the prince of Rome would lead the attack of the nations on Jerusalem.

[4] See further Alexander, "From Poetry to Historiography," 103–28.

[5] Raphael Loewe, "Apologetic Motifs in the Targum to the Song of Songs," 165.

(b) The Poll Tax. A date in the Islamic period has been argued by Loewe on the basis of 8:9, which speaks of Israel giving "her silver to buy the unity of the name of the Lord of the World." He makes out a careful case that the reference here is to the poll tax imposed by the Islamic authorities on the Jews: "Jews, Christians, and certain others, each of them constituting an *ahl al-kitab,* became, by payment of poll tax *(jizya),* licensees, and as such were exempted from the choice between Islam and the sword."[6] He translates: "And she lays out her money to acquire the right to proclaim the uniqueness of the Name of the Master of the world." But there is a problem with this interpretation. In context the Tg. to 8:9 is describing the Messianic Age, when the subjugation enshrined in the payment of *jizya* is not appropriate. It is possible the Targumist has momentarily forgotten where he is in narrative time, but in fact the expression is rather vague. Loewe quotes S. D. Goitein's view, communicated to him personally, that "the emphasis evinced by some Genizah documents on the 'holy character' of certain Jewish communal obligations involving pecuniary sacrifice, such as the redemption of captives (see, for example, Mann, *The Jews in Egypt*, II, 345), is an adequate explanation."[7] My own view is that Goitein is on the right track and that the precise communal obligation alluded to at 8:9 is financial support for the schools (see *Note* 43 *ad loc.*).

8.2. The Provenance of Tg. Cant.

The most likely provenance for Tg. Cant. is Palestine. Two considerations point in this direction.

(1) "This polluted land"

At 8:14 the Targumist refers to his domicile as "this polluted land." Ezra Z. Melamed has suggested that it is unlikely that our author would have referred to the "holy land" as "polluted" and that this indicates that he lived outside the Land, presumably in Babylonia.[8] But the exact opposite is surely the case. The Targumist, like the prophets of old, regarded the Land as susceptible to pollution. Indeed, its susceptibility was directly related to its holiness. Here the pollution of the Land is probably caused, as Loewe remarks, by its "continued occupancy by gentiles."[9] Moreover, the Targumist says that the pollution of the Land drives away the Shekhinah. But since he seems to hold that the Shekhinah can be experienced only in the Land of Israel (see *Intro.* 4.1), then the land here must be Palestine.

(2) The Rabbinic Schools

The references to the schools also point, on balance, in the same direction. As we noted earlier, the Targum can be read as a paean of praise to the schools. But which school or schools are in view? There are only two possibilities, the schools of Babylonia (Sura and Pumbeditha) and the great school of Palestine (which in the period to which our Targum probably belongs was still in Tiberias).[10] The most important references are as follows:

[6] Ibid. 167.

[7] Ibid. 167, n. 39.

[8] Melamed, "Targum Canticles," 215.

[9] Loewe, "Apologetic Motifs in the Targum to the Song of Songs," 163. Note how Tg. Cant. 8:5 envisages the expulsion of the Gentiles from the Land in the Messianic Age as involving even the miraculous slinging out of the corpses of their dead.

[10] Moshe Gil, *A History of Palestine 634–1099*. Translated from the Hebrew by Ethel Broido. (Cambridge: Cambridge University Press, 1992) 499–500.

(A) TARGUM TO 7:3: The Head of your College, through whose merit all the world is sustained, just as the fetus is sustained through its navel in the belly of its mother, shines with [a knowledge of] the Torah like the disc of the moon, when he comes to pronounce pure or impure, innocent or guilty, and the words of the Torah never fail [to flow] from his mouth, just as the waters of the great river which issues from Eden never fail. Seventy Sages surround him, like a round threshing-floor, and their treasuries are full of the holy tithes, votive and free-will offerings, which Ezra the priest, Zerubbabel, Jeshua, Nehemiah, and Mordechai Bilshan, the Men of the Great Assembly, who are compared to roses, ordained for their benefit, so that they might be enabled to engage in the study of the Torah day and night.

(B) TARGUM TO 7:5: The Father of the Law Court who judges your cases, having power over the people to bind and to scourge whoever is condemned to scourging by the court, is like king Solomon, who made the Tower of Ivory, and subdued the people of the House of Israel, and brought them back to the Sovereign of the World. Your scribes are as full of wisdom as pools of water, and they know how to make calculations for intercalation, and they intercalate years, and fix the beginnings of years and the beginnings of months in the gate of the house of the Great Sanhedrin. The chief of the family of the House of Judah is like king David who built the citadel of Zion which is called the Tower of Lebanon; anyone who stands upon it is able to count the towers that are in Damascus.

(C) TARGUM TO 8:13: Solomon the prophet said at the end of his prophecy: The Lord of the World will say to the Assembly of Israel at the end of days: "You, Assembly of Israel, who are likened to a little garden among the nations, and [who] sit in the House of Study with the members of the Sanhedrin, and [with] the rest of the people who listen to the voice of the Head of the College, and learn from his mouth the teachings of the Torah, cause me to hear the sound of your words, when you sit to acquit and to condemn, and I will approve all that you do."

If we combine these references together, the following plausible picture of the College emerges. The College is called both "the House of Study" (Aram. *beit midrasha'* = Heb. *beit ha-midrash*) and the "Sanhedrin" because it functions as a place of study and teaching, as a legislative assembly, and as a court of law. It comprises seventy "members" (Aram. *ḥabrayya'* = Heb. *ḥaberim*) and is governed by the "head of college" (Aram. *resh metibta'* = Heb. *ro'sh ha-yeshibah*). The other major official mentioned, presumably the second in command to the Head of the College, is the Father of the Law Court *('ab beit din)*. The *Beit Din* may have been concerned with the everyday administration of justice and comprised a smaller body of *ḥaberim* within the Sanhedrin. In plenary session the Sanhedrin probably functioned as a legislative assembly, or occasionally as a high court. Another group of officials within the Sanhedrin were "the scribes." They sat in the "gate of the house of the Great Sanhedrin" and were particularly responsible for fixing the calendar. The College claimed that Ezra and the Men of the Great Assembly back in the Persian period had decreed that the community had a duty financially to support the College with "holy tithes, votive and free-will offerings."

The picture is fairly specific, but not quite specific enough. It could broadly apply to either the Babylonian or the Palestinian Yeshibot. Alexander Marx argued that the title *'ab beit din* was distinctively Palestinian,[11] but it is doubtful if this was the case. Perhaps more telling is the term *ḥaberim,* which does not seem to have been used in the Babylonian Yeshibot. It is securely attested for Palestine, as is the title *Ḥaburat ha-Qodesh,* "the Holy Association," for the Palestinian Yeshibah. Moreover, the reference to determining the calendar

[11] "Studies in Gaonic History and Literature," *JQR* n.s. 1 (1910–11) 66–67. Marx also notes that the indiscriminate use of the term "Sanhedrin" for the Yeshibah is post-Talmudic and typical of Palestine.

is important. This prerogative was jealously guarded by the Palestinian Yeshibah, and evidence is lacking before the time of Saʿadya that Babylonia made any attempt to question this role. However, two elements in the description at first sight seem to point to Babylonia rather than Palestine. Melamed saw in the reference in 8:13 to study-sessions attended by the members of the general public a clear allusion to the Babylonian institution of the *pirqaʾ*. It is less easy to find references to such public gatherings in Palestine in the period to which our Targum belongs.[12] The other piece of evidence perhaps pointing to Babylonia is the mention of "the chief of the family of the House of Judah" in 7:5. This could easily be taken as alluding to the Exilarch *(Resh Galutaʾ)* in Babylonia, who claimed Davidic descent. By way of contrast there are grounds for thinking that the corresponding office of the Patriarch *(Nasiʾ)* in the west had died out some time before our Targum was composed. However, Jacob Mann has argued that in some form the office of *Nasiʾ* continued in the west well into Gaonic times, and that at least some of those who laid claim to it asserted their Davidic descent.[13]

But the most telling argument in favor of a Palestinian as opposed to a Babylonian provenance is the simple fact that our text mentions only one Yeshibah. There were *two* great ecumenical schools in Babylonia in our period—Sura and Pumbeditha—but only one in Palestine. The contrast between our Targum and what appears to be a fragment of a midrash on Canticles in British Library ms. Or. 5554a, fol. 12a is instructive. This also probably exploited the text of Canticles to praise the schools, but it clearly has Sura and Pumbeditha in mind.[14] The great Yeshibot collaborated with each other to a considerable degree, carving up the Jewish world between them as their respective spheres of influence. However, rivalry was always bubbling just below the surface. Tg. Cant. was, at least in part, composed as propaganda for the Palestinian Yeshibah. It emphasized its importance and solicited donations on its behalf. It was composed for liturgical use on the festival of Passover (*Intro.* 7), and if, as seems likely, it became popular, it would surely have been effective in promoting the interests of the Palestinian Sanhedrin and Gaonate.[15]

[12] Melamed, "Targum Canticles," 215. At Cant 6:2 the Tg. appears to accept that the founding of the Babylonian Yeshibot dates back to the time of the Babylonian exile, a view exploited in some Babylonian sources to advance the claims of the Babylonian schools against those of Palestine (see David M. Goodblatt, *Rabbinic Instruction in Sasanian Babylonia* [Leiden: Brill, 1975] 13–16). But this does not seem to be the case here. On the *pirqaʾ* see Goodblatt, *Instruction* 170–96, who also notes in passing some references to public lectures in the west, though the term *pirqaʾ* is not used for these.

[13] Jacob Mann, *The Jews in Egypt and in Palestine under the Fatimid Caliphs.* 2 vols. (London: Oxford University Press, 1920–22) 1:274 and *passim.* A law of Theodosius II dated May 30, 429 (*Codex Theodosianus* 16.8.29) refers to the "cessation of the patriarchs" *(post excessum patriarcharum).* See Amnon Lindner, *The Jews in Roman Imperial Legislation* (Detroit: Wayne State University Press, 1987) 320–23. On this basis Michael Avi-Yonah, *The Jews of Palestine: A Political History from the Bar Kokhba War to the Arab Conquest* (Oxford: Blackwell; New York: Schocken, 1976) 225–29, talks of the "end of the Patriarchate." But the evidence for an office of *Nasi* in Gaonic Palestine is compelling. There are two possibilities. Either the "cessation of the patriarchs" refers only to the loss of status and privilege in Roman law, while the office in fact continued to be recognized and to function *within* the Jewish community, or the office did indeed cease for a time, only to be revived later, perhaps under Islamic jurisdiction.

[14] Mann, *Texts and Studies* 1:322, n. 47a. The anti-Palestinian bias of this text seems rather obvious: "The Torah flourished in Jerusalem from the time of the Hasmoneans till the Destruction [of the Temple]. From then on, *Flee, My Beloved, and be like the gazelle . . . upon the mountains of spices* (Cant. 8:14). These are the two Yeshibahs whose scent spreads from one end of the world to the other, as we say; 'Where [is the Shekhinah] in Babylonia? In the synagogue of Huṣal and in the synagogue of Shaf we-Yatib in Nehardea etc.' (b.Meg. 29a). This teaches you that the Shekhinah departed from Jerusalem and took up its abode in Babylonia, as it is written, *Be in pain, and labour to bring forth, O daughter of Zion, [like a woman in travail: for now you shall go forth out of the city, and shall dwell in the field, and shall come even unto Babylon; there shall you be rescued; there shall the Lord redeem you from the hand of your enemies].*" Read against our Tg. to Cant. 8:14 this could be seen as rather pointed: the Shekhinah, when it departs from Palestine in our Targum, does not go to Babylon, or anywhere else in the Diaspora, but to heaven.

[15] On the Yeshibot, in addition to the works of Gil, Mann, Marx, and Goodblatt listed above, see S. D. Goitein, *A Mediterranean Society* (Berkeley: University of California Press, 1971) 2:195–205; Isaiah M. Gafni, *The Jews of Babylonia in the Talmudic Era: A Social and Cultural History* (Jerusalem: The Zalman Shazar Centre for Jewish History, 1990) 177–203 [Hebrew].

9. BIBLIOGRAPHY

For editions of Talmudic and Midrashic texts see Günter Stemberger, *Introduction to the Talmud and Midrash.* Translated and edited by Markus Bockmuehl. 2nd ed. Edinburgh: T & T Clark, 1996.

Abegg, Martin, Jr., Peter Flint, and Eugene Ulrich. *The Dead Sea Scrolls Bible.* San Francisco: HarperSanFrancisco, 1999.

Abelson, Joshua. *The Immanence of God in Rabbinical Literature.* London: Macmillan, 1912.

Abraham, R. D. "The Vocabulary of the Old Judeo-Spanish Translation of the Canticles and their Chaldean Paraphrase," *Hispanic Review* 41 (1973) 1–5.

Abrams, Daniel. *Sexual Symbolism and Merkavah Speculation in Medieval Germany: A Study of the Sod ha-egoz Texts.* Tübingen: J.C.B. Mohr [Paul Siebeck], 1997.

Agus, Ronald E. *The Binding of Isaac and Messiah: Law, Martyrdom and Deliverance in Early Rabbinic Religiosity.* Albany: SUNY Press, 1988.

Alexander, Philip S. "The Targumim and Early Exegesis of 'Sons of God' in Genesis 6," *JJS* 23 (1972) 60–71.

———. *The Toponymy of the Targumim, with special reference to the Table of the Nations and the Boundaries of the Land of Israel.* D.Phil. thesis, University of Oxford, 1974.

———. "3 Enoch," in James H. Charlesworth, ed., *The Old Testament Pseudepigrapha.* 2 vols. New York and London: Doubleday, 1983, 1:223–315.

———. *Textual Sources for the Study of Judaism.* Manchester: Manchester University Press, 1984.

———. "Jewish Aramaic Translations of Hebrew Scriptures," in Martin J. Mulder, ed., *Mikra: Text, Translation, Reading, and Interpretation of the Hebrew Bible in Ancient Judaism and Early Christianity.* CRINT II.1. Assen: Van Gorcum, 1988; Minneapolis: Fortress, 1990, 217–53.

———. "The Aramaic Version of the Song of Songs," in Geneviève Contamine, ed., *Traduction et Traducteurs au Moyen Âge: Actes du colloque international du CNRS organisé à Paris, Institut de Recherche et d'Histoire des Textes les 26–28 mai 1986.* Paris: Éditions du Centre National de la Recherche Scientifique, 1989, 119–31.

———. "Quid Athenis et Hierosolymis? Rabbinic Midrash and Hermeneutics in the Graeco-Roman World," in Philip R. Davies and Richard T. White, eds., *A Tribute to Geza Vermes.* JSOT.S 100. Sheffield: JSOT Press, 1990, 101–24.

———. "Pre-emptive Exegesis: Genesis Rabba's Reading of the Story of Creation," *JJS* 43 (1992) 230–45.

———. "Textual Criticism and Rabbinic Literature: The Case of the Targum of the Song of Songs," in: Philip S. Alexander and Alexander Samely, eds., *Artefact and Text: The Recreation of Jewish Literature in Medieval Hebrew Manuscripts = Bulletin of the John Rylands University Library of Manchester* 75.3 (1993) 159–73.

———. "Tradition and Originality in the Targum of the Song of Songs," in Derek R. G. Beattie and Martin McNamara, eds., *The Aramaic Bible: Targums in their Historical Context.* JSOT.S 166. Sheffield: JSOT Press, 1994, 318–39.

———. "Bavli Berakhot 55a-57b: The Talmudic Dreambook in Context," *JJS* 46 (1995) 230–48.

———. "'A Sixtieth Part of Prophecy': The Problem of Continuing Revelation in Judaism," in Jon Davies, Graham Harvey, and Wilfred G. E. Watson, eds., *Words Remembered, Texts Renewed: Essays in Honour of John F. A. Sawyer.* JSOT.S 195. Sheffield: Sheffield Academic Press, 1995, 414–33.

———. "The Song of Songs as Historical Allegory: Notes on the Development of an Exegetical Tradition," in: Kevin J. Cathcart and Michael Maher, eds., *Targumic and Cognate Studies: Essays in Honour of Martin McNamara.* JSOT.S 230. Sheffield: Sheffield Academic Press, 1996, 14–29.

———. "'Wrestling against Wickedness in High Places': Magic in the Worldview of the Qumran Community," in Stanley E. Porter and Craig A. Evans, eds., *The Scrolls and the Scriptures: Qumran Fifty Years After.* JSOT.S 26. Sheffield: Sheffield Academic Press, 1997, 318–37.

———. "The King Messiah in Rabbinic Judaism," in John Day, ed., *King and Messiah in Israel and the Ancient Near East: Proceedings of the Oxford Old Testament Seminar.* JSOT.S 270. Sheffield: Sheffield Academic Press, 1998, 456–73.

———. "From Poetry to Historiography: The Image of the Hasmoneans in Targum Canticles and the Question of the Targum's Provenance and Date," *JSP* 19 (1999) 103–28.

———. "Jerusalem as the Omphalos of the World: On the History of a Geographical Concept," in Lee I. Levine, ed., *Jerusalem: Its Sanctity and Centrality to Judaism, Christianity and Islam.* New York: Continuum, 1999, 104–19.

———. "Jewish Elements in Gnosticism and Magic c. 70 to c. 270 C.E.," in William Horbury, W. D. Davies, and John Sturdy, eds., *Cambridge History of Judaism.* Vol. 4. Cambridge: Cambridge University Press, 1999, 1052–78.

———. "Torah and Salvation in Tannaitic Literature," in: D. A. Carson, Peter T. O'Brien, and Mark A. Seifrid, eds., *Justification and Variegated Nomism.* Tübingen: J.C.B. Mohr [Paul Siebeck], 2001, 1:261–302.

———. "Notes on Some Targums of the Targum of the Song of Songs," in Paul V. M. Flesher, ed., *Ernest Clarke Memorial Volume.* Leiden: Brill, 2002.

Alexander, Philip S., and Geza Vermes, "4Q285 Sefer ha-Milḥamah," in Philip S. Alexander et al., eds., *Qumran Cave 4. XXVI: Cryptic Texts and Miscellanea, Part 1.* Discoveries in the Judaean Desert XXXVI. Oxford: Clarendon Press, 2000, 228–46.

Altmann, Alexander. "Moses Narboni's 'Epistle on *Shiʿur Qoma*,'" in idem, *Jewish Medieval and Renaissance Studies.* Cambridge, Mass.: Harvard University Press, 1967, 225–88.

Anderson, Andrew R. *Alexander's Gate, Gog and Magog, and the Inclosed Nations.* Cambridge, Mass.: The Medieval Academy of America, 1932.

Arndt, William F., and F. Wilbur Gingrich. *A Greek-English Lexicon of the New Testament and Other Early Christian Literature.* Chicago: University of Chicago Press, 1957.

Astell, Ann W. *The Song of Songs in the Middle Ages.* Ithaca, N.Y.: Cornell University Press, 1990.

Avemarie, Friedrich. *Tora und Leben: Untersuchungen zur Heilsbedeutung der Tora in frühen rabbinischen Literatur.* Tübingen: J.C.B. Mohr, 1996.

Avi-Yonah, Michael. *The Jews of Palestine: A Political History from the Bar Kokhba War to the Arab Conquest.* Oxford: Blackwell; New York: Schocken, 1976.

Bacher, Wilhelm. "The supposed inscription upon 'Joshua the Robber,'" *JQR* o.s. 3 (1891) 354–57.

———. "Une ancienne liste des noms grecs des pierres précieuses relatées dans Exode XXVIII, 17-20," *REJ* 29 (1894) 79–90.

Bauckham, Richard J. *Tudor Apocalypse*: *sixteenth century apocalypticism, millennarianism, and the English Reformation: from John Bale to John Foxe and Thomas Brightman: illustrative texts from The lanterne of lyght . . . [et al.].* Abingdon and Oxford: The Sutton Courtenay Press, 1978.

———. "The List of the Tribes in Revelation Again," *JSNT* 42 (1991) 99–115.

———. *The Climax of Prophecy: Studies in the Book of Revelation.* Edinburgh: T & T Clark, 1993.

———. *The Fate of the Dead: Studies on Jewish and Christian Apocalypses.* Leiden: Brill, 1998.

Bauer, Max. *Edelsteinkunde.* 3rd ed. Leipzig: C. H. Tauchnitz, 1932.

Baxter, Ron. *Bestiaries and Their Users in the Middle Ages.* Stroud: Sutton; London: Courtauld Institute, 1998.

Beattie, Derek R. G. "The Textual Tradition of Targum Ruth," in Derek R. G. Beattie and Martin J. McNamara, eds., *The Aramaic Bible: Targums in their Historical Context.* JSOT.S 166. Sheffield: Sheffield Academic Press, 1994, 340–48.

Ben-Shammai, Haggai. "New Findings in a Forgotten Manuscript: Samuel B. Hofni's Commentary on *Haʾazinu* and Saʿadya's 'Commentary on the Ten Songs,'" *Qiryat Sefer* 61 (1986–87) 313–32 [Hebrew].

Bergmeier, Roland. "Jerusalem, die hochgebaute Stadt," *ZNW* 75 (1984) 86–106.

Beyer, Klaus. *Die aramäischen Texte vom Toten Meer.* Göttingen: Vanderhoeck & Ruprecht, 1984.

Bietenhard, Hans. *Die himmlische Welt im Urchristentum und Spätjudentum.* Tübingen: J.C.B. Mohr [Paul Siebeck], 1951.

Black, Matthew. *The Book of Enoch or 1 Enoch: A New English Edition.* Leiden: Brill, 1985.

Blau, Lajos. *Studien zum althebräischen Buchwesen.* Strassburg: E.K.J. Trübner, 1902.

Bockmuehl, Markus. *Jewish Law in Gentile Churches.* Edinburgh: T & T Clark, 2000.

Bøe, Sverre. *Gog and Magog: Ezekiel 38–39 as Pre-text for Revelation 19, 17-21 and 20, 7-10.* Tübingen: J.C.B. Mohr [Paul Siebeck], 2001.

Bori, Pier Cesare. *The Golden Calf and the Origins of the Anti-Jewish Controversy.* Translated by David Ward. Atlanta: Scholars, 1990.

Bousset, Wilhelm. *The Antichrist Legend: A Chapter in Christian and Jewish Folklore.* London: Hutchinson and Co., 1896.

Boyarin, Daniel. "Two Introductions to the Midrash on the Song of Songs," *Tarbiṣ* 56 (1986–87) 479–500 [Hebrew].

Brockelmann, Carl. *Lexicon Syriacum.* 2nd ed. Halle: Niemeyer, 1928.

Brown, Francis, Samuel R. Driver and Charles A. Briggs. *A Hebrew and English Lexicon of the Old Testament.* Oxford: Clarendon Press, 1966.

Buber, Salomon. *Midrasch Suta: Hagadische Abhandlungen über Schir ha-Schirim, Ruth, Echah und Koheleth.* Berlin: Mʾkize Nirdamim, 1894.

Buchanan, George Wesley. *Revelation and Redemption: Jewish Documents of Deliverance from the Fall of Jerusalem to the Death of Nahmanides.* Dillsboro, N.C.: Western North Carolina Press, 1978.

Charles, Robert Henry. *The Book of Jubilees, or The Little Genesis.* London: A. and C. Black, 1902.

Charlesworth, James H., ed. *The Old Testament Pseudepigrapha.* 2 vols. New York and London: Doubleday, 1983.

Chester, Andrew. *Divine Revelation and Divine Titles in the Pentateuchal Targumim.* Tübingen: J.C.B. Mohr [Paul Siebeck], 1986.

Chill, Abraham. *The Minhagim: The Customs and Ceremonies of Judaism, Their Origin and Rationale.* New York: Sepher-Hermon Press, 1979.

Churgin, Pinkhos. *The Targum to Hagiographa.* New York: Horeb, 1945, 117–39 on Tg. Cant. [Hebrew].

Clark, Elizabeth A. "The Uses of the Song of Songs: Origen and the Later Latin Fathers," in eadem, *Ascetic Piety and Women's Faith: Essays on Late Ancient Christianity.* Lewiston, N.Y.: Edwin Mellen Press, 1986, 386–427.

Cohen, Gerson D., editor and translator. *The Book of Tradition (Sefer Ha-Qabbalah) by Abraham ibn Daud.* Philadelphia: Jewish Publication Society, 1967.

———. "The Song of Songs and the Jewish Religious Mentality," in idem, *Studies in the Variety of Rabbinic Cultures.* Philadelphia: Jewish Publication Society, 1991, 3–17.

Cohen, Jeremy. *The Friars and the Jews: The Evolution of Medieval Anti-Judaism.* Ithaca, N.Y.: Cornell University Press, 1982.

Cohen, Martin S. *The Shiʿur Qomah: Liturgy and Theurgy in Pre-Kabbalistic Jewish Mysticism.* Lanham, Md.: University Press of America, 1983.

———. *The Shiʿur Qomah: Texts and Recensions.* Tübingen: J.C.B. Mohr [Paul Siebeck], 1985.

Cook, Edward M. "A New Perspective on the Language of Onqelos and Jonathan," in Beattie and McNamara, eds., *The Aramaic Bible: Targums in their Historical Context,* 142–56.

Dalman, Gustaf. *Grammatik des jüdisch-palästinischen Aramäisch.* Leipzig: J. C. Hinrich'sche Buchhandlung, 1905.

Dan, Joseph. "The Chambers of the Chariot," *Tarbiṣ* 47 (1977–78) 49–55 [Hebrew].

———. "Armillus: The Jewish Antichrist and the Origins and Dating of the *Sefer Zerubbavelʾ,*" in Peter Schäfer and Mark Cohen, eds., *Towards the Millennium: Messianic Expectations from the Bible to Waco.* Leiden: Brill, 1998, 73–104.

Davies, W. D. *Torah in the Messianic Age and/or the Age to Come*. JBL.MS 7. Philadelphia: Society of Biblical Literature, 1952.

Díez Merino, Luis. "El Targum al Cantar de los Cantares (Tradición Sefardi de Alfonso de Zamora)," *Estudios Biblicos* 38 (1979–80) 295–357.

———. "El Targum al Cantar de los Cantares (Texto arameo del Códice Urbinati 1 y su traducción)," *Anuario de Filología*, Facultad de Filología, Universidad de Barcelona (1981) 237–84.

Dimant, Devora. "Qumran Sectarian Literature," in Michael E. Stone, ed., *Jewish Writings of the Second Temple Period*. CRINT II.2. Assen: VanGorcum; Philadelphia: Fortress, 1984, 505–508.

Draper, Jonathan A. "The Twelve Apostles as Foundation Stones of the Heavenly Jerusalem and the Foundation of the Qumran Community," *Neotestamentica* 22 (1988) 41–64.

Eben-Shmuel, Yehuda. *Midreshei Geʾullah*. 2nd ed. Jerusalem: Mosad Bialik, 1968.

Ego, Beate. *Im Himmel wie auf Erden*. Tübingen: J.C.B. Mohr [Paul Siebeck], 1989.

———. *Targum Scheni zu Ester*. Tübingen: J.C.B. Mohr [Paul Siebeck], 1996.

Eisenstein, Jacob D. *Ozar Midrashim*. 2 vols. New York: J. D. Eisenstein, 1915.

Elbogen, Ismar. *Jewish Liturgy: A Comprehensive History*. Translated by Raymond P. Scheindlin. Philadelphia: Jewish Publication Society; New York: Jewish Theological Seminary, 1993.

Encyclopedia of Islam, new edition. 9 vols. Leiden: Brill, 1960–.

Encyclopaedia Judaica. 16 vols. Jerusalem: Keter, 1972.

Engammare, Max. *Le Cantique des Cantiques à la renaissance: étude et bibliographie*. Geneva: Librairie Droz, 1993 .

Epstein, Abraham. "The Song of Abraham our Father," *Mimmizraḥ umimmaʿarab* 1 (Vienna, 1894) 85–89; reprinted in Abraham M. Haberman, ed., *Kitbei Rabbi A. Epstein*. Jerusalem, 1957, 1:251–54 [Hebrew].

Epstein, Jacob N. *Diqduq ʾaramit bablit*. Jerusalem: Magnes, 1960.

Fine, Lawrence. *Safed Spirituality*. Classics of Western Spirituality. Mahwah, N.J.: Paulist, 1984.

Fishbane, Michael A. "The Qumran-Pesher and Traits of Ancient Hermeneutics," *Proceedings of the Sixth World Congress of Jewish Studies* 6/1 (1977) 97–114.

———. *Biblical Interpretation in Ancient Israel*. Oxford: Clarendon Press, 1986.

Flusser, David. *The Josippon [Joseph Gorionides]. Edited with an Introduction, Commentary and Notes*. 2 vols. Jerusalem: The Bialik Institute, 1980–81.

Fontela, Carlos Alonso. *El Targum al Cantar de los Cantares (Edición Crítica)*. Colección Tesis Doctorales, No. 92/87. Madrid: Editorial de la Universidad Complutense de Madrid, 1987.

Freehof, Solomon B. "The Song of Songs: A General Suggestion," *JQR* 39 (1948–49) 397–402.

Gafni, Isaiah M. *The Jews of Babylonia in the Talmudic Era: A Social and Cultural History*. Jerusalem: The Zalman Shazar Centre for Jewish History, 1990 [Hebrew].

Gaster, Moses. *The Exempla of the Rabbis*. London and Leipzig: Asia Publishing Co., 1924; reprint New York: Ktav, 1968 = *Sefer Maʿasiyyot*.

———. *Studies and Texts*. 3 vols. London: Maggs Bros., 1925–28.

Gil, Moshe. *A History of Palestine 634–1099*. Cambridge: Cambridge University Press, 1992.

Gill, John. *An Exposition of the Book of Solomon's Song . . . to which is added the targum . . . faithfully translated*. 2nd ed. London: Printed for John Ward, 1751.

Ginsburg, Christian D. *The Song of Songs*. London: Longman, 1857.

Ginzberg, Louis. *The Legends of the Jews*. 7 vols. Philadelphia: Jewish Publication Society, 1909–38.

———. *Geonica*. 2 vols. New York: Jewish Theological Seminary, 1909; reprint New York: Hermon, 1968.

———. *Ginze Schechter*. Vol. 1. New York: Beit Midrash ha-Rabbanim, 1928.

Glasson, Thomas F. "The Order of the Jewels in Rev xxi.19-20: A Theory Eliminated," *JTS* 26 (1975) 95–100.

Gliszczynski, S. von. "Versuch einer Identifizierung der Edelsteine im Amtsschild des jüdischen Hohenpriesters auf Grund kritischer und ästhetischer Vergleichsmomente," *Forschungen und Fortschritte* (Berlin) 21–23 (1947) 234–38.

Goitein, S. D. *A Mediterranean Society; The Jewish Communities of the Arab World as Portrayed in the Documents of the Cairo Geniza.* Vol. 2. Berkeley: University of California Press, 1971.

Goldberg, Arnold M. *Untersuchungen über die Vorstellung von der Schechinah in der frühen rabbinischen Literatur (Talmud und Midrasch).* Berlin: de Gruyter, 1969.

Goldin, Judah. *The Song at the Sea: Being a Commentary on a Commentary in Two Parts.* New Haven: Yale University Press, 1971.

———. "This Song," in idem, *Studies in Midrash and Related Literature*, edited by Barry L. Eichler and Jeffrey H. Tigay. Philadelphia: Jewish Publication Society, 1988, 151–61.

Gollancz, Hermann. *The Targum to "The Song of Songs"; The Book of the Apple; The Ten Jewish Martyrs; A Dialogue on Games of Chance.* Translated from the Hebrew and Aramaic. London: Luzac & Co., 1908.

Goodblatt, David M. *Rabbinic Instruction in Sasanian Babylonia.* Leiden: Brill, 1975.

Goodenough, Erwin R. *Jewish Symbols in the Greco-Roman Period.* 13 vols. [New York]: Pantheon,1953–68.

Gordon, Robert P. *Studies in the Targums to the Twelve Prophets: From Nahum to Malachi.* Leiden and New York: Brill, 1994.

Goshen-Gottstein, Moshe H. "The 'Third Targum' on Esther and MS. Neofiti 1," *Biblica* 56 (1975) 301–29.

Greenfield, Jonas C. "Aramaic and Its Dialects. Jewish Languages: Theme and Variations," in Herbert Paper, ed., *Proceedings of Regional Conferences of the Association for Jewish Studies.* Cambridge, Mass.: Association for Jewish Studies, 1978, 29–43.

Greenup, Albert W. *The Commentary of Rabbi Tobia ben Elieser on Canticles.* No publisher: London, 1909.

Grossfeld, Bernard. *Bibliography of Targum Literature.* 3 vols. Cincinnati: Hebrew Union College Press, 1973–90.

_____. *The Targum to the Five Megilloth.* New York: Hermon, 1973.

———. *The Two Targums of Esther.* Collegeville: The Liturgical Press, 1991.

Grözinger, Karl-Erich. *Musik und Gesang in der Theologie der frühen jüdischen Literatur.* Tübingen: J.C.B. Mohr [Paul Siebeck], 1982.

Grünhut, Eleazar. *Midrash Shir Ha-Shirim.* Jerusalem, 1897; reissued with introduction and notes by Joseph Chaim Wertheimer, Jerusalem: Ketav yad ve-sefer, 1971.

Hailperin, Herman. *Rashi and the Christian Scholars.* Pittsburgh: University of Pittsburgh Press, 1963.

Halperin, David J. *The Faces of the Chariot: Early Jewish Responses to Ezekiel's Vision.* Tübingen: J.C.B. Mohr, 1988.

Harari, Yuval. *Ḥarba de-Mosheh.* Jerusalem: Aqademon, 1997.

Harkavy, Abraham E. *Teshubot ha-Geonim.* Mittheilungen aus der kaiserl. öffentlichen Bibliothek zu St. Petersburg 4. Berlin: Selbstverlag des Vereins M'Kize Nirdamim (Dr. A. Berliner), 1885.

Harris, J. S. "The Stones of the High Priest's Breastplate," *Annual of the Leeds University Oriental Society* 5 (1963–65) 40–58.

Hayward, Robert. *Divine Name and Presence: The Memra.* Totowa, N.J.: Allanheld, Osmun, 1981.

Heide, Albert van der. *The Yemenite Tradition of the Targum of Lamentations.* Leiden: Brill, 1981.

Heinemann, Joseph. "The Messiah of Ephraim and the Premature Exodus of Ephraim," *Tarbiṣ* 40 (1970–71) 450–61 [Hebrew].

———. "Targum Canticles and Its Sources," *Tarbiṣ* 41 (1971–72) 126–29 [Hebrew].

_____. *Aggadah and Its Development.* Jerusalem: Keter, 1974 [Hebrew].

———. "The Messiah of Ephraim and the Premature Exodus of the Tribe of Ephraim," *HTR* 68 (1975) 1–16.

Hengel, Martin. *The Zealots: Investigations into the Jewish Freedom Movement in the Period from Herod I until 70 A.D.* Edinburgh: T & T Clark, 1989.

Herde, Rosemarie. *Das Hohelied in der lateinischen Literatur des Mittelalters bis zum 12. Jahrhundert.* Münchener Beiträge zur Mediävistik und Renaissanceforschung 3. Spoleto: Centro Italiano di Studi sull'Alto Medioevo, 1968.

Herr, M. D. "Song of Songs Rabbah," *EJ* 15, cols. 152-54.

Higgins, Reynold A. *Greek and Roman Jewellery.* London: Methuen, 1961; 2nd ed. Berkeley and Los Angeles: University of California Press, 1980.

Hill, Charles E. "Antichrist from the Tribe of Dan," *JTS* n.s. 46 (1995) 99–117.

Hill, Christopher. *The English Bible and the Seventeenth-Century Revolution.* London: Allen Lane; New York: Penguin, 1993.

Himmelfarb, Martha. *Tours of Hell: An Apocalyptic Form in Jewish and Christian Literature.* Philadelphia: University of Pennsylvania Press, 1983.

Hirschberg, Ḥaim Zeev. *A History of the Jews in North Africa.* 2 vols. 2nd revised ed. Leiden: Brill, 1974–81.

Hurwitz, Shimon. *Maḥsor Vitry.* 2nd ed. Nuremberg: Bulka, 1923.

Jart, Una. "The Precious Stones in the Revelation of St. John xxi.18-21," *Studia Theologica* 24 (1970) 150–81.

Jastrow, Marcus. *A Dictionary of the Targumim, the Talmud Babli and Yerushalmi, and the Midrashic Literature.* London: Luzac, 1903.

Jellinek, Adolph. *Bet ha-Midrasch.* 6 vols. Leipzig: F. Nies, 1853–77; 3rd ed. Jerusalem: Wahrmann Books, 1967.

Jerusalmi, Isaac. *The Song of Songs in the Targumic Tradition: Vocalized Aramaic Text with Facing English Translation and La<u>d</u>ino Versions.* Cincinnati: La<u>d</u>ino Books, 1993.

Jewish Encyclopaedia. 12 vols. New York and London: Funk and Wagnalls, 1901–1906.

Joüon, Paul. *Le Cantique des Cantiques: commentaire philologique et exégétique.* Paris: Beauchesne, 1909.

Juusola, Hannu. *Linguistic Peculiarities in the Aramaic Magic Bowls.* Studia Orientalia 86. Helsinki: Finnish Oriental Society, 1999.

Kadushin, Max. *The Rabbinic Mind.* New York: Jewish Theological Seminary, 1952.

Kahle, Paul E. *Masoreten des Westens II.* Stuttgart: Kohlhammer, 1930.

———. *The Cairo Geniza.* 2nd ed. Oxford: Blackwell; New York: Praeger, 1959.

Kamin, Sarah, and Avrom Saltman. *Secundum Salomonem: A Thirteenth Century Latin Commentary on the Song of Solomon.* Ramat Gan: Bar-Ilan University Press, 1989.

Kasher, Menahem M. *Torah Shelemah.* 42 vols. to date. Jerusalem: Beit Torah Shelemah, 1927–1991, continuing.

Kasher, Rimon. *Targumic Toseftot to the Prophets.* Jerusalem: World Union of Jewish Studies, 1996.

Kaufman, Stephen A. "Aramaic," in Robert Hetzron, ed., *The Semitic Languages.* London: Routledge, 1997, 114–30.

Kellner, Menachem. *Commentary on Song of Songs: Levi ben Gershom (Gersonides).* New Haven and London: Yale University Press, 1998.

Kimmelman, Reuven. "Rabbi Yohanan and Origen on the Song of Songs: A Third Century Jewish-Christian Disputation," *HTR* 73 (1980) 567–59.

Kittel, Gerhard, and Gerhard Friedrich, eds., *Theological Dictionary of the New Testament.* Translated and edited by Geoffrey W. Bromiley. 10 vols. Grand Rapids: Eerdmans, 1964.

Klein, Michael L. *The Fragment-Targums of the Pentateuch according to their Extant Sources.* 2 vols. Rome: Biblical Institute Press, 1980.

———. *Targumic Manuscripts in the Cambridge Genizah Collections.* Cambridge: Cambridge University Press, 1992.

Koehler, Ludwig, and Walter Baumgartner. *The Hebrew and Aramaic Lexicon of the Old Testament.* Translated and edited by M. E. J. Richardson. 5 vols. Leiden: Brill, 1994–2000.

Komlosh, Yehuda. *The Bible in the Light of the Aramaic Translations.* Ramat-Gan: Bar Ilan University; Tel Aviv: Dvir, 1973, 77–81 on Tg. Cant. [Hebrew].

Kutscher, Edward Y. "The Language of the Genesis Apocryphon: A Preliminary Study," in Chaim Rabin and Yigael Yadin, eds., *Aspects of the Dead Sea Scrolls.* Scripta Hierosolymitana 4. Jerusalem: Magnes, 1957, 1–35.

Lagarde, Paul de. *Hagiographa Chaldaice.* Leipzig: Teubner, 1873; reprint Osnabrück: O. Zeller, 1967.

Lawson, R. P., ed. *Origen: The Song of Songs, Commentary and Homilies.* Ancient Christian Writers. London: Longmans, Green; Westminster, Md.: Newman, 1957.

Le Déaut, Roger. *La Nuit Pascale: Essai sur la signification de la Pâque juive à partir du targum d'Exode XII:42.* AnBib 22. Rome: Biblical Institute Press, 1963.

Levey, Samson H. *The Messiah: An Aramaic Interpretation.* Cincinnati: Hebrew Union College-Jewish Institute of Religion, 1974.

Lévi, Israel. "L'Apocalypse de Zorobabel," *REJ* 68 (1914) 129–60.

Levine, Étan. *The Targum of the Five Megillot: Ruth, Ecclesiastes, Canticles, Lamentations, Esther: Codex Urbinati 1.* Jerusalem: Makor, 1977, 71–74 on Tg. Cant.

Lichtenstein, Hans. "Die Fastenrolle: Eine Untersuchungen zur jüdisch-hellenistischen Geschichte," *HUCA* 8–9 (1931–32) 257–51.

Liddel, Henry G., and Robert Scott. *A Greek-English Lexicon.* 9th ed., revised by Henry Stuart Jones. Oxford: Clarendon Press, 1961.

Lieberman, Saul. *Greek in Jewish Palestine: Studies in the Life and Manners of Jewish Palestine in the II–IV Centuries C. E.* New York: Jewish Theological Seminary, 1942.

———. *Hellenism in Jewish Palestine: Studies in the Literary Transmission, Beliefs and Manners of Palestine in the I century B. C. E.–IV century C. E.* 2nd ed. New York: Jewish Theological Seminary, 1962.

———. "Mishnat Shir ha-Shirim," in Gershom G. Scholem, *Jewish Gnosticism, Merkabah Mysticism, and Talmudic Tradition.* 2nd ed. New York: Jewish Theological Seminary, 1965, 118–26.

Liebreich, Leon J. "The Benedictory Formula in the Targum to the Song of Songs," *HUCA* 18 (1944) 177–98.

———. "Midrash Leqaḥ Tob's Dependence upon the Targum to the Song of Songs 8:11-12," *JQR* n.s. 38 (1947–48) 63–66.

Linder, Amnon, ed. *The Jews in Roman Imperial Legislation.* Detroit: Wayne State University Press, 1987.

Littledale, Richard F. *A Commentary on the Song of Songs from Ancient and Mediaeval Sources.* London: Joseph Masters, 1869.

Loewe, Raphael. "The Divine Garment and the Shiʿur Qomah," *HTR* 58 (1965) 153–60.

———. "Apologetic Motifs in the Targum to the Song of Songs," in Alexander Altmann, ed., *Biblical Motifs: Origins and Transformations.* Cambridge, Mass.: Harvard University Press, 1966, 159–96.

———. "The Sources of the Targum to the Song of Songs," in Denis Sinor et al., eds., *Proceedings of the Twenty-seventh International Congress of Orientalists at Ann Arbor, Michigan, 1967.* Wiesbaden: Harrassowitz, 1971, 104–105.

Loring, Richard T. *The Christian Historical Exegesis of the Song of Songs and Its Possible Jewish Antecedents: A Chapter in the History of Interpretation.* Th.D. dissertation. New York: General Theological Seminary, 1967.

Mann, Jacob. *The Jews in Egypt and in Palestine under the Fatimid Caliphs.* 2 vols. London: Oxford University Press, 1920–22.

———. *Texts and Studies.* 2 vols. New York: Ktav, 1972.

———. "Some Midrashic Genizah Fragments," *HUCA* 14 (1939) 303–58.

Marcus, Ivan G. "The Song of Songs in German Hasidism and the School of Rashi: A Preliminary Comparison," in Barry Walfish, ed., *The Frank Talmage Memorial Volume I*. Haifa: Haifa University Press, 1994, 181–89. Also printed in Gabrielle Sed-Rajna, ed., *Rashi 1040–1990: Hommage à Ephraïm E. Urbach*. Paris: Cerf, 1993, 265–74.

Marx, Alexander. "Studies in Gaonic History and Literature," *JQR* n.s. 1 (1910–11), 61–104.

Matter, E. Ann. *The Voice of My Beloved: The Song of Songs in Western Mediaeval Christianity*. Philadelphia: University of Pennsylvania Press, 1990.

Mathews, Henry J., ed. *Commentary of Abraham ibn Ezra on the Canticles after the First Recension*. London: Trübner, 1874.

———. "Anonymous Commentary on the Song of Songs," in *Festschrift zum achtzigsten Geburtstage Moritz Steinschneider's*. Leipzig: Otto Harrassowitz, 1896; reprint Jerusalem: Makor, 1970.

Melamed, Ezra Z. *Shir ha-Shirim: Targum ʾArami, Targum ʿIbri, Tafsir bi-leshon Yehudei Paras*. Jerusalem: no publisher, 1971.

———. "Targum Canticles," *Tarbiṣ* 40 (1970–71) 201–15 [Hebrew].

———. "Rejoinder" to Heinemann (see above), *Tarbiṣ* 41 (1971–72) 126–29 [Hebrew].

———. *Bible Commentators*. Vol. 1. Jerusalem: Magnes, 1978, 341–42 on Canticles [Hebrew].

Melamed, Raphael H. *The Targum to Canticles according to six Yemen MSS, compared with the "Textus Receptus" (Ed. de Lagarde)*. Philadelphia: Dropsie College, 1921. Reprinted from *JQR* n.s. 10 (1919–20) 377–410; 11 (1920–21) 1–20; 12 (1921–22) 57–117.

Moore, George Foote. *Judaism in the First Centuries of the Christian Era*. 3 vols. Cambridge, Mass.: Harvard University Press, 1927–30.

Mulder, Martin J. *De targum op het Hooglied: Inleiding vertaling en korte verklaring*. Amsterdam: Ton Bolland, 1975.

———. "1 Chronik 7,21B-23 und die rabbinische Tradition," *JSJ* 6 (1975) 141–66.

Murphy, Roland E. *The Song of Songs*. Hermeneia. Minneapolis: Fortress, 1990.

Nadich, Judah. *Jewish Legends of the Second Commonwealth*. Philadelphia: Jewish Publication Society, 1983.

Nagar, Shalom S. *Ḥamesh Megillot . . . Miqra, Targum, Tafsir ʿim peirushim*. N.p., 1970.

Neri, Umberto. *Il Cantico dei Cantici: Targum e antiche interpretazioni ebraiche*. Rome: Città Nuova, 1976.

Neubauer, Adolf. "Megillat Taʿanit," in idem, ed., *Mediaeval Jewish Chronicles II*. Anecdota Oxoniensia. Oxford: Clarendon Press, 1895, 3–25.

Neusner, Jacob. *Song of Songs Rabbah: An Analytical Translation*. 2 vols. Atlanta: Scholars, 1989.

Ohly, Friedrich. *Hohelied-Studien: Grundzüge einer Geschichte der Hoheliedauslegung des Abendlandes bis zum 1200*. Wiesbaden: Franz Steiner Verlag, 1958.

Origen, *Commentary on Canticles*. Edited and translated by Luc Brésard, Henri Crouzel, and Marcel Borret. *Origène: Commentaire sur le Cantique des Cantiques*. 2 vols. SC 375-76. Paris: Cerf, 1991–92.

Payne Smith, Robert. *Thesaurus Syriacus*. 2 vols. Oxford: Clarendon Press, 1879–1901.

Piattelli, Alberto A. "Una Caratteristica del Targum Aramaico de 'Shir Ha-shirim,'" *Annuario di Studi Ebraici* 2 (1964/5) 123–29.

———. *Targum Shir ha-Shirim: Parafrasi aramaica del Cantico dei Cantici*. Rome: Barulli, 1975.

Pope, Marvin H. *The Song of Songs*. AB 7C. Garden City, N.Y.: Doubleday, 1977.

Qafiḥ, Yosef. *Ḥamesh Megillot . . . ʿim peirushim ʿattiqim*. Jerusalem, 1962.

Quiring, Heinrich. "Die Edelsteine im Schild des jüdischen Hohenpriesters," *Sudhoffs Archiv für Geschichte der Medizin und Naturwissenschaft* 38 (1954) 198–213.

Rabinowitz, Zvi M. *Ginzé Midrash: The Oldest Forms of Rabbinic Midrashim According to Genizah Manuscripts*. Tel Aviv: Chaim Rosenberg School of Jewish Studies, 1976.

Reader, William W. "The Twelve Jewels of Revelation 21:19-20: Tradition History and Modern Interpretations," *JBL* 100 (1981) 433–57.

Reiss, J. "Das Targum zu dem Buche Schir ha-Schirim: Verhältnis des edirten Textes desselben zu dem eines handschriftlichen Codex auf der Breslauer Stadtbibliothek, stammend aus dem 13. Jahrhundert (Codex No. 11)," *Das Jüdische Literaturblatt* 18 (1889) 158–59, 163–64, 169.

Riedel, Wilhelm. *Die Auslegung des Hohenliedes in der jüdischen Gemeinde und der griechischen Kirche.* Leipzig: A. Deichert (Georg Böhme), 1898.

Riedlinger, Helmut. *Die Makellosigkeit der Kirche in den lateinischen Hoheliedkommentaren des Mittelalters.* Münster: Aschendorff, 1958.

Robert, André, Raymond J. Tournay, and André Feuillet. *Le Cantique des Cantiques: traduction et commentaire.* Études Bibliques. Paris: Gabalda, 1963.

Rosenberg, Shalom. "Philosophical Hermeneutics on the Song of Songs: Introductory Remarks," *Tarbiṣ* 59 (1990) 133–51 [Hebrew].

Rosenthal, Judah. "Peirush Rashi ʿal Shir ha-Shirim," in Simon G. Bernstein and Gershon A. Churgin, eds., *Samuel K. Mirsky Jubilee Volume.* New York: The Jubilee Committee, 1958, 130–88.

Rowley, Harold H. "The Interpretation of the Song of Songs," in idem, *The Servant of the Lord and other Essays on the Old Testament.* 2nd, revised ed. Oxford: Blackwell, 1952, 195–246.

Sabar, Yona. *Targum de-Targum: An Old Neo-Aramaic Version of the Targum on Song of Songs.* Wiesbaden: Otto Harrassowitz, 1991.

Safrai, Shemuel. "Education and the Study of the Torah," in Shemuel Safrai and Menahem Stern, eds., with David Flusser and W. C. van Unnik, *The Jewish People in the First Century: Historical Geography, Political History, Social, Cultural and Religious Life and Institutions.* CRINT I.2. Assen: Van Gorcum, 1976, 945–70.

St. Clair, George. "Israel in Camp: A Study," *JTS* 8 (1907) 185–217.

Salfeld, Siegmund. "Das Hohelied bei den jüdischen Erklärern des Mittelalters," *Magazin für die Wissenschaft des Judenthums* 5 (1878) 110–78; 6 (1879) 20–48; 129–69; 189–209. Reissued in book form as *Das Hohelied Salomo's bei den jüdischen Erklärern des Mittelalters, nebst einem Anhange, Erklärungsproben aus Handschriften.* Berlin: Julius Benzian, 1879.

Samely, Alexander. *The Interpretation of Speech in the Pentateuch Targums.* Tübingen: J.C.B. Mohr [Paul Siebeck], 1992.

Schäfer, Peter. "Die Termini 'Heiliger Geist' und 'Geist der Prophetie' in den Targumim," *VT* 20 (1970) 304–14.

———. *Die Vorstellung vom Heiligen Geist in der rabbinischen Literatur.* Munich: Kösel, 1972.

———. *Rivalität zwischen Engeln und Menschen.* Berlin and New York: Walter de Gruyter, 1975.

_____. *Synopse zur Hekhalot Literatur.* Tübingen: J.C.B. Mohr [Paul Siebeck], 1981.

———. *Konkordanz zur Hekhalot Literatur.* 2 vols. Tübingen: J.C.B. Mohr [Paul Siebeck], 1988.

Schechter, Solomon. *Agadath Shir Hashirim, edited from a Parma Manuscript, annotated and illustrated with parallel passages from numerous mss. and early prints, with a postscript on the history of the work.* Cambridge: Deighton Bell & Co., 1896.

———. *Aspects of Rabbinic Theology: Major Concepts of the Talmud.* 1909; reprint New York: Schocken, 1965.

Schiffman, Lawrence H. "A Forty-two Letter Divine Name in the Aramaic Magic Bowls," *Bulletin of the Institute for Jewish Studies* 1 (1973) 97–102.

Schneekloth, L. G. *The Targum of the Song of Songs: A Study of Rabbinic Bible Interpretation.* Ph.D. Dissertation, University of Wisconsin, Madison, 1977.

Scholem, Gershom G. *Jewish Gnosticism, Merkabah Mysticism and Talmudic Tradition.* 2nd ed. New York: Jewish Theological Seminary, 1965.

———. *On the Kabbalah and Its Symbolism.* New York: Schocken, 1969.

———. "Redemption through Sin," in idem, *The Messianic Idea in Judaism.* New York: Schocken, 1971, 78–141.

Schürer, Emil. *The History of the Jewish People in the Age of Jesus Christ, (175 B.C.–A.D. 135).* Translated by T. A. Burkill et al. Revised by Geza Vermes, Fergus Millar, Matthew Black, and Martin Goodman. 3 vols. Edinburgh: T & T Clark, 1973–86.

Sefer Na'awah Qodesh. Livorno, 1875.

Sefer Shir ha-Shirim 'im Targum we-Sharḥ 'Arbi. Livorno: Shelomoh Bilforti va-havero, 1926.

Selwyn, Edward G. *The First Epistle of St. Peter.* London: Macmillan, 1964.

Shirman, Chaim. *Ha-Shirah ha- 'Ibrit bi-Sefarad ubi-Provence.* 3 vols. 2nd ed. Jerusalem: Mosad Bialik; Tel Aviv: Dvir, 1959–60.

Silber, Ephraim. *Sedeh Jerusalem: Ein Kommentar zu Targum Chamesh Megiloth.* Chernovsty: E. Haylpern, 1883 [Hebrew].

Simon, Maurice. "Midrash Rabbah: Song of Songs," in Harry Freedman and Maurice Simon, eds., *Midrash Rabbah.* 9 vols. 3rd ed. London and New York: Soncino, 1983.

———. "On Josephus, *Wars,* V, 5, 7," *JQR* 13 (1901) 547–48.

Singer, Simeon. *The Authorized Daily Prayer Book.* Enlarged Centenary Edition. London: Singer's Prayer Book Publication Committee, 1992.

Smith, Christopher R. "The Portrayal of the Church as the New Israel in the Names and Order of the Tribes in Revelation 7.5-8," *JSNT* 39 (1990) 111–18.

Smolar, Leivy, and Moses Aberbach, "The Golden Calf Episode in Postbiblical Literature," *HUCA* 39 (1968) 91–116.

Sokoloff, Michael. *A Dictionary of Jewish-Palestinian Aramaic.* Ramat-Gan: Bar Ilan University Press, 1992.

Sperber, Alexander. *The Bible in Aramaic, based on old manuscripts and printed texts.* 4 vols. in 5. Vol. IVA, *The Hagiographa.* Leiden: Brill, 1968, 127–41 on Tg. Cant.

Stec, David M. *The Text of the Targum of Job: An Introduction and Critical Edition.* Leiden and New York: Brill, 1994.

Steller, Hans E. "Preliminary Remarks to a New Edition of *Shir Hashirim Rabbah,*" in Gabrielle Sed-Rajna, ed., *Rashi 1040–1990: Hommage à Ephraïm E. Urbach.* Paris: Cerf, 1993, 301–12.

Stemberger, Günter. "Midraschim des Hoheslied und Geschichte Israels," in Gabrielle Sed-Rajna, ed., *Rashi 1040–1990: Hommage à Ephraïm E. Urbach.* Paris: Cerf, 1993, 313–19.

———. *Introduction to the Talmud and Midrash.* Translated and edited by Markus Bockmuehl. 2nd ed. Edinburgh: T & T Clark; Minneapolis: Fortress, 1996.

Strack, Hermann L., and Paul Billerbeck. *Kommentar zum Neuen Testament aus Talmud und Midrasch.* 4 vols. Munich: Beck, 1926–28; Vols. 5–6 edited by Joachim Jeremias and Kurt Adolph. Munich: Beck, 1956–61.

Stuckrad, Kocku von. *Das Ringen um die Astrologie: jüdische und christliche Beiträge zum antiken Zeitverständnis.* Berlin and New York: de Gruyter, 2000.

Sysling, Harry. *Teḥiyyat ha-Metim: The Resurrection of the Dead in the Palestinian Targums of the Pentateuch and Parallel Traditions in Classical Rabbinic Literature.* Tübingen: J.C.B. Mohr [Paul Siebeck], 1996.

Tal, Abraham. *The Language of the Targum of the Former Prophets and Its Position within the Aramaic Dialects.* Tel Aviv: Tel Aviv University, 1975 [Hebrew].

Talmudic Encyclopedia. 24 vols. Jerusalem: Talmudic Encyclopedia Institute, 1951–59, continuing [Hebrew].

Ta-Shma, Israel. "The Library of the Ashkenazi Sages in the 11th–12th Centuries," *Qiryat Sefer* 60 (1984).

———. "The Library of the French Sages," in Gabrielle Sed-Rajna, ed., *Rashi 1040–1990: Hommage à Ephraïm E. Urbach.* Paris: Cerf, 1993, 535–40.

Tishby, Isaiah. *Wisdom of the Zohar: An Anthology of Texts*. 3 vols. Translated by D. Goldstein. Oxford: Littman Library/Oxford University Press, 1989.

Toorn, Karel van der, Bob Becking, and Pieter W. van der Horst, eds., *Dictionary of Deities and Demons in the Bible*. Leiden: Brill, 1995.

Ulmer, Rivka. *The Evil Eye in the Bible and Rabbinic Literature*. Hoboken, N.J.: Ktav, 1994.

Urbach, Ephraim E. "When did Prophecy Cease?" *Tarbiṣ* 17 (1946) 1–11 [Hebrew].

———· "Rabbinic Exegesis and Origines' Commentaries on the Song of Songs, and Jewish-Christian Polemics," *Tarbiṣ* 30 (1960–61) 148–70 [Hebrew]. English: "The Homiletical Interpretations of the Sages and the Expositions of Origen on Canticles, and the Jewish-Christian Disputation," *Scripta Hierosolymitana* 22 (1971) 247–75.

———·*The Sages, Their Concepts and Beliefs*. Translated by Israel Abrahams. Jerusalem: Magnes, 1975; 4th ed. Cambridge, Mass.: Harvard University Press, 1995.

Venture, Mardochée. *Cantique des cantiques, avec la paraphrase chaldaïque*. Paris: M. Lambert, 1774.

Vermes, Geza. "'Car le Liban, c'est le Conseil de la Communauté,'" in *Mélanges bibliques rédigés en l'honneur de André Robert*. Paris: Bloud & Gay, [1956], 316–25.

———· "The Symbolical Interpretation of Lebanon in the Targums," *JTS* n.s. 9 (1958) 1–12.

———· *Scripture and Tradition in Judaism*. Leiden: Brill, 1961.

———· *Jesus the Jew: A Historian's Reading of the Gospels*. London: Collins, 1973.

———· *Post-Bibilical Jewish Studies*. Leiden: Brill, 1975.

Vilnay, Zev. *Legends of Jerusalem*. Philadelphia: Jewish Publication Society, 1973.

Vregille, Bernard de, and Louis Neyrand, eds. *Apponii in Canticum Canticorum Expositionem* [sic]. CCSL XIX. Turnhout: Brepols, 1986.

Vulliaud, Paul. *Le Cantique des Cantiques d'après la tradition juive*. Paris: Presses Universitaires de France, 1925.

Walfish, Barry D. "Annotated Bibliography of Medieval Jewish Commentaries on Song of Songs," in Sarah Yafet, ed., *Ha-Miqra be-reʾi Mefarshav: Sefer Zikkaron le-Sarah Kamin*. Jerusalem: Magnes, 1994, 518–71 [Hebrew].

Weitzman, Michael. *The Syriac Version of the Old Testament: An Introduction*. University of Cambridge Oriental Publications 56. Cambridge: Cambridge University Press, 1999.

Wertheimer, Solomon A. *Batei Midrashot*. 2 vols. New edition by Abraham Y. Wertheimer. 2 vols. Jerusalem: Mosad Ketav ve-sefer, 1968.

Witte, Johannes. *Der Kommentar des Aponius zum Hohenliede*. Inaugural Dissertation, Erlangen: Junge & Sohn, 1903.

Zetterholm, Karin. *Portrait of a Villain: Laban the Aramean in Rabbinic Literature*. Sterling, Va.: Peeters, 2001.

Zimmerli, Walther. *Ezechiel*. BKAT. Neukirchen-Vluyn: Neukirchener Verlag, 1969.

Zohary, Michael. *Plants of the Bible: A Complete Handbook to All the Plants with 200 Full-Color Plates Taken in the Natural Habitat*. London and New York: Cambridge University Press, 1982.

The Targum of Canticles

Translation

CHAPTER 1

1. Hebrew Text:

The Song of Songs,[1] *which is Solomon's.*[2]

Targum:

Songs and praises which Solomon, the prophet, the king of Israel, recited in the holy spirit[a][3] before the Sovereign of all the World,[b] the Lord.

Ten songs[4] were recited in this world;[c] this song is the most excellent of them all.

Apparatus, Chapter 1

[a] D F: "in the spirit of prophecy." Further Tg. 2:12, *Note* 77.

[b] H J L M N: "the Sovereign of the World." A has *rbwn kl ʿlmʾ* here and at 1:4 and 7:12; *rbwn kl ʿlmyʾ* ("Sovereign of all the Worlds") at 5:2; and *rbwn ʿlmʾ* ("Sovereign of the World") at 2:3, but there are variants and the original reading in each case is uncertain. The inconsistency may be original. The formula varies also in the other Targumim: *rbwn kl ʿlmʾ* in Ps-J Gen. 18:30, 31, 32; Num. 23:19; Deut. 32:4; FT Gen. 30:22; CG Gen. 37:33; 38:25; Tg. Micah (v.l. *rbwn kl ʾrʿʾ*); *rbwn ʿlmʾ* in Onq. Exod. 23:17; 34:23; *rbwn ʿlmyʾ* in Ps-J Exod. 34:23. Tg. Cant. is sensitive to stylistic variation. Note how it varies this formula with *mry ʿlmʾ* ("Master of the World") in 1:1, 4; 2:1, 13; 5:3, 5; 6:2, 11; 8:4, 7, 13, 14. Cf. *Apparatus k.*

[c] D F: "in this world"; A B C G H I J K L M N: "in the world."

Notes, Chapter 1

[1] Tg. offers multiple interpretations of "Song of Songs": (1) "A song comprising the songs of Solomon," hence "songs and praises which Solomon . . . recited"—a title for Canticles that sees it as a collection of discrete songs composed by Solomon. (2) "A song which is one of a series of songs." Tg. identifies ten songs in all, of which Canticles is the ninth. (3) "The most excellent song": Cant.R. 1:1 §11, "*The Song of Songs:* as if to say, the best of songs, the most excellent of songs, the finest of songs." This understanding of the Hebrew construction as expressing the superlative may be reflected in Aqiba's famous description of Cant. as "the holy of holies" *(qodesh qodashim)* of Scripture (m.Yad. 3:5). Cf. Origen, *Commentary on Canticles*, Prol. 4.1: "*simile . . . est hoc illis quae in tabernaculo testimonii appellantur* sancta sanctorum *(Exod 30:29), et illis quae in Numerorum libro memorantur* opera operum *(Num 4:47) quaeque apud Paulum dicuntur* saecula saeculorum *(Rom 16:27).*"

[2] Tg. offers a double interpretation of *ʾasher li-Shelomoh.* (1) "Which Solomon composed," the preposition *lamed* being construed as indicating authorship (cf. *mizmor le-David*). (2) "Which [were recited] before God," *Shelomoh* being taken as a title of God ("The One to whom belongs peace *[shalom]*"). Tg. Cant. translates "to Solomon was a vineyard" in 8:11 by "one nation, which is likened to a vineyard, fell to the lot of the Lord of the World, with whom is peace." Cf. Mek. deR. Ishmael, *Pisḥa* 14, which interprets "the litter of Solomon" in Cant 3:7 as "the litter of Him to whom belongs peace" (i.e., the Temple). Further Cant.R. 1:1 §11: "Wherever you find *king Solomon*, the reference is to the King to whom belongs peace; wherever you find *the king* simply, the reference is to the Community of Israel." On the derivation of the name *Shelomoh* from *shalom* see Ginzberg, *Legends* 6:277 n. 2.

[3] On the interchangeability of the terms "holy spirit" and "spirit of prophecy" see *Apparatus a.* Tg. stresses the inspiration of Canticles (see also Tg. to 2:17; 7:2; 8:5, 13) to counter any suggestions to the contrary (*Intro.* 6.1). Cf. t. Yad. 2:14, "The Song of Songs renders the hands unclean, because it was spoken through the holy spirit"; Cant.R. 1:1 §§5, 6, 7, 8, 9: "The holy spirit rested on him and he composed these three works: Proverbs, Song of Songs, and Ecclesiastes."

[4] Tg. adapts a preexistent midrash, the Midrash of the Ten Songs (see Appendix A). It is unlikely, therefore, that the number ten is derived from the supposed redundant *yod* in *ha-shirim* (so *Aggadat Shir ha-Shirim*, ed. Schechter, 53). Rather, ten numerologically indicates completeness, as in the Ten Words (the Decalogue) and the Ten Plagues in the Bible, and the Ten Trials of Abraham in the Midrash (Ginzberg, *Legends* 1:217; 5:218 n. 52; 7:468, under "Ten as a round number"). So here the ten songs cover the whole history of the world from the creation to the consummation. Cf. the Midrash of the Ten Kings (Tg. Sheni Esther 1:1; Pirqei de R. El. 11; *Sefer Maʿasiyyot*, ed. Gaster, 1, and, in a greatly expanded version, Eisenstein, *OM* 2:461–66), the Midrash of the Ten Exiles (Eisenstein, *OM* 2:433–39), and the Midrash of the Ten Famines (Tg. Ruth 1:1). Note

The first song was recited by Adam when his sin was forgiven him[5] and the Sabbath day came and protected him.[6] He opened his mouth and said: "A psalm, a song for the Sabbath day" (Ps 92:1).[7]

The second song was recited by Moses, together with the Children of Israel, on the day when the Lord of the World divided for them the Red Sea. They all opened their mouths in unison[8] and recited a song, as it is written: "Then sang Moses and the Children of Israel this song"[d] (Exod 15:1).

The third song was recited by the Children of Israel when the well of water was given to them, as it is written, "Then sang Israel this song"[e] (Num 21:17).

The fourth song was recited by Moses the prophet,[f] when his time had come to depart from the world, and he reproved with it the people of the house of Israel, as it is written: "Give ear, O heavens, and I will speak" (Deut 32:1).[9]

The fifth song was recited by Joshua the son of Nun, when he waged war against Gibeon and the sun and the moon stood still for him for thirty-six hours.[10] They ceased recit-

Apparatus, Chapter 1

[d] B D F G H I J K L M N omit "this song."

[e] C: "this song"; A K L N: "the song"; B D F H I G omit; J M: "The third song, the song of the well, was recited by Moses and the Children of Israel. All of them opened their mouths in unison and recited the song, as it is written, 'Spring up, O well; sing to it (Num 21:17).'"

[f] J M: "Moses the chief of the prophets."

Notes, Chapter 1

---

also the opening of Midrash Hallel (Eisenstein, *OM* 1:127): "The Book of Psalms uses ten terms for 'praise'" (cf. b. Pesaḥ. 117a; Midrash Ps. 1.6). Most of the songs in the Tg. Cant. version of the Midrash are songs of deliverance. The identification of Canticles as the ninth of the ten songs creates a sense of imminent messianic redemption.

[5] On Adam's repentance see Pirqei de R. El. 20: "Adam said before the Holy One, blessed be He: Sovereign of the Worlds, remove, I pray you, my sins from me and accept my repentance, and all generations will learn that repentance is a reality. What did the Holy One, blessed be He, do? He put forth his right hand, and accepted his repentance, and took away his sin."

[6] From the judgment of Gehenna: see Pirqei de R. El. 18: "At twilight on the eve of Sabbath, he [Adam] was driven forth [from the Garden of Eden] . . . The Sabbath day arrived and became an advocate for the First Man, and it spoke before Him: Sovereign of all Worlds, no murderer has been slain in this world during the six days of creation, and will You commence [to do this] with me? Is this the sanctity, and is this the blessing, as it is said, *And God blessed the seventh day, and hallowed it* (Gen 2:3)? By the merit of the Sabbath day Adam was saved from the judgment of Gehinnom." Cf. b. Shabb. 118a. Pirqei de R. El. 20 defines the protection more broadly: "The Sabbath day protected him from all evil, and comforted him on account of all the doubts of his heart, as it is said, *In the multitude of my doubts within me, Your comforts delight my soul* (Ps 94:19)." In general the Sabbath protects against demons (since evil spirits do not walk abroad on the Sabbath), and against the flames of hell, since no one is sent to Gehenna on the Sabbath, and even the damned in hell have respite.

[7] For the attribution of the anonymous Ps 92 to Adam see Pirqei de R. El. 18 (continuation of quotation in *Note* 6): "When Adam perceived the power of the Sabbath, he said: Not for nought did the Holy One, blessed be He, bless and hallow the Sabbath day. He began to observe [the Sabbath] (v.l. to sing) and to utter a Psalm for the Sabbath day, as it is said, *A psalm, a song for the Sabbath day* (Ps 92:1)." Tg. Ps. 92:1, "Praise and Song which the First Man recited concerning the Sabbath day." b. B. Bat. 14b, however, classifies Ps 92 as a Mosaic psalm. Cf. Gen.R. 22.13. Pirqei de R. El. 18 reconciles the two traditions: "R. Simeon said: The First Man said this psalm, but it was forgotten throughout all the generations till Moses came and renewed it in his own name."

[8] Tg. reflects discussion of Exod 15:1, *ʾaz yashir Mosheh u-Benei Yisraʾel*. Why is Moses mentioned separately? And why is the verb singular? According to one explanation the wording implies that "it was Moses who recited the Song, leading all Israel in it" (Mek. deR. Ishmael, *Shirta* 1), i.e., the song was recited in the form of versicle and response: "first Moses would begin a sentence, and then Israel would repeat after him and with him conclude" (Mek. deR. Ishmael, *Shirta* 1). Tg. takes the opposite view: the wording implies that "when they recited the Song, Moses was on a par with Israel and Israel was on a par with Moses" (Mek. deR. Ishmael, *Shirta* 1). Hence: "they all [Moses and the Israelites] opened their mouths in unison."

[9] Deuteronomy 32 is called a "song" in Deut 31:19, 30. The idea that it is a song of reproof is implicit at 31:19, "that this song might be a witness for me against the Children of Israel" (cf. 31:26; 2 Macc 7:6).

[10] The language of Josh 10:13 is vague ("about a whole day"). For the idea that the sun and moon stood still for precisely thirty-six hours see b. ʾAbod. Zar. 25a and Pirqei de R. El. 52.

ing [their] song, and he opened his mouth and recited [his] song,[11] as it is written: "Then sang[g][12] Joshua before the Lord" (Josh 10:12).

The sixth song was recited by Barak and Deborah on the day when the Lord delivered Sisera and his host into the hand of the Children of Israel, as it is written: "And Deborah and Barak the son of Abinoam sang" (Judg 5:1).

The seventh song was recited by Hannah, when a son was granted her from before the Lord, as it is written: "Hannah prayed in prophecy and said"[h] (1 Sam 2:1).

The eighth song was recited by David, king of Israel, concerning all the wonders which the Lord wrought for him. He opened his mouth and recited the song, as it is written: "David sang in prophecy before the Lord"[i] (2 Sam 22:1).

The ninth song was recited by Solomon, the king of Israel, in the holy spirit[j] before the Sovereign of all the World,[k] the Lord.

The tenth song will be recited by the children of the exile when they depart from their exiles,[l] as is clearly written by Isaiah the prophet:[m] "You shall have this song of joy, as on the night when the festival of Passover is sanctified, and [you shall have] gladness of heart, like the people who go to appear before the Lord three times in the year with all kinds of

Apparatus, Chapter 1

[g] C B G I K L N: "sang" (pf.); A J M have the impf.

[h] D^2 F G H^2: "Hannah prayed in prophecy and said;" A J K L M N: "Hannah prayed in the spirit of prophecy"; B H^1 I: "Hannah prayed in prophecy."

[i] I omits "before the Lord."

[j] C I omit "in the holy spirit."

[k] J K L M N: "Sovereign of the World." Cf. *Apparatus b.*

[l] J M O: "when their exiles depart from among the nations"; D F: "when they depart from the exile"; H: "when they depart from their exile."

[m] H omits "clearly . . . by Isaiah the prophet." The phrase *ktyb wmprsh* has been taken as hendiadys: "as is clearly written." However, *mprsh* may recall the interpretation of *meforash* in Neh 8:8 as alluding to the institution of the Targum (b. Meg. 3a). *Ktyb wmprsh* could, then, effectively mean "as is written in the text and explained in the Targum" of Isa 30:29. This would make sense in this particular case since the text quoted (unlike the other songs) diverges substantially from the literal sense of the Heb. In the Tg. "pipe" translates *tblʾ*. Hesychius says that *tabala* is a Parthian word for "drum." This appears to be the meaning of the word in Arabic, and it would fit some Rabbinic occurrences (b. Sanh. 67b). But here *tblʾ* probably translates Heb. *ḥalil*, which is some sort of flute or pipe (BDB 319b). Note also b. Arakh. 10b where *hdrwlys* = Gk. *hydraulis* (hydraulic organ) is glossed *tblʾ gwrgnʾ*, "mechanical *tabla*." The Arukh correctly explains: "a musical instrument of pipes worked by pressure of water." Rashi's identification of the *tabla* as a bell is less likely (though accepted by Jast. 518a).

Notes, Chapter 1

[11] In Josh 10:12, Joshua literally says, "Sun, be silent *(dom)* in Gibeon, and you moon in the valley of Aijalon." Tg. took this as a command to the sun and the moon to cease their singing, so that Joshua's song could be heard by God (note v. 12, "Joshua spoke *to the Lord,*" and v. 14, "there was no day like that before it or after it, when *the Lord heard* the voice of a man"). Here the sun and the moon are regarded as angels who praise God as part of the heavenly choirs (cf. Ps 19:2; Job 38:7). They fall silent out of respect for Joshua, so that his prayer may be heard. There is an implication that it is the motion of the heavenly bodies that creates their "song" (a possible echo of the doctrine of the music of the spheres), so that to tell them to be silent is in effect to tell them to stop moving. Cf. the idea in the Heikhalot literature that the cherubim create their song by moving their wings (3 Enoch 24:15, with Alexander's comment in Charlesworth, *OTP* 1:279, n. y). If *dom* is taken as "be silent!" then the command is peremptory and may hint at the traditions about the rivalry between Israel and the angels (Schäfer, *Rivalität zwischen Engeln und Menschen*). In the Heikhalot texts the angels crowd round the Throne of Glory and would drown out the praises of Israel if God did not restrain them and tell them to be silent till he hears the praises of Israel on earth, or to recite their praises in the form of a response to Israel's, thus stressing the superiority of his earthly to his heavenly family (b. Ḥag. 12b; Heikhalot Rabbati, Schäfer, *Synopse*, §173; Gen.R. 65.21; Grözinger, *Musik und Gesang*, 86–89 and 93–94; Rev 8:1 with Bauckham, *Climax of Prophecy*, 70–83). The theological purpose of this reading of Josh 10:12-13 is to insist that the Israelites were victorious through *God's* help, not through the help of the sun and the moon. Given that the sun and the moon were widely worshiped as deities, there was an incentive to play down their contribution to Israel's victory.

[12] The Hebrew of Josh 10:12 has literally "then said *(ʾaz yedabber)* Joshua." For the translation "sang" see also the Tg. Josh. 10:12.

musical instruments and [with] the sound of the pipe, [who go] to ascend into the Mountain of the Lord, and to worship before the Mighty One of Israel" (Isa 30:29).[13]

2. Hebrew Text:

Let Him kiss me with the kisses of His mouth[14]—
For Your love is better than wine.[15]

Targum:

Solomon the prophet said: "Blessed[16] be the name of the Lord who gave us the Torah at the hands of Moses, the Great Scribe,[17] [both the Torah] written on the two tablets of stone,

Notes, Chapter 1

[13] The paraphrase of Isa 30:29 given here differs from Tg. Jon. to this verse and may be the remnant of a more expansive Palestinian Tg. to Isaiah. Both renderings agree, however, that the unnamed feast of the Hebrew text is Passover. The "song of joy" that Tg. Cant. associates with Passover is presumably the Hallel, which is sung on the first night of Passover (b. Pesaḥ. 95b). The analogy between the Exodus from Egypt and the final exodus of the Jews from exile at the beginning of the Messianic redemption is picked up again and again in Tg. Cant.

[14] Tg. takes the speaker as Israel, the addressee as God, and the occasion as the giving of the Torah on Sinai. The "kisses of His mouth" recalls God's speaking "mouth to mouth" (Num 12:8), or "face to face" (Exod 33:11; Deut 34:10) with Moses. This is a common Rabbinic understanding of the verse. Cf. Cant.R. 1:2 §1: "*Let Him kiss me with the kisses of His mouth.* Where was this said? . . . R. Judah b. R. Simon said: It was said at Sinai"; Aggadat Shir ha-Shirim, ed. Schechter, 11: "*Let Him kiss me with the kisses of His mouth.* This refers to when they stood before Mount Sinai"; Cant.R. 1:2 §2: "The commandment itself went in turn to each of the Israelites and said to him, Do you undertake to keep me? . . . He would reply, Yes, Yes, and straightway the commandment kisses him on the mouth"; further Exod.R. 30.9; 41.3; Midrash Ps. 149.1. The biblical phrase is doubly interpreted by Tg. It is taken (1) as defining the content of the revelation: "kisses," plural, indicates the twofold Torah (*pihu* may hint specifically at *Torah she-beʿal peh*); and (2) as defining the manner of the revelation: directly, without mediation, and in love. This latter point stands in tension with the biblical account which, though granting that the people heard the voice of God (Exod 20:22; Deut 4:36), says that they were afraid and asked Moses to act as mediator for them (Exod 20:19; Deut 5:24-26). Tg. has, probably for polemical purposes, transferred to the people what the biblical narrative says of Moses: all Israel was present at Sinai and received God's revelation directly.

[15] Tg. interprets: "for Your love for us is better than for all the nations of the world." "Wine" *(yayin)* is taken by *gematria* as seventy = the seventy nations, i.e., the totality of the nations, the number being derived from the Table of the Nations in Genesis 10, with Israel presumably being the seventy-first nation (Ginzberg, *Legends* 5:194–95 n. 72). Cf. Cant.R. 1:2 §3: "*Than wine:* this refers to the Gentile nations. *Yod* is ten, *yod* is ten, and *nun* fifty, alluding to the seventy nations, to show that Israel is more beloved before the Holy One, blessed be He, than all the nations"; further Tanḥuma, *Bemidbar* 10 (ed. Buber, 9); Num.R. 2.3. The same *gematria* of *yayin* is found again at Tg. Cant. 1:4 and 4:10.

[16] As was customary in the Talmudic and Gaonic periods, Solomon opens his *derashah* on Canticles with a benediction. Tg. would have seen nothing incongruous or anachronistic in this, since biblical figures are regularly portrayed in the Aggadah as behaving in Rabbinical fashion. The benedictions that preface the public reading of the Torah stress, as does the Tg. to this verse, the giving of the Torah and the election of Israel: "Blessed are You, the Lord our God, King of the Universe, who has chosen us from all peoples and has given us His Torah. Blessed are You, the Lord, the Giver of Torah" (Singer, *ADPB* 369). Liebreich ("Benedictory Formula" 193ff.) specifically compares the benediction that opens the *derashah* in Tanḥuma, *Noah* 3 (cf. Mishnat R. Eliʿezer, ed. Enelow, 257ff.): "May the name of the King of the kings of kings be blessed, the Holy One, blessed be He, who has chosen Israel from the seventy nations, as it is written, *For the Lord's portion is His people; Jacob is the lot of His inheritance* (Deut 32:9), and He has given to us the Written Torah, with its allusions to concealed and hidden matters that are explained in the Oral Torah, and He has revealed it to Israel." The *derashah* in question was preached on the Exilarch's reception Sabbath, when a sermon was delivered by the Gaon of Sura on the theme of the importance of the Oral Torah and of the Academies of Sura and Pumbedita (Ginzberg, *Geonica* 1:5, n. 1; *Ginze Schechter* 1:18 and 543–44). A major theme also of Tg. Cant. is the importance of the Academies, though the Academy it glorifies is probably the Academy of Tiberias (see *Intro.* 8.2).

[17] Cf. Tg. Cant. to 2:4, "Moses the Great Scribe," and 3:3, "Moses the Great Scribe of Israel." This is not a biblical title for Moses, but note how it is used in Onq. Deut. 33:21 to translate *meḥoqeq*, and how Ezra, *Moses redivivus,* is called "the Scribe of the Law of the God of Heaven" in Ezra 7:12. Cf. Tg. Ps. 62:12; Sifrei Deut. §357 (ed. Finkelstein, 428, v.l., "Moses the Great Scribe of Israel is dead"); b. Soṭah 13b. In Ps-J Gen. 5:24 it is Enoch, in his elevated existence as the archangel Metatron, who is designated "Great Scribe."

and the Six Orders of the Mishnah[18] and Talmud by oral tradition, and [who] spoke with us face to face as a man kisses his friend, out of the abundance of the love wherewith He loved us[19] more than the seventy nations."

3. Hebrew Text:

As to smell, Your ointments [were] good;
[Like] ointment Your name [was] poured forth;[20]
Therefore the maidens[21] *loved You.*

Targum:

At the news of Your miracles and mighty acts[22] which You performed for Your people,[n] the house of Israel, all the peoples trembled,[23] when they heard the report of Your mighty

Apparatus, Chapter 1

[n] D F H: "the people."

Notes, Chapter 1

[18] The Six Orders of the Mishnah are mentioned again in Tg. Cant. 5:10. The doctrine of the two Torahs is central to the Tg., as it is to Rabbinic Judaism. See Cant.R. 1:2 §5; Lev.R. 22.1. Tg. probably implies that the whole of the Oral Torah, in its Mishnaic and Talmudic forms, was given at Sinai. Pesiq. Rab. Kah. 4.7 justifies this strict view by appealing to divine foreknowledge: Moses, when he ascended to heaven to receive the Torah, found the Holy One reciting the Talmudic traditions verbatim in the name of the scholars who would later promulgate them. Exod.R. 26.6 provides a different explanation: the souls of the later authorities (in this case the prophets) were actually present at Sinai and heard the words they were later to speak. They recalled them after they were born in a kind of Platonic *anamnesis*. Cf. Cant.R. 5:14 §2, "All the Talmud was on the two tablets"; Exod.R. 47.1, "God told Moses Scripture, Mishnah, Talmud, and Aggada."

[19] The themes of love and election are closely related: see Deut 7:6-8, "The Lord . . . has chosen you to be a peculiar people unto Himself, above all the peoples that are upon the face of the earth. The Lord did not set His love upon you, because you were more in number than any other people . . . but because the Lord loves you."

[20] With this verse, which is implicitly contextualized to the time of the Exodus from Egypt, Tg.'s historical narrative begins. The interpretation is based on the equation of scent with reputation: cf. also Tg. to 1:12 and 4:10. "Ointments" in the first stich are taken as symbolizing God's miracles, the spread of their scent as the broadcasting of the news of those miracles. "Ointment" in the second stich is identified as the holy oil used to anoint kings and high priests (Exod 30:22-33). Cf. Eccl 7:1, "a good name *(shem)* is better than precious ointment *(shemen)*," which the Tg. renders, "Better is the good name which the righteous acquire in this world than the oil of greatness which is poured profusely on the heads of kings and [high] priests." Cant.R. 1:3 §2 also sees here a reference to the anointing oil but attaches it to the plural "ointments" in stich one: *"As to smell, your ointments [were] good . . .* The reference is to the two anointing oils—the oil of priesthood and the oil of kingship."

[21] Tg. offers a double interpretation of Heb. *ʿalamot* ("maidens"): (1) symbolically = "the righteous"; (2) revocalized *ʿolamot*, "worlds" = "this world and the world to come." The former interpretation was probably dictated by the latter since only the righteous will inherit the world to come. Cf. Cant. Zuta (ed. Buber, 11): *"Therefore do ʿalamot love you*—this world and the world to come. Keep the commandments in this world and He will give you two worlds"; m. Sanh. 10:1, "All Israelites have a share in the world to come, for it is written, *Your people also shall be all righteous; they shall inherit the land for ever* . . . (Isa 60:21)"; m. Parah 6:7; b. ʿAbod. Zar. 35b.

[22] The signs and wonders associated with the Exodus from Egypt. See Deut 4:34; 6:22-23; Ps 135:9. The reference may specifically be to the ten miracles at the crossing of the Red Sea (Ginzberg, *Legends* 3:22).

[23] Exodus 15:13-14, "You in Your love have led the people that You have redeemed . . . The peoples have heard, they tremble" (note Onq. *ad loc.*). Cf. Exod.R. 20.16: "God kept them forty years in the wilderness, because He wished to impress the fear of the Israelites upon the heathen. He illumined their path with the pillar of cloud by day and with the pillar of fire by night, and when all the heathen heard this, trembling seized them, as it says: *Terror and dread falls upon them* (Exod 15:16); and what does it say after this? *You bring them in, and plant them* (v. 17)"; Tg. Cant. 6:4, "The fear of you is on all the nations as in the day when your four camps marched through the wilderness" (repeated in Tg. to 6:10).

acts and Your good signs. And Your holy name, which is more choice than the anointing oil poured on the heads of kings and [high] priests, was heard in all the world. Therefore the righteous loved to walk in the way of Your goodness, so that they might inherit this world[o] and the world to come.[24]

4. Hebrew Text:

Draw me after You,[25] we will run;
May the King bring us into His chambers;[26]
We will be glad and rejoice in You;[27]
We will recall [our] love for You more than [for] wine![28]
Rightly[29] do they love You.

Apparatus, Chapter 1

[o] B C D F G H I J K L M N O: "so that they might inherit this world"; A: "for the sake of this world."

Notes, Chapter 1

[24] Tg. may imply here a spiritualizing interpretation of "the world to come" = Gan ʿEden or immortality. Since "inheriting this world" must in context mean "inheriting the Land," "inheriting the world to come" can hardly mean "inheriting the Land in the Messianic Age." Note Cant.R. 1:3 §3, where two repointings of *ʿalamot* are proposed—*ʿolamot* ("worlds") and *ʿal mawet* ("above death"): "Aquila translates *ʿalamot* by *athanasia,* a word which means immortality. They indicate one to another with the finger and say, For this is the Lord our God for ever and ever; He will guide us above death. He will guide us in two worlds—[in this world,] as it is written, *For the Lord your God will bless you* (Deut 15:6), and in the next, as it is written, *And the Lord will guide you continually* (Isa 58:11)."

[25] Tg., against the Masoretic accentuation, takes *ʾaḥareikha* with the preceding rather than the following word.

[26] Tg. may have read *hebiʾennu* ("he has brought us"), rather than MT's *hebiʾani* ("he has brought me"), and construed the verb as a precative perfect. The third person may be formal and polite, suitable for addressing a king. God's "chambers" have been doubly identified, as (1) Mount Sinai, and (2) the heavenly treasury where he kept the Torah. Tg. rather pointedly avoids a mystical interpretation here. It makes no reference to the idea that Moses at Sinai actually ascended into heaven to receive the Torah, a tradition that it knew (see Tg. to 1:5 [*Note* 42], 1:11, 1:14, and 3:3) and that is easily attached to the words, "the King brought me [sing. = Moses!] into His chambers." The Merkabah mystics may have had this same phrase in mind when they spoke of the "chambers" of the Merkabah (3 Enoch 18:18; 38:1), or of God's heavenly palaces as being "chamber within chamber" (3 Enoch 1:2). Note how Cant.R. 1:4 §1 attaches the story of the four who entered Pardes to the words, "the King has brought me into His chambers." See further *Intro.* 6.2, n. 15.

[27] Tg. interprets Heb. *bakh* by *gematria* as twenty-two, hence the twenty letters of the Hebrew alphabet in which the Torah was written. Cf. Cant.R. 1:4 §1: "*Bakh* means in the twenty-two letters which You have written for us in the Torah." *Beit* is two, *kaf* twenty, thus making up the word *bakh.* Further Pesiq. Rab. 52.7; Pesiq. Rab. Kah. 22.2; 28 (ed. Mandelbaum, 433–34). Midrash Ps. 25.2 interprets *bakh* in Ps 25:2 in the same way (cf. also Midrash Ps. 7:4; 9:6). Thus, in keeping with the Rabbinic doctrine of the inspiration of Scripture, Tg. asserts the priority of the Hebrew text over translations and stresses the importance of scrupulous attention to the letter of the law, not one jot or tittle of which is insignificant.

[28] Tg. takes *yayin* ("wine") by *gematria* as = seventy; hence "the nations"; see above 1:2, *Note* 15.

[29] Tg. takes Heb. *mesharim* ("rightly") as = "the righteous," possibly through repointing as *meyashsherim* [sc. *ʾorḥotam*] = "those who make straight their paths" (for this phrase see Prov 9:15).

Targum:

When the people of the house of Israel went out from Egypt, the Shekhinah[30] of the Master of the World traveled before them in a pillar of cloud by day and a pillar of fire by night.[31] The righteous of that generation said before the Lord of the World: "Draw us after You, and we will run in the way of Your goodness. Bring us near to the foot of Mount Sinai, and give us Your Torah from out of Your heavenly treasury,[32] and we will be glad and rejoice in the twenty-two letters in which it is written. We will remember them and love Your divinity and shun the idols[33] of the nations. And all the righteous who do what is right before You will fear You and love Your commandments."

5. Hebrew Text:

I am black, but comely,[34]
O Daughters of Jerusalem,[35]
[black] as the tents of Qedar,[36]
[comely] as the curtains of Solomon.[37]

Notes, Chapter 1

[30] On the doctrine of the Shekhinah in Tg. Cant. see *Intro.* 4.1.

[31] On the pillar of cloud and the pillar of fire see Exod 13:21.

[32] For the idea of the heavenly treasury see Deut 28:12. Normally the heavenly treasuries contain natural phenomena—rain, snow, hail, etc. Here the treasury contains the Torah, which was stored up in heaven before being revealed on Sinai. Cf. 3 Enoch 8:1-2; 48D:2-3; Alphabet of Aqiba, Jellinek, *BHM* 3:16. On the preexistent, heavenly Torah see Gen.R. 1.1; Eccl.R. 3:1 §1; Midrash Prov. 8:9. The idea may go back to Proverbs 8, where preexistent Wisdom, which was with God in the beginning (vv. 22-23), is said to delight in being with the human race (v. 31). Once revealed on earth, Torah must not be sought again in heaven: cf. Deut 30:11-14, with Deut.R. 8:6: "*For this commandment . . . is not in heaven* (Deut 30:11). Moses said to Israel: Do not say, Another Moses will arise and bring us another Torah from heaven; I therefore warn you, *it is not in heaven,* that is to say, no part of it has remained in heaven." Further b. B. Meṣiʿa 59a-b.

[33] Idolatry is one of the major themes of Tg. Cant. See *Intro.* 4.2. For the phrase "love of God's divinity" see Tg. to 8:6 (*Note* 29).

[34] Tg. sharply contrasts blackness and comeliness: "black" through sin, "comely" through repentance, through good deeds (the making of the Tabernacle), and through intercession (the intercession of Moses). The sin is identified specifically as the making of the Golden Calf (Exod 32:1-6; Deut 9:12-21). Cf. Cant.R. 1:5 §1: "I was black at Horeb, as it says, *They made a calf in Horeb* (Ps 106:19), and I was comely at Horeb, as it says, *And they said: All that the Lord has spoken we will do, and obey* (Exod 24:7). I was black in the Wilderness, as it says, *How often did they rebel against Him in the Wilderness* (Ps 88:40), and I was comely in the Wilderness at the setting up of the Tabernacle, as it says, *And on the day that the Tabernacle was raised up* (Num 9:15)." Further Exod.R. 49.2.

[35] "Daughters of Jerusalem" is not interpreted here, but it lies behind "the nations" in v. 6.

[36] Tg. links "black" with Qedar through derivation of the name from the root *qdr* = "be dark" (BDB 871a).

[37] Tg. takes Solomon as a title of God = "The One to whom belongs peace" (see 1:1, *Note* 2). This leads to a double interpretation of "curtains": (1) as the curtains of the Tabernacle (Exod 36:8-9, "every wise-hearted man among those that wrought the work made the Tabernacle with ten curtains"); and (2) as the heavens, either because they are seen as spread out like a curtain (Job 37:18; Isa 42:5; 44:24), or with particular reference to Vilon (the Curtain), the first of the seven heavens in Rabbinic cosmography (b. Ḥag. 12b; 3 Enoch 17:3). Cf. Cant.R. 1:5 §1: "*Like the curtains of Solomon,* that is, like the curtains of Him to whom belongs peace, at whose word the world came into being, never to be moved from the day when He stretched them [= the heavens] out." The element of "peace" *(shalom)* seen in the name Solomon generates the idea of Moses making peace between Israel and God.

Targum:

When the people of the House of Israel[p] made the Calf,[38] their faces became as dark as [those of] the sons of Cush who dwell in the tents of Qedar,[39] but when they returned in repentance and were forgiven, the radiance of the glory of their faces became as great as [that of] the angels,[q] [40] because they had made curtains for the Tabernacle, and the Shekhinah had taken up its abode among them,[41] and [because] Moses their teacher had ascended to heaven[42] and made peace between them and their King.[43]

6. Hebrew Text:

Do not look down upon me,[44]
Because I am swarthy,
Because the sun has scorched me.[45]

Apparatus, Chapter 1

[p] C: "when Your people, the House of Israel"; D F G: "when the House of Israel."

[q] B C D F G H I J K L M N O: "became as great as [that of] the angels"; A: "changed [to be] like [that of] the angels."

Notes, Chapter 1

[38] The sin of making the Golden Calf was seen as particularly heinous in Rabbinic literature: it was "like a bride playing the harlot while still under the bridal canopy" (Pope, 349) (cf. b. Shabb. 88b; b. Giṭ. 36b; Ginzberg, *Legends* 3:119–24). The story was one of the Forbidden Targumim (m. Meg. 4:10). Jewish embarrassment at the incident was compounded by the fact that Christian apologists often referred to it in the context of arguing the supersession of Israel (Bori, *The Golden Calf*). Cf. Tg. Cant. 1:12, where the sin of the Calf is blamed on the "mixed multitude."

[39] Qedar, a son of Ishmael according to Gen 25:13, was one of the tribes of northern Arabia (Isa 21:16; 42:11; Ezek 27:21). Psalm 120:5, "tents of Qedar" is translated in the Tg. "tents of the Arabs." Yefet ben Ali identifies Qedar with Muhammad's tribe, the Quraish: "she compares the colour of her skin to the blackness of the hair of the tents of the Quraish" (Pope, 319). "Sons of Kush" cannot, therefore, mean Ethiopians, but must be used in the general sense of "black-skinned people," probably with allusion to Amos 9:7, "Are you not as the sons of Kush to Me, O Children of Israel? says the Lord."

[40] The shining of the Israelites' faces recalls the shining of Moses' face when he came down from Mount Sinai with the two tablets of the law (Exod 34:29). The transfiguration of Moses is transferred to the whole people, but more: they are compared not to Moses but to angels.

[41] Cf. Exod.R. 13.2: "When did the Shekhinah rest on earth? On the day when the Tabernacle was erected; as it says, *Then the cloud covered the tent of meeting, and the glory of the Lord filled the Tabernacle* (Exod 40:34)." Parallel: Cant. R. 5:1 §1.

[42] It is the standard Rabbinic view that Moses ascended into heaven at Sinai to receive the Torah. See Tg. to 1:11, 12, 14; 3:3; further b. Shabb. 89a; Exod.R. 28.1; Deut.R. 3.11; 10.2; 11.10; Lev.R. 1.15; Pesiq. Rab. 13.4; Pirqei de R. El. 46; Maʿyan Ḥokhmah, Jellinek, *BHM* 1:58–64; Ginzberg, *Legends* 3:109–19. Gedullat Mosheh (ed. Gaster, *ST* 1:125ff.) also contains an ascension of Moses but attaches it to the incident of the burning bush (cf. Ginzberg, *Legends* 2:304–16).

[43] On Moses' intercession see Exod 32:30-32; 34:9.

[44] Israel addresses the nations (= "the daughters of Jerusalem" in v. 5). Her tone is apologetic: she defends herself against the charge that, as a sinner, she is rejected by her God. Cf. Cant.R. 1:6 §3: "And Israel further says to the other nations: We will tell you what we resemble. We are like a king's son who went out to the waste ground of the city and the sun beat down on his head so that his face became all swarthy. But when he went into the town, with a little water and a little bathing his skin became white again and his former good appearance was restored. So with us, the sun of idolatry may have scorched us, but you are swarthy from your mother's womb; for when a woman is pregnant she goes to her idolatrous temple and bows down to the idol along with her child." Tg. takes Heb. *tirʾuni* in a negative sense = "look down upon," hence "despise."

[45] Tg. interprets: the worship of the sun and the moon have scorched me, i.e., made me black with sin. Cf. Pesiq. Rab. 28.1: "*Because the sun has scorched me.* My deeds have caused me to leave the Holy One and go after the sun and the moon."

The sons of my mother have angered [God] against me;[46]
They have made me a keeper of [others'] vineyards,
But my own vineyard[47] *have I not kept.*

Targum:

The Assembly of Israel said before the nations:[48] "Do not despise me, because I am darker than you, because I did what you did and bowed down to the sun and the moon.[49] For it is the false prophets who have caused the fierceness of the Lord's anger to be visited upon me. They taught me to serve your idols and walk in your laws,[r] but the Master of the World, who is my [own] God, have I not served, nor followed His laws, nor kept His commandments or His Torah."

7. Hebrew Text:

Tell me,[50] *how will You feed*
Her whom my soul loves?[51]

Apparatus, Chapter 1

[r] J K L M N O: "their laws."

Notes, Chapter 1

[46] Tg. interprets "sons of my mother" as false prophets. The equation implies that the prophets are *Jewish* prophets; cf. Deut 13:1-3, "If there arise in your midst a prophet . . . saying, Let us go after other gods, whom you have not known, and let us serve them; you shall not hearken to the words of that prophet." Cant. Zuta (ed. Buber, 14): "*The sons of my mother were angry against me.* These are the kings and false princes [*negidim*, read *nebi'im*, "prophets"]." Tg. has taken Heb. *niḥaru* in a causative sense, "brought [God's] anger upon me," or "angered [God] against me." Cf. Cant.R. 1:6 §4: "*Were angry at me.* They attacked me and filled the Judge with wrath against me."

[47] Tg. takes cultivating a vineyard as symbolic of worshiping a god and keeping his laws.

[48] "The nations" is derived from the "Daughters of Jerusalem" in v. 5 (see v. 5, *Note* 35; further Tg. Cant. 2:2, *Note* 6).

[49] Though the cults of the sun and the moon were probably still active when the Tg. was written, and a disapproving allusion to the use of the image of Helios on synagogue mosaics cannot be ruled out, the reference is probably conventional, and based on passages such as Deut 4:19; 17:3; Ezek 8:16; Job 31:26-28. The worship of the sun and the moon stands for all forms of idolatry.

[50] Tg. identifies the voice in this verse as the voice of Moses and the addressee as God. The setting, at the end of Moses' life (Deut 31:14-29), is piquant: Moses, on the threshold of the Land, foresees the exile, the reversal of entry into the Land. Moses, the great leader and provider, asks how Israel will be led and provided for after his death. His tone toward God is challenging. Tg. probably has Deut 31:27, 29 particularly in mind: "I know your rebellion, and your stiff neck; behold, while I am yet alive with you this day, you have been rebellious against the Lord; and how much more after my death? . . . For I know that after my death you will in any wise deal corruptly, and turn aside from the way that I have commanded you; and evil will befall you in the end of days; because you will do that which is evil in the sight of the Lord, to provoke Him through the work of your hands." Cf. Cant.R. 1:7 §2: "Moses said before God: Sovereign of the Universe, as You are removing me from the world, tell me who are the shepherds whom You are appointing over Your children? Where is this stated? Here, in the words, *Tell me, as for her whom my soul loves*—the people whom my soul loves, the people to whom I have devoted my life—*how You will feed her,* when foreign powers arise, *how You will give [her] rest at noon,* when foreign powers subject her." See further Cant. Zuta (ed. Buber, 14).

[51] Tg. probably took Heb. *she-'ahabah nafshi* as referring not to God but to Israel (cf. Cant.R. 1:7 §2 quoted in the previous note), though the phrase is not formally translated in this verse (note, however, how it is echoed in "that my soul should love her" in the next verse). It is not clear whether Tg. took the Heb. verbs *tir'eh* and *tarbiṣ* as transitive ("how You will feed," "how You will give rest"), or as intransitive ("how she will feed," "how she will rest").

How will You give [her] rest at noon?[52]
For why should I be as one who wanders[53]
Beside the flocks of Your companions?[54]

Targum:

When the time arrived for Moses the prophet to depart from the world he said before the Lord: "It has been revealed[55] before me[s] that this people will sin and go into exile. Now show me[t] how they will be provided for, and how they will settle down[56] among the nations whose decrees are as harsh as the scorching heat of the noonday sun at the summer solstice, and why they should wander among the flocks of Esau and Ishmael who associate with You their idols as [Your] companions?"[57]

8. Hebrew Text:

If you do not know, fairest among women,[58]

Apparatus, Chapter 1

[s] G: "before You, O Lord"; I K L: "before You."

[t] The verb *ḥwy* should here probably be translated "show." There is an allusion to the idea that Moses on the point of death received an apocalypse of Israel's future history.

Notes, Chapter 1

[52] Tg. takes "noon," the time when the flocks are in most distress, as symbolic of the oppression of the nations.

[53] Tg. takes Heb. *ʿoteyah* as meaning "wandering," as though the text had *toʿiyyah*. It should not be assumed, however, that Tg. actually had this reading. Tg. also treats the sentence as if it were third person rather than first (i.e., *tihyeh* rather than *ʾehyeh*).

[54] Since God has no companions, the companions mentioned must be idols falsely associated with Him. "Flocks" in the plural means at least two: hence Esau and Ishmael.

[55] Tg. alludes to the common belief that Moses was granted a vision of the future history of Israel just before he died. This vision is usually linked to Deut 34:1, "The Lord showed him all the land." Moses was shown not only the land but the events that would take place there. See Ps-J Deut. 34:1-4; Sifrei Deut. §357; Mek. deR. Ishmael, *Amalek* 2; Testament of Moses (Charlesworth, *OTP* 1:927–34).

[56] Tg. is redolent of the desire of the exiled and the oppressed for a livelihood and for security. The harsh decrees of the nations keep Israel on the move, so that she cannot settle down. Exile is one of the major themes of Tg. Cant. See *Intro.* 4.1.

[57] Though in Ps 83:7 the "tents of Edom and the Ishmaelites" are arrayed, along with other enemies, against Israel, the singling out of Esau and Ishmael here and elsewhere in Tg. Cant. suggests a coded reference to Christianity (Esau) and Islam (Ishmael). In view of the doctrine of the Trinity, the charge of *shittuf,* of associating other deities with the true God, has obvious relevance in the case of Christianity but seems less apt in the case of fiercely monotheistic Islam. Note, however, how Ps-J Gen. 21:9-21 accuses Ishmael (= Islam) of idolatry. On this problem, and the identification of Esau and Ishmael in Tg. Cant., see *Intro.* 8.1. For the sin of *shittuf* see b. Sanh. 63a: "He who associates the name of God with another shall be eradicated from the world"; Exod.R. 42.3: "The Sages said that they [Israel addressing the Golden Calf] said: *This [zeh] is your God* (Neh 9:18) who redeemed us. R. Haggai b. Eleazar said: It does not say *this [zeh] is your God,* but *these are your gods [ʾeleh ʾeloheikha]* (Exod 32:4), because they associated Him with the Calf and said, God and the Calf redeemed us." On the theme of idolatry in Tg. Cant. see *Intro.* 4.2.

[58] God addresses Israel, "the fairest among women." Tg., however, casts the verse in the third person, in the form of a reply to Moses' question in v. 7. "If you do not know"—how to survive and to end the exile.

Go out in the footsteps of the flock,[59]
And feed your kids[60] *by the shepherds' tents.*[61]

Targum:

The Holy One, blessed be He, said to Moses, the prophet: "If the assembly of Israel, which is likened to a beautiful maiden, desires to blot out the exile,[u] and that My soul should love her, let her walk in the ways of the righteous, let her order her prayer on the instructions of[v] the leaders and guides of her generation,[62] and let her teach her sons, who are likened to the kids of goats, to go to the synagogue and house of study,[63] and in virtue of this[w][64] they will be provided for in exile, until I send them the King Messiah,[65] who will lead them gently[66] to their tents, that is the Temple, which David and Solomon the shepherds[67] of Israel had built for them."[x]

Apparatus, Chapter 1

[u] B G I J K L M N O: "to see the exile" (?).

[v] Lit. "at the mouth of." Though *sdr* (translated "order") can mean little more than "to pray" (cf. *Siddur* = order of prayer, and Jast. 958a), there seems to be some concern here about praying in a fashion approved by the authorities. Cf. the use of *sdr* in b. Ber. 28a for the editing of the ʿAmidah (*Note* 62). "Leader" = Aram. *krzylʾ*, which is ultimately derived from the Akkadian *kuzallu(m)*, "shepherd." The spelling *krzylʾ* is, therefore, original. The common variant *brzylʾ* possibly arose through a graphical confusion that then passed over into speech (so also Syriac: Brockelmann 344). In Rabbinic sources *krzylʾ* appears to be used technically of an "under-shepherd" (b. B. Qam. 56b). The implication here may be that God is the "shepherd" (*roʿeh*) of Israel, and the leaders of the generation are his "under-shepherds" (*karzilin*). However, *krzylʾ* is also used to designate "the one who calls to, leads in prayer" (Jast. 665b) = *sheliaḥ ha-ṣibbur*. Cf. Tg. Eccl. 10:10.

[w] Lit. "through this merit."

[x] A B C H I J M O: "had built"; K L N: "are building"; D F G: "will build."

Notes, Chapter 1

[59] Tg. takes in a double sense: (1) follow in the footsteps of the righteous; and (2) pray with the congregation in synagogue.

[60] Tg. interprets: teach your children. "Kids" metaphorically in the sense of young scholars is a commonplace in Rabbinic literature: Gen.R. 42.3, "Ahaz said likewise: If there are no kids there are no wethers; if there are no wethers there are no sheep; if there are no sheep there is no shepherd; if there is no shepherd there is no world. He reasoned thus to himself: No children, no adults; no adults, no disciples; no disciples, no sages; no sages, no elders; no elders, no prophets; and if there are no prophets, the Holy One, blessed be He, will not cause His Shekhinah to rest upon them" (cf. y. Sanh. X, 28b); y. Sanh. I, 19a: "The kids [young scholars] you left behind in Palestine have become wethers."

[61] Tg. gives a double interpretation of "tents": (1) the synagogue and house of study (picking up the plural *mishkenot* in the Heb.); and (2) the Temple. "Shepherds" is also given a double interpretation: it is obviously equated with David and Solomon, but it is also echoed in the phrase "the leaders and guides of her generation," which skillfully sustains the pastoral imagery of the verse. Thus a parallelism is subtly suggested between the synagogue and house of study under the authority of the Sages in this age and the Temple under the authority of the Messiah in the age to come.

[62] The stress on following the guidance of the Rabbis in prayer suggests the Tg. was composed at a time when reform of the liturgy was in the air and the Rabbis were trying to impose their authority on the synagogue service.

[63] On the synagogue and house of study in Tg. Cant. see *Intro.* 4.4.

[64] The doctrine of merits is a central theme of Tg. Cant.: see *Intro.* 4.3.

[65] On the King Messiah in Tg. Cant. see *Intro.* 4.5.

[66] Cf. Tg. Isa. 40:11, "Like a shepherd that feeds his flock, that gathers the lambs in his arms and carries the young in his bosom, and gently leads *[bnyḥ mdbr]* those that give suck." The words used in Isaiah 40 of God are here transferred to God's agent, the Messiah. See following *Note*.

[67] Cf. Ps 78:70-72, "He chose David also as His servant, and took him from the sheepfolds; . . . He brought him to be a shepherd over Jacob His people . . . So he shepherded them according to the integrity of his heart"; Ezek 34:11-23, "For thus says the Lord God: Behold . . . I will search for my sheep, and seek them out. As a shepherd seeks out his flock . . . so I will seek out My sheep . . . And I will bring them out from the peoples . . . and bring them into their own land; and I will feed them upon the mountains of Israel . . . And I will set up one shepherd over them, and he shall feed them, even My servant David."

9. Hebrew Text:

To a mare in the chariots of Pharaoh
Have I compared you, O My Love.[68]

Targum:

When Israel went out from Egypt, Pharaoh and his hosts pursued after them with chariots[y] and horsemen,[69] and the way was barred to them on their four sides.[70] To the right and the left were deserts full of fiery serpents.[71] Behind them was wicked Pharaoh and his hosts, and in front of them was the Red Sea. What did the Holy One, blessed be He, do? He revealed Himself in the power of His might by the sea and dried up the water,[z 72] but the mud He did not dry up. The wicked, the mixed multitude, and the strangers who were among them said: "He is able to dry up the water,[aa] but the mud He is not able to dry!"[73] At that

Apparatus, Chapter 1

[y] I K L^2: "with mares." Cf. *Apparatus bb.*
[z] B D F G H I K L N O: "the sea."
[aa] D F: "the waters of the sea"; G H I K L N O: "the sea."

Notes, Chapter 1

[68] The mention of "the chariots of Pharaoh" provides one of the primary time-notes in Canticles. Tg. saw a reference to the chariots in which Pharaoh pursued the Israelites to the Red Sea. Thus he contextualized the verse to the events described in Exodus 14–15: note particularly Exod 14:7, *rekheb baḥur . . . rekheb miṣrayim,* which Tg. doubtless saw echoed in *rikhbei farʿoh* in Cant 1:9. Most Rabbinic commentators link Cant 1:9 with the Exodus from Egypt, though they interpret it in different ways: see, e.g., Cant.R. 1:9 §§4-5; Exod.R. 23.14; Num.R. 8.3; Mek. deR. Ishmael, *Beshallaḥ* 7; ARN A.27; Midrash Ps. 18.14; Pirqei de R. El. 42. For another reworking of the Exodus narrative by Tg., see his rendering of Cant 2:14.

God addresses Israel. The comparison with the "mare in the chariots of Pharaoh" is taken negatively, not positively, as an allusion to the rebellion of the Israelites at the Red Sea: I compared you to wicked Pharaoh and his hosts when you rebelled against Me at the Sea, and would have punished you in the same way, but for the intercession of Moses and of the righteous, and the merit of the Fathers. This negative reading makes the address "O My Love" problematic: it is picked up in "Abraham, Isaac, and Jacob, the beloved of the Lord": see *Note* 76.

[69] Cf. Exod 14:8-9, "Pharaoh pursued after the children of Israel . . . the Egyptians pursued after them, all the horses and chariots of Pharaoh, and his horsemen, and his army."

[70] Cf. Exod 14:3, "Pharaoh will say of the children of Israel: They are entangled in the land, the Wilderness has shut them in." Mek. deR. Ishmael, *Beshallaḥ* 2: "*The Wilderness has shut them in.* As soon as the Israelites saw the sea storming and the enemy pursuing them, they turned toward the Wilderness. Immediately the Holy One, blessed be He, ordered wild beasts to come and they did not let them cross, as it is said, *He shut the Wilderness against them.* For shutting here can only mean by wild beasts, as it says: *My God has sent His angels and has shut the lions' mouths* (Dan 6:23)."

[71] Cf. Deut 8:15, "[God] led you through the . . . Wilderness, wherein . . . were fiery serpents"; Num 21:6, "The Lord sent fiery serpents [Heb. *ha-neḥashim ha-serafim;* Onq. *ḥiwyan qalan*] among the people"; Tg. Cant. 2:6, the Cloud of Glory "killed all the fiery serpents *[ḥiwyan qalan]* and scorpions that were in the Wilderness"; Tg. Cant. 2:14, "on their two flanks were deserts full of fiery serpents *[ḥiwyan qalan]* that bite and kill men with their venom."

[72] The drying of the Red Sea was brought about by direct, divine intervention. Note Exod 14:21, "And *Moses* stretched out his hand over the sea, and *the Lord* caused the sea to go back." Cf. Mek. deR. Ishmael, *Beshallaḥ* 5: "When Moses came and stood by the sea, ordering it in the name of the Holy One, blessed be He, to divide itself, it would not consent. He showed it the staff, and still it refused to consent, so that the Holy One, blessed be He, with His glory, had to manifest Himself over it. As soon as the Holy One, blessed be He, with His might and glory manifested Himself, the sea began to flee, as it is said: *The sea saw it and fled* (Ps 114:3)."

[73] Tg. takes Exod 14:10-11 as a rebellion by the Israelites; cf. Ps 106:7, "Our fathers in Egypt gave no heed to Your wonders; they did not remember the multitude of Your mercies, but were rebellious at the Sea, even at the Red Sea." Cant. Zuta to 1:9 (ed. Buber, 15) summarizes the tradition behind the Tg.: "*To a mare in the chariots of Pharaoh have I compared you, O My love.* This refers to the rebellion which the Israelites perpetrated at the sea. Which rebellion? The one in which the Omnipresent tested them by drying up the water but not drying up the mud. Israel began to say: He is able to dry up the water, but the mud

hour the wrath of the Lord waxed hot against them, and He would have drowned them in the waters of the sea, just as Pharaoh and his mares, chariots, and horsemen[bb] were drowned, had it not been for Moses the prophet, who spread out his hands in prayer before the Lord, and turned back from them[cc] the wrath of the Lord.[74] He and the righteous of that generation[dd] opened their mouths, recited the song,[75] and passed through the midst of the sea[ee] on dry land, on account of the merit[ff] of Abraham, Isaac, and Jacob, the beloved of the Lord.[76]

10. Hebrew Text:

[How] comely are your cheeks with circlets![77]
[How comely is] your neck with beads![78]

Apparatus, Chapter 1

[bb] Lag. has a typically full reading: "Pharaoh and his forces—his chariots, his horsemen, and his mares."
[cc] B D F G H I J K L M N O: "from them"; A omits.
[dd] B G H I: "that generation"; A C D F J K L M N O: "the generation."
[ee] D F: "Red Sea."
[ff] J K L M N: "merits."

Notes, Chapter 1

He is not able to dry up! The Omnipresent said to them: I have tested you and you have not stood the test. As the horses of Pharaoh perished and his chariots, so you deserve to perish. But I will act to ensure that My great name is not profaned. Hence it is said: *They rebelled at the Red Sea, but He saved them for the sake of His great name, to make known His power* (Ps 106:7-8). And from where do we know that He dried up the water, but did not dry up the mud? As it is written: *You have trodden the sea with Your horses, through the clay [homer] of mighty waters* (Hab 3:15)." See also the similar traditions in Exod.R. 24.1; Cant.R. 1:9 §4; Mek. deR. Ishmael, *Beshallaḥ* 7.

Here in the Tg. the rebellion is blamed not on Israel as a whole but on "the wicked, the mixed multitude, and the strangers who were among them." For the "mixed multitude" see Exod 12:38 ("a mixed multitude *[ʿereb rab]* also went up with them"), and Num 11:4 ("and the mixed multitude *[ʾasafsuf]* that was among them"). They are again held responsible for the making of the Calf in Tg. Cant. 1:12. For the possible significance of "the mixed multitude" to Tg. see *Intro.* 4.2.

74 The intercession of Moses saved the Israelites when they rebelled at the Red Sea, just as it saved them when they rebelled by making the Calf. See Tg. Cant. 1:5.

75 Tg. seems to imply that the Song at the Sea (Exodus 15) was recited *before* the crossing and that it was a prayer of intercession. Here "the righteous" of Israel (as opposed to "the wicked, the mixed multitude, and the strangers") join Moses as effective intercessors for Israel.

76 The merit of the Fathers is a central theme of Tg. Cant. (*Intro.* 4.3). For the tradition that the crossing of the Red Sea took place in the presence of the three Fathers and the six Mothers see Ginzberg, *Legends* 3:22. The introduction of the Fathers here helps to solve the problem of how God can address Israel as "My Love" in a context of anger and judgment: Israel is still God's beloved, even when she sins, because of the merit of the Fathers.

77 Though it is apparently directly addressed by God to Israel, Tg. casts this verse, like v. 8, in the third person as an address to Moses in reply to his intercession in v. 9. The righteous showed their faith by going into the Wilderness. By the crossing of the Red Sea they expiated the rebellion at the Sea, and were rewarded by the giving of the Torah.

"Circlets" *(torim)* suggests Torah: cf. Cant.R. 1:10 §1: "*With circlets*: with two *Torot*—the Written and the Oral." The word is interpreted in basically the same way in the following verse. "Words of Torah on the cheeks" suggests that Torah is being compared to a horse's bridle: just as a bridle stops the horse from straying, so the words of Torah keep Israel from straying. Cf. ARN A.24: "A man who has good deeds and studies much Torah is like a horse with a bridle (*kalinos* = Greek *chalinos*)." Note the echoing of the equine imagery of the previous verse. There the horse symbolized headstrong rebellion; here it symbolizes biddableness and obedience to God.

78 Tg. takes "beads" as symbolizing the precepts of the Torah. Torah upon the neck suggests the common image of Torah as a yoke (m. ʾAbot 3:5; Tg. Lam. 3:27; the "yoke of the kingdom of heaven" in m. Ber. 2:2 and elsewhere is synonymous: Strack-Billerbeck 1:608–609). "Yoke" in turn generates the image of the plowing ox, which is reinforced by the *toraʾ/Torah* wordplay.

Targum:

When they went out[gg] into the wilderness, the Lord said to Moses: "How comely is this people to be given the words of the Torah, to be like bridles on their cheeks, so that they should not turn aside from the right path, just as the horse on whose cheek is the bridle does not turn aside! And how comely is their neck to bear the yoke of My commandments, so that it should be upon them like a yoke upon the neck of the ox,[hh] that plows the field and supports itself and its master!"[79]

11. Hebrew Text:

We will make for you[80] *circlets*[81] *of gold*
With studs[82] *of silver.*

Apparatus, Chapter 1

[gg] K L: "when the House of Israel went out."
[hh] B G I J K L M N O: "upon the ox."

Notes, Chapter 1

[79] An implicit answer to Moses' question in v. 7 as to how Israel will be sustained in exile: Accept the yoke of the Torah and you will not lack a livelihood *(parnasah)*. It is unclear whether the "master" is introduced simply to stress the general usefulness of the ox, or slyly to hint at the need to support the scholars who study Torah, or to suggest the thought that God is sustained by the praises and obedience of God's people.

[80] Tg. probably took "you" here as Israel rather than Moses (the form *lakh* is ambiguous and could be either feminine or pausal masculine). The verse is seen as addressed by God to Israel. The Torah is Israel's adornment and her reward for her faithfulness in following God into the wilderness. As in vv. 8 and 10, however, the direct address to Israel has been turned in the translation into an address to Moses. "We" = God and Moses: "and I [God] will give them [the Ten Words] by your [Moses'] hand . . . to Israel."

[81] Tg. gives a double interpretation of "circlets *(torim)*": (1) "two tables of stone." The equation is based on seeing *torim* as a play on *Torot* (see *Note* 77). It is reinforced by the use of the word "gold," which is often linked with Torah in Scripture: cf. Cant.R. 5:14 §1: "*Rods of gold*: this refers to the words of Torah of which it is said, *More to be desired are they than gold, yea, than much fine gold* (Ps 19:11)." See further Gen.R. 16.4 (quoting Ps 19:11); Exod.R. 47.7 (quoting Ps 119:72); Midrash Ps. 119.58 (on Ps 119:72). It can further be reinforced by seeing in "we will make *[na'aseh]*" an allusion to "the tables were the work *[ma'aseh]* of God" in Exod 32:16. Cf. Cant.R. 5:14 §1: "*His hands:* this refers to the tables of the covenant, as it says, *The tables were the work of God* (Exod 32:16)." (2) Tg. has also probably related *torim* to Aramaic *tora'* = "row, line" (Jast. 1656b): hence "arranged in lines *(shytyn)*" (see *Note* 85).

[82] "Studs" = the Ten Words. The qualification "of silver" assists the identification: note the allusion to Ps 12:7, "The words *('amarot)* of the Lord are pure words, as silver tried in a crucible on the earth, refined seven times *(mezuqqaq shib'atayim)*." Cf. Num.R. 14.12: "The Torah is called silver, as it is written, *The words of the Lord are . . . as silver tried in a crucible on the earth* (Ps 12:7)." See further Lev.R. 22.1, and Exod.R. 33.1: "It is written, *For I give you good doctrine; forsake not My teaching* (Prov 4:2). Do not forsake the article I have made over to you. When a man purchases an article, if it is of gold, then it is not of silver, of silver then it is not of gold. But the article I have given you has silver therein, for it says, *The words of the Lord are pure words, as silver tried in a crucible* (Ps 12:7); it also has gold therein, for it says, *More to be desired are they than gold, yea than much fine gold* (Ps 19:11)." Here the "gold" is the inner sense *(derash)* of the Torah, the "silver" the outer sense *(peshat)*. In Tg. Cant., because of the link with Ps 12:7, it is the "silver" that symbolizes the multiple senses of Scripture.

Targum:

Then it was said to Moses:[83] "Ascend to the firmament and I will give you two tables of stone,[84] hewn from the sapphire of the throne of My glory,[85] gleaming like fine gold, arranged in lines[86] and written by My finger.[87] Engraved on them are the Ten Words,[88] refined more than silver that has been refined in seven times seven [ways]—that is the sum

Notes, Chapter 1

[83] The passive is curious: why not "then God said to Moses" (contrast vv. 8 and 10)? It might be a residual anti-anthropomorphism, characteristic of Targumic style. Or it may reflect confusion as to who issued the command to ascend, caused by the puzzling wording of Exod. 24:1, "And he said to Moses, Come up to the Lord." Why not "Come up to Me"? According to b. Ḥag. 15a and b. Sanh. 38b the command to ascend here was issued by Metatron.

[84] The closest parallel is Exod 24:12, "And the Lord said to Moses, Come up to Me in the mount . . . and I will give you the tables of stone" (cf. Exod 19:3). However, Tg., following a common Rabbinic tradition, has Moses ascend into heaven itself to receive the Torah (see 1:5, *Note* 42).

[85] The reference here is to the first tables of the Law, which Tg., following Exod 32:16, implies were God's handiwork, and their material, therefore, was of heavenly origin. The "sapphire" is derived from Exod 24:10, "They saw the God of Israel; and there was under His feet as it were a pavement of sapphire." This suggests a connection between "sapphire" and "stone." Ezek 1:26 makes the link between "sapphire" and "the throne of glory": "Above the firmament that was over their heads was the likeness of a throne, as the appearance of a sapphire stone." In Yalqut Shimʿoni, Deut. §854, it is Moses who hews the first tables, though from a celestial quarry: "Moses said to Him, From where am I going to bring the tables of stone? He said to him, I am going to show you the quarry. R. Levi said in the name of R. Ḥama b. Ḥanina, The Holy One, blessed be He, showed Moses the quarry beneath the Throne of Glory, as it is said, *And under His feet as it were a pavement of sapphire* (Exod 24:10) . . . The Holy One, blessed be He, said to him, Hew from here two tables of stone." See also Leqaḥ Tob to Exod 31:18. The second tables of the Law (Exod 34:1, 4; Tg. Cant. 1:14, *Note* 112), were hewn by Moses himself at the foot of the mountain before his second ascent to heaven, following the principle that the middleman bears the loss when goods are damaged before delivery (Deut.R. 3.12). But, since the second tables were to be "like the first," and the first, according to tradition, were of sapphire, God graciously created a sapphire quarry in Moses' tent from which to hew them (and Moses grew rich from the chippings!). See Pirqei de R. El. 46: "The [first] tables were not created out of the earth but out of the heavens, the handiwork of the Holy One, blessed be He, as it is said, *And the tables were the work of God* (Exod 32:16). They are the tables which were of old, and the writing was divine writing . . . When the Holy One, blessed be He, said to Moses, *Hew two tables of stone like the first* (Exod 34:1), a quarry of sapphires was created for Moses in the midst of his tent, and he cut them out from there, as it is said, *And he hewed two tables of stone like the first* (Exod 34:4). Moses ascended [text wrongly has "descended"] with the tables, and spent forty days on the mountain, sitting down before the Holy One, blessed be He, like a disciple who is sitting before his teacher, reading the Written Torah, and repeating the Oral Torah which he had learnt." See further b. Ned. 38a; Exod.R. 46.2; 47.3; Lev.R. 32.2; Eccl.R. 9:11 §2; 10:20 §1; Ginzberg, *Legends* 6:49, n. 258, and 59, n. 306.

[86] For "lines" as a play on "circlets" see *Note* 81. Rabbinic commentators speculate on how the Ten Words were arranged on the two tables: see Cant.R. 5:14 §1 (on "rods of gold"); and Ginzberg, *Legends* 6:49, n. 258. Tg. probably implies that each commandment was written on a separate line, and that there were five lines to a table, as in the standard representation of the *luḥot ha-berit* in synagogue iconography (see *EJ* 4:1340–41; 7:1132 [Sarajevo Haggadah]; 14:1324 [the Regensburg Pentateuch]). See further 5:13, *Notes* 46 and 47.

[87] Cf. Exod 31:8, "And He gave Moses . . . the two tables of testimony, tables of stone, written by the finger of God"; Deut 9:10, "The Lord delivered to me the two tables of stone, written by the finger of God."

[88] Tg. probably sees the Decalogue as the summation of the whole Torah. This idea, already propounded by Philo in the *Decalogue* and the *Special Laws*, was taken up again by Saʿadya, who divided the 613 commandments into ten categories arranged under the headings of the Ten Commandments. Note also the rather quaint expression of the same view in Cant.R. 5:14 §2: "Ḥananiah the son of the brother of R. Joshua said: Between every two commandments [on the Tables of the Law] were written the sections and the minutiae of the Torah. When R. Joḥanan in the course of studying Scripture came to this verse *set with beryls* (Cant 5:14), he used to say: I have to thank the son of the brother of R. Joshua for teaching me this. Just as between every two large waves there are small waves in the sea, so between every commandment and the next one [on the tablets] the sections and the minutiae of the Torah were written." Num.R. 13.15-16: "*Of ten shekels* (Num 7:20). These allude to the Ten Commandments which were inscribed upon the tables . . . *full of incense* signifies that the six hundred and thirteen commandments are included in them." However, midrashic sources of the Talmudic period do not speak of the Decalogue as the summation of the Torah, probably for polemical reasons—lest "heretics" should say only the Decalogue was given at Sinai. See y. Ber. I, 3c: "The Decalogue should be recited daily. Why then is it not recited? Because of the heretics *[minim]*, who would then claim that these commandments alone were given to Moses at Sinai" (cf. b. Ber. 12a and Maimonides to m. Tamid 5:1).

total of the principles by which the forty-nine facets [of the Torah] are expounded.[89] And I will give them by your hand to the people of the house of Israel."

12. Hebrew Text:

While the king was on his banqueting-couch[90]
My spikenard gave off its smell.[91]

Targum:

But while Moses their teacher was in the firmament to receive the two tables of stone[ii]—the Torah and the statute[92]—the wicked of that generation and the mixed multitude among them arose and made the Golden Calf;[93] they made their actions stink and acquired for themselves an evil reputation in the world. Whereas formerly their fragrance had spread

Apparatus, Chapter 1

[ii] C adds "that were hewn from the sapphire of the throne of His glory." Cf. v. 11.

Notes, Chapter 1

[89] Tg. offers a midrash of the implicit quotation of Ps 12:7 (see *Note* 82). "Seven times seven" suggests the inexhaustible meaning latent in Torah: Torah has forty-nine "facets" (Aram. *ʾappin* = Heb. *panim*), each of which can be expounded according to forty-nine different hermeneutical principles (Aram. *ʿinyanin* = Heb. *middot*). Tg. clearly distinguishes the "facets" of the Torah itself from the "principles" applied to its exposition. Sometimes, however, *panim* is used to denote the principles of interpretation. Cf. Cant.R. 2:4 §1: "The Community of Israel said: The Holy One, blessed be He, brought me . . . to Sinai, and from there gave me the Torah which is expounded with forty-nine reasons *[panim]* for declaring clean and forty-nine for declaring unclean, the numerical value of *we-diglo* [and his banner]." Parallel: Num.R. 19.2. Num.R. 13.15-16 speaks of seventy ways of expounding Torah; "As the numerical value of *yayin* (wine) is seventy, so there are seventy modes of expounding the Torah." Tg. indirectly justifies its own highly complex reading of Canticles.

[90] Tg. takes the verse as spoken by Israel and contextualizes it to the incident of the making of the Golden Calf. "The king" is identified not as God (contrast Cant.R. 1:12 §1 quoted in *Note* 91) but as Moses: cf. Cant.R. 1:12 §1: "R. Berekhiah said: While Moses, who is called king, as it says, *And there was a king in Jeshurun, when the heads of the people were gathered* (Deut 33:5), was at his table in the firmament, already God spoke all these words (Exod 20:1)." According to Midrash Moses held the offices both of priest and king, but these did not pass on to his descendants (see Ginzberg, *Legends* 6:28, n. 170). The "banqueting-couch" is seen as an allusion to Moses' ascent to the firmament to receive the Torah: "When the king [Moses] was on his banqueting-couch [in heaven] . . . ." The basis may be Exod 24:9-11, "Then Moses, and Aaron, Nadab and Abihu, and seventy elders went up . . . and they beheld God, and did eat and drink."

[91] Tg. takes "scent" as symbolizing reputation (cf. Tg. Cant. 1:3, *Note* 20), and since, oddly (see *Note* 94), it regards spikenard as evil-smelling, it takes spikenard as symbolizing the wicked, and sees an allusion here to misdeeds by Israel, viz., the making of the Golden Calf. Cf. Cant.R. 1:12 §1: "R. Meir said: While yet the supreme King of kings, the Holy One, blessed be He, was at His table in the firmament, Israel gave off an offensive smell and said to the Calf, *This is your God, O Israel* (Exod 32:4)." Contrast "ointments" = the righteous in 4:10.

[92] Cf. Exod 24:12, "And the Lord said to Moses, Come up to Me into the mount, and be there: and I will give you the tables of stone, and the Torah and the commandment." Tg. probably took "and the Torah and the commandment" as epexegetical of "the tables of stone."

[93] On the sin of the Calf see Tg. Cant. 1:5, *Note* 38. In mitigation Tg. blames the incident on "the wicked and the mixed multitude," the group blamed also for the rebellion at the Sea (Tg. Cant. 1:9, *Note* 73).

through all the world,[94] after that they stank like spikenard,[jj] the odor of which is very bad;[95] and the plague of leprosy came down upon their flesh.[96]

13. Hebrew Text:

The bundle of myrrh , O my Beloved, [is] mine.[97]
Between my breasts He shall lodge.[98]

Targum:

At once[kk] the Lord said to Moses: "Go, descend, for your people[ll][99] have behaved corruptly. Let Me be, so that I may destroy them."[100] Then Moses turned and pleaded for mercy before the Lord,[101] and the Lord remembered for them the binding of Isaac, whose father Abraham[mm] bound him on Mount Moriah upon the altar,[102] and the Lord turned from His anger and caused His Shekhinah[103] to dwell among them as before.

Apparatus, Chapter 1

[jj] Aram. *nirda.* This corresponds to the Heb. and must be original. C reads *gidda,* "wormwood" (Jast. 235a), presumably because a scribe was puzzled that spikenard should be regarded as evil-smelling. See *Note* 95.

[kk] Lit. "at that time."

[ll] J K L M N O: "the people," but "your people" is more pointed.

[mm] B: "whose father Abraham"; A C D F G H I J K L M N O: "whose father."

Notes, Chapter 1

[94] Perhaps a reference to the spread of God's fame through the miracles wrought for Israel at the Sea: see Tg. Cant. 1:3 (*Note* 22).

[95] Spikenard is normally regarded as sweet-smelling. Tg. may reflect a puritanical attitude toward perfume and cosmetics in general. In 4:13, 14 Tg. renders *nerd* by *riqsha* (see Tg. to 4:13, *Note* 52).

[96] Cf. Exod 32:35, "The Lord sent a plague upon *(wayyigof)* the people, because they made the Calf." Tg. has identified the undefined affliction of the Bible with leprosy—the punishment inflicted on Miriam for rebellion against Moses (Num 12:10). Cf. Pesiq. Rab. 7.7.

[97] Addressed by Israel to God (*dodi,* "my Beloved") through Israel's mediator, Moses. The "bundle of myrrh" *(mor)* is the merit of the binding of Isaac on Mount Moriah, which overcomes the stench caused by the sin of the Golden Calf. For "myrrh" = Moriah see Tg. to 3:6 and 4:6. Tg. contextualizes the verse to Exod 32:7-14, which describes Moses' successful intercession for Israel over the sin of the Calf: "The Lord spoke to Moses: Go, descend, for your people . . . have behaved corruptly . . . Let me be . . . that I may destroy them . . . But Moses implored the Lord . . . Turn aside from Your fierce anger . . . Remember Abraham and Isaac . . ." (cf. Deut 9:26-29).

[98] God's lodging between Israel's breasts is interpreted as God's forgiving of Israel for the sin of the Calf and causing the Shekhinah to dwell among them as before. Tg. does not make anything specifically of the "breasts." Cant.R. 1:14 §3 interprets "between my breasts" as "between the two staves of the ark," probably with an allusion to the tradition that the staves of the ark, pressing on the curtain from the inside, caused on the outside two breast-like swellings (see b. Yoma 54a; b. Menaḥ 98a). Hence Rashi: "between the Cherubim"; Ibn Ezra: "between the Cherubim, or in the midst of the congregation of Israel."

[99] "*Your* people" is pointed: cf. Pirqei de R. El. 45: "Moses spoke before the Holy One, blessed be He: Sovereign of all the worlds! Whilst Israel had not yet sinned before You, You called them, My people, as it is said, *And I will bring forth My hosts, My people* (Exod 7:4). Now that they have sinned before You, You say to me, *Go, descend, for your people have corrupted themselves* (Exod 32:7). They are Your people, and Your inheritance, as it is said, *Yet they are Your people and Your inheritance* (Deut 9:29)."

[100] "Let Me be, that I may destroy them": the precise wording of the Tg. is closer to Deut 9:14 than to Exod 32:10.

[101] On the efficacious intercession of Moses see also Tg. Cant. 1:5 and 1:9. Moses stands for the righteous in general in their role as mediators and protectors of Israel: see *Intro.* 4.3.

[102] The theme of the ʿAqedah is central to Tg. Cant. See *Intro.* 4.3. For "Moriah" here as a play on *mor,* "myrrh" see *Note* 97.

[103] On the doctrine of the Shekhinah in Tg. Cant. see *Intro.* 4.1.

14. Hebrew Text:

The cluster of henna, O my Beloved, [is] mine,
In the vineyards of En-gedi.[104]

Targum:

Behold, then Moses descended from the Mount[nn] with the two tables of stone in his hands,[105] but on account of the sins of Israel his hands became heavy, and [the tables] fell and broke.[106] Then Moses went and ground up the Calf, scattered its dust on the brook,[oo] and gave [it] to the Children of Israel to drink,[107] and it killed anyone who deserved death.[108] He went up a second time to the firmament,[109] and prayed before the Lord and made atonement for the Children of Israel.[110] Then he was commanded to make the Tabernacle[pp] and the Ark.

Apparatus, Chapter 1

[nn] B G H I J K L M N O: "from the Mount"; A B C D F omit.

[oo] C: "on the water."

[pp] C adds "and all its utensils," omitting this phrase later in the verse.

Notes, Chapter 1

[104] Israel still addresses God. Tg. detects the parallelism between vv. 14 and 13. The "cluster of henna" *(ʾeshkol ha-kofer)* alludes to a second atonement *(kapparah),* which, like "the bundle of myrrh," overcame the stench of the sin of the Calf. The "cluster of henna" is doubly interpreted. (1) First it is taken as alluding to Moses who, on a second ascent to God (see *Note* 109), after punishing the worshipers of the Calf, made atonement for Israel *(we-khappar ʿal benei Yisraʾel).* Cf. Cant.R. 1:14 §2: *"The cluster (ʾeshkol) of henna (kofer).* What is meant by *ʾeshkol*? A man in whom is everything *(ʾish she-hakkol bo)*—Scripture, Mishnah, Talmud, Toseftas, and Aggadot. *Of kofer*—because he atones *(mekhapper)* for the iniquities of Israel." Yalqut Shimʿoni, Cant. §984: "*ʾEshkol*: a man in whom is everything *(ʾish she-hakkol bo)*; *kofer:* who made atonement for me over the episode of the Calf, when my face grew pallid [from shame] *(nitkarkemu panai).*" *ʾEshkol* as a term for a scholar became commonplace in Rabbinic literature (Jast. 128a). (2) Second, "the cluster of henna . . . in the vineyards of En-gedi" is seen as alluding to the grape clusters from the vineyards of En-gedi that provided the wine libations, which together with the service of the Tabernacle atoned for the sin of the Calf ("the atoning cluster . . . from the vineyards of En-gedi is mine, O my Beloved").

[105] Cf. Exod 32:15, "And Moses turned, and descended from the Mount, with the two tables of the testimony in his hand."

[106] Cf. Exod 32:19, "He cast the tables out of his hands, and broke them beneath the Mount"; Deut 9:17, "And I took hold of the two tables, and cast them out of my hands, and broke them before your eyes." The Bible gives Moses a more active role in breaking the tables. The aggadic addition, "but on account of the sins of Israel his hands became heavy," is intended to exonerate him from all blame. Cf. Pirqei de R. El. 45: "Moses took the tables and descended, and the tables carried their own weight and Moses with them; but when they beheld the Calf and the dances, the writing fled from off the tables, and they became heavy in his hands, and Moses was not able to carry himself and the tables, and he cast them from his hand, and they were broken beneath the mount"; further b. Ned. 38a; b. Shabb. 87b.

[107] Cf. Exod 32:20, "And he took the Calf which they had made, and burned it with fire, and ground it to powder, and strewed it upon the water, and made the children of Israel drink of it"; Deut 9:21, "And I took your sin, the Calf which you had made, and I burnt it with fire, and beat it in pieces, grinding it very small, until it was fine as dust; and I cast the dust thereof into the brook that descended out of the Mount."

[108] Tg. mentions only death by drinking the water, not death at the hands of the Levites (Exod 32:27-28), or death by plague (Exod 32:35). It suggests a trial by ordeal: the waters singled out the guilty, as in the bitter waters of the *sotah* (Num 5:11-31; Num.R. 9.48 links the two events). According to one tradition, a mark appeared on the face of those who had kissed the Calf, when they drank the waters, and the Levites then knew who was guilty and whom to kill: see Ps-J Exod. 32:20; b. ʿAbod. Zar. 44a; Pirqei de R. El. 45; further Ginzberg, *Legends* 6:54, n. 281.

[109] Cf. Exod 34:4, "And he hewed two tables of stone like the first; and Moses rose early in the morning, and went up into Mount Sinai." For Moses' ascent to heaven see Tg. to 1:5 (*Note* 42); 1:11; 1:12; 3:3.

[110] Cf. Exod 34:8-9. There seems to be an implication that Moses' first intercession, during his first ascent of Sinai (Exod 32:11-14), was only partially successful because God still "smote the people, because they had made the Calf" (Exod 32:35), though he did not totally destroy them as he had threatened. The second intercession led to the establishment of the Tabernacle—a perpetual means of atoning for Israel's sins.

At once Moses hurried and made the Tabernacle,[111] and all its utensils, and the Ark, and he placed in the Ark the two later tables.[112] And he appointed the sons of Aaron as priests[113] to offer up the sacrifices[qq] upon the altar and to pour the libation of wine upon the sacrifices.[qq] From where did they get wine to pour as a libation?[114] Were they not residing[rr] in the Wilderness—not a fit place for sowing, nor indeed for figs, or vines or pomegranates? However, they went to the vineyards of En-gedi, and brought from them clusters of grapes. They squeezed from them wine, and poured it as a libation upon the altar, a quarter of a *hin* for each lamb.[115]

15. Hebrew Text:

Behold,[116] *you are fair, My Darling,*[117]
Behold, you are fair;[118]
Your eyes are [like] doves.[119]

Targum:

When the Children of Israel[ss] did[tt] the will of their King, He through His Word[120] was praising them in the household of the holy angels,[121] and saying: "How fair are your deeds,

Apparatus, Chapter 1

[qq] B D F G H K L O: "the sacrifice."
[rr] B D E F G I J K L M N O omit "residing."
[ss] J K L M N O: "House of Israel."
[tt] D E F: "did"; A B C G H I J K L M N O: "do."

Notes, Chapter 1

[111] See Exod 35:4-19.

[112] Cf. Exod 34:1, 4, "The Lord said to Moses: Hew for yourself two tables of stone like the first . . . And he hewed two tables of stone like the first"; Exod 40:20, "And he took and put the testimony in the ark" (see *Note* 85 above).

[113] See Exod 40:12-15.

[114] The style is Midrashic or even Mishnaic, not Targumic.

[115] Cf. Num 15:5, "And wine for the drink offering, a quarter of a *hin,* shall you prepare with the burnt offering, or for the sacrifice, for each lamb"; Exod 29:40, "And with the one lamb a tenth part of an *ephah* of fine flour mingled with a quarter of a *hin* of beaten oil; and a quarter of a *hin* of wine for the drink offering."

[116] Tg. takes the verse as addressed in praise by God to Israel, who has accepted his will. In context this and the following verse can be seen as referring to Israel's acceptance of the Torah at Sinai (cf. Exod 24:7, "All that the Lord has spoken we will do, and obey"). However, neither verse is strongly contextualized to the sacred history, but is read as expressing timeless truths.

[117] "My Darling" is rendered, straightforwardly, "dear Daughter, Congregation of Israel," but note also the wordplay between "darling" *(raʿyah)* and "will" *(reʿutaʾ):* you are My darling *(raʿyati)* when you do My will *(reʿuti).*

[118] "Fair" not in physical form, but in conduct—in the study of the Torah and in good deeds. Cf. Cant.R. 1:15 §1: "Behold, you are fair in the performance of precepts, behold, you are fair in deeds of loving kindness."

[119] *ʿEinayikh,* "your eyes," has been read by *ʾal tiqrei* as *ʿinyanayikh,* which here in parallelism to "your deeds" must mean "your actions." The actions are compared to doves. Cf. Cant.R. 1:15 §4: *"Your eyes are doves*: that is *like* doves." Tg. does not support the idea that the Hebrew here involves a *comparatio decurtata* = "your eyes are like the eyes of doves." The doves, through Lev 1:14, are identified as sacrificial doves (see *Note* 122). Contrast the interpretation of the parallel in 4:1 and 6:5, where "eyes" are taken as a symbol of the Sanhedrin.

[120] It is hard to see what function Memra performs here. It is probably solemn, reverential language, seen by Tg. as typical of Targumic style. See *Intro.* 4.1.

[121] God praising Israel, or the righteous, in the presence of the angels is a theme in the Midrash. In Neof. Gen. 22:10 a *bat qol* praises Abraham and Isaac (in the parallel in Ps-J the praises are spoken by the angels). The idea may ultimately go back to Job 1:6-8.

dear Daughter, Congregation of Israel, when you do My will, and are occupied with the words of My Torah! How upright are your deeds! And your actions [are] like chicks, the offspring of the dove, that are fit to be offered upon the altar."[122]

16. Hebrew Text:

Behold, You are fair, my Beloved,
Yea, pleasant;[123]
Also our couch is luxuriant.[124]

Targum:

The Congregation of Israel replied before the Lord of all the World, and thus said: "How fair is the Shekhinah of Your holiness[125] when You dwell among us and receive with favor our prayer,[126] and when You cause love to dwell in the bridal bed so that our children are many on the earth, and we increase and multiply[127] like a tree that is planted by a spring of water, whose leaves are beautiful and whose fruit is abundant."[128]

Notes, Chapter 1

[122] The implication is that good deeds and the study of the Torah are as efficacious as the sacrifice of doves in atoning for Israel. Cf. Cant.R. 1:15 §2: "Just as the dove produces a fresh brood every month, so Israel every month produces fresh learning and good deeds." The equation of good deeds with sacrifice is a Rabbinic commonplace. "The offspring of the dove" echoes Lev 1:14, "If his offering to the Lord be a burnt-offering of fowls, then he shall bring his offering of turtle-doves *[torim]*, or of young pigeons [lit. "offspring of the dove," *benei ha-yonah*]"; cf. Lev 12:8.

[123] Israel replies to God. Tg. transfers God's beauty reverentially to God's Shekhinah, and interprets God's "pleasantness" as God's acceptance of Israel's prayer.

[124] The "couch" is interpreted as the marriage bed; "luxuriant" is therefore taken as indicating an abundance of children. The arboreal metaphor latent in "luxuriant" is then drawn out to compare Israel to a flourishing tree.

[125] Israel's relationship to God in Tg. Cant. is expressed primarily in terms of her experience of God's Presence (the Shekhinah). Here God's Presence not only shows that he hears the prayers of his people but guarantees an abundant progeny, possibly by warding off Liliths and other evil spirits that attack children and pregnant women. On the link between God's Presence and progeny see Cant.R. 1:16 §3: *"Also our couch is luxuriant:* Just as a couch is only for being fruitful and multiplying, so before the Temple was built [David could say] *Go, number Israel* (1 Chr 21:2), but after it was built [and the Shekhinah took up residence] *Judah and Israel were many as the sand which is by the sea in multitude* (1 Kgs 4:20). Another interpretation: *Also our couch is luxuriant:* Before the [Second] Temple was built, *The whole congregation together was forty and two thousand* (Ezra 2:64), but after the Temple was built they increased rapidly, as stated by R. Joḥanan: From Gabbata to Antipatris there were sixty myriads of towns, and they had a population twice as numerous as the Israelites who went out from Egypt." On the Shekhinah in Tg. Cant. see *Intro.* 4.1.

[126] "Lord of all the World . . . receive with favor our prayer." The language is liturgical. Cf., e.g., the ʿAmidah: "Receive in mercy and with favor our prayer *(qabbel be-raḥamim u-beraṣon ʾet tefillatenu)* (Singer, *ADPB* 83). But note here, as in the previous verse, the implication that prayer is as efficacious as sacrifice. Again cf. the ʿAmidah: "Restore the service to Your most holy house, and receive in love and with favor the fire-offerings of Israel and their prayer. May the service of Your people Israel [whether sacrifice or prayer] always be acceptable to You" (Singer, *ADPB* 83).

[127] Cf. Gen 1:28, "be fruitful and multiply."

[128] Cf. Ps 1:3, "He shall be like a tree planted by streams of water, that brings forth its fruit in its season, and whose leaf does not wither; and whatsoever he does shall prosper"; Jer 17:8, "For he shall be as a tree planted by the waters, that spreads out its roots by the river, and it shall not see when heat comes, but its foliage shall be luxuriant; and it shall not be anxious in the year of drought, neither shall cease from yielding fruit." In both these verses, however, the tree represents the righteous individual. Note, however, how in Ezek 17:22-24 Israel at the end of days is compared to a flourishing cedar. The phrase "whose leaves are beautiful and whose fruit is abundant" is taken from Dan 4:12.

17. Hebrew Text:

The beams of our houses are cedars,
Our joists cypresses.[129]

Targum:

Solomon the prophet said: "How fair is the Temple of the Lord that has been built from cedar-wood, but fairer still will be the Temple that is going to be built in the days of the King Messiah, the beams of which will be of cedars from the Garden of Eden, and its joists[130] will be of cypress, teak, and cedar."[uu][131]

Apparatus, Chapter 1

[uu] B G I J K L M N O read "the beams of which will be of cypress, teak, and cedar," by parablepsis (*min* to *min*).

Notes, Chapter 1

[129] Since cedar and cypress wood figured prominently in the construction of the Temple (1 Kgs 5:10; 6:15-18), Tg. sees here a reference to the Temple; cf. Cant.R. 1:17 §2: *"Our floor-boards (rahitenu) are cypresses*: the place on which the priests ran *(rehutim)* was floored with cypresses, as it says, *And he covered the floor of the house with boards of cypress* (1 Kgs 6:15)." The plural "houses" suggests an allusion to two Temples *(batei miqdash)*—Solomon's and the Temple that will be built in the Messianic Age. The reference to the Temple here takes this verse out of the chronological sequence of the narrative, which at this point is dealing with the wilderness period of Israel's history. Tg., therefore, turns the verse into an aside by Solomon the narrator, in which he praises the Temple he has built and anticipates prophetically the Messianic Temple. This reminds the reader that Solomon is the narrator and that the narrative is being told from the chronological standpoint of his reign. The anticipation of the Messianic Age here matches the similar anticipation at Tg. Cant. 1:8, " . . . until I send them the King Messiah who will gently lead them to their tents, that is the Temple, which David and Solomon the shepherds of Israel will build for them." On Messianism in Tg. Cant. see *Intro*. 4.5.

[130] Tg. interprets Heb. *rahit* as "beam" or "joist," Cant.R. 1:17 §2 (quoted in *Note* 129) as "floor-board."

[131] The three types of tree mentioned here are probably derived from Ezek 31:8, which speaks of the trees that grow in Eden: "The cedars in the Garden of God could not hide him: the cypresses were not like his boughs, and the plane trees (Heb. *'armon,* probably identified by the Tg. here as *sha'ga,* teak) were not as his branches; nor was any tree in the Garden of God like him in his beauty. I made him fair by the multitude of his branches: so that all the trees of Eden, that were in the Garden of God, envied him." The Messianic Temple will be constructed of indestructible materials. See Midrash Ps. 90.19.

CHAPTER 2

1. Hebrew Text:

I am a narcissus of the Sharon,
A rose of the lowlands.[1]

Targum:

The Congregation of Israel says: "When the Master of the World causes His Shekhinah to dwell in the midst of me I may be compared to a fresh[2] narcissus from the Garden of Eden[a], and my deeds[b] are as fair as the rose[c] that is in the plain of the Garden of Eden."[d3]

2. Hebrew Text:

Like a rose among thorns,[4]
So is My Darling among the daughters.[5]

Apparatus, Chapter 2

[a] J K L M N O: "a narcissus fresh from the Garden of Eden."
[b] B G H[1] I L: "its deeds."
[c] B I: "like nard": *nrd'*, a miscopying for *wrd'* = "rose."
[d] *Ginnunita' de-'Eden.* Earlier in the verse the Tg. has the more usual *Ginta' de-'Eden,* and so B C I J K L M N O read here; but the variation is typical of Tg. Cant.'s careful style. *Ginnunita'/Ginnanita'* = garden of a house, pleasure garden, especially the Garden of Eden, Paradise (Ps-J Gen. 46:17). See Jast. 258a.

Notes, Chapter 2

[1] This and the following verse continue the interlude that began at 1:15. Note the continuity of the themes of the Shekhinah, good deeds, and the Garden of Eden. Israel, the speaker, is fair as a "narcissus" when the divine Presence is with her, and fair as a "rose" through her good deeds. The bases for interpreting "the Sharon" as "the Garden of Eden" and "the lowlands" as "the plain of the Garden of Eden" are unclear. b. B. Bat. 84a mentions "the rose-garden" of Paradise (Jast. 375b).

[2] "Fresh": Aramaic *rattib.* The same verbal root is used frequently in the Midrash in connection with this verse: cf., e.g., Cant.R. 2:1 §1: *"I am a ḥabaṣṣelet of the Sharon:* I am the one and beloved am I. I am she that was hidden in the shadow *(ḥabuyah ba-ṣel)* of Mount Sinai, and in a brief space I blossomed forth *(hirtabti)* with good deeds before Him, like a rose, with hand and heart, and I said before Him, *All that the Lord has said we will do, and obey"* (Exod 24:7).

[3] That is, like the rose of Eden, Israel's good deeds do not wither and fade. The idea is the same as in Cant.R. 2:1 §3: "R. Eliezer said: The righteous are compared by Scripture to the most excellent of plants and to the most excellent species of that plant. To the most excellent of plants, viz., the rose of the lowlands. Not to the rose of the mountains, which soon withers, but to the rose of the lowlands, which goes on blooming."

[4] Tg. takes the verse as addressed by God to Israel, but presents it as a third-person report by Israel of what God says. This enables him to link v. 2 very closely with v. 1, which is also spoken by Israel. The thorns are a symbol of political oppression by the gentiles ("harsh decrees"). Cf. Lev.R. 23.5: "R. Ḥanina son of R. Abba interpreted the verse (Cant 2:2) as applying to foreign governments. How is it with the rose? When she is placed among thorns a north wind goes forth and bends her toward the south and a thorn pricks her, and a south wind goes forth and bends her toward the north and a thorn pricks her; yet, for all that, her core is directed upward. It is the same with Israel. Although *annonae* and *angariae* are collected from them, their hearts are directed towards their Father who is in heaven. What is the proof? *My eyes are ever toward the Lord; for He will bring forth my feet out of the net* (Ps 25:15)." The parallel in Cant.R. 2:2 §5 is corrupt.

[5] "The daughters" is interpreted as "the provinces" *(pilkhayya'),* which, being without further qualification, are identified as the lands outside the Land of Israel. The basis of the equation is probably the use of Heb. *banot*

Targum:

"But when I stray from the path that is established before Him,[e] and He removes the Shekhinah of His holiness from me, I may be compared to a rose that blooms[f] among thorns, whose petals are pricked and torn, just as I am pricked and torn by harsh decrees in exile[6] among the provinces[g] of the nations."

3. Hebrew Text:

Like a citron among the trees of the wood,[7]
So is my Beloved among the sons.[8]
In His shade I longed to sit,
And His fruit was sweet to my palate.[9]

Apparatus, Chapter 2

[e] B I J K L M N O omit "but when I stray from the path that is established before Him."
[f] "That blooms" *(dmlblbʾ);* J K L: "that is mixed up" *(dmblblʾ).*
[g] "Provinces" *(pylky);* Miq.Ged.: "kings" *(mlky).*

Notes, Chapter 2

("daughters") of the satellite villages of a city or town, or its surrounding territory (Num 21:25; Josh 17:11; further BDB 123b). The gentile lands are seen as satellites of the Land of Israel. Cf. Tg. Cant. 3:10, "daughters of Jerusalem" = "cities of the Land of Israel"; 3:11, "daughters of Zion" = "inhabitants of the districts *(pilkhayyaʾ)* of the Land of Israel"; 6:9, "the daughters" = "the inhabitants of the districts *(pilkhayyaʾ)*." See further Tg. Cant. 6:9, *Note* 30.

[6] Exile is one of the major themes of Tg. Cant. (see *Intro.* 4.1). Deviation from the true path leads to removal of the Shekhinah. Removal of the Shekhinah leads to exile and political oppression. The Shekhinah is experienced only in the Land of Israel, and does not follow Israel into exile.

[7] Tg. returns to the giving of the Torah at Sinai, after the interlude of 1:15–2:2. Israel is the speaker, and she describes God, her Beloved. Tg. translates Heb. *tappuaḥ* (English versions "apple") by "citron" *(ʾethrogaʾ),* and *ʿaṣei ha-yaʿar* ("trees of the wood") by *ʾilanei seraq,* trees that do not bear edible fruit (see *Note* 11).

[8] "The sons" are equated with "the angels" on the basis of Gen 6:2 ("sons of God" = angels: Alexander, "'Sons of God' in Genesis 6") and Job 38:7 ("all the sons of God" = Tg. "all the companies of the angels"). God being praised in the presence of the angels by Israel at Sinai neatly balances Israel being praised in the presence of the angels by God at Sinai (Tg. Cant. 1:15).

[9] God's "shade" = " the shade of His Shekhinah"; his "fruit" = "the words of His Torah."

Targum:

"Just as the citron[h10] is fair and praised among the wild trees,[i11] and all the world acknowledges it,[12] so the Lord of the World was fair[j] and praised among the angels[k] at the time that He was revealed on Mount Sinai,[13] when He gave His Torah to His people. At that hour I longed to sit in the shade of His Shekhinah, and the words of His Torah were sweet to my palate,[l14] and the reward[m] [for the keeping] of His commandments is stored up for me in the world to come."[n15]

Apparatus, Chapter 2

[h] "Citron" = ethrog. J K L M N: "Matrona." This is probably more than a simple miscopying, and betrays Qabbalistic influence. Matrona = the Shekhinah, which is also designated "the field of holy apple-trees" (Scholem, *Kabbalah and its Symbolism* 140). Then "wild trees" may have been taken as an allusion to the gods of the nations among whom the Matrona/Shekhinah wanders (see Rashi quoted in *Note* 11).

[i] "Wild trees" = *ʾilanei seraq:* see Jast. 1030a.

[j] F omits "fair."

[k] E: "the kings."

[l] "Sweet *(besiman)* to my palate"; B D E F G I: "fixed *(besisan)* upon my palate," i.e., I recite them constantly, but the sense is weak.

[m] "Reward" = *shakhar* (? a Hebraism); B G H J K L M N have the Aramaic synonym *ʾagar.*

[n] J K L M N: "and the reward of my commandments [*piqqudai* = ? Heb. *miṣwotai* in the sense of "good deeds"] is stored up for the world to come."

Notes, Chapter 2

[10] The citron *(ʾethrog)* recalls the festival of Sukkot, which commemorates the forty years' wandering in the Wilderness. This Wilderness association strengthens the contextualization of the verse to the Wilderness period.

[11] Tg. may be classifying the citron as an *ʾilan seraq* on the basis of m. Kil. 6:5, "all trees are *seraq* trees, except for the olive tree and the fig tree." Or it may be contrasting the citron with the *ʾilanei seraq* (Rashi: *"Like a tappuaḥ among the trees of the wood:* that is to say, better than *ʾilanei seraq"*). The citron produces (edible) fruit but little shade; the *ʾilanei seraq* produce much shade but no (edible) fruit. If Tg. is thinking of the citron's lack of shade, then the following, "I longed to sit in the shade of His Shekhinah," becomes pointed and may contain an allusion to the midrash found in Cant.R. 2:3 §1: "R. Ḥuna and R. Aḥa in the name of R. Zimra said: The *tappuaḥ* [Tg. citron] is shunned by all peoples when the sun beats down because it provides no shade. So all the nations refused to sit in the shadow of the Holy One, blessed be He, on the day of the giving of the Torah. Do you think Israel was the same? No, for it says, *For His shade I longed, and I sat [there]*: I longed for Him and I sat; it was I that longed, not the nations." On this interpretation one would expect the *ʾilanei seraq* to represent the gods of the nations, who might provide shade for their devotees but not the fruit of the Torah. So Rashi: *"So is my Beloved among the sons*: that is to say, among other gods, *For the Lord is a great God and a great king above all gods* (Ps 95:3). And just as no one sits out of choice beneath the *tappuaḥ* tree, because it has no shade, so the nations did not run to rest beneath Him to receive the Torah." However, Tg. actually equates the *ʾilanei seraq* with the angels. The equation may be polemical: angels did not give the Torah; angels should not be worshiped (see *Note* 13).

[12] There is probably an allusion to Lev 23:40 where the "goodly tree" *(ʿeṣ hadar)* is traditionally identified as the *ʾethrog.*

[13] The Midrash commonly claims that the angels were present at the Sinai theophany, appealing in proof to Ps 68:18, "The chariots of God are myriads, even thousands upon thousands; the Lord is among them, as at Sinai, in holiness" (Tg.: "The chariots of God are two myriad chariots of burning fire, with two thousand angels driving them; the Shekhinah of the Lord rested upon them at Mount Sinai in holiness"). Cf. Pesiq. Rab Kah. 12.22: "R. Abdimi of Haifa said . . . I learned that twenty-two thousand ministering angels came down with the Holy One on Mount Sinai . . . as many as there were males in the camp of the Levites came down: *The chariots of God: two myriads, and two thousand angels.*" See further Ginzberg, *Legends* 3:94; 6:38, n. 207. Christian exegetes used this tradition polemically to argue that the Torah was actually given at Sinai by angels, and was therefore inferior to God's direct revelation in Christ (Gal 3:19; Acts 7:53; Heb 2:2). Some Rabbinic authorities, probably aware of this argument, denied that the angels were present at Sinai (see, e.g., Pesiq. Rab. 33.10; further Ginzberg, *Legends* 6:47, n. 248). Tg. is careful to stress that it was God who gave the Torah, and the angels praised God for doing so.

[14] For the sweetness of Torah see Ps 19:11; 119:103; Ezek 3:1.

[15] "The world to come" here probably refers to the Messianic Age, which is not treated in the Tg. till ch. 8 but is anticipated several times earlier (e.g., 1:8, 17). At 1:3, however, Tg. may use the expression to denote immortality or the state of bliss after death (see *Note* 24 *ad loc.*).

4. Hebrew Text:

He brought me into the House of Wine,
And His banner was upon me in love.[16]

Targum:

The Congregation of Israel said: "The Lord brought me into the House of the Seat of Study[o]—Sinai[17]—to learn the Torah from the mouth of Moses the Great Scribe,[p][18] and the banner of His commandments I received upon myself in love,[q][19] and I said: All that the Lord commands I will do and I will obey."[20]

5. Hebrew Text:

Sustain me with raisin-cakes,[21]
Refresh me with apples,[22]
For I am sick with love.

Apparatus, Chapter 2

[o] "The House of the Seat of Study"; E: "the House of Assembly [= the Synagogue] and the House of Study [= the Yeshibah]."

[p] K L: "Moses the Great"; cf. "Shem the Great": Ps-J Gen. 22:19, "and the angels on high took Isaac and brought him to the Academy of Shem the Great"; and see Jast. 211a.

[q] G J N: "and the banner of His commandments was upon me in love." Cf. Hebrew.

Notes, Chapter 2

[16] Tg. takes this verse as Israel's description of how she was brought to Sinai, given the Torah, and accepted it with love. "Wine" = Torah: see Deut.R. 7.3 and Yalqut Shimʿoni, both quoting Prov 9:5, "Come, eat of my [Wisdom's] bread, and drink of the wine I have mingled." "House of Wine" symbolizes the House of Study, and then Sinai, where the Torah was first taught. God's "banner" is symbolic of God's commandments, which Israel takes upon herself. Cf. Num.R. 2.3; Cant.R. 2:4 §1: "What then is meant by *He brought me into the House of Wine?* The community of Israel said: The Holy One, blessed be He, brought me to a great cellar *[martef]* of wine, viz., Sinai. There He gave me banners of Torah *[diglei Torah]* and precepts and good deeds, and in great love I accepted them."

[17] The study of Torah and the House of Study (Beit Midrash) are central themes of Tg. Cant. (see *Intro.* 4.4). It is not surprising, therefore, that Tg. envisages the revelation of the Torah at Sinai essentially as a Beit Midrash experience—both for Moses (Pirqei de R. El. 46: "Moses spent forty days on the mountain, sitting down before the Holy One, blessed be He, like a disciple who sits before his teacher, reading the Written Torah, and repeating the Oral Torah which he had learnt"), and for Israel (Cant.R. 2:3 §4: "Israel spent twelve months in front of Sinai regaling themselves with the words of Torah").

[18] For Moses as "the Great Scribe" see 1:2, *Note* 17.

[19] The language echoes the common expression "taking upon oneself the yoke of the Torah/Kingdom of Heaven" (see 1:10, *Note* 78).

[20] Cf. Exod 24:7, "All that the Lord has spoken we will do, and obey"; parallels: Exod 19:8 and 24:3.

[21] Tg. takes this verse as addressed by Israel to Moses and Aaron at Sinai, asking them to mediate between her and God, and to teach her God's Torah. "Raisin-cakes" (Heb. *ʾashishot*) is interpreted as "the words of the Torah upon which the world is founded," probably by linking the word with Aramaic *ʾush,* "foundation" (Ezra 4:12; 5:16; 6:3; Tg. Mic. 1:6 [Heb. *yesod*]; b. B. Qam. 50a).

[22] Tg. takes the "apples" as symbolizing "the interpretation of the holy words that are sweet as apples." Thus for Tg. "apples" = Oral Torah, and "raisin-cakes" = Written Torah. Cant.R. 2:5 §1, according to one interpretation, equates "raisin-cakes" with "well-founded (*meʾushashot*) *halakhot*" and "apples" with "*haggadot*, which have a fragrance and taste like apples." According to another interpretation "raisin-cakes" on its own alludes to the dual Torah: "*Sustain me with raisin-cakes*: with two fires *(ʾishot)*—the Written Torah and the Oral Torah." It is unclear how Tg. got from "refresh me" (Heb. *rappeduni*) to "put [as] chains upon my neck" (see *Note* 27).

Targum:

But when I heard His voice speaking[r] from the midst of the flame of fire, I trembled and shrank back in fear. Then I approached Moses and Aaron[s23] and said to them: "*You* receive the sound[t] of the utterance[u] of the Holy One, blessed be He[v], from the midst of the fire,[24] and bring me into the house of study,[25] and sustain me with the words of the Torah upon which the world is founded,[w26] and put [as] chains upon my neck[27] the interpretation[x] of the holy words that are as sweet to my palate as apples from the Garden of Eden,[28] and I will be occupied with them. Perhaps I will be healed by them, for I am sick from love."[29]

6. Hebrew Text:

His left hand is under my head,
His right hand embraces me.[30]

Apparatus, Chapter 2

[r] C omits "speaking."

[s] I omits "Aaron" (see *Note* 23), but keeps the plural verbs and prepositions.

[t] "Sound" = *ql*; B reads "all" = *kl,* but it was the sound that caused the panic.

[u] "Utterance" = *ptgm'*; B D F I: "utterances" = *ptgmy*; E: "utterances of the Torah."

[v] "Of the Holy One, blessed be He"; D E F: "of the Lord" *(YYY).*

[w] G I J K L M N: "is founded" *('tbs[y]s).* A erroneously: *'tbsm.* Scribes regularly confuse the roots *bss* and *bsm.*

[x] "Interpretation" = *mpshr;* I J K L M N: *mprsh.* The latter may be preferable since *mpshr* should, strictly speaking, be used of interpreting a dream or riddle, whereas *mprsh* has a broader, more generic sense (see Jast. 1242a and 1249a).

Notes, Chapter 2

[23] Aaron is not in the biblical text (see *Note* 24). He has been added by the Tg. to explain the plural imperatives in Cant.

[24] Tg. contextualizes to Exod 20:15-16, where the people, overwhelmed by the theophany, require support: "And all the people perceived the thunderings, and the lightnings, and the voice of the horn, and the mountain smoking; and when the people saw it, they trembled, and stood afar off. And they said to Moses, Speak you with us, and we will hear; but let not God speak with us, lest we die"; Deut 5:22-27, ". . . We have heard His voice out of the midst of the fire . . . If we hear the voice of the Lord our God any more, then we shall die . . . Go you near, and hear all that the Lord our God shall say: and you speak unto us all that the Lord our God shall speak unto you; and we will hear it and do it." On the basis of Deut 5, Mek. deR. Ishmael, *Baḥodesh* 9, concludes that the people heard directly only the Ten Commandments.

[25] For Sinai as a House of Study see 1:4, *Note* 18.

[26] It is unclear whether Tg. means that the physical world or the moral order is based on Torah, or both. Both ideas are found in the Midrash. For the former see Gen.R. 1.1: "God looked into the Torah and created the world, as Torah declares, *In the beginning (re'shit) God created* (Gen 1:1), *beginning (re'shit)* referring to Torah, as in the verse, *The Lord made me as the beginning (re'shit) of His way* (Prov 8:22)"; m. 'Abot 3:15, "Beloved is Israel, for to them was given the precious instrument; still greater was the love, in that it was made known to them that to them was given the precious instrument by which the world was created, as it is written, *For I give you good doctrine; forsake not my Torah* (Prov 4:2)." For the latter see m. 'Abot 1:2, "The world rests on three pillars: the Torah, divine service, and acts of kindliness"; Tg. Cant. 1:15, "His righteous ones are the pillars of the world, set upon sockets of fine gold, that is [upon] the words of the Torah."

[27] The primary idea is that the Torah is an adornment for Israel (like a necklace or torque), but the wording also suggests obedience by alluding to the image of the Torah as a yoke (see Tg. Cant. 1:10, *Note* 78).

[28] "Sweet to my palate" echoes 2:3. On the sweetness of Torah see 1:10, *Note* 15. Cf. "apples from the Garden of Eden" with the "narcissus . . . from the Garden of Eden" and the "rose . . . of the Garden of Eden" in Tg. Cant. 2:1.

[29] On the basis of Exod 15:26 ("If you . . . will keep all His statutes, I will put none of these diseases upon you . . . for I am the Lord who heals you"), it was believed that keeping the Torah literally protected from disease, and words of Torah were frequently used as charms on Jewish amulets. Here, however, Israel's yearning for God—her lovesickness—is assuaged by study of the Torah. For Israel sick with love for God see Tg. Cant. 5:8; Midrash Ps. 9.17; 116.1.

[30] Israel describes God's protection in the wilderness, specifically during the period of wandering: cf. Num 10:33-34 (*Note* 34). Tg.'s treatment is uncharacteristically impressionistic (with exact equivalents unclear), and incoherent: a general

Targum:

When the people, the House of Israel,[y] were wandering in the Wilderness, four clouds of glory[31] surrounded them on four sides,[z] so that the evil eye[32] should have no power over them: one above them,[aa] so that the heat and the sun should not overwhelm them, nor rain and hail; one below them which carried them as a nursing-father carries the infant in his bosom;[33] one ran three days' journey before them to flatten mountains and to level valleys.[34]

Apparatus, Chapter 2

[y] A reads "Children of Israel," but the other mss. have the usual "House of Israel."

[z] "On four sides": lit. "from the four winds of the world," i.e., the four cardinal points of the compass; cf. "from the four sides of the world" (Tg. 2:14, *Apparatus bbb*).

[aa] C J K L M N omit, by parablepsis, "so that the evil eye should have no power over them: one above them." L^2, however, adds the words.

Notes, Chapter 2

statement asserts that the "clouds" protect from the evil eye, but when Tg. lists the benefits conferred by the clouds they are different, and only three clouds are itemized rather than four (the cloud that went behind is missing). "His left hand is under my head" is interpreted as God's continuing protection of Israel, "His right hand embraces me" as Israel's continuing communion with God through study of the Torah as she marched on from Sinai. Tg. interprets the repetition of this verse in 8:3 differently, though in both cases it sees a reference specifically to protection from demonic attack.

[31] The single biblical "cloud" (Num 10:34), symbol of the Shekhinah, has become four clouds to express the thought of God's all-round protection of Israel. The expression "cloud of glory" is not biblical (though note Exod 16:10 and the *ʿanan kabed* in Exod 19:16), but is common in the Midrash. For speculation on the "clouds" see Mek. deR. Ishmael, *Beshallaḥ* 1: "*And the Lord went before them by day* (Exod 13:21): You will have to say: There were seven clouds . . . four on the four sides of them, one above them, one beneath them, and one that advanced before them on the road, raising the depressions and lowering the elevations, as it is said: *Every valley shall be lifted up, and every mountain and hill made level, and the rough places a plain* (Isa 40:2). It also killed the snakes and the scorpions, and swept and sprinkled the road before them. R. Judah says: There were thirteen clouds, two on every side, two over them, two beneath them, and one that advanced before them. R. Josiah says: There were four, one in front of them, one behind them, one above them, and one beneath them. Rabbi says: There were two."

[32] It is unclear whether Tg. uses "evil eye" here in a precise, technical sense, or generally to represent the demonic powers against which the Shekhinah protected Israel. According to the Midrash the "evil eye" was active in inducing Israel to make the Golden Calf (it is, in effect, equivalent to Israel's *yeṣer ha-raʿ*). It was, therefore, responsible for Moses breaking the first tables of the Torah, when he saw the Calf. But the Midrash equally insists that the erection of the Tabernacle led to the expulsion of demons from Israel's midst. See Ginzberg, *Legends* 3:140, 186–87; further Ulmer, *The Evil Eye in the Bible and Rabbinic Literature*.

[33] Cf. Num 11:12, "Have I [Moses] conceived all this people? Have I brought them forth, that You [God] should say to me, Carry them in your bosom, as a nursing-father carries the sucking child, unto the land which You swore unto their fathers?"; Deut 1:31, ". . . and in the Wilderness, where you have seen how the Lord Your God carried you, as a man carries his son, in all the way that you went, until you came to this place." The language inevitably recalls the "eagles' wings" of Exod 19:4. Cf. Mek. deR. Ishmael, *Baḥodesh* 2, which links the two images: "*How I bore you on eagles' wings* (Exod 19:4): How is the eagle distinguished from all other birds? All the other birds carry their young between their feet, being afraid of other birds flying higher above them. The eagle, however, is afraid only of men who might shoot at him. He, therefore, prefers that the arrows lodge in him rather than his children. To give a parable: A man was going on the road with his son walking in front of him. If robbers, who might seek to capture the son, come from the front, he takes him from before him and puts him behind him. If a wolf comes from behind, he takes his son from behind and puts him in front. If robbers come from in front and wolves from behind, he takes his son and puts him on his shoulders. As it is said: *And in the Wilderness, where you have seen how the Lord Your God carried you, as a man carries his son* (Deut 1:31)."

[34] Cf. Num 10:33-34, "And they set forward from the Mount of the Lord three days' journey; and the ark of the covenant of the Lord went before them three days' journey, to seek out a resting place for them. And the cloud of the Lord was over them by day, when they set forward from the camp." See Ps-J Num. 10:34 and Sifrei Num. §83. The flattening of the mountains and the raising of the valleys echoes Isa 40:4, which Tg. doubtless took as a description of the straightening of the path of the exiles through the wilderness in the Messianic Age. Thus again Tg. anticipates the Messianic Age.

It killed all the fiery serpents and scorpions that were in the Wilderness,[bb][35] and it spied out for them a fit place to lodge, so that they could engage in the study of the Torah[36] which had been given to them by the right hand[37] of the Lord.

7. Hebrew Text:

I adjure you,[38] Daughters of Jerusalem,[39]
By the gazelles, or by the hinds of the field,[40]
That you do not awaken or stir up love,
Until it please.[41]

Targum:

After that Moses was told by prophecy from before the Lord[42] to send messengers to spy out the land of Canaan.[cc][43] When they returned from spying they put out a bad report about the land of Israel,[44] and they [the Israelites] were detained for forty years in the wilderness.[45] Moses the teacher of Israel[dd] opened his mouth and said: "I adjure you, congregation

Apparatus, Chapter 2

[bb] E omits "it killed all the fiery serpents and scorpions that were in the wilderness."

[cc] B D E F G I J M N omit "of Canaan."

[dd] D E F omit "the teacher of Israel."

Notes, Chapter 2

35 For the fiery serpents see Tg. to 1:9 (*Note* 71) and 2:14. Cf. Mek. deR. Ishmael, *Beshallaḥ* 1 (quoted in *Note* 31 above).

36 Again Tg. stresses the study of the Torah: Israel's procession through the Wilderness was one long Shiʿur (cf. *Note* 17).

37 Cf. Deut 33:2, "The Lord came from Sinai . . . at His right hand was a fiery law for them" (see Sifrei Deut. §343). God's right hand delivered Israel at the Sea (Exod 14:30), gave the Torah at Sinai (Deut 33:2), and will redeem Israel at the end of days (see 3 Enoch 48A:1-10; and cf. the representations of the right hand of God in synagogue art in late antiquity, e.g., at Beit Alpha in the mosaic panel depicting the ʿAqedah).

38 Tg. takes this verse as addressed by Moses to the Israelites after the spies returned from spying out the Land (see *Note* 44). The same adjuration occurs again at 3:5 and 8:4 (cf. also 5:8), and in the two other occurrences Tg. takes it, as here, as an exhortation not to force God's will or try to hasten the redemption by going up prematurely to the Land (cf. *Note* 49). For the possible relevance of such an exhortation to the Tg.'s own times see *Intro.* 4.6.

39 "Daughters of Jerusalem" = Congregation of Israel.

40 "Gazelles" *(ṣebaʾot)* is taken as referring to the Lord of Hosts *(YYY ṣebaʾot),* and "hinds *(ʾaylot)* of the field" to "the mighty ones of the Land of Israel" (cf. Heb. *ʾayil,* "leader, chief": see BDB 18a and note especially *ʾeilei ha-ʾareṣ* = the Judean aristocracy in Ezek 17:13). It is unclear what an adjuration by "the mighty ones of the Land of Israel" might signify. Perhaps Moses invokes all heavenly and earthly authority. The Midrash speculates at length on the phrase: cf. Cant.R. 2:7 §1: "*I adjure you, daughters of Jerusalem.* With what did God adjure Israel? R. Eliezer said: He adjured them by the heavens and the earth (cf. Deut 30:19)—*by the gazelles (bi-ṣebaʾot)*: by the upper hosts *(ṣebaʾot)* and the lower hosts, by two hosts."

41 Tg. takes this as an exhortation not to arouse prematurely the desire to go up to the Land until God's time to go up has come: "until it [= God's will] should please." Cf. Cant.R. 2:7 §1: "*Until it please*: the *it* here refers to the kingdom of heaven. When the Attribute of Justice shall please of itself, then *I* shall bring the deliverance with loud trumpetings and shall not delay. Hence it says, *Until it please*" (see *Notes* on 8:4).

42 Tg. faithfully reproduces the reverential, anti-anthropomorphic Targumic style (cf. *Note* 47).

43 Cf. Num 13:1, "The Lord spoke to Moses, saying: Send men that they may spy out the land of Canaan."

44 Cf. Num 13:25, 32, "And they returned from spying out the Land at the end of forty days . . . and they spread an evil report about the Land they had spied out." For the forty years see *Note* 45.

45 Cf. Num 14:21-36, ". . . your carcasses shall fall in the wilderness, and all that were numbered of you, according to your whole number, from twenty years old and upwards . . . shall not come into the Land . . . and your children shall be wanderers in the Wilderness forty years, until your carcasses be consumed in the Wilderness . . . And . . . those men who brought an evil

of Israel, by the Lord of hosts and by the mighty ones of the Land of Israel,[ee] not to presume[46] to go up to the land of Canaan, until it should be the will of the Lord,[47] and until all the generation[ff] of the men of war perish utterly from the midst of the camp[48]—as your brothers, the sons of Ephraim, presumed when they went out from Egypt thirty years before the [appointed] time had arrived, and they fell at the hands of the Philistines who dwelt in Gath, and they killed them.[49] Rather wait out the period of forty years, and after that your sons will enter and possess it [the land of Israel]."[50]

Apparatus, Chapter 2

[ee] J K L M N omit "by the Lord of Hosts and by the mighty ones of the Land of Israel."

[ff] J K L M N omit "generation." The singular emphatic *dara'* is syntactically awkward. N^2 and Miq. Ged. read plural construct *darei,* but this, like the omission of the word, is probably a secondary correction. It is better to emend to singular construct *dar* and assume a dittography of *'alef.*

Notes, Chapter 2

report of the Land have died of the plague before the Lord." See further *Note* 48. Tg. expects the reader to know that the bad report of the spies led to a full-scale rebellion against Moses and Aaron (Num 14), and this is why "the Israelites were detained for forty years in the wilderness."

[46] The language is strong. "Presumption" *(zadon)* involves premeditated and willful rebellion against God (BDB 267b; Jast. 380b).

[47] Lit. "until there should be a will from before the Lord": again, reverential Targumic style (see *Note* 42).

[48] Cf. Deut 2:14, "And the days in which we came from Qadesh-barnea, until we were come over the brook Zered, were thirty and eight years; until all the generation of the men of war were consumed from the midst of the camp." See further *Note* 45.

[49] According to a widespread Rabbinic tradition a company of Ephraimites left Egypt thirty years before the Exodus, marched to Canaan, attacked Gath, and were exterminated. They miscalculated the time of the Exodus by reckoning the four hundred years to the end of the Egyptian captivity from the date of the covenant with Abraham between the pieces (Gen 15:13-14), rather than from the birth of Isaac (for the calculation see Abraham ibn Daud, *Sefer ha-Qabbalah* 1; further *Note* 55 below). This story, which was frequently used to counsel against calculating the end or forcing the redemption (e.g., Ibn Daud, *Sefer ha-Qabbalah* 1, ". . . until the emergence from Ephraim and Gilead (?) of the false prophets who misled Israel and were killed"; Maimonides, *Epistle to the Yemen* 3; cf. Tg. to 8:13, *Note* 55), was based on exegesis of Ps 78:9 and 1 Chr 7:20-22, but it also has certain similarities to Num 14:40-45, where the Israelites "presume" to go up "to the top of the mountain" without the accompanying presence of God and are defeated by the Amalekites and Canaanites. Like the Tg., Cant. R. 2:7 §1 sees in Cant 2:7 an allusion to the premature exodus of the Ephraimites: "R. Ḥelbo said: Four adjurations are mentioned here (Cant 2:7; 3:5; 5:8; 8:4). God adjured Israel that they should not rebel against the governments, that they should not seek to hasten the end, that they should not reveal their mysteries to other nations, and that they should not attempt to go out from the Diaspora by force, for if they do, why should the King Messiah come to gather the exiles of Israel? R. Onia said: He addressed to them four adjurations corresponding to the four generations who tried to hasten the end and came to grief, namely once in the days of Amram, once in the days of Dinai, once in the days of Ben Koziba, and once in the days of Shuthelah the son of Ephraim (see 1 Chr 7:20-21), as it says, *The Children of Israel were as archers handling the bow* (Ps 78:9). Some say, once in the days of Amram, once in the generation of the great persecution, once in the days of Ben Koziba, and once in the days of Shuthelah the son of Ephraim, as it says, *The Children of Ephraim were as archers handling the bow.* They reckoned [that the four hundred years to the termination of the Egyptian bondage began] from the time when the decree was pronounced (Gen 15:13-14), but it really began from when Isaac was born. [*Your seed* in Gen 15:13 = Isaac, on the basis of Gen 21:12, *In Isaac shall your seed be called.* But Isaac was not born till thirty years later.] What did they do? They assembled and went forth to battle, and many of them were slain. Why was this? *Because they did not believe in the Lord and did not trust in His salvation* (Ps 78:22), but anticipated the end and transgressed the adjuration." On the exodus of the Ephraimites see further Mek. deR. Ishmael, *Beshallaḥ* 1 and *Shirta* 9; Mek. deRashbi 37-38; b. Sanh. 92b; Exod.R. 20.11; Pirqei de R. El. 48; Ps-J Exod. 13:17; Tg. Ps. 78:9; Tg. 1 Chr. 7:21-22; Ginzberg, *Legends* 3:17–18; 6:2, n. 10; Heinemann, "The Messiah of Ephraim," *Tarbiṣ* 40 and *HTR* 68; Mulder, "1 Chronik 7,21B-23 und die rabbinische Tradition."

[50] Cf. Num 14:31, "But your little ones . . . shall know the Land you have rejected." In the Tg. here the forty years in the wilderness is seen as punishment for the rebellion after the return of the spies. Moses exhorts the Israelites to "wait out" the full term of their punishment, and not to try to shorten it. In Tg. to 3:5 the forty years in the wilderness is seen in a more positive light.

8. Hebrew Text:

The voice of my Beloved![51]
Behold He comes,
Leaping over the mountains,
Jumping over the hills.[52]

Targum:

King Solomon said: "When the people, the House of Israel, were dwelling[gg] in Egypt, their complaint went up to the heavens above.[53] Behold, then the Glory of the Lord was revealed to Moses[hh] on Mount Horeb, and He sent him to Egypt to deliver them and to bring them out[ii] from the oppression of the tyranny of the Egyptians,[54] and He leaped[jj] over the [appointed] time on account of the merit of the Patriarchs who are likened to mountains, and

Apparatus, Chapter 2

[gg] C E F G: "dwelling" *(ytbyn)*. A B D H I have *yhybyn,* which yields little sense in context. K L N: "serving" *(plhyn);* J: *yhybyn plhyn,* a conflate reading.

[hh] A accidentally omits "to Moses." The words are added in the margin and in the other mss.

[ii] E K L N omit "and to bring them out" by parablepsis.

[jj] The mss. are very unsure as to the form of the verb here. Read either *tpz* with A N^2 (Jast. 545b) or, better, *qpz* with the Arukh (Jast. 1399a; Sokoloff 499b).

Notes, Chapter 2

[51] Tg. takes this verse as spoken by Israel during her captivity in Egypt: she hails her Deliverer, who hastens to her rescue. God is the "Beloved"; God's "voice," God's spokesperson, is Moses (cf. Exod 3:18, "they shall hearken to your voice"; 4:12, "I will be with your mouth and teach you what you shall speak"; 4:16, "you shall be to him [Aaron] in God's stead"). Having in the previous verse brought the reader to the borders of the Promised Land, Tg. now backtracks to the Egyptian bondage and begins his third and final reprise of the Exodus and the Wilderness wanderings. Both verses are thematically linked, however, by an interest in the chronology of the Exodus.

[52] The primary equation of "mountains" with the Patriarchs and of "hills" with the Matriarchs is helped by the fact that *harim* is masculine and *geba'ot* feminine. (Exod.R. 15.4 derives mountains = Patriarchs from Mic 6:2; cf. Gen.R. 50.11, "mountain" in Gen 19:17 = Abraham.) The interpretation is standard in the Midrash (see *Note* 56). But Tg. also takes "mountains" and "hills" secondarily as denoting chronologies or calculations of time: thus God "leaping over the mountains and jumping over the hills" shows God's disregard for chronology and his hastening of the redemption from Egypt (cf. Cant.R. 2:8 §1 quoted in *Note* 55). Canticles 2:8 was widely cited in the Midrash in the context of explaining the conflicting biblical chronologies of the Exodus (see *Note* 55).

[53] Cf. Exod 2:23, ". . . the Children of Israel sighed by reason of the bondage, and they cried, and their complaint [Onq. *qebilathon*] came up to God by reason of the bondage"; Exod 3:7, "The Lord said: I have surely seen the affliction of my people that are in Egypt, and have heard their complaint [Onq. *qebilathon*] by reason of their taskmasters; for I know their pains."

[54] Cf. Exod 3:1–4:17, ". . . and he [Moses] came to the mountain of God, to Horeb. And the Angel of the Lord appeared to him in a flame of fire . . . Come now, therefore, and I will send you to Pharaoh, that you may bring forth my people the Children of Israel out of Egypt . . . and I will bring you up out of the affliction of Egypt . . . ."

He jumped one hundred and ninety years[55] over the time of slavery on account of the righteousness of the Matriarchs[56] who are compared[kk] to hills."[ll]

9. Hebrew Text:

My Beloved[57] *is like a gazelle or the young of the harts;*[58]
Behold, He stands behind our wall,

Apparatus, Chapter 2

[kk] A F accidentally omit "who are compared." The other mss. have the words.

[ll] "Hills" = *galmata'*. B G H I J K L M N read *gib'ata'* as in the Hebrew.

Notes, Chapter 2

[55] The duration of the Egyptian bondage and the date of the Exodus are among the major problems of Jewish chronography. According to Gen 15:13 the bondage would last 400 years. According to Exod 12:40-41 it lasted 430 years. However, the internal chronology of Genesis and Exodus suggests that the actual duration was much shorter. On one common calculation, from Jacob's entry into Egypt until the Exodus was only 210 years: thus Jochebed, who was born in the year Jacob went down to Egypt, was 130 when Moses was born, and Moses was 80 in the year of the Exodus (see Pirqei de R. El. 48). One way of reconciling the contradiction was to calculate the 400 years from the birth of Isaac (*Note* 49), or the 430 years from the Covenant between the Pieces (Mek. deR. Ishmael, *Piṣha* 14). Another was to suppose that the period of the Egyptian bondage (from Jacob's entry into Egypt till the Exodus) was meant to be 400 or 430 years, but God graciously shortened it. Tg., which adopts the 400-year calculation of Gen 15:13, takes this line. However, he seems to be guilty of double counting, because in v. 7 he implied that the 400 years were to be reckoned from the birth of Isaac (*Note* 49)—unless he holds that God's shortening of the time involved recalculating the starting point as being the birth of Isaac (cf. Rashi to Cant 2:11, "*For lo, the winter is past*. These are the four hundred years that I skipped over, so as to reckon them from the birth of Isaac"). This would fit well with his assertion that the time was shortened on account of the merits of the Patriarchs. Tg. is probably thinking primarily of the 'Aqedah: God, in effect, decided to backdate the 400 years to the Binding of Isaac. Tg.'s interpretation agrees broadly with Cant.R. 2:8 §1: "R. Judah said: *The voice of my Beloved, behold he comes*. This refers to Moses. When he came he said to Israel, In this month you shall be delivered. They said to him, Our teacher Moses, how can we be delivered? Did not the Holy One say to Abraham, *And they shall serve them; and they shall afflict them four hundred years* (Gen 15:13), and so far only two hundred and ten have passed? He said to them: Since God desires to deliver you, He takes no heed of your reckonings, but *leaps over the mountains*. The *mountains* and *hills* mentioned here refer to the calculations and periods. He leaps over calculations and periods and terminuses, and in this month you are to be delivered."

[56] "The merit of the Patriarchs . . . the righteousness of the Matriarchs": the variation in wording is purely stylistic. The doctrine of *zekhut 'abot* is central to Tg., the most meritorious act being the Binding of Isaac (cf. Tg. to 1:13). Tg., interestingly, includes here the *zekhut 'immot* (see *Intro.* 4.3). Neofiti and FT to Deut. 33:15 identify the Patriarchs as Abraham, Isaac, and Jacob, and the Matriarchs as Sarah, Rebecca, Rachel, and Leah: the land of Joseph will be fruitful "through the merit of our Fathers, Abraham, Isaac, and Jacob, who are compared to *mountains*, and through the merit of the Mothers, Sarah, Rebecca, Rachel, and Leah, who are compared to *hills* (Neof.)." The idea that "mountains" and "hills" here refer to the Patriarchs and the Matriarchs, on whose account the Israelites were redeemed from the Egyptian bondage, is common in the Midrash: see, e.g., b. Rosh. Hash. 11a; b. Soṭah. 11b; Exod.R. 15.4; Pirqei de R. El. 48.

[57] Tg. contextualizes to the night of the first Passover in Egypt: Israel dramatically describes how God "went through the land of Egypt" (Exod 12:12; cf. 11:4; 12:23). Tg. interweaves Cant 2:9 with Exodus 12: "(7) And they shall take of the blood and put it on the two side-posts and on the lintel, upon the houses wherein they shall eat it. (8) They shall eat the flesh . . . roast with fire, and unleavened bread; with bitter herbs shall they eat it. . . . (12) For I will go through the land of Egypt in that night, and will smite all the firstborn of the land of Egypt. (13) And the blood shall be to you for a sign (*'ot*) upon the houses where you are; and when I see the blood, I will pass over you. . . . (22) And you shall take a bunch of hyssop, and dip it in the blood that is in the basin. . . . (23) For the Lord will pass through to smite the Egyptians; and when He sees the blood upon the lintel, and on the two side-posts, the Lord will pass over the door, and will not suffer the destroyer to come into your houses to smite you. . . . (27) It is the sacrifice of the Lord's passover, for that He passed over the houses of the Children of Israel in Egypt, when He smote the Egyptians and delivered our houses . . . ."

[58] "Gazelle" and "young hart" are taken as symbols of God's swiftness and eagerness in bringing the redemption. Cf. Mek. deR. Ishmael, *Piṣha* 7: "*And you shall eat it in haste* (Exod 12:11) . . . Abba Ḥanin in the name of R. Eliezer says: This refers to the haste of the Shekhinah. And though there is no proof for this, there is a hint of it: *The voice of my Beloved! Behold He comes . . . behold He stands behind our wall* (Cant 2:8-9)."

He looks in through the windows,
He peers through the lattices.[59]

Targum:

The Congregation of Israel said: "At the time when the Glory of the Lord was revealed in Egypt on the night of the Passover, and He slew every firstborn, He rode upon the swift cloud[60] and ran like a gazelle and like the young of the hart,[mm] and He protected the houses wherein we were. He took up a position behind our wall, looked in through the windows[nn] and peered through the lattices, and He saw the blood of the Passover sacrifice[oo] and the blood of the decree of circumcision marked on our doors.[61] He hastened from the heavens above[pp] and saw His people eating the festival sacrifice, roasted with fire, together with

Apparatus, Chapter 2

[mm] Cant.R. 2:9 §1 appears to quote a Targum text here not found in any of the extant mss. *(ʾwrzyhwn dʾyltʾ).*

[nn] Reading *kwwtʾ* with C D[2] F H I J K L M N (Jast. 617a). A has *bktʾ*, a corruption of *kbtʾ*, a phonetic spelling of *kwwtʾ;* cf. B *kbʾtʾ*.

[oo] "Sacrifice" = *nksʾ*; K L: "libation" = *nyskʾ*.

[pp] J K L M N add "and took pity" by vertical dittography from the line below.

Notes, Chapter 2

59 The "wall," the "windows," and the "lattices" belong to the houses of the Israelites in Egypt. The Beloved's action is not seen as sinister, threatening, or furtive, but as protective.

60 Cf. Isa 19:1, "Behold the Lord rides upon a swift cloud [Tg. the cloud of His Glory] and comes to Egypt: and the idols of Egypt shall be moved at His presence, and the heart of Egypt shall melt in the midst of it." The cloud, the outward manifestation of the Shekhinah, here symbolizes God's returning presence, echoes the clouds of Tg. 2:6, and links Passover and Sinai, where God also descended in a cloud to give the Torah (Exod 19:9; cf. Midrash Ps. 104.6).

61 The connection between the Passover blood and the blood of circumcision is based partly on Exod 12:48, "Let all his males be circumcised . . . no uncircumcised person shall eat thereof [the Passover meal]," and partly on the fact that both are called "signs" *(ʾotot)*: see Exod 12:13 and Gen 17:11. Tg. probably reflects the late tradition that the Israelites actually mixed together the blood of the Paschal lamb with the blood of circumcision and marked their doors with that. According to the Midrash the Israelites "abolished the covenant of circumcision after the death of Joseph, saying, Let us become like the Egyptians" (Exod.R. 1.8). Hence they had to be circumcised before they could eat the Passover. See Ps-J Exod. 12:13, "Take care to mix the blood of the Paschal sacrifice with that of the circumcision, to make with it a sign on the houses where you dwell. I will see the merit of the blood and I will have mercy on you, and the Angel of Death, to whom has been granted the power to exterminate, will have no power over you." The thought may be that the Passover blood was efficacious because it reminded God of the blood of the covenant. Cf. the tradition, which Tg. could well have used here but did not, that it was efficacious because it reminded God of the blood of the ʿAqedah (Mek. deR. Ishmael, *Pisḥa* 7, "*When I see the blood* [Exod 12:13], I see the blood of the Binding of Isaac"; Exod.R. 15.11 dates the ʿAqedah to Passover). The Midrash claims that the Israelites were godless in Egypt, worshiping idols, and filling the theatres and circuses (Ginzberg, *Legends* 5:395, n. 29), but because they obeyed the two divine commandments of killing the Paschal lamb and circumcision they were saved: see Pesiq. Rab Kah. 7.6: "Or, by *because of the judgments* (Ps 119:62), David meant: Because of the judgments which You brought upon the Egyptians in Egypt; and because of the mercy which You showed our fathers in Egypt at a time when they did not have the merit of obedience to Your various commandments, obedience whereby they might have gained redemption; for at that time they were obedient to only two of Your commandments, those concerned with the blood of the Passover and with the blood of circumcision. Of His mercy, then, it is written, *When I passed by you, and saw you wallowing in your blood, I said: Through your bloods live* (Ezek 16:6)—*through your bloods*, that is, through the blood of the Passover lamb and the blood of circumcision." Cf. FT to Exod. 12:13; Tg. Ezek. 16:16; Pesiq. Rab Kah. 5.6; Pesiq. Rab. 15.17; Mek. deR. Ishmael, *Pisḥa* 5; Exod.R. 12.10; 12.22; further Le Déaut, *La nuit pascale* 209–12.

chervil, endives,[62] and unleavened bread, and He took pity on us, and did not give permission to the Destroying Angel[63] to do us any harm."

10. Hebrew Text:

My Beloved answered and said to me:
Rise up, My Darling, My Fair One, and come away![64]

Targum:

And when it was morning[65] my Beloved answered and said to me: "Rise up,[qq] Congregation of Israel, My Darling from of old,[66] fair in deeds! Come, depart from the slavery of the Egyptians!"

11. Hebrew:

For lo, the winter is past,
The rain is over and gone.[67]

Apparatus, Chapter 2

[qq] N adds "from the slavery of the Egyptians" by vertical dittography.

Notes, Chapter 2

[62] Tg. offers "chervil" *(tamkha')* and "endives" *('ulshin)* as examples of the "bitter herbs" (Heb. *merorim*) that Exod 12:8 stipulates should be eaten on Passover. Ps-J uses the same two plants to translate "bitter herbs" in Exod 12:8, "They shall eat it [the flesh] roast with fire, and unleavened bread, together with chervil and endives." Cf. the list of bitter herbs in m. Pesaḥ. 2:6, "These are the herbs by [the eating of] which at Passover a man fulfils his duty: lettuce *(ḥazeret)*, endives *('ulshin)*, chervil *(tamkha')*, snakeroot *(harhabina')*, and dandelion *(maror)*." The identifications of these plants are much debated: see the discussion in y. Pesaḥ. II, 29c and b. Pesaḥ. 39a, where other examples of "bitter herbs" are given.

[63] Exodus 12:23 speaks only of "the Destroyer" (Heb. *ha-mashḥit*), Tg. Cant. of "a Destroying *Angel*" *(mal'akh meḥabbel)*, through assimilation of this passage to 2 Sam 24:16 and 1 Chr 21:15-16, where the Destroying *Angel (ha-mal'akh ha-mashḥit* = Tg. *mal'akha' dimeḥabbel)* is described as a gigantic figure, sword in hand. The Targumic *mal'akh meḥabbel* recalls the common Rabbinic expression *mal'akhei ḥabbalah*, "angels of destruction" (e.g., b. Ber. 51a; Pesiq. Rab. 10.9). Originally this phrase probably meant "agents of destruction" and denoted demons. In the Gaonic period, however, *mal'akhei* was taken in its normal sense as referring to angels. Ps-J Exod. 12:23 also speaks of "the Destroying *Angel*," which earlier (to Exod 12:13) it had identified with the Angel of Death, i.e., Death personified. See further on Tg. Cant. 4:6.

[64] Israel tells how God addressed her on the morning after the first Passover and told her to leave Egypt. "Fair one" = "fair in deeds." The contextualization of this verse to the Exodus is common in the Midrash: cf. Cant.R. 2:9 §§4-5: "*My Beloved answered and said to me.* What did He say to me? *This month shall be to you the beginning of months* (Exod 12:2). Another explanation: *My Beloved answered and said to me.* R. Azariah said: Are not 'speaking' and 'saying' the same thing? What it means, however, is: He spoke to me by the hand of Moses and said to me by the hand of Aaron. What did He say to me? *Rise up My Darling, My Fair One. Rise up* means 'bestir yourself' [to keep the precepts of Passover and circumcision]. Another explanation: *Rise up,* O Daughter of Abraham, to whom were addressed the words, *Get out of your country and from your kindred* (Gen 12:1). *My Darling, My Fair One,* O Daughter of Isaac, who drew close to me and glorified me on the altar." See also Exod.R. 15.1.

[65] Cf. Exod 12:22, "None of you shall go out of the door of his house until the morning."

[66] Cf. Jer 31:3, "The Lord appeared of old [Heb. *meraḥoq* = Tg. *milleqadmin*] to me, saying, I have loved you with everlasting love: therefore with loving-kindness have I drawn you."

[67] God continues to address Israel. "Winter" = "the time of servitude"; "is past" = "has been cut short"; "the rain" = "the tyranny of the Egyptians." Broadly similar interpretations of the verse are common in the Midrash: cf. Cant.R. 2:11 §1: "*For*

Targum:

"For lo,[rr] the time of servitude, which is likened to winter, has ended, and the years about which I spoke to Abraham between the pieces have been cut short,[68] and the tyranny[69] of the Egyptians, which is compared to the [period of] incessant[ss] rain has passed and gone. You shall not see them ever again."[70]

12. Hebrew Text:

The flowers have appeared in the land;[71]
The time of pruning[72] *has come,*
And the voice of the turtledove has been heard in our land.[73]

Apparatus, Chapter 2

[rr] B G H I J K L M N omit "lo," but cf. Hebrew.

[ss] "Incessant" = *tryd'* (Prov 19:13; 27:15; Jast. 550a). C substitutes the more common synonym *tdyr'* (Jast. 1647b). B H I G omit. "The word *geshem* always designates heavy rain, as in Gen 7:12, and is occasionally accompanied by words to emphasize the point. 1 Kgs 18:41; Ezek 13:11, 13" (Pope). *Tryd'* makes clear that the comparison is with the period of continuous rain during winter. See *Note* 69.

Notes, Chapter 2

lo, the winter is past. This refers to the four hundred years during which our ancestors were condemned to be in Egypt. *The rain is over and gone.* This refers to the two hundred and ten years [that they actually spent there: see *Note* 55]. Are not 'rain' and 'winter' the same thing? R. Tanḥuma said: The real hardship [of winter] is its rainy period. So the real bondage of Israel in Egypt was the eighty-six years from the birth of Miriam." Further: Exod.R. 15.1; Pesiq. Rab. 15.10, 11; Pesiq. Rab Kah. 5.9.

[68] Cf. Gen 15:10-16, especially 13, "And He said to Abraham: Know of a surety that your seed shall be a stranger in a land not theirs, and shall serve them; and they shall afflict them for four hundred years." On the cutting short of the four hundred years see *Note* 55.

[69] "Tyranny" (Aram: *marwat*) plays on the "bitterness" *(√mrr)* of the Egyptian bondage. It probably does not cover precisely the same period as the "servitude" mentioned earlier, but refers to the eighty-six years of particular oppression beginning, according to Rabbinic tradition, with the birth of Miriam, who was so called because the Egyptians had begun to make the Israelites' lives especially bitter (Exod 1:14). Just as the period of incessant rain (note Tg.'s addition of the adjective!) is shorter than the whole winter, so the time of harshest tyranny in Egypt was shorter than the period of total servitude (see *Note* 67).

[70] Cf. Exod 14:13, ". . . for whereas you have seen the Egyptians today, you shall see them again no more forever." Tg. Cant. here agrees exactly with Onq.'s rendering of "you shall see them again no more forever." It is possible that Tg. interpreted the dative *lo* in *halakh lo* as the negative, and hence saw an allusion to the emphatically negative statement in Exod 14:13. Cf. Pesiq. Rab. 29/30A where *lh* in Ruth 2:14 (without *mappiq*) is taken as the negative *lo'*.

[71] God continues to address Israel on the point of her departure from Egypt. Hebrew *niṣṣanim* is found only here in the Bible, but it is obvious to relate it to *neṣ* and *niṣṣah,* "blossom" (BDB 665a; Jast. 927a). The basis of Tg.'s rendering, "palm branches" *(lulabei de-tamar),* is uncertain, but the identification with Moses and Aaron is found also in the Midrash (see *Note* 74). "The land" is taken as the land of Egypt, possibly in contrast to "our land" at the end of the verse, which has implicitly been identified with the Land of Israel.

[72] Hebrew *zamir* could be related either to √*zmr* = "sing," or √*zmr* = "prune." Tg. clearly takes the latter derivation, and relates the "pruning" to the cutting off of the Egyptian firstborn (see further *Note* 76).

[73] Tg. takes "the voice of the turtledove" as referring to the proclamation of the redemption uttered by the holy spirit in fulfillment of the promise to Abraham "between the pieces" (Gen 15:14)—an event that happened in the Land of Israel ("our Land"). See *Note* 77.

Targum:

And Moses and Aaron, who are compared to palm branches,[tt][74] have appeared in order to work miracles in the land of Egypt.[75] The time for cutting off the firstborn has arrived,[76] and the voice of the holy spirit,[77] [proclaiming] the redemption[uu] of which I spoke[vv] to Abraham, your forefather,[ww] you have already heard[xx]—how I said to him: "Moreover, the people whom they shall serve will I judge, and after that they will depart with much possessions."[78] Now[yy] I want[zz] to perform what I promised to him through My Word.[79]

Apparatus, Chapter 2

[tt] Reading *llwlby* with the rest of the mss. for A's *llwby.*

[uu] Reading *pwrq'n'* with the rest of the mss. for A's *pwrq'*. The *d-* that precedes this word is *d- recitativum* after the verb of saying implicit in *ql*.

[vv] Reading *d'mryt* with the rest of the mss. for A's *w'mryt.*

[ww] D E F read "to your forefather" instead of "to Abraham, your forefather."

[xx] K L omit "the redemption of which I spoke to Abraham, your forefather, you have already heard" by parablepsis (*d'mryt* to *d'mryt*)

[yy] "Now" = *kdw*; B D E F G I J K L M N have the synonym *k'n.*

[zz] J K L M N omit "I want," but a verb is necessary.

Notes, Chapter 2

[74] A number of Midrashim, like the Tg., identify the *niṣṣanim* with Moses and Aaron, though none understands *niṣṣanim* as "palm branches." Cf. Cant.R. 2:12 §1: "*The flowers (niṣṣanim) have appeared on the earth.* The conquerors *(naṣohot)* have appeared on the earth. Who are they? Moses and Aaron, as it says, *And the Lord spoke to Moses and Aaron in the land of Egypt, saying* (Exod 12:1)." Further Pesiq. Rab. 15.11; Pesiq. Rab Kah. 5.9: "*The flowers have appeared on the earth*—[the fame of] Moses and Aaron flourishes."

[75] The "miracles" are both the signs by which Moses convinced the Israelites that he was God's emissary (Exod 4:1-9, 29-31), and the signs he and Aaron performed to persuade Pharaoh to let the Israelites go (7:8–11:10).

[76] Cf. Exod 12:12, "I will go through the land of Egypt in that night, and I will smite all the firstborn." Cant.R. 2:12 §1: "*The time of pruning has come*: the time has come for the uncircumcision to be cut off; the time has come for the Egyptians to be pruned"; cf. Pesiq. Rab. 15.11. Pesiq. Rab Kah. 5.9 plays on both senses of the word *zamir* (*Note* 72): "*The time of zamir has come*: the time has come for the foreskin to be cut; the time has come for the Egyptians to be cut down; the time has come for their idols to be cut out of the world . . . the time has come for singing the song at the Red Sea . . . "

[77] The expression "holy spirit" (Heb. *ruaḥ ha-qodesh*) occurs only three times in the Hebrew Bible (Ps 51:13; Isa 63:10-11), but is common in Rabbinic literature. Synonymous with "the spirit of prophecy" *(ruaḥ ha-nebu'ah),* it usually denotes a divine power that invades a human being, in virtue of which he or she speaks the word of the Lord. Less commonly it denotes a divine agent or intermediary (almost like an angel, though the holy spirit never manifests itself in human form), who conveys a specific message from God to an individual. Here in the Tg. the "voice of the holy spirit" is effectively synonymous with *bat qol* (see *Note* 92). Tg. envisages God's words to Israel in vv. 10-12 being delivered, as in v. 14, by a *bat qol*. The Israelites have "just heard"—in the preceding verse—the heavenly voice alluding to the promise of redemption to Abraham. In contrast to the Tg., Cant.R. 2:12 §1, 2:13 §2 and Pesiq. Rab Kah. 5.9 identify the "voice of the turtledove" with the voice of Moses, or Joshua, or the King Messiah. On the holy spirit in the Targumim and in Rabbinic literature see Schäfer, "Die Termini 'Heiliger Geist' und 'Geist der Prophetie' in den Targumim."

The symbolizing of the "holy spirit" by a dove, standard in Christian iconography because of Matt 3:16 ("he saw the spirit of God descending as a dove"); Mark 1:10; Luke 3:22; John 1:32 (cf. Origen, *Commentary on Canticles* II, 12, "the dove is the Holy Spirit"), is harder to parallel in Rabbinic literature (Strack-Billerbeck 1:123–25 [to Matt 3:16]). The comparison of the spirit of God to a bird is implicit in Gen 1:2, "and the spirit of God was hovering upon the face of the waters"—"like a bird hovering and flapping with its wings, its wings barely touching [the nest]" (Gen.R. 2.4), though the bird envisaged by t. Ḥag. 2:5 in Gen 1:2 (on the basis of Deut 32:11) is an eagle rather than a dove (cf. y. Ḥag. II, 77a; b. Ḥag. 15a).

[78] Cf. Gen 15:14. Tg. Cant. agrees with Onq.'s rendering of the verse.

[79] *Memri*. Tg. Cant. appears to use *Memra* simply as characteristic of Targumic style, without any strong theological meaning. See *Intro.* 4.1.

13. Hebrew Text:

The fig tree grew fragrant;[80]
Its green figs and the budding vines
gave forth their fragrance.[81]
"Rise up, My Darling, My Fair One,
and come away."[82]

Targum:

The Congregation of Israel, that is compared to the first-fruits of figs,[83] opened her mouth and recited the Song at the Red Sea. Moreover, the youths and the babes praised the Master of the World with their tongues.[84] At once the Master of the World said to them:[aaa] "Rise up, Congregation of Israel, My Darling and My Fair One. Come away from here to the Land I promised to your forefathers."[85]

14. Hebrew Text:

O My Dove,[86] *who is in the clefts of the rock,*
in the hiding-place of the cliff,[87]
Let Me see your form, let Me hear your voice,
For your voice is sweet, and your form comely.[88]

Apparatus, Chapter 2

[aaa] F omits "with their tongues. At once the Master of the World said to them" by parablepsis.

Notes, Chapter 2

[80] The "fig tree" stands for Israel (*Note* 83); the fragrance given off by the fig tree in spring symbolizes the Song Israel sang to God at the Red Sea (Exodus 15). Tg. takes the first two stichs of the verse as historical narrative rather than direct speech, an interpretation assisted by the past tenses of the verbs.

[81] Tg. has probably divided the verse contrary to the accents, taking *paggeiha* ("its green figs") with *ha-gefanim* rather than with *ḥanetah*. The "green figs" = immature youths (cf. m. Nid. 5:7; b. Nid. 47a; Jast. 1132a, *paggah* = undeveloped puberty, childhood); "the budding vines" = the babes; "gave forth their fragrance" = praised the Lord.

[82] Spoken by God directly to Israel (cf. 2:10) in response to her praise.

[83] Cf. Hos 9:10, "I found Israel like grapes in the wilderness; I saw your fathers as the first fruit on the fig tree *(bikkurah bi-te'enah)* at her first season." See Pesiq. Rab. 15.11.

[84] That even the babes joined in the singing of the Song at the Sea is a commonplace in the Midrash. Tg.'s "with their tongues" emphasizes the miracle: according to one more restrained view the babes at their mothers' breasts indicated their praise with their fingers; the Tg. here, however, has them actually singing. The most extreme tradition has even the babes in their mothers' wombs joining in: see Neof. and Ps-J to Exod. 15:2-3; Mek. deR. Ishmael, *Shirta* 1; t. Soṭah 6:4; y. Soṭah VI, 29c; b. Soṭah 30b; Midrash Ps. 8.77.

[85] Cf. Exod 13:5, ". . . the land . . . which He swore to your fathers to give you . . ."; Exod 33:1, ". . . the land which I swore unto Abraham, to Isaac, and to Jacob, saying: Unto your seed will I give it . . . ."

[86] Addressed by God to Israel. The dove is a well-known symbol of Israel: cf. Cant.R. 2:14 §1: "R. Joḥanan said: The Holy One, blessed be He, said: I call Israel *My Dove*, as it is written, *And Israel is like a silly dove, without understanding* (Hos 7:11)." See also b. Ber. 53b; Cant.R. 2:14 §2; Midrash Ps. 18.30; 33.1; 119.1; Pirqei de R. El. 28. Further Tg. to 5:2 (*Note* 9) and 6:9 (*Note* 29).

[87] Tg. takes this as describing Israel trapped at the Red Sea.

[88] "Let Me see your comely form" = let me see your good deeds; "Let Me hear your voice" = let me hear your prayer. If Israel prays to God and performs good deeds God will rescue her from tight corners.

Targum:

When wicked Pharaoh pursued after the people of the House of Israel, the Congregation of Israel resembled a dove shut up in the clefts of the rock, with a serpent threatening her from within, and a hawk threatening her from without. So the Congregation of Israel was shut up from the four points of the compass:[bbb] in front of them was the sea; behind them pursued the enemy;[89] and on their two flanks were deserts full of fiery serpents that bite and kill men with their venom.[90] At once she opened her mouth in prayer before the Lord,[91] and a *bat qol*[92] fell-[ccc] from the heavens above and thus said: "O Congregation of Israel, that resembles the spotless dove shut up in the clefts of the rock and in the hiding-places of the cliff, let Me see your form and your upright deeds. Let Me hear your voice, for your voice is sweet when you pray in the Little Sanctuary,[93] and your form is comely through good deeds."[94]

15. Hebrew Text:

The foxes would have seized us,
The little foxes,
That destroy the vineyards,
But our vineyards were giving off scent.[95]

Apparatus, Chapter 2

[bbb] Lit. "from the four sides of the world"; cf. "from the four winds of the world" (Tg. to 2:6, *Apparatus z*).

[ccc] = *nplt,* but most other mss. have the more common *npqt* ("went forth"). Cf. 4:1, *Apparatus a.*

Notes, Chapter 2

[89] Cf. Cant.R. 2:14 §2: "It was taught in the school of R. Ishmael: When Israel went out from Egypt, what did they resemble? A dove which was fleeing from a hawk and flew into the cleft of a rock, and found a serpent lurking there. When it tried to get right in, it could not, because a serpent was lurking there, and when it tried to turn back it could not, because a hawk was hovering outside. What then did the dove do? It began to cry and beat its wings, so that the owner of the cote should hear and come to its rescue. This was the position of Israel by the Red Sea. They could not go down into the sea, because it had not yet been divided before them. They could not turn back, because Pharaoh had already drawn near. What did they do? *And they were sore afraid; and the Children of Israel cried out to the Lord* (Exod 14:10). Then straightway, *Thus the Lord saved Israel that day* (Exod 14:30)." See also Mek. deR. Ishmael, *Beshallaḥ* 3; Exod.R. 21.5.

[90] For the fiery serpents see Tg. to 1:9 (*Note* 71) and 2:6 (*Note* 36).

[91] Cf. Exod 14:8-10, "Pharaoh pursued after the Children of Israel. . . . The Children of Israel cried out unto the Lord."

[92] A heavenly voice (lit. "daughter of a voice") by which God communicated with humankind both in the prophetic period and after the end of prophecy. Tg. Cant. seems roughly to equate the *bat qol* with God's *Memra* and with the Shekhinah. See b. Sanh. 11a; t. Soṭah 13:2. Further: L. Blau, *JE* 2:588; A. Rothkoff, *EJ* 4:324; Kadushin, *The Rabbinic Mind* 261ff; Strack-Billerbeck 1:125; Lieberman, *Hellenism* 194–99; *TDNT* 9:288–90.

[93] *Beit maqdash ze'ir.* Cf. Ezek 11:16, "Thus says the Lord God: Although I have removed them afar off among the nations, and although I have scattered them among the countries, yet I have been to them as a Little Sanctuary *[miqdash me'at]* in the countries where they are come." The Little Sanctuary has traditionally been taken as a reference to the synagogue (see Tg. Ezek. 11:16). The fact that a reference to the synagogue here would be anachronistic would not trouble Tg. The *darshanim* often assumed that the institutions of their own days (the synagogue, the Beit Midrash) went back to time immemorial, and found it hard to imagine the ancient Israelites leading a religious life different from their own.

[94] Cf. Mek. deR. Ishmael, *Beshallaḥ* 3: "When it says *For your voice is sweet, and your form is comely,* it means, for your voice is sweet in prayer and your form is comely in the study of the Torah. Another interpretation: For your voice is sweet in prayer and your form is comely in good deeds." For other interpretations see Cant.R. 2:14 §§2 and 5; Mek. deR. Ishmael, *Beshallaḥ* 3; b. Qidd. 40b; b. B. Qam. 17a; Midrash Ps. 18.30; 33.1; 39.1; 119.1; 149.4, 5.

[95] Tg.'s reading of this verse turns on the standard equation of Israel with a vineyard: cf. Cant.R. 2:15 §2, "*That destroy the vineyards:* this signifies Israel, as it says, *For the vineyard of the Lord of Hosts is the House of Israel* (Isa 5:7)." The foxes

Targum:

After they had crossed the sea they murmured for water, and wicked Amalek came against them,[96] who bore a grudge against them on account of the birthright and the blessing which Jacob*[ddd]* had taken from Esau.[97] He came to wage war against Israel, because they had ceased to observe the words of the Torah.[98] And wicked Amalek was stealing from beneath the wings of the clouds of glory souls from the tribe of Dan,*[eee]*[99] and was killing them, because they had in their hands the idol of Micah.[100] At that hour the people of the house of

Apparatus, Chapter 2

[ddd] D E F add "our father."
[eee] Reading "tribe of Dan" with J M N. A and other mss. oddly have "tribes of Dan."

Notes, Chapter 2

that attack the vineyard then become the enemies of Israel, their precise identification with Amalek being determined by the chronology of the Tg.'s ongoing interpretation, though "*little (qetannim)* foxes" may have reminded Tg. of Obad 2 where Edom (= Amalek, both descendants of Esau: see Gen 36:9 and *Note* 97 below) is described as "little" *(qaton)* among the nations (cf. Cant.R. 2:15 §2, "The *little foxes* are Esau and his generals, as it says, *behold I made you little among the nations* [Obad 2]"). The vineyards "giving off scent" is taken as an allusion to the righteous, whose merit saved Israel from destruction. It is unclear how Tg. has interpreted *ʾeḥezu*: the verb seems to be echoed in "wicked Amalek *was stealing* . . . souls," in which case Tg. may have repointed *ʾeḥezu* as *ʾaḥazu*: the foxes would have seized and destroyed us if our vineyards had not given off their scent. The words would then be spoken by the narrator (Solomon), or Israel, recalling the events at Rephidim. Alternatively he may have taken *ʾeḥezu* as spoken by God, giving instructions (to the angels?) to prevent the foxes from destroying the vineyards, because they are giving off their scent. The first person plurals ("us," "our") could then be taken as *plurales majestatis*. Cf. Rashi *ad loc.*

[96] Cf. Exod 17:1-8, "But the people thirsted there [at Rephidim] for water, and the people murmured against Moses . . . Then came Amalek and fought with Israel at Rephidim."

[97] For Amalek as a grandson of Esau see Gen 36:12, "And Timna was concubine to Eliphaz, Esau's son; and she bore to Eliphaz Amalek" (cf. 1 Chr 1:36). Elaborating on Gen 27:41, "Esau hated Jacob because of the blessing wherewith his father blessed him," a late midrashic tradition claimed Esau enjoined on Amalek a war of annihilation against Israel (Ginzberg, *Legends* 3:55; 6:23, n. 138).

[98] Cf. Mek. deR. Ishmael, *ʿAmalek* 1: "*Then came Amalek*. . . . It is impossible for Israel to exist unless they busy themselves with the words of Torah. And because they separated themselves from the Torah the enemy came upon them. For the enemy comes only because of sin and transgression. . . . Rephidim means only 'feebleness of hands.' Because they relaxed their hold on the words of the Torah the enemy came upon them. For the enemy comes only because of feebleness of hands in upholding the Torah." See also Mek. deR. Ishmael, *Wayyassaʿ* 7: "Because they separated themselves from the words of the Torah, therefore the enemy came upon them. For the enemy comes only because of sin and transgression."

[99] Cf. Mek. deR. Ishmael, *ʿAmalek* 1: "R. Eleazar of Modiʿim says: *Then came Amalek.* Because Amalek would come in under the very wings of the Shekhinah and steal souls of Israel and kill them." Tg. seems to represent the war of Amalek against Israel essentially as spiritual: Amalek attempted to seduce the Israelites from allegiance to the Torah and lead them into apostasy. "Stealing souls" may mean no more than "kidnapping," but it suggests deviousness and cunning (see Ginzberg, *Legends* 3:56–57 on Amalek's cunning in attacking Israel). In this context the "killing" may be figurative and denote spiritual death, though Tg. may allude to the tradition that Amalek not only killed the Israelites but mutilated their bodies, cutting off the foreskins and throwing them heavenwards with the taunt, "Here, have what you desire!" (Ginzberg, *Legends* 3:57). The "clouds of glory" are the protective clouds with which God surrounded Israel during the Wilderness wanderings (see Tg. to 2:6 and *Note* 32 *ad loc.*). The phrase "wings of the clouds of glory" recalls the phrase "wings of the Shekhinah"—an expression normally used in the context of conversion to Judaism (proselytes are said to come "under the wings of the Shekhinah": see Jast. 651a), but here in a context of apostasy.

[100] The Shekhinah does not protect idolaters or the ritually impure (Sifrei Num. §83; Pirqei de R. El. 44), so the Danites were particularly vulnerable to Amalek's attack because they worshiped the "idol of Micah" (cf. Pesiq. Rab Kah. 3.12; 10.8; Pesiq. Rab. 12.13; 29/30.1; Sifrei Deut. §296; Pirqei de R. El. 44; Ps-J Exod. 17:8 and Num. 11:1; Ginzberg, *Legends* 6:24, n. 141). The "idol of Micah" was the idol made by Micah of the hill country of Ephraim in the time of the Judges, which he set up in a private sanctuary. The Danites carried it off and installed it in their cult center in the city of Dan: "And the children of

Israel, who are compared to a vineyard, would have been condemned to be destroyed but for the righteous of that generation, who are compared to good perfume.[101]

16. Hebrew Text:

"My Beloved is mine, and I am His!" [102]
The Shepherd [was] among the roses.[103]

Targum:

At that hour they returned in repentance, and Moses*fff* the prophet prepared himself and prayed before the Lord,[104] and Joshua his minister[105] armed himself and went out from beneath the wings of the clouds of glory,*ggg*[106] along with mighty men, the righteous of [that]

Apparatus, Chapter 2

fff D E F: "thereupon *(wkn)* Moses."
ggg J K L M N[1] omit "the wings of"; N[2] adds the words in a different hand.

Notes, Chapter 2

Dan set up for themselves the graven image [of Micah]: and Jonathan, the son of Gershom, the son of Moses, he and his sons were priests to the tribe of the Danites until the day of the captivity of the Land" (Judges 17–18, especially 18:30-31). The statement that the Danites already worshiped the idol in the wilderness alludes to the tradition that Micah had been in Egypt and had already made the image there, and that it had crossed the Red Sea with the Israelites (Mek. deR. Ishmael, *Bo* 14; *Wayyassa'* 1; *Beshallaḥ* 3; Exod.R. 24.1; 41.1; b. Sanh. 103b; b. Pesaḥ. 117a; Pesiq. Rab Kah. 10.8; ARN A.34; Sifrei Num. §84: Ginzberg, *Legends* 6:13, n. 72). Another tradition claims that Micah was responsible for making the Golden Calf, perhaps hinting that the Calf was the idol of Micah (Ginzberg, *Legends* 6:209, n. 126). Because one of Jeroboam's golden calves was set up at Dan (1 Kgs 12:26-33; 2 Chr 11:14-15), the Danites are seen in the Midrash as being particularly prone to idolatry (Mek. deR. Ishmael, *'Amalek*, 2; Pesiq. Rab. 11.3; 12.13; 46.3; Pirqei de R. El. 27; 38; Midrash Ps. 101.2). Cf. the Christian tradition that Antichrist is from the tribe of Dan (Bousset, *Antichrist*, Index, "Dan"; Hill, "Antichrist from the Tribe of Dan").

[101] Once again the merit of the righteous protects Israel and atones for her sins. See *Intro.* 4.3. For "good perfume" = "good reputation" see Tg. to 1:3 (*Note* 20), 1:12 and 2:16.

[102] Tg.'s interpretation is impressionistic and largely dictated by the flow of his narrative. He probably took the words "My Beloved is mine and I am His" as addressed by Israel to God in repentance and renewed fidelity, but it is puzzling that he did not integrate the direct speech into his translation: e.g., "At that hour they returned in repentance and said, My Beloved is mine, and I am His." Cf. Cant.R. 2:16 §1: "*My Beloved is mine, and I am His.* He is my God and I am His [chosen] people."

[103] Tg. does not make clear who says these words—Israel, or the narrator. "The shepherd" is apparently identified as Joshua, possibly on the basis of the common designation of a ruler or leader as a "shepherd" (BDB 945a). "The roses" = "righteous men, who are compared in their deeds to the rose." The parallels in 4:4 and 6:3 are treated differently.

[104] Cf. Exod 17:9-11, "I will stand on top of the hill . . . Whenever Moses held up his hand, Israel prevailed . . . ." Tg. depicts Moses in typical intercessory role: the raising of his hands is taken as an act of prayer. "Moses did not go out to battle, but through his prayer . . . the battle was won" (Ginzberg, *Legends* 3:59–60). Moses prepares himself *('it'attad)* for prayer: cf. Mek. deR. Ishmael, *'Amalek* 1: "*Tomorrow I will stand.* Tomorrow we shall be prepared *(me'uttadim)* and stand. *Upon the top of the hill,* to be taken literally—these are the words of R. Joshua. R. Eleazar of Modi'im says: Let us declare tomorrow a fast day and be ready *(me'uttadim),* relying upon the deeds of the forefathers, for *top* refers to the deeds of the fathers, and *hill* refers to the deeds of the mothers." Cf. Ps-J Exod. 17:9. According to Pirqei de R. El. 44, while Moses prayed on the hill the people prayed in the camp, following him like a precentor in the synagogue.

[105] On Joshua as the minister of Moses see Exod 24:13; 33:11 (cf. Onq. *ad loc.*). The central figure in the defense of Israel is Moses: Joshua and the righteous act as his agents.

[106] Cf. Mek. deR. Ishmael, *'Amalek* 1: "*And go out, fight with Amalek* (Exod 17:9). R. Joshua says: Moses said to him: Joshua, go out from under the protection of the cloud and fight with Amalek." Ps-J Exod. 17:9, "Go out from beneath the clouds of glory and draw up the battle-lines against the hosts of Amalek."

generation,[hhh] who are compared in their deeds to the rose,[107] and they waged war on Amalek, and they crushed him and his people by the curse of the Lord,[108] which kills and destroys according to the law of the sword.[iii][109]

17. Hebrew Text:

Until the day came,
When the shadows fled away.[110]
"Turn, my Beloved, and picture to Yourself
The gazelle, or the young of the hart,
Upon the Mountains of Division."[111]

Apparatus, Chapter 2

hhh Reading "mighty men, the righteous of [that] generation" *(gybry ṣdyqy dr')* with J L M. N has "the mighty men of [that] generation" = Heb. *gedolei ha-dor.* A B C and some other western mss. have the rather weak *gwbryn ṣdyqyn* = "righteous men," "certain righteous men."

iii The syntax is awkward here and this is reflected in the variant readings of the mss. A and many other mss. have *bshmt' dyyy dqtl' wtbr' bptgm ḥrb,* which should probably be translated as above. D E F have *dshmt' dyyy wqtl' wtb(y)r' bptgm ḥrb,* which implies that *qtl'* and *tb(y)r'* are nouns and not participles. Translation: "by the curse of the Lord and [by] death and destruction according to the law of the sword." The first reading suggests that Joshua's warfare is purely spiritual: it is the divine curse that does the damage. The second reading, however, appears to envisage both spiritual and physical warfare.

Notes, Chapter 2

107 Cf. Mek. deR. Ishmael, *'Amalek* 1: "*Choose us out men* (Exod 17:9): *Choose us out,* that is, heroes; *men,* that is, fearers of sin. R. Eleazar of Modi'im says: *choose us out,* that is, fearers of sin; *men,* that is, heroes." The link between "roses" and "righteous men" is probably through the equation of scent with reputation: see Tg. to 1:3 (*Note* 20), 1:12 and 2:15.

108 Probably a reference to God's decree of extermination against Amalek (Exod 17:16, "The Lord has sworn [lit.: because there is a hand upon the throne of the Lord]: the Lord will have war with Amalek from generation to generation"; cf. Num 24:20; Deut 25:19: see Pirqei de R. El. 44), though Tg. may be alluding to the tradition that Amalek was a magician and used sorcery against Israel, and Joshua and Moses countered his attack by magical means (y. Rosh. Hash. III, 59a; Ginzberg, *Legends* 3:59–60). Note how the following verse of Tg. reveals that the weapons of the Israelites were engraved with "the Great Name expressed in seventy names."

109 Cf. Exod 17:13, "And Joshua discomfited Amalek and his people with the edge of the sword." Tg.'s "according to the law of the sword" *(le-fitgam de-ḥereb)* translates "the edge of the sword" *(le-fi ḥereb)* in Exod 17:13 (cf. Onq. *ad loc.*). Tg. is referring to decapitation with a sword, the least shameful of the four forms of capital punishment (m. Sanh. 7:1, 3: "The ordinance of those that are to be beheaded [is this]: they used to cut off his head with a sword as the government does"; *pitgam de-ḥereb* = Latin *ius gladii*). Mek. deR. Ishmael, *'Amalek* 1: "*And Joshua discomfited Amalek and his people.* R. Joshua says: He went down and cut off the heads of the mighty men that were with Amalek, those standing in the battle lines . . . *With the edge of the sword.* R. Joshua says: He did not disfigure them [cf. *Note* 99], but treated them with some degree of mercy."

110 Tg. treats the parallel in Cant 4:6 differently. Here the shadows fleeing away is taken as symbolizing the departure of the Shekhinah when Israel made the Calf. It is unclear how Tg. has understood the Hebrew *'ad she-yafuaḥ ha-yom* (lit. "till the day breathes"): he may have taken it simply as meaning "until the day arrived." He probably saw the phrase as part of the narrative framework.

111 Tg. probably took these words as addressed by Moses to God. He apparently caught here an echo of Moses' prayer of intercession when Israel made the Golden Calf: "Moses besought the Lord . . . and said . . . Why should the Egyptians speak, saying, For evil did He bring them forth . . . to consume them from the face of the earth? Turn from Your fierce wrath . . . Remember Abraham, Isaac, and Israel, Your servants, to whom You did swear by Your own self, and said to them: I will multiply your seed as the stars of heaven" (Exod 32:11-13). The promise here to multiply Israel's seed echoes Gen 22:16-17 (the 'Aqedah) and Gen 15:5 (the Covenant between the Pieces). Tg. holds that both these events took place on the same mountain. He saw an allusion to the Covenant between the Pieces *(betarim)* in the Mountains of Division *(beter),* and to the 'Aqedah in the "gazelle" (Abraham) and the "young of the hart" (Isaac). He probably repointed the Hebrew *demeh lekha,* "be like" as *dammeh lekha,* "picture to yourself," "think about" (for this sense of the verb see Ps 48:10). Moses says: "Turn [from Your anger], my Beloved, and picture to Yourself Abraham and Isaac on Mount Moriah." Tg. treats the partial parallel in 8:14 differently: see *Notes ad loc.*

Targum:

But within a short time the children of Israel had made the Calf,[jjj][112] and the clouds of glory that were shading them departed. They were left exposed and were bereft of the adornment of their weaponry,[kkk] on which was engraved the Great Name,[113] expressed in seventy names.[114] And the Lord wanted to destroy them from the world, but He remembered[lll] the covenant which He had made through His Word with Abraham, Isaac, and Jacob,[115] who were swift in service like the gazelle and like the young of the hart, and [He remembered] the sacrifice which Abraham had offered of Isaac his son[mmm] on Mount Moriah,[nnn][116] and [how] before that he had offered there the offerings[ooo] and divided them equally.[117]

Apparatus, Chapter 2

[jjj] D F: "the Golden Calf."

[kkk] A: *w'trwqnw yt tyqwn zyynyhwn*. The resumptive pronoun in *byh* indicates that *zyynyhwn* should be singular; hence we should probably read *zy(y)nhwn* with D E F J K L M N. *Tyqwn* = "adornment": see Jast. 1666a. For the phrase *tyqwn zynhwn* see Onq. and Ps-J to Exod. 33:4, 6 (*Note* 113).

[lll] Lit. "there was remembered before Him."

[mmm] B J K L M N omit "his son."

[nnn] J M: "the Mount of Worship"; cf. Ps-J Gen. 22:2, and 3:6, *Apparatus ee*; 4:6, *Apparatus t*.

[ooo] L N: "the offering"; C D E F: "his offering," but the singular conflicts with the resumptive plural pronoun in *ythwn* and with Gen 15:9-10.

Notes, Chapter 2

[112] Cf. Exod 32:1-4; Tg. Cant. 1:5; 1:12. Sinai, where the Calf was made, was the stage in the desert wanderings after Rephidim (Exod 19:2, "And when they were departed from Rephidim, and were come to the Wilderness of Sinai, they pitched in the Wilderness, and there Israel camped before the Mount"). Hence Tg.'s "within a short time."

[113] An allusion to Exod 33:4-6, "And when the people heard these evil tidings, they mourned: and no man put on him his adornments (*ʿadi*). The Lord said to Moses: Say to the Children of Israel: You are a stiff-necked people; if I go up into the midst of you for one moment, I shall consume you; therefore now put off your adornments from you, that I may know what to do to you. And the Children of Israel stripped themselves of their adornments from Mount Horeb onward." The Midrash speculated on the nature of these "adornments," and according to one tradition they included magical weapons, inscribed with the Name of God, which had been given to the Israelites at Sinai. Cf. Ps-J Exod. 33:4, ". . . and no man put on his weapons [*tyqwn zynyh* = Onq.; cf. Tg. Cant. here], which had been given to them at Sinai [and] on which had been engraved all the letters of the Great and Holy Name"; Exod. R. 45.3: "*Therefore put off your adornments* (Exod 33:5). This refers, said R. Simeon b. Yoḥai, to the weapons which God gave them and upon which the Ineffable Name was inscribed"; Exod.R. 51.8: "He gave them [at Sinai] weapons on which was engraved the Ineffable Name, and as long as this sword was in their possession, the Angel of Death could exercise no power over them. Whence do we derive this? From the verse: *Therefore now put off your adornments from you, that I may know what to do to you* (Exod 33:5)"; Cant.R. 4:12 §2; 8:5 §1; Lam.R. Proem 24; b. Shabb. 88a; Pesiq. Rab Kah. 16.3; Pesiq. Rab. 10.6; 23.10; Pirqei de R. El. 47. On the Name of God as a weapon in battle see 1 Sam 17:45; Ps 20:8 (ET 20:7, with Mek. deR. Ishmael, *Shirta* 4, "With His Name does He fight and He does not need all these accoutrements of war"); Exod 2:12 (with Exod.R. 1.29, "The Rabbis say that he pronounced God's Name against him and thus slew him"). Further *Note* 114 below, Tg. Cant. 3:1 (*Note* 3), and Urbach, *The Sages* 149, 748.

[114] By the "Great Name" Tg. probably does not mean the Tetragrammaton, but a secret magical name of God, passed down by esoteric tradition allegedly from Moses (see Tg. to 3:7 and *Note* 38). This was sometimes said to consist of numerous letters (forty-two or sixty or seventy/seventy-two: Num.R. 14.5; Pesiq. Rab. 15.17; Pesiq. Rab Kah. 5.11; Sefer Raziʾel 24b; Tg. Cant. 3:7), or, as here, of a series of seventy separate magical names: 3 Enoch 48B = Alphabet of R. Aqiba (Wertheimer, *BM* 2:350ff); cf. Num.R. 14.12. See Alexander in Charlesworth, *OTP* 1:310; Schiffman, "A Forty-two Letter Divine Name." Tg. Cant. shows considerable interest in magic, and may be following the tradition that the "weapons" of the Israelites were not literally "swords," but magical incantations employing the Names of God. Cf. the Jewish magical text containing a long magical name of God known as The Sword of Moses (Harari, *Ḥarba deMosheh;* see Alexander, "Incantations and Books of Magic").

[115] Cf. Exod 32:11-13 (*Note* 111 above).

[116] The ʿAqedah theme is prominent in Tg. Cant. See *Intro*. 4.3.

[117] Cf. Gen 15:10, "And he [Abraham] . . . cut them in two (*wa-yebatter*) and laid each half against the other (*ʾish bitro*); Cant.R. 2:17 §1: "*Upon the Mountains of Division (beter)*: for the sake of the promise which I made to your father Abraham between the pieces (*betarim*), as it says, *In that day the Lord made a covenant with Abraham, saying* . . . (Gen 15:8)."

CHAPTER 3

1. Hebrew Text:

Upon my bed at night[1]
I sought Him whom my soul loves;
I sought Him but did not find Him.[2]

Targum:

But when the people of the House of Israel saw that the clouds of glory had departed from them, and the holy crown[3] that had been given to them at Sinai had been taken away from them, and they had been left in darkness as in the night, they sought the holy crown[a] that had departed from them, but they did not find it.

2. Hebrew Text:

"I will arise now and go about the city,
In the streets and in the squares;[4]

Apparatus, Chapter 3

[a] G omits "that had been given to them . . . holy crown" by parablepsis.

Notes, Chapter 3

[1] The onward impetus of Tg.'s reading largely determines its interpretation. The verse is spoken by Israel and represents her repentance after the creation of the Calf—an event not obviously found in the biblical narrative. Tg.'s rendering of the following verse suggests that he is thinking particularly of Exod 33:7-10 and taking the Israelites' honoring of Moses and their worshiping at the doors of their tents as a sign of contrition (see *Note* 6). Tg. interprets "night" as symbolizing the darkness left by the withdrawal of the clouds of glory.

[2] Since Tg. identifies the object of Israel's search as "the crown of holiness" it might be supposed that he rendered the Hebrew "I sought that which my soul loves; I sought it but did not find it." However, since the crown = the Shekhinah (see *Note* 3), God is still implicitly the object of the search and the personal reference can be left.

[3] Among the "adornments" granted to Israel when she accepted the Torah at Sinai (Tg. Cant. 2:17, *Note* 113) was "a crown," which was removed after the sin of the Calf (Ps-J Exod. 32:25, ". . . for they had lost by Aaron's act the holy crown which they had on their heads, on which was inscribed in all its letters the Great and Glorious Name"; also Neof. *ad loc.;* Exod.R. 45.2; Pesiq. Rab. 10.6; b. Shabb. 88a). The "crown" could be identified as the Torah itself; see Num.R. 14.10: ". . . the three crowns which the Holy One, blessed be He, gave to Israel . . . viz., the crown of Torah, the crown of priesthood, and the crown of royalty" (cf. m. ʾAbot 4:13; ARN A.41). Pirqei de R. El. 47 implies that it was the Ineffable Name: "R. Eleazar ben ʿArakh said: When the Holy One, blessed be He, descended upon Mount Sinai to give the Torah to Israel, sixty myriads of ministering angels descended with Him, corresponding to the sixty myriads of the mighty men of Israel, and in their hands were swords and crowns, and they crowned the Israelites with the Ineffable Name." There is probably an allusion here to the plate on the high priest's turban on which the divine name was inscribed (Exod 28:36; 39:30; Lev 8:9; see *Notes* to Tg. Cant. 5:14): thus Israel became "a kingdom of priests" (Exod 19:6). It is clear, however, that Tg. Cant. identifies the crown as the Shekhinah: see v. 2, "Let us seek . . . the holy Shekhinah that has departed from us." Cf. Cant.R. 4:12 §2, which, contextualizing God's adorning of Israel in Ezek 16:11-12 at Sinai, comments: "*And a beautiful crown upon your head* (Ezek 16:12): this is the Shekhinah, as we read, *You shall also be a crown of beauty in the hand of the Lord* (Isa 62:3), and it is written, *And their king has passed on before them, and the Lord at the head of them* (Mic 2:13)."

[4] Tg. contextualizes to Exod 33:7-11, where Moses pitches a tent outside the camp. The words are spoken by Israel in repentance, as she turns back to God: the first three stichs are a soliloquy ("the Children of Israel said one to another"), the fourth

I will seek Him whom my soul loves."
I sought him but did not find Him.[5]

Targum:

The Children of Israel said one to another: "Let us arise and go around[b] the Tent of Meeting which Moses has pitched outside the camp,[6] and let us seek instruction from the Lord,[7] and [let us seek] the holy Shekhinah[c] that has departed from us." They went round the cities, the streets, and the squares, but did not find [it].

Apparatus, Chapter 3

[b] Lit. "let us go and surround" *(wnyzyl wnsḥr),* but the expression is here a hendiadys. N omits *wnyzyl.*

[c] G I: "the Shekhinah"; N[1]: "His Shekhinah," but N[2] adds "holy" in a different hand. "Holy Shekhinah" is the stronger reading since it helps to make the connection with the previous verse. The syntax is rather awkward: *shkynt qwdshʾ* is to be construed as the second object of the verb *ntbʿ*.

Notes, Chapter 3

a comment by Israel on the futility of her efforts. The "city," "streets," and "squares," which are rendered literally, are probably taken as describing the Israelite camp, from which both Moses and the Shekhinah have removed their presence. "City," however, seems to have been taken also as an allusion to the tent (see v. 3).

[5] "Him whom my soul loves" = "the holy Shekhinah" = "the holy crown" (v. 1).

[6] Cf. Exod 33:7, "Now Moses took the tent and pitched it outside the camp, afar off from the camp; and he called it the Tent of Meeting." This tent should not be confused with the Tabernacle, which does not begin to be built till Exodus 35–39 (see Tg. to v. 4). It was at this tent—outside the camp—that the Shekhinah met with Moses (Exod 33:9). Tg. saw this as evidence of the withdrawal of the Shekhinah from Israel because of the sin of the Calf. The Midrash saw it also as evidence of Moses' anger at Israel: he left the camp in solidarity with God, citing the principle that "the disciple may not have intercourse with people whom the master has excommunicated": "When Moses saw how they had squandered the precious gifts they had acquired, he was filled with anger against them, as it says, *Now Moses took the tent and pitched it outside the camp, afar off from the camp* (Exod 33:7). . . . Why was he angry with them? R. Joḥanan and R. Simeon ben Laqish discussed this. Because, said R. Joḥanan, Moses argued thus: One excommunicated by a teacher must be treated as such by his disciples; for this reason *Now Moses took the tent.* R. Simeon ben Laqish said: It can be compared to a king whose legion rebelled against him. What did the commander of the mutinous legion do? He took the imperial standard and fled. Moses did likewise: when Israel perpetrated that heinous sin, he took up his tent and departed—hence it says, *Now Moses took the tent*" (Exod.R. 45.3; Ginzberg, *Legends* 3:132). Exodus 33:12, "Moses said unto the Lord, See, You say to me, Bring up this people . . ." was interpreted as God remonstrating with Moses and telling him to return and lead the people (Exod.R. 45.2). Rashi logically assumes that the tent Moses pitched outside the camp was his own tent: "He did this to his tent when the people sinned with the Calf, and continued to do so till the erection of the Tabernacle. Since, he said, God has withdrawn from the camp, I must do likewise" (cf. Exod.R. 45.3 quoted above).

[7] The Tent of Meeting (Heb. *ʾohel moʿed*) is a place of instruction (Aram. *ʾulpan* = Heb. *moʿed*). This fits with Tg. Cant.'s tendency to see the Tabernacle and the Temple not just as places of sacrifice but also as Batei Midrash (see, e.g., Tg. to v. 4, and further *Intro.* 4.4). Cf. Onq. Exod. 33:7, "And Moses took a tent, and spread it for himself outside the camp, at a distance from the camp, and called it the Tent of the House of Instruction; and it came to pass that everyone who sought instruction from before the Lord went out to the Tent of the House of Instruction." Note also Neof. *ad loc.*: ". . . he called it the Tent of Meeting, and whoever sought instruction from before the Lord went out to the Tent of Meeting." Ps-J links the instruction with confession of sin, which fits well with Tg. Cant.'s understanding of this passage in Exodus as having to do with repentance: ". . . he called it the Tent of the House of Instruction, and whoever had repented with a perfect heart before the Lord would go out to the Tent of the House of Instruction, which was outside the camp; he would confess his sins and would pray for his sins, and, through prayer, he would be pardoned."

3. Hebrew Text:

The Guardians who go around the city found me.
"Have you seen Him whom my soul loves?"[8]

Targum:

[d]Moses, Aaron, and the Levites, the Guardians of the watch[9] of the Word of the Lord in the Tent of Meeting,[e10] who encompass it round about, found me, and I asked them about the Shekhinah of the Glory of the Lord that had departed from me. And Moses, the Great Scribe[f] of Israel, replied and thus said: "I will ascend to the highest heavens, and I will pray before the Lord. Perhaps He will pardon[g] your sins, and will cause His Shekhinah to dwell[h] among you as before."[11]

Apparatus, Chapter 3

[d] D E F add: "The Congregation of Israel said."

[e] Reading "Guardians of the watch of the Word *[Memra]* of the Lord in the Tent of Meeting" with B G H I J K L M N. A and several other mss. read "Guardians of the Word *[Memra]* of the Tent of Meeting." Cf. Onq. to Num 3:7 and see further *Note* 10.

[f] Reading "the Great Scribe" with C D E F J K L M N. A reads simply "the Great."

[g] *Ykpr:* lit. "He will atone for"; N: "I will atone for" *(ʾkpr)*. The first person looks the more obvious reading since God is less usual as subject of the verb *kpr* (though see Ps 65:4; 78:38), and Exod 32:20 has the first person (= Moses). But *ykpr* has the support of the vast majority of the mss. and is *lectio difficilior.*

[h] D E F make it clear that they construe the verbal form *yshry* as *ʾafʿel* by putting the object marker *yt* before *shkyntyh* (cf. v. 4). So most Yem. mss., J K L M, point the verb *(yashrei)*, but one, N, points as *peʿal (yishrei)*, suggesting it understood the sense to be "and His Shekhinah shall dwell . . . ." However, this involves a lack of concord in gender between the subject and the verb.

Notes, Chapter 3

[8] Israel continues to speak. The second stich, addressed by her to "the Guardians," is not directly represented in the Tg., though it is replied to by Moses! This illustrates how Tg. did not intend his translation to be read on its own, but only in conjunction with the Hebrew original. The "city" is identified as the Tent of Meeting (*Note* 7), and the Guardians as Moses, Aaron, and the Levites (*Note* 9).

[9] The link between the Levites and the Guardians *(ha-shomerim)* is easily made on the basis of passages such as Num 3:5-7, "The Lord spoke to Moses, saying: Bring the tribe of Levi near, and set them before Aaron the priest, that they may minister to him. And they shall keep his charge, and the charge of the whole congregation *(we-shameru ʾet mishmarto we-ʾet mishmeret kol ha-ʿedah)* before the Tent of Meeting, to do the service of the Tabernacle." Cf. Cant.R. 3:3 §1: "*The Guardians who go around the city found me:* these are the tribe of Levi, as we read, *Go to and fro from gate to gate* (Exod 32:27)." The positive evaluation of Moses and the Levites in the context of the story of the Calf is easily explained from the Bible: the latter sided with Moses in punishing the wrongdoers (Exod 32:26-27). Aaron's role seems to be more questionable in the Bible (see Exod 32:21-25). However, there is a tendency in the Midrash to exonerate him from blame for the making of the Calf (Ginzberg, *Legends* 3:121–24).

[10] The expression "the guardians of the watch of the Word *(Memra)* of the Lord in the Tent of Meeting" is intended to assign to Moses, Aaron, and the Levites a teaching role. Cf. v. 2, where the Tent of Meeting is represented as a Beit Midrash. "The Word *(Memra)* of the Lord" here, then, may (somewhat unusually) effectively mean the Torah. Tg. may have had at the back of his mind the famous aggadah in which the true "guardians of the city *(netorei qartaʾ)*" are said to be "the instructors in Bible and Mishnah": Lam.R. Proem 2: "Rabbi sent R. Assi and R. Ammi on a mission to organize [religious education in] the cities of the Land of Israel. They came to a city and said to the people, Bring us the guardians of the city. They fetched the captain of the guard and the magistrate. The Rabbis exclaimed, Are these the guardians of the city? These are its destroyers! The people inquired, Who then are its guardians? And they answered, The instructors in Bible and Mishnah, who meditate upon, teach, and preserve the Torah day and night. This is in accordance with what is said, *You shall meditate therein day and night* (Josh 1:8); and it is similarly stated, *Except the Lord build the house, they labor in vain who build it; [except the Lord keep the city, the watchman stays awake in vain]* (Ps 127:1)." Alternatively *Memra* here could be equivalent to the Shekhinah. Moses, Aaron, and the Levites tend the Shekhinah, which resides in the Tabernacle.

[11] Cf. Exod 32:30-31, "And it came to pass on the morrow that Moses said to the people: You have sinned a great sin; and now I will go up to the Lord; peradventure I shall make atonement for your sin. And Moses returned unto the Lord, and said . . . ." For Moses' ascent into heaven see Tg. to 1:5, *Note* 42.

4. Hebrew Text:

Scarcely had I left them
When I found Him whom my soul loves.[12]
I held him and would not let Him go,
Until I had brought Him into my mother's house,
Into the chamber of her that conceived me.[13]

Targum:

Scarcely a moment passed[i] before the Lord turned from His fierce anger[j] and commanded[k] Moses the prophet[l] to make the Tent of Meeting and the Ark,[14] and He caused His Shekhinah to dwell therein.[15] And the people of Israel were bringing their offerings[m] and

Apparatus, Chapter 3

[i] Reading *kz'yr syb ḥd hwh* with the Yem., mss. J K L M N. *Syb ḥd* is sometimes written as one word, *sybḥd,* but the Yem. tradition correctly recognizes its etymology as two words = "a small piece, a morsel," here of time (Sokoloff 462b). A and other mss. have the common corruption *s(y)bḥr.* The whole phrase literally means "scarcely a morsel [of time] had been when . . . ." For *z'yr* = Hebrew *me'at* see Neof. Gen. 43:2.

[j] *mtqwp rwgzyh;* J K L M N: *mrwgzyh* ("from His anger").

[k] A reads "and the Lord commanded." Omit "the Lord" with most other mss.

[l] J K L M N omit "the prophet."

[m] Reading the plural "their offerings" *(qwrbnyhwn)* with C F G H J K. A B D L N have the singular, "their offering" *(qwrbnhwn).*

Notes, Chapter 3

[12] Tg. implies that Israel here describes the return of the Shekhinah and the restoration of her communion with God, but he presents his rendering of the verse in the form of a third-person report. "Them" = Moses, Aaron, and the Levites, the "Guardians" of v. 3. In keeping with the drift of his narrative he contextualizes the verse to the making of the Tabernacle (*Note* 14).

[13] Israel cleaves steadfastly to God through worship and study. The Tabernacle, like the Tent of Meeting of Exod 33:7-11 and the Temple (see *Note* 7), functions both as a place of worship and as a place of study. Both activities—worship (Tg. deliberately uses a vague word *[qurban]* that could cover both sacrifice and prayer) and study of Torah—effect the descent of the Shekhinah. For the idea that the Shekhinah resides in the Beit Midrash just as it did in the Tabernacle and Temple see m. ʾAbot 3:6, "If ten men sit together and occupy themselves with the Torah, the Shekhinah resides among them . . . ." "My mother's house" = Moses' Beit Midrash; "the chamber of her that conceived me" = Joshua's Beit Midrash, though not to be envisaged as a separate institution (see *Note* 16). Moses and Joshua could be described as "mothers" of Israel because they engendered Israel spiritually through their teaching. Tg. clearly saw an allusion in *horati* ("her that conceived me") to *horaʾah* ("instruction"). Cf. Lev.R. 1.10: "Said R. Eleazar: Even though the Torah was given as a fence at Sinai, they were not punishable in respect thereof until it was repeated in the Tent of Meeting. This may be compared to an edict which has been written and sealed and brought into the province, but the inhabitants of the province are not punished for violating it until it has been clearly explained to them in the public meeting place of the province. So, too, with the Torah: even though it was given to Israel at Sinai, they were not punished for violating it until it had been repeated in the Tent of Meeting. This is indicated by what is written, *Until I had brought it into my mother's house, and into the chamber of her that conceived me* (Cant 3:4). *My mother's house* means Sinai; *the chamber of her that conceived me (horati)* means the Tent of Meeting, for thence Israel were commanded the instruction *(horaʾah).*" Parallels Cant.R. 2:3 §4; 3:4 §1. Tg. might also have seen a reference in "mother" to Torah: see Tg. to 6:9, *Note* 29, and 8:1, *Note* 1.

[14] Here "Tent of Meeting" means the Tabernacle, as the addition "and the Ark" is intended to indicate (see *Note* 7). Cf. Exod 35:4–40:33.

[15] Cf. Exod 40:33-34, ". . . so Moses finished the work. Then the cloud of glory covered the Tent of Meeting, and the glory of the Lord filled the Tabernacle."

engaging in the study of the words of the Torah in the chamber of the house of study of Moses their teacher,[n] and in the room of Joshua son of Nun, his minister.[o16]

5. Hebrew Text:

I adjure you, Daughters of Jerusalem,
By the gazelles, or by the hinds of the field,
That you do not awaken or stir up love
Until it please.[17]

Targum:

When the seven nations[p] heard[18] that the Children of Israel were about to take possession of their land they rose up as one and cut down the trees, stopped up the wells of water, laid waste their cities, and fled.[19] The Holy One, blessed be He, said to Moses, the prophet[q]: "I swore through my Word[r] to the fathers of these[20] that I would bring up their sons to possess a land[s] flowing with milk and honey.[21] How, then, can I bring up their sons to a land[s] devastated and empty? Now[t] I am detaining them for forty years in the Wilderness, so that

Apparatus, Chapter 3

[n] J K L M N omit "their teacher."

[o] J K L M N omit "son of Nun, his minister," but see Exod 33:11. N adds "his minister" in the margin in a different hand.

[p] Some mss. (e.g., A C G J K L M N[1]) have *ʿammayyaʾ*, others (e.g., D E F) *ʾummayyaʾ*. The standard Rabbinic phrase is *shebaʿ ʾummot ha-ʾareṣ*.

[q] J K L M N omit "the prophet."

[r] = "through My Memra" *(bmymry)*. D E F omit.

[s] B D E F G H read "the land" on both occasions.

[t] K L omit "then, can I bring up their sons to a land devastated and empty. Now" by parablepsis *(ʾnʾ* to *ʾnʾ)*.

Notes, Chapter 3

[16] Tg. probably understood the synonymous parallelism of the original correctly, and is not referring here to two separate institutions, but to one—the Beit Midrash of Moses, and of his successor as teacher of Israel, Joshua, which was located in the Tabernacle. Thus he carries back to Moses the founding of the most important Rabbinic institution of his own day. Tg. exploits the parallelism to introduce Joshua, not only because of Exod 33:11 ("but [Moses'] minister Joshua, the son of Nun, a young man, departed not out of the tent"), but because he was Moses' successor in the line of transmission of oral Torah (m. ʾAbot 1:1). In general Joshua comes well out of the episode of the Calf in the Midrash (Ginzberg, *Legends* 3:128). For Joshua as Moses' "minister" see Tg. to 2:16 (*Note* 105). The words "chamber" and "room" skillfully pick up the suggestion of intimacy in the original: the intimacies of communion with God through Torah are like the intimacies of the marriage chamber.

[17] As in the parallel in 2:7, Tg. sees here an adjuration by Moses to the Israelites (the "daughters of Jerusalem") not to stir up prematurely the desire to enter the Promised Land. Instead they should remain in the Wilderness studying the Torah, as described by the Tg. in the preceding verse. See *Notes* to 2:7, and further Tg. to 7:13, *Note* 55.

[18] Tg. follows Deut 7:1's enumeration of seven Canaanite nations. Exod 13:5 lists five, and Exod 33:2 has six. See the discussion in Mek. deR. Ishmael, *Pisḥa* 17.

[19] The scorched-earth policy that Tg. here describes the Canaanites as adopting is so extreme that it would obviously have made the Land uninhabitable by themselves as well as by the Israelites. Tg. may be thinking of some version of the "Joshua the Robber" traditions, according to which there was an emigration of Canaanites from the Land when the Israelites approached: see Procopius, *De Bello Vandalico* II, 10. 13-22; Bacher, "Joshua the Robber"; Hirschfeld, *Jews in North Africa* 45–48; Alexander, *Toponymy* 92–105.

[20] "These," rather than "the Children of Israel," is nicely dramatic.

[21] Cf. Exod 3:8; 33:3; Deut 26:9, 15. Tg. renders Hebrew *ʾereṣ zabat ḥalab u-debash* by *ʾaraʿ ʿabedaʾ ḥalab u-debash* (lit. "a land making/producing milk and honey") = Onq., but Ps-J (sometimes) and Neof. (always) render differently.

My Torah should be absorbed into their [very] bodies, and [meanwhile][u] those wicked nations will build [again] what they have laid waste."[22] So Moses said to the Children of Israel: "I adjure you, Assembly of Israel, by the Lord of Hosts and the Mighty Ones of the land of Israel,[v] that you should not presume to go up to the land of the Canaanites till forty years are completed, when it shall be the Lord's pleasure to deliver the inhabitants of the land into your hands. You shall cross over the Jordan[w] and the land shall be subdued before you."[23]

6. Hebrew Text:

Who is this going up from the Wilderness,[24]
Perfumed as with pillars of smoke,
[Sustained] with myrrh and frankincense,
From all the powders of the merchant?[25]

Apparatus, Chapter 3

[u] A B I J K L M N read *w'(y)nwn*. The syntax is nuanced and needs no improvement. D E F's *wmbtr kn 'ynwn* ("and after this they . . .") is an unnecessary attempt to clarify the sense. The *wth'* clause is final; the *w'ynwn* clause is nominal and relates a circumstance that will materialize contemporaneously with the *wth'* clause ("and all the while those nations . . ."). The *w'ynwn* clause is not final.

[v] J K L M N omit "Assembly of Israel, by the Lord of Hosts and the Mighty Ones of the Land of Israel" by parablepsis.

[w] J K L M N omit "you shall cross over the Jordan."

Notes, Chapter 3

[22] Unlike 2:7, Tg. here sees the forty years in the wilderness in a positive light, as giving time for the Israelites to absorb the teachings of the Torah, and time for the Canaanites to be tricked into reversing their scorched-earth policy. Cf. Mek. deR. Ishmael, *Beshallaḥ* 1: "Should God not all the more have brought them in by the straight road? But God said: If I bring Israel into the Land now, every one of them will immediately take hold of his field or his vineyard and neglect the Torah. But I will make them go round about through the desert forty years, so that, having the manna to eat and the water of the well to drink [= Miriam's well: b. Ta'an. 9a], the Torah will be absorbed into their very bodies. On the basis of this interpretation R. Simon the son of Yoḥai said: Only to those who eat manna is it given really to study the Torah. Like them are those who eat *Terumah*. Another interpretation: Should God not all the more have brought them in by the straight road? But, as soon as the Canaanites heard that the Israelites were about to enter the Land, they arose and burnt the seeds, cut down the trees, destroyed the buildings, and stopped up the wells. God, then, said: I promised Abraham to bring them not into a desolate land, but into a land full of all good things, as it is said: *And houses full of good things* (Deut 6:11). Therefore I will make them go round about through the desert forty years, so that the Canaanites will arise and repair what they have spoiled." See also Exod.R. 20.15-16. Mekilta contains a barely concealed exhortation to the community to support financially the scholars studying in the Beit Midrash, just as the priests were supported by *Terumah*. It was only because Israel was relieved in the Wilderness of the cares of earning a livelihood (because she was sustained by the manna and the water from Miriam's well) that her studies were so effective. For the Tg. the Beit Midrash was an important institution (see *Intro.* 4.4), and similar ideas may have been at the back of his mind. It is unclear, however, from where both Mek. and Tg. derive the idea of the Torah being absorbed into the bodies of the Israelites. Behind this may lie a spiritualization of the manna and the water from Miriam's well as heavenly instruction.

[23] Cf. Josh 1:2, "Moses My servant is dead; now, therefore, arise, go over the Jordan, you and all the people, unto the Land which I am giving to them, even to the Children of Israel. Every place that the sole of your foot shall tread upon, to you I have given it . . . ."

[24] Said by "the peoples of the Land" = "the seven nations" of v. 5, when they see Israel emerging from the Wilderness to occupy the Promised Land. The feminine pronoun and participle *(mi zo't 'olah)* support the identification with Israel, the "Bride" according to Tg.'s reading of the Song. *'Olah* is suggestive of going up to the Land, making *'aliyyah;* "from the Wilderness" provides an important time note, like "the mare in the chariots of Pharaoh" in 1:9, and suggests contextualizing the verse to the entry into Canaan. The parallel in 8:5 is interpreted of the exiles returning to the Land in the Messianic Age.

[25] Tg. appears to have translated here a text that conflated 3:6 and 8:5, "Who is this going up from the Wilderness, perfumed (Heb. *mequttoret* = Aram. *mitgammera/mitmareqa'*) as with pillars of incense, sustained (Heb. *mitrappeqet* from 8:5 =

Targum:

When the Children of Israel went up from the Wilderness and crossed the Jordan with Joshua, the son of Nun,[x][26] the peoples of the land said: "What chosen nation is this that goes up[y] from the Wilderness, perfumed[z] with the incense of spices,[aa] and sustained by the merits[bb][27] of Abraham who worshiped[cc] and prayed[dd] before the Lord on Mount Moriah,[ee][28] [a nation] scented[ff] with the oil of high office,[29] through the righteousness of Isaac who was

Apparatus, Chapter 3

[x] J K L M N omit "son of Nun."

[y] Reading *dslq'* ("that goes up") with the majority of the mss. for A's *dslyqt* ("that went up").

[z] "Perfumed" = *mtgmr'*. Jast. 254b explains *gmr* as a denominative from *mugmar,* "spices put on burning coals, offered after dinner, perfume" (m. Ber. 6:6; Jast. 738b). Hence *gmr,* "to perfume (clothes with spices)"; *itpe.,* "to be perfumed, soaked with perfume." N's *wmtgmr'* is stylistically weaker than *mtgmr'*.

[aa] Correcting A's *qtryt* to *qt(w)rt* with the rest of the mss.

[bb] A, with several other mss., reads the plural, *zkwwtyh,* "merits, meritorious acts" (cf. J K L M N: *zkwwt'*); B C D E F H read the singular *zkwtyh,* "merit." This is a common variant in the mss.

[cc] N: "Abraham, Isaac, and Israel who worshiped." Israel, as a people, worshiped on Mount Moriah (= the Temple Mount) after the Temple was built.

[dd] J K L M N omit "and prayed."

[ee] J M: "Mount of Worship *(pwlḥn')*"; cf. 2:17, *Apparatus nnn*; 4:6, *Apparatus t.*

[ff] "Scented" = *mtmrq'*. The verb *mrq* can mean "to cleanse." The reference might be to the use of oil in

Notes, Chapter 3

Aram. *se'ida'*) with myrrh and frankincense . . . ." Tg. took the "pillars of smoke" as alluding not, as one might have expected (see Cant.R. 3:6 §2), to the pillars *('ammudim)* of fire and cloud that followed Israel in the wilderness and symbolized the Shekhinah (Exod 13:21-22; 14:19, 24; Ps 99:7; Neh 9:12, 19), but to the pillars of incense in the Temple. Cf. Cant.R. 3:6 §4: "The House of Abtinas were expert in the making of the incense, in the mixing of the spices, and their incense used to send up a straight pillar of smoke." "Myrrh" *(mor)* alludes to Moriah (cf. Tg. to 1:13 and 4:6), and "frankincense *(lebonah)*" to the Temple mount, not only because frankincense was commonly used in the Temple cult, but also because of the wordplay *lebonah—Lebanon* (= the Temple: cf. 1 Kgs 7:2, where "the House of the forest of Lebanon" is identified by Num.R. 11.3 as the Temple; see further Tg. Cant. 3:9 [*Note* 48]; 4:8, 15; Num.R. 12.4; Cant.R. 3:10 §4; Sifrei Deut. §6; b. Giṭ. 56a; b. Yoma 39b; Vermes, "'Car le Liban, c'est le Conseil de la Communauté'"; Vermes, "The Symbolical Interpretation of Lebanon in the Targums"). The wordplay *lebonah—Lebanon* occurs again in Tg. to Cant 5:11. The *hapax legomenon* "powders *('abqat)*" alludes to the story of Jacob wrestling with the angel (Gen 32:25, "and a man wrestled *[wayye'abeq]* with him . . ."; see *Note* 32). Hence "myrrh" = Abraham, "incense" = Isaac, and "powders of the merchant" = Jacob. Cf. Cant.R. 3:6 §2: "*Perfumed with myrrh:* this refers to our father Abraham. Just as the myrrh is the foremost of spices, so our father Abraham was the foremost of all the righteous . . . *And frankincense:* this refers to our father Isaac, who was offered on the altar like a handful of frankincense. *With all the powders of the merchant:* this refers to our father Jacob, whose couch was flawless before God and in whose seed no defect was found."

[26] Cf. Josh 3:1–4:1.

[27] Israel arrives from the Wilderness perfumed with the merits of the fathers. For the doctrine of the merit of the fathers in Tg. Cant. see *Intro.* 4.3. "Merit of Abraham" . . . "righteousness of Isaac" . . . "piety of Jacob" is simply stylistic variation; the reference in each case is to the *zekhut 'abot.*

[28] Genesis 22 speaks of Abraham "worshiping" on Mount Moriah (Gen 22:5), but not of him "praying." However, the Midrash commonly interprets *wayyiqra' 'Abraham shem ha-maqom ha-hu'* in Gen 22:14 as meaning "and Abraham called upon the Name [of the Lord] in that place." See Onq. *ad loc.*: "And Abraham worshiped and prayed there in that place. He said before the Lord: Generations shall worship here. It will, therefore, be said, On this day in this mountain Abraham worshiped before the Lord." Ps-J: "And Abraham gave thanks and prayed there in that place, and said: When I prayed for mercy from before You, O Lord, it was revealed before You that there was no deviousness in my heart, and I sought to perform your decree with joy, that when the descendants of Isaac, my son, shall come to the hour of distress you may remember them, and answer them, and deliver them; and that all generations to come may say, In this mountain Abraham bound Isaac, his son, and there the Shekhinah of the Lord was revealed to him." Further FT and Neof. *ad loc.*; Gen.R. 56.10; Lev.R. 29.9; y. Ta'an. II, 65d; Pesiq. Rab Kah. 23.9.

[29] The "oil of high office" refers to the oil with which kings and high priests were anointed. Here, however, since it is the nation as a whole that is anointed there is probably an allusion to Exod 19:6, "You shall be to Me a kingdom of priests." Cf. Cant.R. 3:6 §1: "Royalty came from the Wilderness, as it says, *And you shall be to me a kingdom of priests* (Exod 19:6)." Tg. attributes this special status to the merit of Isaac.

bound at the site of the Temple, that is called the Mountain of Frankincense,[30] [a nation] for whom miracles are performed,[gg] through the piety of Jacob,[31] with whom a man[hh] wrestled till the dawn broke, and [Jacob] prevailed over him,[32] and was delivered, he and his twelve tribes."[33]

7. Hebrew Text:

Behold, the litter of Solomon![34]
Sixty mighty men are round about her,
From the mighty men of Israel.[35]

Apparatus, Chapter 3

place of soap, a practice common in antiquity, but one would not use "the oil of high office" (= kingship) for one's toilet, hence Jast. 847a is probably correct to see the sense here as "scented, perfumed"—a learned synonym for *mtgmrʾ*. He links with the biblical *tamruq*. For *tamruqei nashim* see Esth 2:3, 9, 12, where the context suggests the reference is to ointments and perfumes. The balanced clauses here and the learned synonyms indicate an attempt at high style.

[gg] Reading *wmtʿbdyn* with the majority of the mss. for A's *wmtʿbdn*.

[hh] "A man" = *gbr;* cf. Gen 32:25; G J K L M N: "the man" *(g(w)brʾ);* D F omit, but some word is needed. Jerusalmi secondarily supplies *mlʾkʾ*, "the angel."

Notes, Chapter 3

[30] Cf. Gen 22:9, "And Abraham . . . bound Isaac his son, and laid him on the altar." The location of the ʿAqedah on the Temple mount, already implicit in the Bible (Gen 22:14; 2 Chr 3:1), is standard in the Midrash (Ginzberg, *Legends* 5:253, n. 253). The Temple Mount is nowhere in the Bible called "the Mountain of Frankincense." Note, however, Cant 4:6, where "the mountain of myrrh" and "the hill of frankincense" are identified as the Temple Mount. Cf. Gen.R. 55.7: "*And get you into the Land of Moriah* . . . The Rabbis said: To the place where incense would be offered, as you say, *I will get me to the mountain of myrrh [to the hill of frankincense]* (Cant 4:6)." The parallelism between the incense in the Temple and the merits of the fathers suggests the idea that the Temple cult was efficacious in appeasing God's anger only because it recalled the merit of the ʿAqedah (see *Intro.* 4.3).

[31] Cf. Tg. to 1:3, "At the news of Your miracles and the mighty acts which You performed for Your people, the House of Israel, all the peoples trembled" (see *Note* 22 *ad loc.*). In context here the miracle of the crossing of the Jordan may be particularly in mind (Josh 3:14-16). According to Cant.R. 4:4 §4, Israel crossed the Jordan only through the merit of Jacob: "R. Judan said in the name of R. Joḥanan: We find it stated in three places—in the Torah, in the Prophets, and in the Writings—that Israel crossed the Jordan only through the merit of Jacob our father . . . " (cf. Gen.R. 76.5).

[32] Cf. Gen 32:24-30, ". . . and there wrestled a man with him until the breaking of the day . . . You have striven with God and with men and have prevailed . . . ." For Jacob's wrestling as a sign of his merit see Cant. R. 3:6 §3: "R. Ḥaninah said: The Holy One, blessed be He, said to Esau's guardian angel [= the "man" of Gen 32:24]: Why do you stand there? He comes against you with five charms in his hand; his own merit, the merit of his father, the merit of his mother, the merit of his grandfather, and the merit of his grandmother. Measure yourself with him [and you will find that] you cannot stand up even against his own merit."

[33] Since Tg. envisages not only Jacob himself but his children as having been threatened by the angel, he presumably accepts the tradition that the angel was the guardian angel of Esau (cf. Cant. R. 3:6 §3 [*Note* 32 above]; Gen.R. 77.3), who, had he overcome Jacob, would then have attacked the children, as Jacob feared Esau would do: see Gen 32:11, "Deliver me, I pray You, from the hand of my brother, from the hand of Esau: for I fear him, lest he come and smite me, the mother with the children." Gen 32:22 states that Jacob only had eleven children at the time (Benjamin was not yet born), so Tg.'s "he and his twelve tribes" looks like a slip. However, in keeping with the Rabbinic principle that he who kills a man kills his unborn offspring, Benjamin too, in a sense, would have been killed.

[34] Tg. leaps forward in time to the completion of Solomon's Temple—the climax of the entry into the Promised Land. The words are spoken by God in praise of the Temple, and answer Solomon's own expression of satisfaction in 1:17. The "litter" is symbolic of the Temple. Cf. Num.R. 11.3: "*Behold, the litter* alludes to the Temple." And Solomon here refers to King Solomon and is not used as a title of God. Cf. Num.R. 11.3: "*Behold the litter of Solomon.* R. Simeon b. Yoḥai expounded this as referring to Solomon, *Behold the litter of Solomon,* i.e., King Solomon"; further b. Shabb. 35b. Contrast Tg. to 1:1 (*Note* 2), and Num.R. 11.3: *"Behold the litter of Solomon,* namely of the Holy One, to whom belongs peace."

[35] The "sixty mighty men" are the sixty letters of the Priestly Blessing (Num 6:24-26), which protects Israel like an encircling wall. Cf. Cant.R. 3:7 §1, "*Sixty mighty men are about it*: this refers to the sixty letters of the Priestly Blessing. *Of the mighty men of Israel*: because they make Israel mighty." Parallels: Num.R. 11.3; 14.18; 18.21. The "mighty men of Israel" are "the Priests, the Levites, and all the Tribes of Israel" (v. 8, *Note* 41).

Targum:

When Solomon, the King of Israel, built the Temple of the Lord in Jerusalem, the Lord said through His Word:[ii] "How lovely is this Temple that has been built for Me by Solomon, son of David![jj][36] And how lovely are the priests when they spread out their hands and, standing upon their dais,[kk][37] bless the people of the house of Israel with the sixty letters that I passed on to Moses their teacher. That blessing surrounds them like a high and strong wall,[ll] and by it all the mighty men of Israel prevail and prosper."[38]

8. Hebrew Text:

All of them are girded with the sword,
And taught in war,[39]
Each with his sword on his thigh,
Against fear in the night.[40]

Apparatus, Chapter 3

[ii] "Through His Word" = *bmymryh.*

[jj] J K L M N omit "that has been built . . . son of David."

[kk] C E F G H J K L M read the plural "daises," but there was only one *dukhan* in the Temple (m. Mid. 2:6).

[ll] B G H I: "and that blessing surrounds them with a high and strong name"—*bshwm* ("with a name") instead of *kshwr* ("like a wall"), an easy mistake in context. G^2: "another text: *kshwr.*" J K L M N: "and that blessing surrounds them, and they are strong through it."

Notes, Chapter 3

[36] Tg. is probably thinking of 1 Kgs 9:1-3, "And it came to pass, when Solomon had finished the building of the house of the Lord, and the king's house, and all Solomon's delight which he was pleased to do, that the Lord appeared to Solomon the second time, as He had appeared to him at Gibeon. And the Lord said to him: I have heard your prayer and your supplication, that you have made before Me: I have hallowed this house, which you have built, to put my name there forever; and My eyes and My heart shall be there perpetually." Tg. picked up here the potential cross-reference to the Priestly Blessing: God's Name was put in the Temple through the recitation there by the priests of the Priestly Blessing (note especially Num 6:27, "so shall they put My Name upon the Children of Israel"; further *Note* 37).

[37] The reference is to the Priestly Blessing of Num 6:24-26. The "spreading of the hands" (with the fingers separated to form a V) while reciting the blessing is traditional and not biblical (cf. b. Ber. 55b; Chill, *The Minhagim* 58; *EJ* 13:1062). For the dais *(dukhan)* on which the priests stood in the Temple to pronounce the blessing see m. Mid. 2:6; m. Qidd. 4:5; m. ʿArak. 2:6; Ps-J Num. 6:23.

[38] The Priestly Blessing was regarded as one of the most potent spells in Jewish magic, and was often used on amulets. Cf. Cant.R. 3:7 §1: "*Each with his sword upon his thigh, against fear in the night* (Cant 3:8). For should a man see in his dream a sword cutting his thigh, if he goes to the synagogue and recites the *Shemaʿ* and says his prayer [= the ʿAmidah] and hears the Priestly Blessing, and answers Amen after them, no harm will come to him. Therefore the text exhorts the sons of Aaron, saying to them, *On this wise shall you bless the Children of Israel* (Num 6:23)." There is probably an antimilitaristic emphasis here, which is continued by Tg. in the next verse. Israel will be saved not by literal swords or armies but by spiritual, "magical" means. For antimilitarism in Tg. Cant. see *Intro.* 4.6.

[39] God continues his commendation of Israel for her studious pursuit of Torah, and for her observance of the covenant of circumcision. The "mighty men of Israel" of the previous verse are here identified as "the Priests, the Levites, and all the Tribes of Israel," specifically in their capacity as students of Torah, which is symbolized by the sword (see *Note* 42). Cf. b. Sanh. 7a and b. Yebam. 109b, where the "mighty men" are identified as the Rabbinic scholars. "Taught in war" means "skilled in argument"—a reference to the debates in the academies, which are seen as a kind of ritualized combat (see *Note* 43).

[40] The "sword on the thigh" is taken as an allusion to the "seal" of circumcision, which protects its bearer against "harmful spirits and demons that walk at night." Cf. Cant.R. 3:7 §4: "*Every man with his sword upon his thigh.* This refers to the fact that Moses said to them, Thus said God to me in one word, *No uncircumcised person shall eat thereof* (Exod 12:48); straightway each one took his sword from his thigh and had himself circumcised." (For the idea that the Israelites had given up circumcision in Egypt, and so needed to be circumcised, see Cant.R. 1:12 §3.) "Each with his sword on his thigh" probably recalled to Tg.'s mind Exod 32:26-27, "And all the sons of Levi gathered themselves together to [Moses]. And he said to them:

Targum:

The Priests, the Levites, and all the tribes of Israel[41]—all of them are equipped[mm] with the words of the Torah, which is likened to a sword,[42] and are debating[nn] with them like mighty men taught in war.[43] And every one of them [bears] the seal of circumcision upon his flesh, just as it was sealed upon the flesh of Abraham their father.[44] And by it[45] they prevail,

Apparatus, Chapter 3

[mm]Cf. Tg. Cant. 6:9. J K L M N omit "equipped," but the text then becomes problematic and the link with the Hebrew is lost (Aram. *ʾaḥid* = Heb. *ʾaḥuz*). N secondarily supplies *ʾlpyn* ("studying [the words of Torah]").

[nn] On the idiom *shql wtry* = Hebrew *nasaʾ we-natan* see Jast. 552b.

Notes, Chapter 3

Thus says the Lord, the God of Israel: Put every man his sword upon his thigh, and go to and fro from gate to gate throughout the camp . . . ." Tg., like Cant.R. 3:7 §4 quoted above, probably saw here a reference to circumcision.

Tg. heard in "fear in the night *(paḥad ba-leilot)*" an echo of Ps 91:5-6, "You shall not be afraid of the terror by night *(paḥad laylah),* nor the arrow that flies by day; of the pestilence that walks in darkness, nor of the destruction that wastes by noonday." See also Tg. to 4:6, where the same verse is alluded to. Psalm 91 was regarded in Rabbinic magic as an incantation against demons (y. ʿErub. X, 26c; b. Shebu. 15b). Cf. Num.R. 11:3: "*Against fear in the night*: because he [Solomon] was afraid of the spirits."

[41] Probably a secondary exegesis of the "sixty mighty men" of v. 7 (see *Note* 35 *ad loc.*). Cf. Num.R. 11:3: "*Sixty mighty men are round about it.* This alludes to the twenty-four priestly watches, the twenty-four levitical watches, and the twelve divisions *[maʿamadot]. Of the mighty men of Israel* serves to allude to the rest of the people who were in Jerusalem."

[42] Torah = sword is a commonplace. Cf. Pesiq. Rab Kah. 12.5: "R. Samuel bar Naḥman used to say, Words of Torah are like weapons. Just as weapons stand up in battle for their owners, so do words of Torah stand up for him who valiantly gives them the labor they require to be understood. And the proof? *The high praises of God are in their throats and a two-edged sword [lit. a sword of mouths: ḥereb pifiyyot] is in their hands* (Ps 149:6) . . . R. Judah says: *Pifiyyot* is the plural of *peh*: two mouths, two Torahs, the Written Torah and the Oral Torah *(Torah she-beʿal peh).*" Cf. Midrash Ps. 45.6. The image is as old as the New Testament: Eph 6:17 ("the sword of the spirit, which is the word of God"); Heb 4:12 ("the word of God is . . . sharper than any two-edged sword"); Rev 1:16; 2:12. See further Tg. Cant. 2:17 with *Notes* 113 and 114. Gen.R. 21.9 links the sword with both Torah and circumcision: "*Sword* (Gen 3:24) refers to circumcision, as it is written, *Make knives [lit. swords, ḥarbot] of flint, and circumcise again* (Josh 5:2). Our Rabbis said: *Sword* refers to the Torah, as it is written, *The high praises of God are in their throats and a two-edged sword is in their hands* (Ps 149:6)." Further *Note* 43.

[43] Just as the equation of Torah with the sword is justified in the Midrash by appealing to Ps 149:6 (*Note* 42), so the common use of military metaphors to describe the scholars and their debates is justified by appealing to Num 21:14. Num.R. 11.3: "*All of them are girded with the sword.* . . . R. Meir says that they all polished up their study to a point of law, till it was as sharp as a sword. . . . *All of them are girded with the sword,* as you read, *And a two-edged sword in their hand* (Ps 149:6). *And taught in war,* namely in the battle of the Torah; as you read, *The Book of the Wars of the Lord* (Num 21:14)." Lam.R. 2:2 §4: "*They fled from the swords . . . and from the grievousness of war* (Isa 21:15). [This happened to them] because they did not thrust and parry in the warfare of the Torah, of which it is written, *Wherefore it is said in the Book of the Wars of the Lord* (Num 21:14)." See further Cant. Zuta and Rashi to 2:8. The transfer of the language of war to the description of the scholars reinforces Tg.'s point that the true defense of Israel resides in study of the Torah rather than in military action. See Tg. to 3:3 (*Note* 10), and *Intro.* 4.6.

[44] Cf. Gen 17:11, 26, "And you shall be circumcised in the flesh of your foreskin; and it shall be a sign of the covenant *(ʾot berit)* between Me and you . . . In the selfsame day was Abraham circumcised." The description of circumcision as a "seal" is not biblical, though it appears to be old (see Rom 4:11). Tg. probably chose "seal" *(ḥotam)* rather than the biblical "sign" *(ʾot)* because of the use of the word "seal" to denote a remedy, or protection, against demons or hostile angels (see Tg. to 4:12, *Note* 45; further Schäfer, *Konkordanz*, at *ḥotam;* Alexander, "Jewish Elements in Gnosticism and Magic").

[45] "By it" could mean "by Torah" or "by circumcision." That Israel "prevails" (i.e., in context "is protected against demons") through the Torah is a common enough sentiment; prevailing through circumcision is less common, but note how in Tg. to 2:9 the blood of circumcision protected Israel against the Destroyer in Egypt (see *Note* 61 *ad loc.*). For the *mezuzah* and *tefillin* as amulets against the Destroyer see Tg. to 8:3 (*Note* 13).

like a mighty man[oo] with a sword strapped upon his thigh. Therefore they do not fear the malicious demons and evil spirits that walk in the night.[46]

9. Hebrew Text:

King Solomon made for himself a palanquin,
Out of woods from Lebanon.[47]

Targum:

King Solomon built for himself a holy Temple from woods of ginger, teak, and cedar, which he brought from Lebanon,[48] and he overlaid it[pp] with pure gold.[49]

10. Hebrew Text:

He made its pillars of silver,
Its support of gold,
Its covering of purple;
Its inside was filled with love [for Jerusalem],
More than for the daughters of Jerusalem.[50]

Apparatus, Chapter 3

[oo] A has "like a man, like someone" *(kgbr)*, but this seems weak. Read "like a mighty man, a hero" *(kgybr)* with C.

[pp] "It" = the Temple (see *Note* 49). N: "them" = the different kinds of wood.

Notes, Chapter 3

[46] By "demons that walk in the night" Tg. may be thinking specifically of Liliths, whose name was derived in folk-etymology from *laylah,* "night" (see M. Hutter, "Lilith," *DDD* 973–76; *EJ* 5:576).

[47] Tg. puts this and the following verse in the mouth of the narrator, Solomon, though it is somewhat awkward that Solomon speaks of himself in the third person. The word "palanquin" *(ʾappiryon)* is a *hapax legomenon* in the Hebrew Bible. Tg., following b. Sotah 12a (cf. Mishnah *ad loc.*), probably took it as a sedan chair, or covered litter, for the transporting of nobles and brides. He may, therefore, have seen it as being synonymous with the "litter" *(mittah)* of v. 7, identified it, like the "litter," with the Temple, and so contextualized the verse to 1 Kings 5–6. The identification is supported by the reference to "woods from Lebanon," which played a major role in the construction of the Temple (*Note* 48), to such an extent that "Lebanon" became a symbolic name for the Temple (*Note* 25). "Solomon" is the earthly king, not God (*Note* 34). Cf. Cant.R. 3:10 §3: "*A palanquin*: this refers to the Temple. *King Solomon made for himself*: Solomon literally. *Out of woods from Lebanon*: as it says, *And we will cut woods out of Lebanon* (2 Chr 2:15)." Parallel: Num.R. 12.4. Contrast Pesiq. Rab Kah. 1.2 and b. B. Bat. 14a, which identify the *ʾappiryon* as the Tabernacle.

[48] "Woods from Lebanon" reminded Tg. of 1 Kgs 5:8-9, "timber of cedar . . . and timber of fir . . . my servants shall bring down from Lebanon," and 2 Chr 2:15, "And we will cut woods [note plural] out of Lebanon." Cf. also the tradition that "the House of the forest of Lebanon" in 1 Kgs 7:2 was the Temple (Tg. to 3:6, *Note* 25). In typical Targumic fashion, Tg. specifies the woods as ginger, teak, and cedar: cf. Ps-J Gen. 22:3 where the unspecified "woods" are identified as the olive, the fig, and the palm.

[49] Cf. 1 Kgs 6:21, "So Solomon overlaid the house within with pure gold"; m. Mid. 4:1, "For all the house was overlaid with gold, save only for the backs of the doors."

[50] Solomon, the narrator, continues to celebrate his own achievements in building the Temple. The verse is contextualized to 1 Kgs 8:6-16, which describes the bringing of the Ark of the Covenant into the Temple: "The priests brought in the Ark of the Covenant of the Lord into its place . . . under the wings of the cherubim. For the cherubim covered the Ark and the staves thereof . . . There was nothing in the Ark save the Two Tables of Stone which Moses had put there at Horeb . . . And it came

Targum:

When he had completed it he placed in it the Ark of the Testimony,[51] which is the pillar of the world,[52] and inside it were the two Tablets of Stone (which Moses had hidden there at

Notes, Chapter 3

to pass . . . that the cloud filled the house of the Lord . . . And [Solomon] said: Blessed be the Lord . . . who spoke to David my father . . . saying, Since the day that I brought forth My people Israel out of Egypt, I chose no city out of all the tribes of Israel to build a house, that My name might dwell there."

Tg.'s exegesis is atomistic and rather disregards the syntax. "Pillars" = the Ark of the Testimony, the plural apparently being ignored (*Note* 52). "Silver" and "gold" = the Two Tables of the Law. Cf. Cant.R. 3:10 §4: "*Its support of gold*: this refers to the words of Torah, of which it says, *More to be desired are they than gold, yea than much fine gold* (Ps 19:11)" (*Note* 53). It is unclear how Tg. understood the *hapax legomenon refidah,* but at 2:5 it took √*rpd* as meaning "sustain, support" (hence our translation "its support").

"Purple" = the Curtain *(parokhet).* Tg. seems to have taken *merkabo* as meaning "screen" or "cover" rather than "seat." Cf. Cant.R. 3:10 §1: "*Its covering of purple,* as it says, *You shall make a curtain of blue and purple* (Exod 26:31)." Parallel: Pesiq. Rab Kah. 1.2. Perhaps Tg. was deliberately avoiding the possible mystical connotations of the word. Contrast Cant.R. 3:10 §4: "*Its seat of purple*: as it says, *To Him who rides [rokeb] upon the heaven of heavens, which are of old* (Ps 68:34). *Its inside was inlaid with love.* R. Berekhiah and R. Bun in the name of R. Abbahu said: There are four lordly creatures. The lord among the birds is the eagle; the lord among cattle is the ox; the lord among beasts is the lion; and the lord over all of them is man. The Holy One, blessed be He, took them and engraved them on the throne of glory." Yalqut Shimʿoni: "*Its seat of purple*: this is the Throne of Glory." For Tg.'s possible avoidance of Merkabah mysticism see *Intro.* 6.2.

"Its inside" = the ark-cover *(kapporet),* and "love" = the Shekhinah, which in the form of the cloud of glory resided upon the ark-cover. Cf. Cant.R. 3:10 §1: "*Its inside was inlaid with Love*: R. Azariah said in the name of R. Judah, who had it from R. Simon: This refers to the Shekhinah." Parallel: Pesiq. Rab Kah. 1.2. "Daughters of Jerusalem" = cities of the land of Israel, with the preposition *min* being understood in a comparative sense, "more than . . . ": cf. Tg. to 2:2 (*Note* 6).

[51] Tg. uses the priestly expression "Ark of the Testimony" (*ha-ʾaron la-ʿedut*/*ʾaron ha-ʿedut*: Exod 25:22; 31:7; Num 4:5; Josh 4:16), rather than the Deuteronomistic expression "Ark of the Covenant" (*ʾaron ha-berit*: Josh 3:6; 1 Kgs 8:6).

[52] The "pillars of the world" are commonly identified in Rabbinic thought as the patriarchs or other righteous men, but for whose merit the world would return to chaos. See Tg. to 5:15, "His righteous ones are the pillars of the world"; to 4:4, "The Head of your College . . . upon the utterances of his mouth the world depends"; and to 7:3, "The Head of your College, through whose merit all the world is sustained, just as a fetus is sustained through its navel in the belly of its mother" (Ginzberg, *Legends* 5:12, n. 28; 6:104, n. 590). The Ark of the Testimony as a "pillar of the world" is, however, hard to parallel. The Ark may stand for the Tabernacle *pars pro toto,* and Tg. may be thinking of the idea that the erection of the Tabernacle marked the culmination of the work of creation. See Num.R. 12.11-12: "Before the Tabernacle was set up the world was unstable, but when the Tabernacle was erected the world was firmly established. . . . We have learned elsewhere [m. ʾAbot 1:2], On three things the world stands *(ʿomed)*: on the Torah, on the [Temple] service, and on deeds of loving-kindness, and Moses mentioned them all in one verse [Exod 15:13, *You in Your mercy have led the people whom You have redeemed; You have guided them in Your strength to Your holy habitation*]. . . . *You in Your mercy have led the people whom You have redeemed,* for He redeemed them as an act of lovingkindness. *You have guided them in Your strength.* He guided them for the sake of the Torah which they had received, until the erection of the Tabernacle. To what was the world at that time like? To a camp-stool on two legs which cannot stand erect but wobbles, and when they make for it a third leg it becomes steady and stands firm. In the same way, as soon as the Tabernacle was constructed—as you read, *To Your holy habitation*—the world was immediately set on a firm foundation and stood erect. For at first the world had only two legs, loving-kindness and Torah, so that it was unstable. When a third leg was made for it, namely the Tabernacle, it straightway stood firm." (See Alexander, "Pre-emptive Exegesis," 230.) The Ark, of course, contained the Two Tables of the Torah, and was associated with the Shekhinah, both of which sustain the world. It was also physically associated with the *ʾeben shetiyyah*—the foundation stone of the world. Cf. Cant. R. 3:10 §4: "*Out of woods from Lebanon*: this intimates that it [the world] was formed out of the earthly Holy of Holies, as we have learnt [b. Yoma 53b; 54b]: When the Ark was taken away [after the destruction of the first Temple], a stone was left in its place, which had been there from the days of the early prophets, and which was called *shetiyyah.* Why was it called *shetiyyah?* Because on it the whole world was founded *(hushtat).*" Tanḥuma, *Qedoshim* 10 (ed. Buber, 39b): "The Land of Israel is the centre of the world, Jerusalem is the centre of the Land of Israel, the Temple is the centre of Jerusalem, the Holy of Holies is the centre of the Temple, the Ark is the centre of the Holy of Holies; and in front of the Ark was a stone called *ʾeben shetiyyah,* the foundation stone of the world." (See Alexander, "Jerusalem as the Omphalos of the World"; Vilnay, *Legends of Jerusalem* 5–19.)

Horeb[qq]), which are more precious[rr] than smelted silver, more beautiful than fine gold.[53] And he spread out and draped over it the curtain of blue and purple.[54] And between the cherubim which were upon the ark-cover was residing[ss] the Shekhinah of the Lord,[55] who caused His Name to dwell in Jerusalem out of all the cities of the land of Israel.[56]

11. Hebrew Text:

Go forth, daughters of Zion,
And look at King Solomon,
At the crown with which his mother has crowned him,
On the day of his espousals,
On the day of the gladness of his heart.[57]

Apparatus, Chapter 3

[qq] J K L M N omit "which Moses had hidden there at Horeb."

[rr] "Precious" = *yqyryn*; J: "choice" *(bhyrn)*; N: "brilliant" *(zhyryn)*; K L: *dhyryn* = (?) a dialectal variant of *zhyryn*.

[ss] Reading "was residing" with B D E F G H I J K L M N. A has simply "was."

Notes, Chapter 3

[53] For "silver" and "gold" as symbols of Torah see Tg. to 1:11 (*Notes* 81-82).

[54] The reference is to the *parokhet* of Exod 26:31 (*Note* 50). However, the precise wording of the Aramaic suggests that Tg. thought of this curtain as somehow draped over the Ark rather than as hanging in front of it. Tg. may have confused the *parokhet* with the blue cloth with which the Israelites were supposed to have covered the Ark in the Wilderness (Ginzberg, *Legends* 3:157).

[55] Cf. Num 7:89, "And when Moses went into the Tent of Meeting that he might speak with Him, then he heard the voice speaking to him from above the ark-cover *(kapporet)* that was upon the Ark of the Testimony, from between the two cherubim."

[56] Cf. 1 Kgs 8:16 (*Note* 50); Deut 12:11, ". . . the place which the Lord your God shall choose to cause His name to dwell there." Neof. and Ps-J to Deut 12:11 identify God's name with his Shekhinah.

[57] Tg. contextualizes the verse to Solomon's dedication of the Temple. The words were spoken by the herald sent to summon the people to the celebration. Cf. 1 Kgs 8:63-66, "So the king and all the Children of Israel dedicated the House of the Lord . . . So Solomon held the festival, and all Israel with him, a great congregation, from the entering in of Hamath to the brook of Egypt, before the Lord our God, seven days and seven days, even fourteen days. On the eighth day he sent the people away, and they blessed the king, and went to their tents joyful and glad of heart for all the goodness that the Lord had showed to David his servant and to Israel his people." Tg. heard in Canticles' "gladness of heart" *(simḥat leb)* an echo of "joyful and glad of heart" *(semeḥim we-tobei leb)* in 1 Kgs 8:66.

"Daughters of Zion" is taken in a double sense: (a) as districts of the Land of Israel; and (b) as inhabitants of Zion. The expression is interpreted very inconsistently in the Tg.: see Tg. to 2:2, *Note* 6. Tg.'s double, comprehensive interpretation here has probably been influenced by the statement in 1 Kgs 8:65 that *all* Israel, "from the entering in of Hamath to the brook of Egypt," celebrated with Solomon.

"King Solomon" is taken as the earthly king, and not as a title of God (Tg. to 3:7 [*Note* 34] and to 1:1 [*Note* 2]), and "his mother" is identified as the people of the House of Israel, probably by *ʾal tiqrei* (*ʾimmo* to *ʿammo*). Cant.R. 3:11 §2 also identifies Israel as the "mother," but implies that Solomon is a title of God: "*The crown with which His mother has crowned Him*: . . . The Holy One, blessed be He, loved Israel exceedingly and called them 'daughter' . . . 'sister' . . . and . . . 'mother,' as it says, *Attend to me, O My people, and give ear to Me, O My nation* (Isa 51:4)—*lʾwmy* (= *leʾummi*, My people) is not written, but *lʾmy* (= *leʾimmi*, to My mother)" (see *Minḥat Shai ad loc.*). Parallel: Num.R. 12.8. See also Sifra to Lev. 9:1 (§99): "*And it came to pass* (Lev 9:1). This teaches that on high there was rejoicing before God as on the day when heaven and earth were created. . . . When Moses saw that the Children of Israel had finished making the Tabernacle he came and bestowed a blessing on them . . . About this Scripture says, *Go forth, daughters of Zion, and look at King Solomon etc.* (Cant 3:11) . . . *King Solomon:* the King to whom belongs peace [= God]. *At the crown with which His mother has crowned Him: crown* refers to the Tent of Meeting,

Targum:

When Solomon came to celebrate the dedication of the Temple, a herald went forth with strength[tt] and thus said: "Go forth, you who dwell in the districts of the land of Israel, and you people of Zion, and look at the diadem and the crown with which the people of the House of Israel have crowned King Solomon on the day of the dedication of the Temple,[uu] and rejoice with the joy of the Festival of Tabernacles[vv] for fourteen days."[58]

Apparatus, Chapter 3

[tt] The expression *krwzʾ npq bḥyl* is simply a brachylogy for *krwzʾ npq wʾkryz bḥyl:* "a herald went forth and announced with strength," i.e., loudly.

[uu] A accidentally omits "King Solomon on the day of the dedication of the Temple." All other mss. have the words.

[vv] A and several other Western mss. add *dʿbd shlmh mlkʾ bʿydn hhyʾ yt hgʾ dmtlltʾ*, but these words are missing from B G H I J K L M N. At first sight the A text looks original, the omission having occurred through parablepsis. But the syntax of the A text is awkward: "and rejoice with the joy of the Festival of Tabernacles, which King Solomon celebrated at that time—the Festival of Tabernacles for fourteen days." And the addition spoils the historical realism of the herald's announcement. It is more satisfactory, therefore, to exclude the words as an intrusive marginal gloss. The gloss ("King Solomon celebrated the Festival of Tabernacles at that time for fourteen days") was simply intended to draw attention to the fact that unusually on this occasion Sukkot had lasted fourteen days (see *Note* 58).

Notes, Chapter 3

which was decorated in blue, purple scarlet, and marble; *His mother* refers to Israel, as it is written . . . (Isa 51:4). *On the day of His espousals*: the day on which the Shekhinah came to rest on the house. *The day of the gladness of His heart*: the day on which fire came down from heaven and consumed the burnt-offering and fat upon the altar." Note the echo of this interpretation in the Shir Ha-Kabod: "for grace and glory, for beauty and for splendor, His people have crowned Him with a crown" (Singer, *ADPB* 421).

"The day of his espousals" = the day of the dedication of the Temple, the dedication being seen as a kind of sacred marriage. Cf. Cant.R. 3:11 §2: "*On the day of his espousals*: this refers to [the consecration of] the Tent of Meeting. *And on the day of the gladness of his heart*: this refers to [the consecration of] the Temple." The Midrash normally takes "the day of the gladness of his heart" as alluding to the dedication of the Temple (m. Taʿan. 4:8; b. Taʿan. 26a; Cant. Zuta). Tg., however, in keeping with the verbal parallel in 1 Kgs 8:66 (see above), takes it as alluding to the Festival of Booths, which celebrated the dedication of the Temple.

[58] In line with 1 Kgs 8:2, Tg. identifies the "festival" of 1 Kgs 8:65 as being Sukkot, and interprets the "seven days and seven days, even fourteen days" of 1 Kgs 8:65 as meaning that on this occasion Sukkot lasted fourteen days rather than the stipulated seven (Lev 23:34). 2 Chron 7:8-9 has two festivals—Sukkot for seven days followed by a special seven-day festival for the dedication of the altar. See Rashi to 1 Kgs 8:65 and b. Moʿed Qaṭ. 9a.

CHAPTER 4

1. Hebrew Text:

Behold, you are beautiful, My Love,
Behold, you are beautiful![1]
Your eyes are [like] doves
Within your veil.[2]
Your hair is like the "flock of goats"
That made a memorial on Mount Gilead.[3]

Targum:

On the day that King Solomon offered up a thousand burnt offerings on the altar,[4] and his offering was accepted with favor before the Lord, a *bat qol*[5] went

Notes, Chapter 4

[1] Parallels: Cant 1:15 and 6:5. The words are addressed by God to Israel in response to the holocausts offered when the Temple was dedicated. Cf. 1 Kgs 8:62/9:3, "And the King and all Israel with him offered sacrifice before the Lord . . . And God said to him, I have heard your prayer and your supplication, which you have made before Me."

"My Love" = Assembly of Israel. The first occurrence of the word "beautiful" is applied to the Assembly as a whole, the second to the leaders of the Assembly and the Sages.

[2] "Eyes" = the leaders and Sages. Cf. Tg. to 4:9, where "eyes" = leaders of the Sanhedrin; 5:12, where "eyes" = the Sanhedrin; 6:5, where "eyes" = your teachers, the Sages of the Great Assembly; and 7:5 where "eyes" = specifically the scribes within the Sanhedrin. Behind the equation lies not only the gematria *ʿayin* = 70 (the number of the members of the Sanhedrin) but also a simile: just as the eyes give light to the body, so the Sages give light (= instruction) to Israel (cf. Cant. Zuta to 4:1). Cant.R. 4:1 §2 identifies the eyes with the Sanhedrin: "*Your eyes* refers to the Sanhedrin, who are the eyes of the community, as it says, *If it be done in error, without the eyes of the congregation* (Num 15:24). There are two hundred and forty-eight limbs in the human body, and they move only by the direction of the eyes, so Israel can do nothing without their Sanhedrin." Parallels: Cant.R. 1:15 §2; 5:12 §1. Tg. here, however, while in substance adopting the same interpretation, correlates "eyes" with the Sages and the "veil" *(ṣammah)* with the Sanhedrin, perhaps through deriving the latter from √*ṣmt,* pa., "to assemble, gather together, summon to a meeting" (Jast. 1290a). Cf. "veil" = the king's counselors and officers in Tg. to 4:3. Tg. probably took Hebrew *mi-baʿad* as meaning "within" (cf. Rashi and Ibn Ezra *ad loc.*: contrast 4:3, *Apparatus i*). It is also possible that Tg. took "veil" as referring to the Temple, where the Sanhedrin sat (cf. Cant.R. 4:1 §3): your eyes [= the Sages] are like doves, [when sitting] within your "veil" [= the Sanhedrin/Temple].

Tg. does not explain why the Sages are compared to doves. Cant.R. 4:1 §2 suggests: "Just as the dove when it enters its cote recognizes its nest, its cote, its young, its fledglings, and its apertures, so when the three rows of disciples sit before the Sanhedrin, each knows his place."

[3] "Your hair" = the rest of your Assembly, by *ʾal tiqrei: sheʿar* ("hair") to *sheʾar* ("remainder").

Mount Gilead reminded Tg. of the story of Jacob and Laban in Genesis 31, the only other passage in the Bible where the term Mount Gilead is found (Gen 31:21, 23, 25). The "flock of goats" = the sons of Jacob (cf. Tg. to 1:4, ". . . her sons, who are likened to the kids of goats"). The verb *galash* (*she-galeshu,* "that trail down") is a *hapax legomenon* in biblical Hebrew and greatly puzzled the ancient versions and commentators. Tg. renders "made a heap" by *ʾal tiqrei: she-galeshu* to *she-gal ʿasu.* See further *Note* 8.

[4] Cf. 2 Chr 7:7, "for there he [Solomon] offered the burnt offerings and the fat of the peace offerings." The parallel 1 Kgs 8:64 speaks of "the burnt offering" in the singular. 2 Chronicles does not give the number of the burnt offerings. 1 Kgs 8:63 says the peace offerings amounted to "twenty-two thousand oxen and one hundred and twenty thousand sheep," but 2 Chr 7:5 appears to give this figure as the total for all the animal sacrifices.

[5] The agent by which God's praise is announced is here "a heavenly voice" *(bat qol).* In the parallels in Cant 1:15 and 6:5 the agent is God's Word *(Memra).* In Tg.'s mind the two were probably functionally equivalent.

forth[a] from the heavens and thus said: "How beautiful are you, Assembly of Israel, and how beautiful are the leaders of the assembly and the Sages sitting in the Sanhedrin,[b6] who enlighten the people[c] of the House of Israel, and [who are] like fledglings, the young of the dove. And even the rest of the members of your assembly, and the ordinary people,[7] are as righteous as the sons of Jacob, who gathered stones and made a memorial[d] on Mount Gilead."[8]

2. Hebrew Text:

Your teeth are like a flock [of ewes] that are shorn,
That have come up from washing,
All of which bear twins,
And not one among them miscarries.[9]

Apparatus, Chapter 4

[a] = *nplt,* but most other mss. have the more common *npqt* ("went forth"). Cf. 2:14, *Apparatus ccc.*

[b] J K L M N: "How beautiful is the Assembly of Israel, and how beautiful are the leaders and the Sages, the Sanhedrin." I omits "and how beautiful are those leaders of the Assembly" by parablepsis.

[c] D E F: *lʿlmʾ lʿmʾ*. The translation of *lʿlmʾ* is uncertain here. There are two possibilities: (1) "who enlighten *forever* the people of the house of Israel"; or (2) "who enlighten *the world,* the people of the House of Israel." In the latter case *lʿmʾ* stands in apposition to *lʿlmʾ*, which could denote specifically the *ʾynshy dʿlmʾ* = the common people, in contrast to the scholars (b. Qidd. 80b; Jast. 1085a), or more generally "everyone" (cf. *kl ʿlmʾ*: Jast. 620a). Graphically the presence of *ʿlmʾ* could be explained by dittography, its absence just as easily by haplography.

[d] = *glshwshytʾ*. The word seems to be attested only here and at 6:5. Some mss. write it as two words *(gl shwshytʾ).*

Notes, Chapter 4

[6] On the importance of the Sanhedrin in Tg. Cant. see *Intro.* 4.4.

[7] "The ordinary people": lit. "the people of the land" (Aram. *ʿammaʾ de-ʾarʿa* = Heb. *ʿam ha-ʾareṣ*), an expression normally used in Rabbinic Hebrew in a pejorative sense = someone ignorant, or unobservant of tithes and purity (cf. m. Soṭah 9:15; Jast. 125b). Here there are three categories: the Sages, the members (lit. "sons") of the Assembly, and the people of the land. In the parallel in 6:5 we have the Sages, the students, and the people of the land. This suggests that with "the members of your Assembly" here Tg. is thinking primarily of the students. In Cant 7:6 Tg. equates "hair" with "the poor of the people." Cf. Rashi to 6:5, "*Your hair is like a flock of goats*: even the young, tender and insignificant among you are praiseworthy."

[8] Cf. Gen 31:46-47, "And Jacob said to his brethren, Gather stones; and they took stones and made a heap: and they ate beside the heap. And Laban called it Jegar-sahadutha; but Jacob called it Galeed." Tg. takes Jacob's "brethren" as being, in fact, his sons, who were called his "brethren" because they were "his peers in piety" (Ginzberg): hence "*righteous* like the sons of Jacob." Cf. Ps-J Gen. 31:46, "Jacob said to his sons, whom he called his brethren"; Gen.R. 74.13: "*And Jacob said to his brethren* (Gen 31:46). How many brothers had he then? But one, and would that he had buried him! It refers, however, to his sons, whom he calls brethren in the holy tongue. R. Ḥunia said: They were as valiant as he and as righteous as he. R. Judan said: When a man dons his father's raiment, he is like him." Further Pirqei de R. El. 36; Rashi to Gen 31:46; Ginzberg, *Legends* 1:375; 5:302, n. 226.

[9] Tg. renders the parallel in 6:6 in the same way. Here the *bat qol* continues its praise of the Temple service.

"Teeth" = the two matching orders of Priests and Levites who eat the priestly gifts. The "flock" to which the priestly gifts are compared is not just any flock, but Jacob's flock, at a significant moment in the sacred history, namely when he is about to wrestle with the angel (see *Note* 11 below). Tg. is fond of such historical flashbacks. The reference to Jacob was not strictly necessary here, but it adds depth and texture to the Tg., like the historical similes in Homer. For another reference to the incident at the Jabbok see Tg. to 3:6. The priestly gifts are like Jacob's flock in two respects: (a) they do not result from robbery: thus the cleanliness of the flocks ("come up from washing") is taken in a moral sense; and (b) they are physically perfect and unblemished ("bearing twins," "none barren/bereaved").

Hebrew *matʾimot* is taken in a double sense = "bearing twins" and "matching"; so too *shakkulah* = "barren" *and* "miscarrying," though in the latter case Tg. may have Exod 23:26 in mind: "none shall miscarry or be barren" (*meshakkelah*

Targum:

"How beautiful are the Priests and Levites who offer up your offerings, and eat holy flesh, tithe and heave-offering,[e] which are pure from any violence or robbery,[f][10] just as Jacob's flock of sheep was pure, when they were shorn and had come up from the brook Jabbok;[11] and none of them was [acquired] by violence or robbery.[g][12] All of them were alike one to the other, and bearing twins every time, and none of them was barren or miscarried."[13]

3. Hebrew Text:

Your lips are like a thread of scarlet,
Your speech is fair;[14]

Apparatus, Chapter 4

[e] *ʾprshwtʾ* = Hebrew *terumot*; cf. Num 18:8 with Onq. *ad loc*.

[f] Alternatively "and who [= the Priests and the Levites] are pure from/innocent of any violence or robbery." This is somewhat supported by the parallel in 6:6: see *Apparatus x ad loc.* J M read "violence, or robbery or oppression *(wʿwshqʾ)*" (Jast. 1059b).

[g] J M: "violence or oppression"; K L N: "violence or robbery;" see *Apparatus f* above.

Notes, Chapter 4

wa-ʿaqarah: cf. Onq. *ad loc*.). Tg. probably heard in *shakkulah* an echo of Gen 31:38, "This twenty years I have been with you, your ewes . . . have not miscarried *(shikkelu)*." This would have encouraged him to interpret Canticles in the light of the incident at the Jabbok.

[10] That is to say, the priestly gifts have not been exacted by oppressing the poor or by demanding more than was the priestly due.

[11] Cf. Gen 32:23-24, "And [Jacob] rose up that night, and took his two handmaids, and his eleven children, and passed over the ford of the Jabbok. And he took them over the stream, and sent over that which he had," which included sheep (see v. 14: "two hundred ewes and twenty rams"). Tg. envisages the flock as wading through the water and hence emerging "washed" on the other side. For "the brook *(naḥal)* Jabbok" see Deut 2:37; 3:16. Genesis 32:23 speaks of the "ford" *(maʿabar)* of the Jabbok.

[12] The assertion seems somewhat ironic in the light of Jacob's trickery in Gen 30:37-43, but the Midrash insists that Jacob was a righteous man (cf. Gen 31:36-42). Further Zetterholm, *Portrait of a Villain*.

[13] On the strength of Jacob's flocks see Gen 30:42, "But when the flock were feeble, he put them not in; so the feebler were Laban's, and the stronger Jacob's."

[14] The *bat qol*'s praises of Israel continue, but its words are reported in the third person.

The "thread of scarlet" *(shani)* reminded Tg. of the crimson thread that was tied to the scapegoat on the Day of Atonement: m. Shabb. 9:3 (cf. m. Yoma 4:2), "Whence do we learn that they tie a strip of crimson *(zehorit)* on the head of the scapegoat? Because it is written, *Though your sins be like scarlet (shanim) they shall be as white as snow; [though they be red like crimson (tolaʿ*; Tg. *zehoritaʾ) they shall be as wool]* (Isa 1:18)." (According to m. Yoma 6:8 the crimson thread was tied to the door of the Sanctuary, and when the scapegoat reached the wilderness it turned white.) Hence the "lips" were identified as the lips of the High Priest making intercessory prayer on Yom Kippur. Hebrew *midbar* is taken in the sense of "speech" (cf. Rashi and Ibn Ezra *ad loc*.), the speech in question being also the High Priest's prayer, "which turns back the sins of Israel." Cant.R. 4:4 §9 gives a generally similar reading, but by taking the "lips" as denoting Israel's prayer and the *midbar* as denoting the scapegoat it is able to claim that prayer is as efficacious as sacrifice: "*Your lips are like a thread of scarlet*; this refers to the crimson strip [tied to the scapegoat or the door of the Sanctuary on Yom Kippur]. *And your midbar is fair*: this refers to the scapegoat [which was sent into the Wilderness—the *midbar*]. Israel said before the Holy One, blessed be He, Sovereign of the Universe, we have no crimson strip or scapegoat. He replied: *Your lips are like a thread of scarlet:* the utterance of your lips is as beloved to Me as the strip of crimson. R. Abbahu cited in this connection, *So shall we render for bullocks the offering of our lips* (Hos 14:3): what shall we pay in place of bullocks and in place of the scapegoat? [The utterance of] our lips. *And your midbar is fair:* your Wilderness is fair; your utterance is fair." Though Tg. does not work the text in precisely the same way, it is noteworthy that he does not actually mention the scapegoat, but stresses rather the efficacy of the High Priest's *prayer.*

Your brow is like a slice of pomegranate
Behind your veil.[15]

Targum:

The lips of the High Priest were making intercession in prayer[16] before the Lord on the Day of Atonement, and his words were turning back the sins of Israel, which are like a thread of scarlet, and making them as white as clean wool.[17] And the King, who was their head,[h] was as full of precepts as a pomegranate, not to mention[i] the counselors and magistrates[j] who were close to the King, who were righteous, and in whom was no iniquity.

4. Hebrew Text:

Your neck is like the tower of David,
Built upon courses;
A thousand shields depend upon it—
All the weapons of the warriors.[18]

Apparatus, Chapter 4

[h] Reading singular *ryshhwn* with E J M for A's plural *ryshyhwn*. J M have "who was leading at their head" *(dhwh mdbr* [= Heb. *mdbr!*] *bryshhwm)* for A's "who was their head" *(dhwh r'sh(y)hwn)*.

[i] = *br mn*, an unexpected rendering of Hebrew *mi-ba'ad* (see *Intro*. 2.1, n. 9).

[j] "Counselors and magistrates": the sonorous pair *'mrkly' w'rkwnyn* must refer to secular officials, since they are "close to the King." Tg.'s ideal polity is divided into the three estates of the priests, the king with the secular officers, and the scholars. *'mrkl* and *'rkwn* are used in the Targumim to render a variety of Hebrew terms: for the former see Jast. 79b, and for the latter (= Gk *archōn*) see Jast. 121b.

Notes, Chapter 4

[15] "Brow" = head = king: the king is as full of *miṣwot* as a pomegranate with seeds. Cf. Cant.R. 4:3 §1: "*Your brow [raqqatekh] is like a slice of pomegranate:* as if to say, The emptiest *[reqan]* among you is packed with religious acts *[reṣuf miṣwot]* as a pomegranate with seeds; how much more those who are *behind your veil (ṣammatekh)*, the modest and self-restrained *(meṣummatim)* among you." The phrase "as full of precepts as a pomegranate" became almost proverbial in Rabbinic literature. See Tg. to 6:7; Cant.R. 4:4 §3; 6:7 §1; Gen.R. 32.10; b. Sanh. 37a; b. Ḥag. 27a; b. Ber. 57a; b. 'Erub. 19a.

"Veil" = the king's counselors and officers. Cf. "veil" = Sanhedrin in Tg. to 4:1. Tg. here, as in v. 1, may have linked "veil" *(ṣammah)* with *ṣmt*, pa., "to assemble, gather together, summon to a meeting" (*Note* 2 above). He may also have thought of the king's counselors who went behind the veil and saw the king face to face (cf. Esth 1:10).

[16] Tg. is probably thinking specifically of the High Priest's prayer of confession over the scapegoat (m. Yoma 4:2).

[17] Note the clear allusion to Isa 1:18 (see *Note* 14 above). "White as wool" in that passage may have been linked in Tg.'s mind with the Temple, through the association of "white" *(laban)* with Lebanon = the Temple. Cf. Sifrei Deut. §6: "Why is the Temple called Lebanon? Because it whitens *(malbin)* the transgressions of Israel, as it is said, *Though your sins be as scarlet, they shall be white (yalbinu) as snow* (Isa 1:18)." Parallel Cant.R. 7:5 §3. For the idea that Israel is especially pure on the Day of Atonement see Deut.R. 2.36: "On the Day of Atonement Israel are as pure as the ministering angels."

[18] The *bat qol* continues its praises of Israel, but the text slips back into the second person.

"Neck" = Head of the College. Cf. Tg. 7:5 where "neck" = the Father of the Law Court. The "tower *(migdal)* of David" alludes to David's "greatness" *(gedullah)*, which, characteristically, is interpreted in a moral sense ("strong in meritorious acts and great in good deeds").

"Built upon courses" *(banui le-talpiyyot)* = "upon the utterance of his mouth the world was built." Perhaps Tg. has somehow, secondarily, equated "the tower of David" with the world. Tg. has clearly derived the *piyyot* element of *talpiyyot* from *peh*, "mouth." Cf. Cant.R. 4:4 §9: "*Built upon courses* refers to the Temple, for which all mouths pray *(piyyot mitpallelot)*." See further b. Ber. 30a.

Hebrew *'elef ha-magen talui 'alayw* has been read by Tg. as meaning "as for [his] teaching [*'elef* = *'ulpan*], the shields [of Israel], all the weapons of [her] warriors [= Israel's physical security], depend upon it."

Targum:

"The Head of the College,[k][19] who is your teacher, is as strong in meritorious acts[l] and as great in good deeds as was David, King of Israel. Upon the utterance of his mouth[m] the world was built,[20] and on the teaching of the Torah, in which he was engaged, the people of the House of Israel were depending, and [through it][n] they were victorious in battle as if they were holding in their hands all kinds of weapons of the warriors."[o][21]

5. Hebrew Text:

Your breasts are like two fawns,
Twins of a gazelle.
Who feed [their flock] with roses.[22]

Apparatus, Chapter 4

[k] E: "your college."

[l] A J M clearly indicate the plural *zkwwtʾ,* which balances *ʿwbdyn;* B C D E F G H seem to read the singular *zkwtʾ* ("merit").

[m] It matters little whether the pronoun refers back to David or the Head of the College, since the latter is compared to the former (though the switch to the past tense favors David). The intention, whether directly or indirectly, is to assert that the world is founded upon and sustained by the Torah, which the Head of the College teaches.

[n] *bʾwlpn ʾwrytʾ* governs the *mnṣḥyn*-clause as well as the *hww rḥyṣyn*-clause.

[o] = *gybryn*; B I K: *gbryn*.

Notes, Chapter 4

[19] Israel's ideal polity, according to the Tg., embraces the High Priest and the King (see v. 3), and the Head of the College (v. 4). Note how the ideal polity envisaged by the ʿAmidah also embraces the Temple (Benediction 14), the judges (Benediction 11), and kingship (Benediction 15). The introduction of the College at the time of Solomon is anachronistic, but Tg., like the Midrash in general, carries the establishment of this institution back to Sinai (Tg. to 3:4, *Note* 16), and regards it as being at least as important as the Temple or the Tabernacle. See further *Intro.* 4.4.

[20] Tg. deliberately transfers to the College the function of the Temple as the "pillar" of the world (Tg. to 3:10 [*Note* 52], and to 7:3 [*Note* 11]).

[21] Once again Tg.'s anti-militaristic stance should be noted. Israel will be protected not by force of arms but by study of the Torah. Cf. Tg. to 3:3 (*Note* 10) and to 3:7 (*Note* 38); see further *Intro.* 4.6.

[22] The *bat qol* predicts the coming of the Messiah son of David and the Messiah son of Ephraim, who will lead Israel in an eschatological exodus, just as Moses and Aaron led Israel in the Wilderness. Tg. renders the parallel in 7:4 in the same way.

"Two breasts" = the Messiahs of David and Ephraim. "Two fawns" = Moses and Aaron. "Gazelle" = Jochebed, the mother of Moses and Aaron. Cf. Yalqut Shimʿoni *ad loc.*: "Why is Jochebed likened to a gazelle *(ṣebiyyah)*? Because she reared the beauties *(ṣebiyyot)* of Israel [i.e., Moses and Aaron]."

"Who feed [their flock] *(ha-roʿim)*" = Moses and Aaron. Tg. is probably aware of the midrashic designation, based on Zech 11:8, of Moses, Aaron, and Miriam as "the three shepherds *(roʿim)*" of Israel: cf. Sifrei Deut. §305: "Three righteous persons died in the same year, Moses, Aaron, and Miriam . . . as it is said, *And I cut off the three shepherds in one month* (Zech 11:8)"; Cant.R. 4:5 §2: "*Twins of a gazelle:* R. Joshua of Sikhnin said in the name of R. Levi: Just as when one of two twins leaves the breast, the breast runs dry, so it is written, *And I cut off the three shepherds (ha-roʿim) in one month* (Zech 11:8)." See further t. Soṭah 11:10; b. Taʿan. 9a; Ginzberg, *Legends* 3:317; 6:110, n. 623.

It is unclear whether Tg. took the "roses" as symbolic of the meritorious deeds of Moses and Aaron or of the sustenance by which Israel was sustained in the Wilderness (the manna, the quails, and the water from Miriam's well), or both. For the former cf. 2:16, where the "roses" = "righteous men, who are compared in their deeds to the rose." For the latter see 6:3, where "roses" = the delicacies with which God feeds Israel. For Tg.'s identification of the *shoshannah* as the rose see 2:1 and 2:16.

Cant.R. 4:5 §§1-2 (cf. Exod.R. 1.35; Cant. Zuta; Rashi) also refers this verse to Moses and Aaron, but sees them as symbolized by the two breasts. The twin fawns simply indicate that Moses and Aaron were equal in knowledge and destiny. Tg.'s reading is closer and more nuanced: he sees *two* distinct pairs here—two breasts (= two Messiahs); two fawns (= Moses and Aaron). Thus Tg. is able to introduce, from his narrative standpoint in the age of Solomon, both a flashback (to the Exodus) and a flashforward (to the Messianic Age), and to establish a parallelism between the first and last exoduses of Israel.

Targum:

"Your two deliverers, who will deliver you, the Messiah son of David and the Messiah son of Ephraim,[23] are like Moses and Aaron, the sons of Jochebed, who are compared[p] to two fawns, twins of a gazelle.[24] In virtue of their meritorious deeds[q25] they were feeding the people of the House of Israel for forty years in the wilderness with manna, plump fowl, and water from Miriam's well."[26]

6. Hebrew Text:

So long as the day continues,
The shades shall flee away.
I will get me to the Mountain of Myrrh,
And to the Hill of Frankincense.[27]

Apparatus, Chapter 4

[p] Correcting A's *ʾymtylw* to *ʾytmylw* with the rest of the mss.

[q] C D E G H K L N: "their merit" *(zkwthwn);* see v. 4, *Apparatus l* above.

Notes, Chapter 4

[23] The Messiah son of Ephraim (known also as the Messiah son of Joseph, and the Anointed for War), is the messianic forerunner of the Messiah son of David. He will be killed in the eschatological battle against the anti-Messiah Armillus, or against Gog and Magog, and his death will be avenged by the Messiah son of David. See Sefer Zerubbabel; b. Sukkah 52a; b. Soṭah 14a; Gen.R. 75.6; Pesiq. Rab. 36 on Isa 60:1 (ed. Friedmann, 161ff.); Ps-J Exod. 40:9, 11; Tg. Tos. to Zech 12:10 (ed. Kasher, *Toseftot to the Prophets* 223–24); Tanḥuma, *Wayyigash* 3 (ed. Buber, 103a); Midrash Ps. 60.9; 87.4; Yalqut Shimʿoni to Isa 60:1 (§499); Strack-Billerbeck, 2:292–99; Heinemann, "The Messiah of Ephraim," *Tarbiṣ* 40 and *HTR* 68; Vermes, *Jesus the Jew* 139, 253.

[24] Cf. Exod 6:20, "And Amram took for himself Jochebed his father's sister to wife; and she bore him Aaron and Moses." Since there is no suggestion in Scripture that Moses and Aaron were literally twins, the Midrash interprets twins here metaphorically: Moses and Aaron were equal in their knowledge of Torah, or died at the same time (see Cant.R. 4:5 §§1-2, and *Note* 22 above).

[25] On the importance of the merits of the righteous in Tg. Cant. see *Intro.* 4.3, and following *Note*.

[26] Cf. Cant.R. 4:5 §2: "R. Jose said: Three good patrons arose for Israel, namely, Moses, Aaron, and Miriam; and for the sake of them three precious gifts were bestowed on Israel—the well, the manna, and the clouds of glory: the manna for the sake of Moses, the well for the sake of Miriam, and the clouds of glory for the sake of Aaron. When Miriam died the well ran dry . . . and it was restored for the sake of Moses and Aaron. When Aaron died, the clouds of glory departed . . . Then both were restored for the sake of Moses. When Moses died all three departed and were never restored." See also Num.R. 1.2. Note, however, that in Tg. the three gifts are the manna, the quails, and Miriam's well. For the manna and the quails see Exod 16:13, "And it came to pass at evening that the quails came up and covered the camp; and in the morning there was a layer of dew round about the camp . . . ." Though Miriam's well alludes to the drawing of the water from the rock at Meribah in Num 20:1-13 (note the reference to Miriam in v. 1), Tg. clearly knows the midrashic tradition that the well created at Meribah miraculously followed the Israelites during their wilderness wanderings and provided them with a constant supply of water. Cf. Num.R. 1.2: "How was the well constructed? It was rock-shaped like a kind of bee-hive, and whenever they journeyed it rolled along and came with them. When the standards [under which the tribes journeyed] halted and the Tabernacle was set up, that same rock would come and settle down in the court of the Tent of Meeting, and the princes would come and stand upon it and say, *Rise up, O Well* (Num 21:17), and it would rise." See b. Shabb. 35a; b. B. Meṣiʿa 86b; Lev.R. 22.4; Midrash Ps. 24.6; Cant.R. 4:12 §3; further Ginzberg, *Legends* 3:50–54; 6:21, nn. 125-126. That this tradition is as old as the first century is evident from 1 Cor 10:1-3, "I want you to know, brethren, that our fathers were all under the cloud, and passed through the sea, and all were baptized into Moses in the cloud and in the sea, and all ate the same supernatural food and all drank the same supernatural drink. For they drank from the supernatural rock which followed them, and the rock was Christ."

[27] God continues speaking and expresses his determination to take up residence in the Temple. His words are reported by Tg. in the third person.

Targum:

So long as the people of the House of Israel were holding in their hands the instrument[r] of their righteous fathers,[28] malicious demons—[harmful] spirits that walk at night, in the morning, and at noon[s29]—were fleeing from them, because the Shekhinah of the Glory of the Lord was dwelling in the Temple that was built on Mount Moriah.[t30] All the malicious demons and harmful spirits[u] were fleeing from the smell of the incense of the spices.[31]

7. Hebrew Text:

All of you is beautiful, My Love,
And there is no blemish in you.[32]

Apparatus, Chapter 4

[r] All mss. clearly read *ʾ(w)mnwt:* see *Note* 28.

[s] I have paraphrased here to bring out the allusion to Ps 91:5-6 (*Note* 29). The Tg. lists four kinds of evil spirit: *mzyqy wtlny wspdydy* [read *wspryry* with B D E F I] *wtyhryry. Spryry* is derived from *safraʾ* = "morning," hence "morning demon" (Jast. 1299a), and *tyhryry* from *tiharaʾ* = "noonday," hence "noonday demon." The etymology of *tlny* is less certain, but Tg. probably linked the word with *telal,* "shade, shadow" (note *ṣelalim* in the Hebrew here), hence "demon of darkness, night demon." *Tlny* are described in Tg. to 3:8 as "walking at night." *Mzyqy,* "those who do harm," is a generic term for demon (Jast. 755a). *Tlny, spryry,* and *tyhryry* are species of the genus *mzyqy:* hence the translation.

[t] J M: "the Mount of Worship"; see 2:17, *Apparatus nnn;* 3:6, *Apparatus ee.*

[u] = *mhblyʾ,* "destroyers" (Jast. 757a), like *mzyqy,* a generic term for demon.

Notes, Chapter 4

The Hebrew *ʿad she-yafuaḥ ha-yom* (lit. "till the day blows") is taken by Tg. as meaning "all day long" (morning, noon, and night). The "shades/shadows" *(ṣelalim)* are identified as the demons, which flee from the divine presence. The "Mountain of Myrrh" is equated with Mount Moriah through a play on "myrrh" *(mor)* and Moriah (see Tg. to 1:13 and 3:6, *Note* 25; further Gen.R. 55.7; Pesiq. Rab. 40.6), and the Hill of Frankincense is identified with the Temple Mount through a play on "frankincense" *(lebonah)* and Lebanon as a symbolic name for the Temple (see Tg. to 3:6, *Note* 25).

The parallel in 2:17, though treated rather differently, introduces the same themes as here: the Shekhinah, Mount Moriah, and the spiritual weapons of Israel.

[28] The "instrument" *(ʾumanut)* is the Torah. There is probably an allusion to Prov 8:30 where Torah/Wisdom is described as acting as God's *ʾAmon* in creation, that is to say as God's "working tool" *(keli ʾumanut):* see Gen.R. 1.1, and cf. the description of Torah as "the precious instrument *(keli ḥemdah)* by which the world was created" in m. ʾAbot 3:15. That Tg. is thinking concretely here is suggested by his precise wording ("holding in their hands"), and by the parallels in 2:17 and 3:8 that talk of Israel's "weaponry" and of the "sword of the Torah." However, there is doubtless an implicit play on *ʾumanut ʾabahateihon* and *ʾemunat ʾabahateihon* ("so long as Israel holds fast to the faith of their fathers"). Cf. the wordplay *be-ʾemunatam—be-ʾumanutam* in y. Sukkah V, 55d, with reference to 1 Chr 19:22.

[29] Note the echo of Ps 91:5-6—a psalm seen traditionally in Jewish magic as a sovereign protection against demonic attack: "You shall not be afraid of the terror by night, nor the arrow that flies by day, of the pestilence that walks in the darkness, nor of destruction that wastes at noonday." See *Apparatus s,* and cf. Tg. Ps. 91:5 and Midrash Ps. 91.5; further Tg. Cant. 3:8, *Note* 40.

[30] Tg. here succeeds in linking together three of his central themes—the Temple, the Shekhinah, and the ʿAqedah. See further *Intro.* 4.

[31] The wording "incense of spices" is characteristically precise, since the Temple incense was composed of a cocktail of different spices (*JE* 6:570). For the idea that demons are driven off by incense see the story of Joḥanan ben Zakkai and the Red Heifer in Pesiq. Rab. Kah. 4.7, and the story about Eleazar and the ring of Solomon in Josephus, *Ant.* 8.45–49. Tg. lists here three remedies against demons: Torah, the Shekhinah, and incense.

[32] God continues his praise of Israel, now not through a *bat qol* issued to the world at large, but through a statement addressed to the angels "in the heavens above." Cf. the parallel in 1:15, "*Behold you are fair, My Darling . . .* When the children of Israel did the will of their King, He through His *Memra* was praising them in the household of the holy angels." God praising Israel to the angels is a theme of the Midrash. Cant.R. 4:7 §1 contextualizes the verse to Sinai, Tg., implicitly, to the Solomonic era, after the building of the Temple. But Tg. in effect treats it as a timeless principle of God's dealings with his people.

Targum:

Whenever the people[v] of the house of Israel do the will of the Lord of the World He praises them in the heavens above, and thus says: "All of you is beautiful, Assembly of Israel, and there is no defect in you."[33]

8. Hebrew Text:

Come with me to Lebanon, My Bride,
With Me to Lebanon.[34]
A gift from the head of Amana,[35]

Apparatus, Chapter 4

[v] E F: "your people." This more or less forces the translation "whenever your people, O House of Israel . . . ."

Notes, Chapter 4

[33] Tg.'s "defect" *(mahata')* does not elaborate on the "blemish" *(mum)* of the biblical text. However, he is probably thinking not of moral defect (since that would produce a weak tautology: "when Israel keeps the Torah she is righteous"), but of physical defect, which is seen as the result of sin. Cf. Cant.R. 4:7 §1: "*All of you is beautiful, My Love*: R. Simeon taught: When Israel stood before Mount Sinai and said, *All that the Lord has spoken we will do, and obey* (Exod 24:7), at that moment there were among them neither persons suffering from the flux nor lepers nor lame nor blind, no dumb and no deaf, no lunatics and no imbeciles, no dullards and no doubters. With reference to that moment it says, *All of you is beautiful, My Love*. After they had sinned, not many days passed before there were among them persons suffering from the flux, and lepers, lame and blind, dumb and deaf, lunatics and dullards. Then the order was given, *Let them put out of the camp every leper, and every one that has an issue* (Num 5:2)." Note also how this verse is used in the Talmud to establish that no one with a physical defect or with a genealogical taint could serve in the Sanhedrin (b. Sanh. 36b; b. Qidd. 76b; b. Yebam. 101b). Thus Tg. here complements its reading of 1:15, where Israel's beauty is definitely moral ("how fair are your deeds, dear Daughter, Congregation of Israel"). Contrast Num.R. 4.1 which interprets Cant 3:7 as freedom from moral blemish by linking it to Isa 60:21, "Your people shall be all righteous."

[34] God addresses Israel through his *Memra* (= the *bat qol* of 4:1) as his "chaste bride," promising to dwell with her and predicting the tribute that the surrounding nations would pay to Israel during Solomon's reign.

"Lebanon" again is taken as a symbolic name for the Temple (see Tg. to 3:6 [*Note* 25], 3:9 [*Note* 48], and 4:15). Tg. interprets "*to* Lebanon," despite the use of the preposition *min*. Note, however, Pope (p. 474): "The rendering 'to Lebanon' (Haller, Zapletal) is possible, but there is no clear warrant here to choose that sense." Cf. Cant.R. 4:8 §1: "R. Levi said: The text in this case should have said, Come with Me *to* Lebanon, O My Bride, and you say, *From* Lebanon? What it means, however, is that at first He leaps forth from the Sanctuary, and then He punishes the nations of the world." Mek. deR. Ishmael, *Pisḥa* 14: "And when they return in the future, the Shekhinah, as it were, will return with them, as it is said, *Then the Lord will return with your captivity* (Deut 30:3). Note that it does not say, The Lord will bring back (*we-heshib*), but it says, He will return *(we-shab)*. And it is also said: *With Me from Lebanon, My Bride* (Cant 4:8). Was she really coming from Lebanon? Was she not rather going up to Lebanon? What then does Scripture mean by saying, *With Me from Lebanon*? Merely this: You and I, as it were, were exiled from Lebanon; you and I will go up to Lebanon."

Tg., in keeping with his historical reading, applies the verse to the reign of Solomon, but the Messianic interpretation is so strong in the Midrash (see also Mek. deR. Ishmael, *Beshallaḥ* 7), that an eschatological subtext cannot be excluded from Tg: the Messiah will restore the Solomonic kingdom. Tg. probably had at the back of his mind Ps 72:1, which is interpreted messianically by the Tg. *ad loc*.: "By the hand of Solomon, spoken through prophecy: O God, give the King Messiah the laws of Your justice, and Your righteousness to the Son of David . . . Those who dwell on the mountains shall bring peace to the House of Israel, and the hills with merit . . . The kings of Tarsus and the Isles of the Great Sea of Ocean shall render tribute *(tqrbwt')*, the kings of Sheba and Seba shall offer a gift *(dwrwn)*."

[35] Tg. related Heb. *tashuri* (usually translated "look": BDB 1003b, √*shwr* II) to *teshurah*, "gift" in 1 Sam 9:7, a *hapax legomenon*, the meaning of which is inferred from the context. Cf. Cant.R. 4:8 §2 (quoted in *Note* 36 below); Midrash Ps. 87.6.

Tg. identifies Amana not as a mountain, as might seem to be implied by *ro'sh* ("head, top": note "from the top of Senir and Hermon"), but as the river of Damascus mentioned in 2 Kgs 5:12. The spelling of the name there is disputed. Some Hebrew mss. have Ketib *'Abanah*, with Qerei *'Amanah*, but other mss. read *'Amanah* in the main text, with no Qerei, and this is the

From the top of Senir[36] *and Hermon.*
From the habitations of lions,
From the mountains of leopards.[37]

Targum:

The Lord said through His Word:[w] "You shall dwell with Me, Assembly of Israel, which is likened to a chaste bride,[38] and with Me you shall go up to the Temple. The heads of the people who dwell by the River Amana,[x] the inhabitants[y] who dwell on the top of the Mountain of Snow, and the nations that are on Hermon shall bring you gifts. Those who dwell in fortified cities, which are mighty as lions, shall bring up to you tribute, and offerings from the towns of the mountains, which are stronger than leopards."

9. Hebrew Text:

You have transfixed My heart, My Sister, My Bride;
You have transfixed My heart with one of your eyes,
With one bead of your necklace.[39]

Apparatus, Chapter 4

[w] = *bmymryh.*
[x] Reading "by the River Amana" with B D E F G H I; A has "in Amana." See *Note* 35.
[y] J K L M N omit "who dwell by the River Amana, the inhabitants" by parablepsis.

Notes, Chapter 4

spelling followed by the Tg. *ad loc*. This identification here forces Tg. to take *ro'sh* figuratively: "the heads of the peoples who dwell by the River Amana." Cant.R. 4:8 §2 takes Amanah as a mountain, identifying it with the Taurus Amanus range near Antioch in Syria, which traditional Jewish geography saw as lying on the northern border of the Messianic Land of Israel (see Alexander, *Toponymy* 203–206, 234; Bockmuehl, *Jewish Law in the Gentile Churches* 61–70). But it also records a tradition that implies, as in the Tg., the identification of Amana with the River of Damascus: "*Sing [ʾal tiqrei tashuri,* but *tashiri] from the top of Amana*: R. Ḥunia said in the name of R. Justa: The exiles are destined to break into song when they reach Taurus Munus, and the nations are destined to bring them like princes [but emend with Radal to "bring them as gifts"] to the Messiah. How do we know? Because it says, *Tashuri from the head of Amanah:* the word *tashuri* indicates an offering, as it says, *There is not a gift (teshurah) to bring to the man of God* (1 Sam 9:7). . . . Have I not already done as much for you in the days of Hazael, as we read, *So Hazael went to meet him [Elisha], and took a present with him, even of every good thing of Damascus, forty camels' burden* (2 Kgs 8:9)." Thus "head of Amana" = Hazael, the chief of Damascus, an equation based on identifying Amana here with Amana, the River of Damascus, in 2 Kgs 5:12.

[36] Tg. identifies Senir as "the Mountain of Snow"—a standard equivalent in the Targumim. Deut 3:9 implies that Senir and Hermon are identical ("The Sidonians call Hermon Sirion, while the Amorites call it Senir"), but Tg., possibly following 1 Chr 5:23, treats them as distinct. Note Ps-J Deut. 3:9, "The Sidonians call Hermon the Mountain of Rotten Fruit, while the Amorites call it the Mountain of Snow, because it is always covered with snow both in summer and winter." See also Onq. and Neof. *ad loc*., and Ps-J Num. 34:11; Neof. Num. 34:15; Ps-J and Neof. Deut. 4:48; Tg. 1 Chr. 5:23; LAB 40.4-5 (reading *montes Telag*); Ben Sira 24:13 (Syriac).

[37] "Habitations *(meʿonot)* of lions" = "fortified cities, which are mighty as lions." "Mountains of leopards" = "towns of the mountains, which are stronger than leopards."

[38] Cf. Cant.R. 4:10 §1 (parallel: Deut.R. 2.37): "In ten places in Scripture Israel is called *bride,* six here (Cant 4:8, 9, 10, 11, 12; 5:1), and four in the Prophets (Isa 49:18; 61:10; 62:5; Jer 7:34)."

[39] God continues to praise Israel, and once again the scholars are brought in as members of the ideal polity, here as the equals of royalty (see further *Intro.* 4.4).

The interpretation is somewhat impressionistic. The Hebrew *libbabtini* has been taken as expressing God's undying love for Israel. "One of your eyes" has been given a double reading: (1) "one of your poor ones" (*ʿaniyyim* by *ʾal tiqrei* for *ʿeinayim*);

Targum:

"Fixed upon the tablet of My heart is love for you,[z] O My Sister, Assembly of Israel, who is compared to a chaste bride.[aa] Fixed upon the tablet of My heart is as much affection for the least among you, if he is righteous,[bb] as for one of the leaders of the Sanhedrin, or for one of the kings of the house of Judah, on whose neck is placed the wreath[cc] of kingship."

10. Hebrew Text:

How beautiful is your love, My Sister, My Bride!
How much better is your love than wine![40]
And the scent of your ointments[41]
Than all spices!

Targum:

"How beautiful to Me is your love,[dd] O My Sister, Assembly of Israel, who is compared to a chaste bride! How much better to me is your love[dd] than [that of] the seventy nations! The good name of your righteous ones is more fragrant[ee] than all their spices."[ff]

Apparatus, Chapter 4

[z] "Love for you" = *rḥymtyk*. The suffix is objective; similarly *ḥbt zwtr*, "affection for the least."

[aa] The Yem. text (J K L M N) of this verse is incoherent. At some point in the common ancestry of the Yem. mss. a scribe accidentally omitted by parablepsis "fixed upon the tablet of My heart . . . chaste bride." Some of the missing words were added in the margin but subsequently inserted in the text in the wrong place. This is a good example of the general inferiority of the Yem. textual tradition. See further *Intro*. 1.3.

[bb] = *whwʾ ṣdyqʾ*: circumstantial clause expressing a conditional, "if he is righteous."

[cc] = *klylʾ*. This normally denotes a crown, but here a wreath or diadem strung around the neck must be envisaged (Jast. 642b). See further 5:7, *Apparatus jj*.

[dd] The forms of the agreeing adjectives *(shpyrn, tbn)* indicate that *ḥybtyk* is to be read as a plural = Hebrew *dodayikh*.

[ee] A adds "and better" *(wtb)*. Omit with the majority of mss.

[ff] Reading "their spices" with the majority of mss. A: "their spice." B (corrected to "their spices") D E F I have "spices," which corresponds to the Hebrew *besamim*, but is less pointed.

Notes, Chapter 4

and (2) "one of the leaders of the Sanhedrin." For "eyes" = leaders of the Sanhedrin see 4:1, *Note* 2. The fact that the one Hebrew item can be given these two senses is seen as showing that the pious poor are the equals of the leaders of the Sanhedrin in God's affection.

The "necklace" is taken as a reference to the "wreath of kingship." One "bead" of the necklace is one of the kings of the house of Judah. Tg. may have taken *ʿanaq* ("bead") in the sense of "giant, hero": hence "(heroic) king." Cf. Josh 15:14, where Tg. translates *ʿanaq* as *gibbarayyaʾ*, "heroes."

Cant.R. 4:9 §1 contextualizes this verse to various events in the sacred history (e.g., the crossing of the Red Sea, Sinai, and the erection of the Tabernacle). It takes "one of your eyes" as symbolizing Phineas, and "one bead of your necklace" as symbolizing Moses.

[40] "Wine" = the seventy nations, by gematria. Tg. thus introduces the doctrine of the divine election of Israel. Cf. Tg. to Cant 1:2, "for your love is better than wine" = "out of the abundance of the love wherewith He loved us more than the seventy nations" (see further *Note* 15 *ad loc*.).

[41] "Scent" = good name (see Tg. to 1:3, *Note* 20), and "ointments" = the righteous. Contrast "spikenard" = the wicked in Tg. to 1:12 (*Note* 91).

11. Hebrew Text:

Your lips drip [like] honeycomb, O Bride,
Honey and milk are under your tongue,[42]
And the scent of your robes is like the scent of Lebanon.[43]

Targum:

"And whenever the priests pray in the holy courts,[gg] their lips[hh] drip like honeycomb,[ii] and your tongue, O Chaste Bride, when you utter songs and praises is as sweet as milk and honey, and the scent of the robes of your priests is like the scent of frankincense."[jj][44]

12. Hebrew Text:

A locked garden is My Sister, Bride;
A locked chest, a sealed fountain.[45]

Apparatus, Chapter 4

[gg] The tradition is uncertain whether to vocalize *ʿzrtʾ* as singular or plural; m. Mid. speaks of the *ʿazarah* in the singular (1:4; 2:6), but also of the "*ʿazarah* of the women" and the "*ʿazarah* of Israel" (2:5), etc. Note also the plural "courts" in Isa 1:12 (see Tg. *ad loc.*). B H I have "courts of the Holy One" *(qaddishaʾ)*, but God is unlikely to refer to himself as "the Holy One," and "Holy One" in the Tg. is normally not *qaddishaʾ* but *qudshaʾ berikh huʾ* (Tg. to 3:5).

[hh] A and several mss. oddly have "his lips." Read "their lips" with C. Also possible is "your lips" (cf. H), i.e., the priests are Israel's lips.

[ii] Read "like honeycomb" with J K L M N. A has simply "honeycomb." Tg.'s *yʿrt dwbshʾ*, derived from 1 Sam 14:27 [Heb. *yaʿrat ha-debash* = *qnʾ ddwbshʾ* in Tg. Jon. *ad loc.*], indicates that it took Hebrew *nofet* here as "honeycomb" and not as "liquid honey." Cf. Tg. Ps. 19:11 (*kwbrytʾ*: Jast. 610a); Prov 5:3; 24:13; 27:7. But since lips cannot drip honey*comb*, it must surely have construed the Hebrew as a simile. Hence the reading "*like* honeycomb" is preferable.

[jj] Lit. "like the scent of the spice of frankincense" = *kryḥ bwsm ʾwlybnwn*. But *bwsm* seems redundant and is omitted by B D[2] E F G. *ʾwlybnwn*, which is supported with variant spellings by B C D E F I, is probably simply a variant of *lbwntʾ* = "frankincense." Jast. 25b suggests "unguent made from incense." J K L M: *kryḥ lbnn* = "like the scent of Lebanon" or "like the scent of frankincense" (? *lbnn* = a variant of *lbwntʾ*).

Notes, Chapter 4

[42] Tg. takes both "your lips drip liquid honey" and "honey and milk are under your tongue" as indicating sweetness of speech, but refers the former to the priests praying in the Temple, and the latter to the general congregation singing God's praises. Note the stress on the Temple as a place of prayer, thus bringing it closer in function to the synagogue. Cf. Midrash Ps. 33.1 and 149.4. Cant.R. 4:11 §1 applies the verse to the Sages discoursing on Torah (the "bride" *[kallah]* = the Sages). Cf. Tg. to 5:13, "His lips are lilies, dripping flowing/liquid myrrh" = "the lips of His Sages who engage in the study of the Torah drip with [legal] reasonings on every side, and the utterance of their mouths is like choice myrrh."

b. Ḥag. 13a takes "honey and milk" as symbolizing the mystical doctrine of the Chariot, and so uses the verse to assert that such doctrine should not be talked about in public, but should be kept "under the tongue."

[43] "Lebanon" has been given a double reading: (1) implicitly it has been taken as a designation of the Temple; hence the "robes" become the priestly robes; and (2) by wordplay it has been taken as alluding to frankincense *(lebonah)*. See Tg. to 3:6 (*Note* 25) and to 2:9 (*Note* 48).

[44] Tg. may be thinking of Lev 8:30, "And Moses took of the anointing oil, and of the blood which was upon the altar, and sprinkled it upon Aaron, and upon his garments, and upon his sons, and upon his sons' garments with him" (cf. Exod 30:22-25, 30).

[45] Tg. sees a contrast between the "garden" on the one hand and the "chest" and "fountain" on the other, the former referring to the married women of Israel, the latter to the unmarried virgins. Lev.R. 32.5 takes a similar view but applies the imagery of the sealed fountain, appropriately, to the males: "R. Phinehas explained that *a locked chest* applies to the virgins, *a locked garden* applies to the married women, and *a fountain sealed* applies to the males." Cf. Cant.R. 4:12 §2; Num.R. 3.6; 20.22; Pesiq. Rab Kah. 11.6, though the parallels sometimes differ as to which symbol applies to which human category.

Targum:

"Your women who are married are chaste like a chaste bride, and like the Garden of Eden,[46] which no one has permission to enter save the righteous, whose souls are borne thither by angels.[47] Your virgins are hidden away like treasures in money-chests,[kk] and sealed thus they are like the spring of living water that issues from beneath the roots of the

Apparatus, Chapter 4

[kk] Reading *tmyrn kgnzyn bʾnpylyn*. A: *tmyrn wgnyzn bʾnpylyn* = "hidden and concealed in *ʾnpylyn*." *ʾnpylyn* is problematic: the most plausible interpretation is "money-chests" (Jast. 78a). Other suggestions ("inner chambers," "curtains") are unsupported. But it does not make sense to say that the virgins are "concealed in money-chests." Hence read *kgnzyn* for *wgnyzn* (cf. N: *kgnzyn;* J K L M: *kgnzn*) = "like treasures." Tg. seems somehow to have taken the troublesome Hebrew *gal* here as meaning "a chest."

Notes, Chapter 4

The fact that the garden, the chest, and the fountain are described as "locked" or "sealed" indicates that the women are chaste and modest (see further *Note* 50). Cf. Exod.R. 52.1. The "locked garden" is taken as an allusion specifically to the Garden of Eden from which humanity has been excluded, and which only the righteous dead can re-enter. The Hebrew *gal* is problematic. It is commonly translated "spring," but this sense is unique (BDB 164b). Some Hebrew mss., LXX, Peshitta, and Vulgate read *gan* ("garden"). Tg. probably read *gal* but took the word as meaning a "money-chest" (see *Apparatus kk*). The symbolizing of a woman, from a sexual point of view, by an enclosed space (a garden, room, or chest) that has to be entered seems to be universal to human speech (for "garden" = woman see also Cant 4:15, 16; 5:1; 6:2, 11). Pirqei de R. El. 21 is fully aware of the sexual connotations of the imagery and, like the Tg. here, links the garden with the Garden of Eden: "*But of the fruit of the tree which is in the midst of the garden* (Gen 3:3). It was taught in a Baraita: R. Zeʿera said, *Of the fruit of the tree*—here *tree* can only mean man, who is compared to the tree, as it is said, *For man is the tree of the field* (Deut 20:19). *Which is in the midst of the garden*—*in the midst of the garden* is here merely a euphemism. *Which is in the midst of the garden*—for *garden* here can only mean woman, who is compared to a garden, as it is said, *A locked garden is My Sister, Bride* (Cant 4:12). Just as with this garden, whatever is sown therein, it produces and brings forth, so (with) this woman; what seed she receives, she conceives and bears through sexual intercourse." See further *Note* 46.

In keeping with "garden" = Garden of Eden, Tg. takes the "fountain" specifically as the fountain of Gen 2:10, the source of the rivers of Paradise (see *Note* 48). "Sealed" is interpreted in a magical sense = sealed with a great seal (i.e., a magical name of God). Cf. Heikhalot Rabbati 22:2 (Schäfer §236), "show them a great seal and a fearful crown—TʾDS WBR MNWGYH WKʿShPTSh YHWH," and frequently in Jewish magical literature (see further *Note* 49 below and Tg. to 3:8, *Note* 44).

[46] Tg. clearly regards Gan Eden as the place where the souls of the righteous are rewarded after death: cf. m.ʾAbot 5:20, "the shameless are for Gehinnom and the shamefast for Gan Eden"; and the popular prayers, "May his soul rest in Eden!" (*nishmato ʿEden*), and "May his repose be in Gan Eden" *(Be-Gan ʿEden teheʾ menuḥato)*. It is probable that, in keeping with the dominant Rabbinic view, he would have located Gan Eden somewhere in heaven, perhaps beneath the Throne of Glory: see, e.g., b.Shabb. 152b: "The souls of the righteous dead are hidden under the Throne of Glory"; Eccl.R. 3:21 §1: "The souls of the righteous ascend after death and are placed in the divine treasury"; further b. Ḥag. 12b; Sifrei Deut. §344; ARN A.12; 3 Enoch 43:1-3. Note how in Rev 6:9 the souls of the martyrs are stored beneath the heavenly altar. The location and nature of Gan Eden were much discussed in later Rabbinic literature: see the various tractates on the subject in Eisenstein, *OM* 1:83ff., and further Bietenhard, *Himmlische Welt* 161–86.

The comparison of the joys of sexual union to the joys of Paradise is bold and opens the way for an allegorization of the Paradise narrative, which Pirqei de R. El. 21 is beginning to exploit (see *Note* 45), and which is fully developed in the Qabbalah (Zohar, Gen. 35b). Ginzberg claims that allegorization of the Garden of Eden only begins, within Rabbinic tradition, in the Islamic period (*Legends* 5:91, n. 50).

[47] On angels as psychopomps see Pesiq. Rab. 2.3, "When a just man departs from the world, three companies of angels take care of him"; Luke 16:22, "And it came to pass that the beggar died, and that he was carried away by the angels to Abraham's bosom" (Ginzberg, *Legends* 1:304, 306; 5:78, n. 20; Strack-Billerbeck 2:223–25). It is uncertain whether Tg.'s statement that only righteous *souls* can enter Gan Eden is intended to deny the tradition that some have entered alive (b. Ketub. 77b; Ginzberg, *Legends* 5:95, n. 67).

Tree of Life,[ll] and that divides into four heads of rivers;[48] and were it not sealed by the Great and Holy Name[49] it would gush out and inundate the whole world."[50]

13. Hebrew Text:

Your saplings are a paradise of pomegranates,[51]
With choicest fruits—
Cypresses with crocus.[52]

Apparatus, Chapter 4

[ll] K L M N add "like the river that issues from Eden"; J adds "in the river that issues from Eden."

Notes, Chapter 4

[48] The primary reference is to Gen 2:10, "A river went out from Eden to water the garden; and from thence it was parted, and became four heads." But from what follows it is evident that Tg. is also thinking of the "fountains of the abyss" that burst out and inundated the world at the time of the Flood and had to be sealed up again before the Flood would abate (Gen 7:11; 8:2). The idea that the source of the rivers of Paradise is beneath the Tree of Life is not found in the Bible, but in the Midrash. See Ginzberg, *Legends* 1:70: "From beneath [the tree of life] flows forth the water that irrigates the whole earth, parting thence into four streams, the Ganges, the Nile, the Tigris, and the Euphrates" (5:91, n. 50 indicates that the sources for this tradition are late). The unitary source of the rivers of Paradise is here called "the spring of living water": cf. b. Tamid 32b; note further the "living waters" *(mayya' ḥayya')* in 1 Enoch 17:4 (where, *pace* Black, *Book of Enoch* 156, the text is defensible), and the "fountain of the water of life" in Rev 21:6 (cf. 22:17; John 4:14; 7:38; Ginzberg, *Legends* 5:92, n. 51).

[49] For the sealing of the abyss see Prayer of Manasseh 3-4, "Who has bound the sea by the word of Your command; who has shut up the abyss, and sealed it with Your terrible and glorious Name"; Rev 9:1; 20:3; further *Note* 50. For the "Great and Holy Name" see Tg. to 2:17, "the Great Name expressed in seventy names" (*Note* 114 *ad loc.*).

[50] Tg. alludes to the folk tradition that the "waters of the abyss" are sealed with a capstone on which is inscribed the name of God. The capstone is sometimes identified with the *'eben shetiyyah* (see Tg. to 3:10, *Note* 52). Tg. may have this tradition in mind here, since it would link Paradise with the Temple, and would fit the context here, which is focused on Jerusalem and the Temple.

The attitude of Tg. toward sex in this verse is richly ambivalent. He regards female chastity and modesty as central to the ideal polity. "Locked" is probably taken in a double sense, as indicating moral self-restraint on the part of the married women and physical seclusion on the part of the unmarried virgins (cf. 2 Macc 3:19). The social seclusion of women was common in the Mediterranean world and in the Middle East at all periods, and would doubtless have been approved by Tg. The power of his similes suggests the strength of his conviction. Women, through wanton behavior, have the capacity to destroy the world. The allusion to the Flood is significant, since the Midrash regarded sexual immorality as one of the major causes of the Flood; there may be a distant echo of the myth of the fallen "sons of God" in Gen 6:1-5 (Ginzberg, *Legends* 1:147ff.). However, the implication that the joys of sexual intercourse are an anticipation of the joys of Paradise is remarkably positive.

[51] Tg.'s description of the ideal polity neatly brings in the Torah-observant young men to balance the chaste young women of the previous verse.

Tg. takes the problematic Hebrew *shelaḥayikh* as "saplings, shoots": hence, metaphorically, "young men." Note the use of the *shalaḥ* of trees sending forth roots (Jer 17:8) or branches (Ps 80:12), and cf. expressions such as *pirḥei kehunah* ("flowers of the priesthood") = young priests (Jast. 614b) and *neti'ot* ("plants") = young men, young scholars (Jast. 899b). Note also the imagery of b. Ber. 43b: "Rab Zutra bar Tobiah said in the name of Rab: The young men of Israel [Munich ms. + who have not tasted sin] are destined to emit a sweet fragrance like Lebanon, as it says, *His branches shall spread and his beauty shall be like the olive tree, and his fragrance as Lebanon* (Hos 14:7)." b. Pesaḥ. 87a: "Rab Zutra bar Tobiah said in Rab's name: What is meant by the verse, *We whose sons are as plants [neti'im] grown up in their youth; whose daughters are as corner-pillars carved after the fashion of the Temple* (Ps 144:12)? *We whose sons are as plants* alludes to the young men who have not tasted sin, *whose daughters are as corner-pillars* to the virgins who reserve themselves [lit. seal their openings] for their husbands."

"Paradise" *(pardes)* = the Garden of Eden, thus repeating a motif introduced in the previous verse. The equation Pardes = Gan Eden, though as old as LXX (Gen 2:8) and 1 Enoch (e.g., 32:3), is rare in classic Rabbinic literature. Just as the Garden of Eden, which is full of aromatic trees (cypress, frankincense, saffron, etc.), gives off a sweet scent, so the young men, by fulfilling the commandment to procreate, acquire a good reputation. For scent = reputation see 1:3, *Note* 20, and 1:12, *Note* 91.

"Pomegranates" is taken, as in Tg. to 4:3, as an image of someone full of religious precepts *(miṣwot)*.

[52] "Choicest fruit" *(peri megadim)* = sons righteous like themselves. Cf. the expression "fruit of the womb" *(peri ha-beten:* Ps 127:3), and note also the commandment to procreate, "Be fruitful and multiply" *(peru u-rebu:* Gen 1:28).

Targum:

"Your young men are full of precepts like pomegranates: they love their wives and beget sons righteous[mm] like themselves, and as a result their scent is like the sweet spices of the Garden of Eden,[53] cypress and crocus."

14. Hebrew Text:

Crocus and saffron, calamus and cinnamon,
With all the trees of frankincense;
Myrrh and aloes with all the chief spices.[54]

Targum:

"Crocus and saffron, sweet calamus and cinnamon, with all the trees of frankincense, pure myrrh and aloes,[nn] with all kinds of valuable spices."[oo][55]

Apparatus, Chapter 4

[mm] D F read *bgyn kn,* "because of this" for *bnyn,* "sons" ("because of this they beget righteous ones . . .").

[nn] *ʾqsyl ʾlwgwn* in A, with variant spellings in other mss., should be written as one word = Gk *xulaloe,* "aromatic aloes" (Jast. 113a; *LSJ* 1191a). A more accurate transcription would be *ʾqsylʾlwʾyn.* For the various spices mentioned here see Exod 30:23-25 (*Note* 50); Ps 45:9, *mor wa-ʾahalot* = Tg. *myrʾ dkyʾ wʾqsyl ʾlwʾyn;* but contrast Prov 7:17, *mor ʾahalim weqinnamon* = Tg. *mwrʾ wkwrqmʾ wqwnmʾ.* Aramaic *kurkemaʾ* = "crocus," Sanskrit *kurkema* (Jast. 625b).

[oo] Aramaic *kl myny shbḥ bwsmnyn.* D E F omit *shbḥ,* but it represents the Hebrew *raʾshei.*

Notes, Chapter 4

"Cypress with crocus," together with the spices listed in v. 14, are taken as belonging to Paradise. Tg. identifies *neradim* here, and *nerd* in the following verse, as *riqsha* = "crocus." The plant in question must, in context, be sweet-smelling. In Cant 1:12, however, he identifies *nerd* as = spikenard (*nirdaʾ*: see *Note* 52 *ad loc.* on the reading), and takes it as giving off a bad odor.

[53] Following Gen 2:8-9, Paradise is often described as full of aromatic trees, the scent of which can sometimes be detected by humans in the habitable world. See, e.g., 1 Enoch 30 and 32. In the Books of Adam and Eve 29:3-6 the ingredients of the Temple incense (Exod 30:34-36) are said to have been brought by Adam from Paradise: "But your father [Adam] said to [the angels], Behold you cast me out [of Paradise]. I pray you, allow me to take fragrant herbs from Paradise, so that I may offer an offering to God after I have gone out of Paradise, so that He hear me. . . . And the angels let him enter [Paradise], and he took four kinds, crocus and nard and calamus and cinnamon." The righteous, even in death, are said to carry about with them the scent of Paradise, an idea adopted also in Christian tradition in the notion of "the odor of sanctity" (Ginzberg, *Legends* 1:289, 334). It is unlikely, however, that Tg. is here thinking of a physical aura; rather, it is taking scent metaphorically as = reputation (see *Note* 51).

[54] Tg. takes the spices as spices of Paradise (see preceding verse), but Cant.R. 4:14 §1 takes them as perfumes miraculously supplied by Miriam's well, which the women of Israel wore during the wilderness wanderings "to gladden their husbands": "*Spikenard (nerd) and saffron (karkom). Nerd* is nard oil. *Karkom* has its literal meaning. *Kaneh*: this is sweet calamus, as it says, *And of sweet calamus* (Exod 30:23). *And cinnamon*: R. Ḥuna said in the name of R. Jose, Cinnamon used to grow in the Land of Israel, and the goats and deer used to eat it. *Mor*: this is oil of myrrh. *And ʾahalot (aloes)*: R. Jassa said, This is foliatum . . . Now whence did the daughters of Israel obtain wherewith to deck themselves and gladden their husbands all the forty years that they were in the wilderness? R. Joḥanan said: From the well [= Miriam's well: see *Note* 26 above]; and so it says, *A fountain of gardens, a well of living waters* (Cant 4:15)."

[55] Tg. heard in Canticles an echo of the recipe for the anointing oil of Exod 30:23-25, "Take you also for yourself the chief spices *(besamim roʾsh*; cf. Canticles' *raʾshei besamim*), of flowing myrrh *(mor deror* = Onq. *moraʾ dakhyaʾ)* five hundred shekels, and of sweet cinnamon *(qinnemon-besem)* half so much, even of two hundred and fifty, and of sweet calamus *(qeneh-bosem)* two hundred and fifty, and of cassia *(qiddah)* five hundred, after the shekel of the sanctuary, and of olive oil a *hin:* and you shall make it a holy anointing oil, a perfume compounded after the art of the perfumer." Hence Tg's "*sweet* calamus and cinnamon" *(qenei busmaʾ we-qinnamon),* and his "*pure* myrrh" *(meraʾ dakhyaʾ).* The Temple allusion fits perfectly his reading here.

15. Hebrew Text:

A fountain of gardens,
A spring of living waters,
flowing from Lebanon.[56]

Targum:

And the waters of Shiloah are led[pp] gently,[57] with the rest of the waters which flow from Lebanon, to irrigate the land of Israel, because they[qq] engage in the study of the words of the Torah, which are likened to a well of living waters,[58] and in virtue[rr] of the libation of water[59] which is poured upon the altar in the Temple built in Jerusalem, which is called Lebanon.[60]

Apparatus, Chapter 4

[pp] The tradition is uncertain whether to point *mdbryn* as ʾitpaʿal *middabberin,* "are led," or as paʿel/ʾafʿel *medabberin/madberin,* "lead." The active is supported by Tg. Isa. 8:6 where "the waters of Shiloah" are equated with the House of David who "lead [the people] gently" (*Note* 57), but this does not fit here, where "the waters of Shiloah" are basically taken in a literal sense.

[qq] The nearest antecedent of "they" is the young men of v. 13.

[rr] "Because . . . and in virtue of . . ." = *bgyn d- . . . bzkwtʾ d-* (reading the singular *zkwtʾ* with the majority of the mss. for A's plural *zkwwtʾ*). The careful and rather mannered variation is typical of the style of Tg. Cant. Two parallel reasons are given why the rivers flow and the land is fertile.

Notes, Chapter 4

[56] God's praise of Israel continues, but is now presented in the voice of the narrator in the third person.

Tg. offers a double interpretation of the "waters": (1) literally, as indicating the streams that irrigate the Land of Israel: hence "fountain of gardens" = the "waters of Shiloah," and Lebanon = the literal mountain range; (2) allegorically, as symbolizing both the study of Torah and the Temple service: hence "Lebanon" = the Temple (seen as place of study and worship), and the "waters" = both the study of Torah and the water-libations of the Temple cult. The fertility of the Land, the well-being of Israel, depend upon the study of Torah by the young men, and upon the proper observance of the Temple cult.

[57] Cf. Isa 8:6, "Because this people has refused the waters of Shiloah that go gently *(mei ha-shiloaḥ ha-holekhim leʿat) . . . .*" Tg. Isa. translates: "Because this people has rejected the rule of the House of David that led them gently *(medabberaʾ lehon bineyaḥ)* like the waters of Shiloah that flow gently *(negidin bi-neyaḥ).*" But our Tg. probably took the "waters of Shiloah" as symbolic of the "words of the Torah."

[58] The equation of Torah with lifegiving water is a commonplace in Rabbinic literature. For the phrase "Torah, which is likened to . . . water," see Gen.R. 41.9; 66.1; 69.5; ARN A.41; Midrash Ps. 1.18; cf. Gen.R. 97.3 ("the waters of the Torah"). Note also the traditional interpretations of the "evil waters" in m. ʾAbot 1:11. The basis of the equation water = Torah is normally given as Isa 55:1: see Gen.R. 84.16: "*There was no water in it* (Gen 37:24)—there were in it no Torah teachings, which are likened to water, as you read, *Ho, every one that thirsts, come for water* (Isa 55:1)." And Deut.R. 7.3: "The Rabbis say: The Torah is compared to five things: water, wine, honey, milk, and oil. Whence to water? [As it is written,] *Ho, every one that thirsts, come for water* (Isa 55:1)." However, Tg.'s precise wording, "well of living waters" (which is based on the biblical text), suggests a link with Gen 26:19 ("and Isaac's servants found there a well of living water *[be'er mayim ḥayyim]*"), and with Jer 2:13 ("for My people have committed two evils: they have forsaken Me, the fountain of living waters *[meqor mayim ḥayyim]*, and hewed out for themselves cisterns, broken cisterns that can hold no water").

[59] Water in connection with the Temple service ("Lebanon") brought to the Tg.'s mind specifically the water-libation on the Festival of Sukkot, and that in turn may have prompted the reference to "the waters of Shiloah," since this libation was brought from Shiloah: m. Sukkah 4:9, "The water-libation *(nissukh mayim)*—what was the manner of this? They used to fill a golden flagon holding three *logs* with water from Shiloah . . . ."

[60] For the equation Lebanon = Temple see Tg. to 3:6 (*Note* 25), to 3:9 (*Note* 48), and to 4:8. In keeping with the close association between study and worship in Rabbinic thought, Tg. sees the Temple not only as a place of sacrifice but also as a place for the study of the Torah. It is the seat of the Sanhedrin and a school for instruction in the Law (see *Intro.* 4.4). For the general sentiment here cf. m. ʾAbot 1:2, "On three things the world stands: on Torah [= study of Torah], on the Temple service, and on deeds of loving kindness."

16. Hebrew Text:

Awake, O North,
And come, O South;
Give off scent, my Garden,
And let His spices flow.
Let my Beloved come into His Garden,
And eat His precious fruit.[61]

Targum:

On the north side was the table upon which was [placed] the showbread.[ss] On the south was the lamp[tt] to give light. Upon the altar the priests were making the offering,[uu] and causing the incense of spices to ascend.[vv] And the Assembly of Israel said: "Let my God, my Beloved, come into His Temple, and receive with favor the offerings[ww] of His people."

Apparatus, Chapter 4

[ss] Cf. Onq. Exod. 25:30.

[tt] "Lamp" = *bwṣyn*ʾ. The singular indicates that the reference is to the menorah, "the lampstand," but the rendering is somewhat problematic. *Bwṣyn*ʾ is a small "lamp" and is used by Onq. in Exod 40:25 for the lamps that stood upon the menorah (Onq. *mnrt*ʾ). J K L M N read *bwṣyny*ʾ, "lamps," and omit *hwwt* ("on the south [were] the lamps"). This may be preferable. However, the variation *hwh . . . hwwt . . . hww* is typical of the Tg.'s style.

[uu] B C G: "offerings," but the singular is appropriate since the reference is to the altar of incense and only one kind of offering is in view.

[vv] Cf. Onq. Exod. 40:27.

[ww] Reading "offerings" with C E G I for A's "offering." Here the plural seems appropriate.

Notes, Chapter 4

[61] Israel responds to God's praises and invites him to commune with her by taking up residence in the Temple.

Tg. takes "north," "south," and "spices" as alluding respectively to the table of showbread, the lampstand, and the altar of incense in the Temple. The background lies in Exod 40:22-27, "And [Moses] put the table in the Tent of Meeting, upon the side of the Tabernacle northward . . . And he set a row of bread in order upon it before the Lord . . . And he put the lampstand in the Tent of Meeting . . . on the side of the Tabernacle southwards . . . And he lighted the lamps before the Lord . . . And he put the golden altar in the tent of meeting . . . and he burnt thereon incense of sweet spices." Cf. 1 Kgs 7:48-49. Given this context, the "garden" easily becomes a symbol of the Temple, and "eating the precious fruit" becomes a reference to God "consuming" the Temple offerings. When linked with vv. 12 and 13 the equation garden = Temple suggests a connection, geographic or symbolic or both, between the Temple and Paradise.

For a similar interpretation see Cant.R. 1:2 §1: "*Awake, O North, and come, O South* . . . The Rabbis say that this was said in the Temple . . . *Awake, O North*: this refers to the burnt-offering which was killed on the north side [Lev 1:10-11]. *And come, O South*: this refers to the peace offerings which were killed on the south side [in fact they could be killed on any side of the altar]. *Give off scent, my Garden*: this refers to the incense of spices. *Let my Beloved come*: this refers to the Shekhinah. *And eat of His precious fruit*: this refers to the offerings." Cf. Gen.R. 22.5; 34.9; Lev.R. 9.6; Num.R. 13.2; Pesiq. Rab. 5.4. But note the originality of the Tg., and how he manages to link the Canticles verse to a single pentateuchal passage, viz., Exod 40:22-27. In Cant.R. 1:2 §1 and parallels Cant 4:16 is quoted to support the claim that peace offerings were newly instituted with the establishment of the Tabernacle and had not been offered by the sons of Noah: hence "*Awake, O North*" indicates the revival of an older practice, and "*Come, O South*" the institution of a new practice.

CHAPTER 5

1. Hebrew Text:

I have come into My garden, My Sister, Bride;
I have gathered My myrrh with My spice;
I have consumed My honeycomb with My honey;
I have drunk My wine with My milk.
Eat, friends, drink;
Be drunk, lovers![1]

Targum:

The Holy One, blessed be He, said to His people, the House of Israel: "I have come into My Temple,[a] which you have built for Me, My Sister, Assembly of Israel, who is likened to a chaste bride. I have caused My Shekhinah to reside among you.[2] I have received with favor[b] the incense of your spices which you have offered for My name's sake. I have sent fire from heaven and it has consumed[c] the burnt offerings and the sacrifices of holy things.[3] The

Apparatus, Chapter 5

[a] H J K L M N: "the Temple," but note Hebrew "*My* garden."

[b] E F omit "with favor."

[c] L: "and I have consumed" *(ʾklyt)*, probably through dittography of the following *yt*.

Notes, Chapter 5

[1] God responds positively to Israel's invitation to take up residence in the Temple (4:16). For Tg. this verse marks the climax of his description of the ideal polity. God's communion with Israel is depicted under the image of a banquet. The language, which is strongly realistic and anthropomorphic, contains, perhaps, a hint of the Messianic banquet (cf. Tg. to 8:2).

"Garden" = Temple (see Tg. to 4:16, *Note* 21). God's "coming into" his garden is interpreted as his causing his Shekhinah to reside in the Temple. The "gathering of myrrh with spice" = God's acceptance with favor of the incense offerings. Tg. assumes that myrrh is one of the ingredients of the Temple incense: it is not actually listed in Exod 30:34, though it was part of the anointing oil (see Exod 30:23 and cf. Tg. to 4:14, *Note* 55, and to 5:5, *Note* 23). "Honeycomb" = the burnt offerings; "honey" = the sacrifices of the holy things; "consume" = accept with favor. "Wine" and "milk" = the libations offered in the Temple, the former alluding to red wine, the latter to the white. Tg. may have linked "milk" *(ḥalab)* with *yen ḥelbon* in Ezek 27:18, interpreted in the sense of "white wine" (cf. Gen.R. 98.9). "Drink" = receive with favor. "Friends . . . lovers" = "priests, lovers of My precepts"; "drink, be drunk" = "enjoy to the full the bounty prepared for you."

Cant. R. 5:1 §1 offers a similar interpretation but refers the verse to the dedication of the Tabernacle and identifies the "friends" with Moses and Aaron, and the "lovers" with Nadab and Abihu (see *Intro.* 6.4[1]). Cf. Num.R. 13.2; Seder ʿOlam Rabba 7; Pesiq. Rab. 5.4.

[2] Cf. 1 Kgs 8:10-13, "And it came to pass . . . that the cloud filled the house of the Lord . . . for the glory of the Lord filled the House of the Lord. Then Solomon said: The Lord has said that He would dwell in thick darkness [Tg.: the Lord has chosen to cause His Shekhinah to reside in Jerusalem]. I have surely built You a house of habitation, a place for You to dwell in forever [Tg.: a place prepared as the House of Your Shekhinah for ever]."

[3] Cf. 2 Chr 7:1, "Now when Solomon had made an end of praying, the fire came down from heaven, and consumed the burnt-offerings and the sacrifices *[wa-toʾkal ha-ʿolah weha-zebaḥim];* and the glory of the Lord filled the house." Note also Lev 9:24.

libations of red[d] and white wine which the priests pour[e] upon My altar[f][4] have been received with favor before Me. Now come, priests, lovers of My precepts, eat what is left of the offerings, and enjoy the bounty[g] that has been prepared for you!"[5]

2. Hebrew Text:

I was asleep, though my heart was being wakened
[By] the voice of my Beloved knocking:
"Open to me, My Sister, My Love, My Dove, My Perfect One;
For My head is full of dew,
My locks [are full] of the drops of night."[6]

Targum:

After all these things[h] the people of the House of Israel sinned, and the Lord gave them over into the hand of Nebuchadnezzar king of Babylon, and he[i] carried them off[j] into exile, and in their exile[k] they were like a man asleep,[l] who cannot be roused from his slumber. But

Apparatus, Chapter 5

[d] C: "vintage red."

[e] Emending A's *nsybw* to *nsykw* with the majority of the mss.

[f] J K L M N: "the altar."

[g] *w'ytpnq mn twb'*. The verb is strong, "indulge in, delight in"; see Tg. Ps. 37:4, 11 (= Heb. *'ng* on both occasions). But the preposition *mn* is awkward. K L N read *bm'* and K L N *m'* for *mn twb'* ("and enjoy what has been prepared").

[h] Or "words" *(ptgmy')*, i.e., the words of love and communion uttered in the preceding verses.

[i] B H I: "the Lord." There are three readings here: (1) *msr yyy . . . w'wbyl yyy,* "the Lord gave [them] over . . . and the Lord carried [them] off" (so, e.g., B); (2) *msr . . . w'wbyl,* probably with the same sense, "He gave [them] over . . . and He carried [them] off" (so, e.g., D); (3) *msr yyy . . . w'wbyl,* "and the Lord gave [them] over . . . and he [Nebuchadnezzar] carried [them] off" (so, e.g., A).

[j] F omits "into the hand of Nebuchadnezzar, and he carried them off" by parablepsis.

[k] Reading "in their exile" with B C G H I K L N. A and other mss. read "in their exiles."

[l] J K L M N omit "carried them off into their exiles like a man asleep" by parablepsis.

Notes, Chapter 5

[4] Silber *ad loc.* quotes b. B. Bat. 97b as stating that white wine is not permissible for libations. Cf. b. Zebaḥ. 78b. See further *Talmudic Encyclopedia* 24, cols. 249-52 (sub *yayin*).

[5] For the priests eating of the offerings see Exod 29:32 and Lev 8:31-32.

[6] A new section begins here, covering the late monarchic period and the Assyrian and Babylonian exiles, the present verse being connected with the latter. Israel muses on how she fell into the slumber of sin and was punished by exile, and how God tried to awaken her through his prophets to repentance.

"Sleep," like death, is a common biblical image of the state of sin and distance from God, "awakening" of return in repentance to God (cf. Isa 51:17; 52:1). Cant. R. 5:2 §1: "The Community of Israel said before the Holy One, blessed be He, Sovereign of the Universe! I am asleep in the neglect of religious observance . . . I am asleep in respect of righteous deeds . . . ."

It is unclear how the Tg. has read *we-libbi 'er.* He seems to take the heart as being Israel's own heart, which was being roused by the prophets' call to repentance. The heart is the seat of intellect and emotion, and the reference to it here suggested to him that spiritual, not physical slumber is in view: hence "the holy spirit . . . was rousing them from the sleep of their hearts." However, it is possible that he took "my Heart" as a title of God: "though I was asleep, my Heart [God] remained awake and watchful, and tried to rouse me." So Rashi, "*My Heart was awake*: this is the Holy One, blessed be He," citing Pesiq. Rab Kah. 5.6: "*I sleep*—in lack of redemption; *but my Heart is awake* to redeem me. Indeed, R. Ḥiyya bar Abba asked, where do we find that the Holy One is actually identified as the heart of Israel? In the verse, *God is the Rock, my Heart and my Portion forever* (Ps 73:26)." Cf. Cant.R. 5:2 §1.

the voice of the holy spirit was admonishing them through the prophets,[7] and was rousing them from the slumber of their hearts. The Lord of all the Worlds[m] spoke and thus said:[n] "Return in repentance;[8] open your mouths in prayer and praise to Me, My Sister, My Love, Assembly of Israel, who are compared to the dove[9] in the perfection of your deeds. For the hair of My head is full of your tears, like a man the hair of whose head is soaked with the dew of heaven, and the locks of My crown are full of drops from your eyes,[o10] like a man the locks of whose crown are full of the drops of rain that falls in the night."

3. Hebrew Text:

I have put off my cloak;
How shall I put it on [again]?
I have washed My feet;
How shall I defile them [again]?[11]

Apparatus, Chapter 5

[m] B C D E F G H I J K L M N: "Lord of all the World."

[n] Lit. "answered and thus said." Deliberately prophetic style but mixing two constructions: (1) *wayyaʿan wayyoʾmer,* and (2) *koh ʾamar yyy.*

[o] Reading "are full of drops from your eyes" with D E F. A and other mss. omit the words, but the longer text is better balanced and the words could easily have fallen out by parablepsis.

Notes, Chapter 5

The "voice" = the voice of the holy spirit speaking through the prophets. "Knocking" = "admonishing . . . and rousing." Cf. Rashi: "God caused His Shekhinah to rest upon the prophets and admonished [Israel] through them, *daily rising up early and sending them* (Jer 7:25)."

"Open" is taken in a double sense: (a) Repent: for the same interpretation of this verb see Tg. to 5:5; cf. Cant. R. 5:2 §2: "*Open to Me.* R. Yassa said: The Holy One, blessed be He, said to Israel, My sons, present to Me an opening of repentance no bigger than the eye of a needle, and I will widen it into openings through which wagons and carriages can pass." (b) Open the mouth in prayer and praise. Cf. Ps 51:15, "Lord, open my lips, and my mouth shall show forth Your praise"—a verse much used in the synagogue liturgy. The beginning of repentance is prayer and confession in the synagogue.

"My Perfect One"—*morally* perfect, such perfection being symbolized here, as elsewhere in Canticles, by the pure dove.

"Dew" and "drops" are taken as symbolizing Israel's tears as she bewails the harsh night of exile. Her tears fall on God's head: he is not indifferent to them. Tg. shows no embarrassment with the extreme anthropomorphism of the language.

[7] Here the purveyor of the divine speech is the "holy spirit," just as elsewhere in the Tg. it is a *bat qol* or God's *Memra.* Tg. follows the standard Rabbinic view that the prophets spoke under the influence of the holy spirit. There may be an echo of Jer 7:25-26: "Since the day that your fathers came forth out of the land of Egypt unto this day, I have sent unto you all my servants the prophets, daily rising up early and sending them: yet they hearkened not unto Me, nor inclined their ear."

[8] Cf. Jer 3:12, "Return, backsliding Israel, says the Lord."

[9] For Israel as God's "sister" see Midrash Ps. 23.1. For Israel as the dove see b. Giṭ. 45a and further Tg. to Cant. 2:14 (*Note* 86) and to 6:9 (*Note* 29).

[10] For Israel weeping in exile see Lam 1:2, "She weeps sore in the night, and her tears are on her cheeks; she has none to comfort her among all her lovers"; 2:18, "their heart cried unto the Lord: O wall of the daughter of Zion, let tears run down like a river day and night . . . Arise, cry out in the night, at the beginning of the watches; pour out your heart like water before the face of the Lord." See Tg. *ad loc.,* which connects the themes of "exile," "tears in the night," " prayer," and "repentance."

[11] Tg. detects here two different voices—the voice of Israel and the voice of God. He contextualizes this and the following verses to the late monarchic period, and takes them as chronicling the deteriorating relationship between God and Israel. This climaxed in the Babylonian exile, to which he returns in v. 7.

"I have put off my cloak; how shall I put it on [again]?" curiously is said *both* by Israel *and* by God, as if in unison. In the case of Israel = "I have removed from myself the yoke of the commandments." In the case of God = "I have removed My Shekhinah." The comparison of the Shekhinah, the visible manifestation of God, to a "cloak" is apt, and may allude to the doctrine of the divine garment *(ḥaluq).* See 3 Enoch 12:1 with Alexander's note *ad loc.,* in Charlesworth, *OTP* 1:265. Further Loewe, "The Divine Garment and the Shiʿur Qomah."

Targum:

The Assembly of Israel answered and said[p] before the prophets: "Behold, I have already removed from myself the yoke of His commandments,[q][12] and have worshiped the idols of the nations, so how can I have the face to return to Him?" The Sovereign of the World replied through the prophets: "As for Me, I too have already taken up from among you My Shekhinah,[13] so how can I return while you are doing evil deeds? I have purified My feet from your uncleanness, so how can I defile them [again] among you with your evil deeds?"[r][14]

4. Hebrew Text:

My Love stretched out his hand from the hole,[15]
And my inwards were stirred for him.[16]

Targum:

When it was revealed before the Lord that the people[s] of the House of Israel were unwilling to repent and return to Him, He stretched out the stroke of His power against the tribe of Reuben and of Gad, and the half-tribe[t] of Manasseh, that were across the Jordan,[17] and He gave them over into the hand of Sennacherib, the king of Assyria, and he carried them

Apparatus, Chapter 5

[p] N: "and thus said"; D E F omit "and said."

[q] B J K L M N: "my commandments" (= the commandments to me); C: "the commandments."

[r] Adding "I have purified My feet from your uncleanness, so how can I defile them [again] among you with your evil deeds?" with B D E F G J K L M N. A and some other mss. omit. Conversely B G H J K L M N omit "I have taken up from among you My Shekhinah, so how can I return while you are doing evil deeds." The omissions were caused by parablepsis: two successive clauses begin with the pronoun "I" and conclude with the phrase "evil deeds."

[s] J K L M N: "When the Glory of the Lord was revealed to the people (. . . they were unwilling . . .)."

[t] F omits "of Reuben and of Gad, and the half-tribe" by parablepsis.

Notes, Chapter 5

"I have washed my feet; how shall I defile them [again]?" is said by God. The "purifying of the feet" is seen as a reference to God's departure from the defiled Temple, his "footstool." Cf. Ezek 43:7-8, "He said to me: Son of man, this [Temple] is the place of My throne, and the place of the soles of My feet . . . and the house of Israel shall no more defile My holy name . . . by their harlotry . . . they have defiled My holy name by their abominations." Note also Lam 1:8-9, "Jerusalem has grievously sinned, therefore she has become as one unclean . . . Her filthiness is in her skirts. . . ."

[12] The "yoke of the commandments" (Heb. *ʿol ha-miṣwot*) is the obligation to obey the commandments: cf. m. Ber. 2:2, "R. Joshua b. Qorḥa said: Why does the section *Hear, O Israel* precede *And it shall come to pass if you shall hearken?*—so that a man may first take upon himself the yoke of the kingdom of heaven and afterwards take upon himself the yoke of the commandments." m. ʾAbot 3:5, "R. Neḥunya b. Ha-Qanah said: He who takes upon himself the yoke of the Torah, from him shall be taken away the yoke of the kingdom and the yoke of worldly care; but he who throws off the yoke of the Torah, upon him shall be laid the yoke of the kingdom and the yoke of worldly care."

[13] Cf. Ezek 10:18, "And the glory of the Lord went forth from over the threshold of the house . . . ."

[14] Again, Tg. does not shrink from extremely anthropomorphic language: God is defiled by the defilements of Israel.

[15] Israel reflects on the fate of the northern tribes. Tg. has interpreted the Hebrew *shalaḥ yado* in a hostile sense: "he stretched out His hand (to do harm)"; cf. Exod 24:11, "Against the nobles of the children of Israel He [God] did not stretch out His hand *[loʾ shalaḥ yado]*." The "harm" is identified as the exile God inflicted on the northern tribes, specifically for the sin of the molten calves. It is unclear how Tg. has understood "from the hole" *(min ha-ḥor)*. Unusually he seems to have ignored the phrase. Ibn Ezra: "*From the hole*: from the window of heaven."

[16] "My inwards were stirred for him": Tg. interprets as an expression of compassion by the southern tribes for the fate of their northern brethren. They read the exile of the northern tribes as a warning, and turn in repentance, only to find the doors of repentance shut in their face (v. 5).

[17] Cf. Josh 14:3, "For Moses had given the inheritance of the two tribes and the half-tribe beyond the Jordan."

off to exile[u] in Laḥlaḥ[v18] and Ḥabor, the river[w] of Gozan and the cities of the Medes, and he had seized[x] from their hands the molten calf[y19] (which wicked Jeroboam had set up at Leshem of Dan,[z] which is called Pamias)[20] in the days of Pekah the son of Ramaliah.[aa21] "And when I heard [this], my compassion was stirred for them."[22]

Apparatus, Chapter 5

[u] K L omit "into the hand of Sennacherib, the king of Assyria, and he carried them off to exile" by parablepsis.

[v] J K L M N: "to Lahlah"; G H: "in Halah" (see *Note* 18).

[w] Reading "river" with J K L M N. A and other mss. have "rivers," but see 2 Kgs 17:6; 18:11; 1 Chr 5:26.

[x] J K L M: "and he had already seized," *wkbr dbr,* but *kbr* is probably a dittography of *dbr.*

[y] B H I: "molten calves." The plural could be supported by 1 Kgs 12:28; 2 Kgs 17:16. On the other hand only one calf was set up at Dan (1 Kgs 12:29). Cf. Exod 32:4 and see further *Note* 19.

[z] J K L M N omit "of Dan."

[aa] The following words are clearly said by Israel, but oddly there is no rubric ("The Assembly of Israel said . . .").

Notes, Chapter 5

[18] According to 2 Kgs 17:6 and 1 Chr 5:26 the name of the place was Ḥalaḥ. Tg. misread the preposition "to" *(la-Ḥalaḥ)* in the latter verse as part of the name. See further *Note* 21.

[19] Tg. may be thinking of Hos 10:5, "The inhabitants of Samaria shall be in terror for the calves [LXX, Peshitta: calf] of Beth-aven [Tg. Beth-el] . . . It also shall be carried to Assyria." It is natural that the idols of a conquered people should be carried off in triumph by the conqueror: see Isa 46:2; Jer 48:7. For the taking of the calves to Assyria see Seder ʿOlam Rabba 22.

[20] The reference to Jeroboam's making of the molten calves echoes 1 Kgs 12:28-29, "Whereupon the king [Jeroboam] took counsel, and made two calves of gold . . . And he set the one in Beth-el, and the other he put in Dan." Doubtless Tg. stresses the sin of the molten calves as a cause of the exile of the northern tribes because he saw it as a repetition of the sin of the Golden Calf, which Israel worshiped in the Wilderness (see Tg. Cant. 1:5, 12; 2:17).

Tg., somewhat gratuitously, shows his learning by linking Dan with Leshem, on the basis of Josh 19:47, and further identifying Dan with Pamias = Paneas (modern *Banias*). Dan = Paneas is a well-known identification in Rabbinic literature: Pirqei de R. El. 27: "And Abraham pursued after them as far as Dan, which is Pamias"; b. Bekh. 55a: "R. Ḥiyya b. Abba reported in the name of R. Joḥanan: Why is it called *Yarden* [Jordan]? Because it comes down from Dan [= *yrd* + *dan*]. Said R. Abba to R. Asi: You learned it from the name, but we learn it from here: *And they called Leshem Dan after the name of their father* (Josh 19:47). R. Isaac said: Leshem is Paneas. And it has been taught: The Jordan issues from the cave of Paneas." See further b. Meg. 6a and Gen.R. 63.8. Paneas remained in Roman times a noted site of pagan worship.

[21] Biblical history distinguishes three exiles of the northern tribes. (a) An exile of the transjordanian tribes, mentioned in 1 Chr 5:25-26: "The God of Israel stirred up the spirit of Pul king of Assyria, and the spirit of Tilgath-pilneser king of Assyria, and he carried them away, even the Reubenites, and the Gadites, and the half-tribe of Manasseh, and brought them to Ḥalaḥ, and Ḥabor, and Hara, and to the river of Gozan, unto this day." The parallel in 2 Kgs 15:19, which does not mention the exiling of the tribes, seems to date this event to the reign of Menaḥem. (b) An exile of the tribes in the Galilee and in the northern part of the northern kingdom during the reign of Pekah: 2 Kgs 15:27-29, "Pekah the son of Remaliah began to reign over Israel in Samaria. And he did that which was evil in the sight of the Lord; he departed not from the sins of Jeroboam the son of Nebat, wherewith he made Israel to sin. In the days of Pekah king of Israel came Tiglath-pileser king of Assyria, and took Ijon, and Abel-beth-maacah, and Janoah, and Kedesh, and Hazor, and Gilead, and Galilee, all the land of Naphthali; and he carried them captive to Assyria." (c) An exile of the remaining northern tribes during the reign of Hoshea: 2 Kgs 17:6-23, "In the ninth year of Hoshea, the king of Assyria [= Shalmaneser according to 2 Kgs 17:3 and 18:9] took Samaria, and carried Israel away to Assyria, and placed them in Ḥalaḥ, and in Ḥabor, on the river of Gozan, and in the cities of the Medes. And it was so, because the children of Israel had sinned against the Lord their God . . . and had served idols . . . Yet the Lord forewarned Israel . . . by the hand of every prophet . . . Notwithstanding they would not hear, but . . . made two images, even two golden calves . . . The Lord was very angry with Israel and removed them out of His sight . . . And the children of Israel walked in the sins of Jeroboam which he did; they departed not from them, until the Lord removed Israel out of His sight . . . So Israel was carried out of their own land to Assyria."

According to standard Rabbinic historiography all three of these exiles were effected by Sennacherib. So Num.R. 23.14: "You will find that Sennacherib carried them off in three exiles. In the first exile he exiled the Reubenites, the Gadites, and the half-tribe of Manasseh. In the second he exiled the tribe of Zebulun and the tribe of Naphthali, as it says, *In the former time he has lightly afflicted the land of Zebulun and the land of Naphthali* (Isa 8:23). In the third he exiled the rest of the tribes, as it says, *But in the latter time he has dealt a more grievous blow (hikhbid)* (Isa 8:23)—*hikhbid* implies that he swept them away *(hikhbidan)* as with a broom *(makhbed).*" Cf. Tanḥuma, *Masʿei* 10 (ed. Buber, 84b); Seder ʿOlam Rabba 22-23; Lam.R. Proem 5. This tradition appears to fly in the face of the biblical evidence that Sennacherib is not mentioned by name till 2 Kgs 18:13, in the fourteenth year of Hezekiah. b.Sanh. 94a, however, states that Sennacherib had eight names (Tiglath-pileser, Pul, Tilgath-pilneser, Shalmaneser, etc.). See further Einhorn's note to Num. R. 23.14 (Midrash Rabba, ed. Vilna, 2:190) and his appendix to Ruth Rabba (Midrash Rabba, ed. Vilna, 2:26). Tg. here seems somewhat confused. He appears to have conflated all three exiles into one.

[22] Israel bewailing the loss of the northern tribes reflects the widespread concern in apocalyptic and Rabbinic literature about the disappearance of the northern tribes, and the insistence that when the Messiah comes *all* Israel will be gathered in (see Tg. to 5:7, *Note* 29, and Ginzberg, *Legends* 6:407, n. 56).

5. Hebrew Text:

I rose to open to my Beloved;
And my hands dripped with myrrh,
My fingers with liquid myrrh,
Upon the handles of the lock.[23]

Targum:

"And when the stroke of the Lord's power was heavy upon me, I was sorry[bb] for my deeds,[24] and the priests brought the offering[cc] and caused to ascend the incense of[dd] spices, but it was not received with favor,[ee] because the Sovereign of the World closed the doors of repentance in my face."[25]

Apparatus, Chapter 5

[bb] Note the stylistic variation in the Tg: "repent" = *thy* here, and *ḥrt* and *twb* in v. 4.
[cc] C G H: "offerings."
[dd] K L N omit "incense of."
[ee] A omits "with favor." The rest of the mss. have the words.

Notes, Chapter 5

[23] Israel responds to the punishment of the northern tribes with contrition and with renewed dedication to the cult, but finds this of no avail.

"To open" = "to repent," as in 5:2. Cf. Cant.R. 5:5 §1, "*To open to my Beloved* in repentance," though Cant.R. contextualizes the verse to the time of the return from the Babylonian exile. Tg. probably contextualizes to the time of Hezekiah or Josiah: see *Note* 24.

"Myrrh" = the daily offering in the Temple (the Tamid); "liquid myrrh" *(mor ʿober)* = the incense offering: cf. the *mor deror* of Exod 30:23, though there myrrh is an ingredient of the holy anointing oil, not of the incense (Exod 30:34-38). See further Tg. to 5:1 (*Note* 1) and 4:14 (*Note* 55). Israel's "hands" and "fingers" are the priests, who act as agents of the body politic.

"The handles of the lock" are seen as a reference to the locked "doors of repentance." See *Note* 25.

[24] Tg. is probably thinking specifically of the reigns of Hezekiah and Josiah, who are depicted in the Bible as righteous, yet their righteousness, in the end, did not save Israel. This is how Rashi understands Cant 5:5-6, probably in the light of the Tg. (cf. b. Sanh. 94b). For Hezekiah see 2 Kgs 18:3-4, "He [Hezekiah] did that which was right in the eyes of the Lord . . . He removed the high places, and broke the pillars, and cut down the Asherah . . . "; yet cf. Isa 39:5-6, "Then said Isaiah to Hezekiah, Hear the word of the Lord of hosts: Behold the days come when all that is in your house, and all that your fathers have laid up in store until this day, shall be carried to Babylon." For Josiah see 2 Kgs 23:25-26, "And like unto him [Josiah] was there no king before him, that turned to the Lord with all his heart, and with all his soul, and with all his might, according to all the Torah of Moses. Notwithstanding the Lord turned not from the fierceness of his great wrath, wherewith his anger was kindled against Judah."

[25] The "doors of repentance" probably allude to the heavenly treasuries containing spiritual gifts (understanding, prudence, humility, reverence, prayer, etc.) that God bestows on the righteous (for a mythological statement of this idea see 3 Enoch 8:1-2). Full repentance is a gift from God. Israel performed the first stage of repentance by showing contrition *(ḥaratah)* for her past sins ("I was sorry for my deeds"), but there was no response from God; he did not grant them the spiritual gift of full repentance. Contrast Cant.R. 5:2 §2: "*Open to Me.* R. Yassa said: The Holy One, blessed be He, said to Israel, My sons, present to Me an opening of repentance no bigger than the eye of a needle, and I will widen it into openings through which wagons and carriages can pass." This is Tg.'s theological explanation as to why the piety of Hezekiah and Josiah failed to save Israel.

6. Hebrew Text:

I opened to my Beloved,
But my Beloved had turned away, and was gone.
My soul went out [in longing] to hear Him speak;
I sought Him, but did not find Him;
I called Him, but He did not answer me.[26]

Targum:

The Assembly of Israel said: "I desired to seek instruction from before the Lord, but He removed His Shekhinah from my midst. My soul longed for the sound of His words. I sought the Shekhinah of His glory,[ff] but I did not find [it]. I prayed before Him, but He covered the heavens with clouds and did not accept my prayer."[27]

Apparatus, Chapter 5

[ff] J K L M N: "His Shekhinah."

Notes, Chapter 5

It is unusual in Rabbinic theology to deny the possibility of repentance. Note, e.g., Lam.R. 3:44 §9, "the gates of repentance are always open" (*Note* 27 below). See also Ezek 33:11, which is quoted in the liturgy for Yom Kippur, and classical works of *musar* such as Jonah Gerondi's *Sha'arei Teshuvah*. However, Rabbinic sources do have a concept of an unforgivable sin (like the Christian idea of the "sin against the Holy Ghost" [Matt 12:31-32]). Thus the "heretics" Elisha ben Abuya (Aḥer) and Jesus are both denied the possibility of repentance (Aḥer: y. Ḥag. II, 77b; b. Ḥag. 15a //3 Enoch 16:1-5; Jesus: b. Sanh. 107a-b; b. Sotah/ 47a). Significantly, the sin in both cases was leading Israel into idolatry (cf. t. Sanh. 13.5; m. Sanh. 10.1). Note also Lam 3:8-9 and 3:44, on which see *Note* 27.

[26] Israel continues to seek God without success.

"Open" = "seek instruction," but in the preceding verse = "repent": see *Note* 23.

"Had turned away, and was gone" *(ḥamaq 'abar)* is taken as indicating God's rejection of Israel. Cf. Cant.R. 5:6 §1: "*But my Beloved had turned away, and was gone:* He had become peevish and was filled with wrath against me." Tg., as usual, expresses God's departure in terms of the removal of his Shekhinah.

"My soul went out" *(nafshi yaṣe'ah)* is taken as expressing longing rather than fainting or dying (contrast Gen 35:18); "to hear Him speak": Hebrew *bedabbero*, lit. "for His speaking," hence "for the sound of His words."

"I sought Him, but did not find Him" echoes Cant 3:2, where Tg. translates: " . . . Let us seek instruction from the Lord, and [let us seek] the holy Shekhinah that has departed from us. They went round in the cites, the streets and the squares, but did not find [it]." These echoes within Canticles doubtless confirmed to Tg. the symmetry of Jewish history.

"I called" = "I prayed." Tg. plays on the Hebrew *'anani* ("answered me") by seeing in it a reference to the "clouds" *('ananim)* with which God covered himself—an allusion to Lam 3:44: see *Note* 27.

[27] Cf. Lam 3:8-9, "Yea, when I cry and call for help He shuts out my prayer. He has fenced up my ways with hewn stone, He has made my paths crooked"; 3:44, "You have wrapped Yourself with a cloud so that no prayer can pass through." Lam.R. 3:44 §9 comments: "R. Ḥelbo asked R. Samuel b. Naḥman: Since I have heard of you that you are a master of Haggadah, what means that which is written, *You have covered Yourself with a cloud, so that no prayer can pass through?* He replied: Prayer is like a *miqweh* and repentance like the sea. Just as the *miqweh* is sometimes open and sometimes locked, so the gates of prayer are sometimes locked and sometimes open; but the sea is always open, and similarly the gates of repentance are always open. R. 'Anan said: The gates of prayer are likewise never locked; that is what is written, *As the Lord our God is [nigh] whensoever we call upon Him* (Deut 4:7), and *call* signifies nothing else than prayer, as it is said, *And it shall come to pass that, before they call, I will answer* (Isa 65:24)." Tg., however, unlike Lam.R., holds that the gates of repentance and of prayer may be closed. He expresses the doctrine of the mysterious "hiding of God's face" *(hester panim)*, which was to play a significant part in later Jewish theology and mysticism. Cf. b. B. Meṣi'a 59a (= b. Ber. 32b), and see further *Note* 25.

7. Hebrew Text:

The guards who go around the city found me;
They struck me [down], they wounded me;
The guards of the walls took away my mantle from me.[28]

Targum:

"The Chaldeans who were guarding the ways[gg] and besieging the city of Jerusalem round about[hh] overtook me.[ii] Part of me they killed with the sword; part of me they led off into captivity. They removed the robe[jj] of kingship from around the neck of Zedekiah, king of Judah,[kk] and they led him away to Riblah,[ll][29] and the people of Babylon who were besieging the city and guarding the walls blinded him."

Apparatus, Chapter 5

[gg] J K L M N: "the way." There may be an allusion to *derekh ha-ʿarabah* in 2 Kgs 25:4; Jer 52:7. If so, the singular is preferable.

[hh] "Besieging round about" = *mʿyqyn ḥzwr ḥzwr*. The verb *ʿwq* is not used in Tg. Jon. 2 Kings 25 or Jeremiah 52 with reference to the siege of Jerusalem, and Tg. Jon. uses *sḥwr sḥwr* rather than *ḥzwr ḥzwr* (2 Kgs 25:1, 4; Jer 52:4, 7 [Heb. *sabib*]). Tg. Cant. possibly did not know Tg. Jon. to 2 Kings 25 and to Jeremiah 52 in its present form.

[ii] Echo of 2 Kgs 25:5, *wayyassigu ʾoto* = Tg. Jon., *wʾdbyqw ytyh*.

[jj] "Robe" = *kbyntʾ*. This translates the Hebrew *redid* ("mantle"), which occurs only here and in Isa 3:23 in a list of fine female garments. Tg. there also translates *kbyntʾ* = "a garment pinned or buckled on" (Jast. 608a). However, A^2 and the majority of the other mss. read *tgʾ*, "the crown," instead of *kbyntʾ* here. The expression "to remove a crown from the neck" seems odd, but see Tg. to 4:9 *(Apparatus cc)*. E has "they removed the crown of kingship from his head." This is straightforward but is almost certainly a secondary correction.

[kk] I J K L M N omit "of Judah."

[ll] Reading "to Riblah" with J K L M N; cf. 2 Kgs 25:6; Jer 52:9. A has "in Riblah."

Notes, Chapter 5

[28] Israel describes the fall of Jerusalem to the Babylonians and the capture and blinding of king Zedekiah. Cf. 2 Kgs 25:1-7, "Nebuchadnezzar king of Babylon came, he and all his army, against Jerusalem, and encamped against it round about. So the city was besieged . . . Then a breach was made in the city and all the men of war [fled] by night . . . Now the Chaldeans were against the city round about . . . and the king went by way of the Arabah. But the army of the Chaldeans pursued after the king, and overtook him in the plains of Jericho . . . Then they took the king, and carried him up to the king of Babylon to Riblah . . . and they put out the eyes of Zedekiah . . . " (parallels: Jer 39:1-9; 52:4-11).

"The guards" *(ha-shomerim)* are here identified as the Chaldeans, but in the parallel in Cant 3:3 as "Moses, Aaron, and the Levites." Cant.R. here too sees a reference to the Levites who at Moses' command struck down the idolatrous Israelites who had made the Calf: "*The guards . . . found me*: the tribe of Levi, of whom it is written, *They have guarded Your word* (Deut 33:9). *That go around the city*: as it says, *Go to and fro from gate to gate* (Exod 32:27). *They struck me, they wounded me*: as it says, *And slay every man his brother* (ibid.)" (Cant.R. 5:7 §1). Tg. would not have been troubled by depicting the Chaldeans as performing a similar role to the Levites, since both were acting as the agents of God's punishment against sinful Israel. Cf. Rashi: "*The guards:* Nebuchadnezzar and his forces; *that go round the city*: to exact the vengeance of the Lord [cf. Jer 25:9, *Nebuchadnezzar the king of Babylon, My servant*]."

Tg. made a distinction between "striking" and "wounding": the former was taken as a mortal blow = death by the sword; the latter was interpreted as exile.

"The guards of the walls" = the people of Babylon. It is unclear how Tg. has interpreted "my mantle" *(redidi)*. Probably he took it as an article of royal dress, hence = "the robe of kingship" (v. l. "crown": see *Apparatus jj*), the removal of which was seen in context as alluding to the deposition of Zedekiah.

[29] Riblah is derived from 2 Kgs 25:6, but cf. Pesiq. Rab. 31.10, which identifies it as one of three places of exile of the northern tribes: "The Messiah will bring back the Ten Tribes who were separated . . . into three companies of exiles, one of which was banished to the Sambation, one . . . to the region beyond the Sambation, and one to Riblah, where it was swallowed up." See further Tg. to 5:4, *Note* 22.

8. Hebrew Text:

I adjure you, O daughters of Jerusalem,
If you should find my Beloved,
This is what you should tell Him,
That I am sick for love.[30]

Targum:

The Assembly of Israel said: "I adjure you, O prophets, by the decree of the Word of the Lord,[31] if the Merciful One[mm] should reveal Himself[nn] to you, say before Him that I am sick for His love."

9. Hebrew Text:

What makes your Beloved different from another beloved,
O fairest among women?
What makes your Beloved different from another beloved,
That thus you adjure us?[32]

Targum:

The prophets answered and said to the House of Israel: "Which God do you seek to worship, Assembly of Israel, who are the fairest of all the nations? Which God do you desire to reverence,[oo] that thus you adjure us?"

Apparatus, Chapter 5

[mm] = *rhmn'*, an unusual equivalent for Hebrew *dodi*, which is elsewhere rendered *rḥymy* (2:10; 4:16; 5:16; 6:3; 8:14). D E F: "your Love" *(rḥymtkwn);* K: *rḥmny* = (?) *rḥymy*. See further *Note* 30.

[nn] Reading *ytgly* with J K L M N for A's *'ytgly*.

[oo] "Seek to worship . . . desire to reverence" = *bʿy' lmplḥ . . . ṣbyy' lmdḥl*. Note the careful stylistic variation, which is continued in the following verse with *rʿwty lmplh* ("my pleasure is to worship").

Notes, Chapter 5

[30] Israel in exile asks the prophets to tell God of her yearning for him.

"Daughters of Jerusalem" = the prophets; 1:5 = the nations (see *Note* 35 *ad loc.*); 2:7 = Congregation of Israel; 3:5 = Assembly of Israel; 3:10 = cities of the land of Israel; 3:11 = districts of the Land of Israel; 5:16 = prophets who prophesy in Jerusalem; 8:4 = people of the House of Israel. Tg. treats the term according to context.

"My Beloved" = "the Merciful One" (*raḥamana'*: see *Apparatus mm*), which is picked up by "His mercies" *(raḥamohi)* later in the verse. Tg.'s treatment of the term *dod* in this and subsequent verses shows the care with which he crafted his translation. He begins with equivalents that express Israel's sense of distance from God ("the Merciful One," "God"), and reserves direct, emotionally charged renderings for the climax of Israel's hymn of praise (v. 16: "God my Beloved" *['elahi reḥimi]*, "my dear Master" *[mari ḥabibi]*).

"I am sick from love": see Tg. to 2:5, *Note* 30.

[31] Lit. "by the decree of the *Memra* of the Lord."

[32] The prophets reply to Israel's adjuration by asking for a description of her God, so that they may know him if they find him. Tg. takes the obscure question *mah dodekh middod* as a request for a description of what distinguishes Israel's God from the gods of the nations. The question is pointed, since in context Israel is in exile and so especially tempted by the worship of other gods.

"Fairest among women" = "fairest among the nations."

Cant.R. 5:9 §1 takes the verse as addressed by the nations to Israel: "The other nations say to Israel: What makes your Beloved better than another beloved? What makes your God better than other deities? What makes your Protector better than other protectors?" Cf. Mek. de R. Ishmael, *Shirta* 3.

10. Hebrew Text:

My Beloved is white and ruddy,
Conspicuous above ten thousand.[33]

Targum:

Then Israel began to speak in praise of the Sovereign of the World, and thus she said: "My pleasure is to worship that God who, wrapped by day in[pp] a robe[qq] white as snow,[34] engages in [the study of] the Twenty Four Books[35] [comprising] the Torah, the words of the Prophets,[rr] and the Writings, and [who] by night engages in [the study of] the Six Orders of

Apparatus, Chapter 5

[pp] Reading the preposition with the majority of the mss.

[qq] = *ʾysṭlʾ*. The word, which has many variant spellings in Hebrew and Aramaic, is ultimately from the Greek *stolē* (Sokoloff, 51b). It tends to denote a *splendid* garment in Rabbinic texts (m. Yoma 7:1; cf. *ʾiṣṭallit shel melakhim* in the Heikhalot texts: Schäfer, *Synopse* §29).

[rr] Reading "words of the prophets" with J K L M N. A has "words of prophecy."

Notes, Chapter 5

[33] Israel's description of her God (vv. 10-16), in answer to the prophets' request, balances God's description of Israel's ideal polity (4:1–5:1). The distinctive characteristic of Israel's God is that he engages in the study of the Torah (both Oral and Written), just as Torah study is the distinctive characteristic of Israel on earth and makes her "fairest among the nations." Thus the Tg. once again stresses the spiritual supremacy of the Torah Sage: the Sage on earth is the image of God in heaven.

"Above ten thousand" *(merebabah)* suggested to Tg. the angels who serve God in their thousands and recalled Dan 7:9-10, "I beheld till thrones were placed, and one that was Ancient of Days did sit: His raiment was as white snow *(lebusheh kit-lag ḥiwar)* . . . A fiery stream *(nehar di-nur)* issued from before Him; thousands upon thousands ministered to Him *(yeshammeshunneh)* and myriads upon myriads *(ribbo ribwan)* stood before Him *(qodamohi)*; the judgment was set and the books *(sifrin)* were opened." Tg. then related *dagul* ("conspicuous") to *degel,* "a banner." God's "banner" is over the angels, just as it is over Israel (Tg. Cant. 2:4). Cf. Cant.R. 5:9 §1: "*Conspicuous above ten thousand.* R. Abba b. Kahana said: An earthly king is known by his robes, but in the case of God, He is fire and His ministers are fire [and yet He can be distinguished], as it says, *He came (ʾathah) from the myriads of holy ones* (Deut 33:2): He stands out like an ensign *(ʾot)* in the midst of the myriads of holy ones." See also Mek. de R. Ishmael, *Shirta* 1.

Tg. took Hebrew *ṣaḥ* ("white") and *ʾadom* ("ruddy") in a contrastive sense: the former alludes to God's appearance as he sits in his white robe studying the written Torah by day, the latter to his fiery appearance as he sits studying the oral Torah by night. Cant.R. 5:9 §1 also takes the two epithets contrastively, but correlates *ṣaḥ* with the attribute of mercy and *ʾadom* with the attribute of justice.

For the same interpretation of this verse see Midrash Ps. 19.7: "And from where do we learn that the Holy One, blessed be He, studies Bible by day and Mishnah by night? From the verse, *My Beloved is white and ruddy.* When He studies Bible by day, His face is as white as the snow (*Beloved [dodi]* alludes to the Twenty-four Books, because *dodi* by gematria is twenty-four). And when He studies Mishnah by night, His face is ruddy."

[34] The "robe *(ʾiṣṭallit)* white as snow" is derived from Dan 7:9 (see *Note* 32 above). As Loewe observes, "the Targumist's formulation suggests that the wrapping on of a garment reminiscent of the 'robe *[ḥaluq]* of the rabbis' is a necessary or invariable preliminary to God's delivering a discourse on the Bible. It is, so to speak, a symbol of the Deity's standing as an *Alttestamentler*" ("Apologetic Motifs," 186). In other words, the motif further stresses that the Rabbis are engaged in an *imitatio Dei.* However, Loewe's further suggestion that the "robe" here alludes to the doctrine of the Deity's mystic garment (a notion linked to Shiʿur Qomah speculation), which had become so widespread by the Targumist's time that "he felt unable completely to bypass it," despite his generally anti-mystical stance ("Apologetic Motifs," 186; Loewe, "The Divine Garment and the Shiʿur Qomah"), is much less convincing. The evidence that our Tg. is reacting to Shiʿur Qomah traditions is slender (*Intro.* 6.2) and it is surely significant that he does not use the mystics' word *ḥaluq*. One need look no further than Dan 7:9 for the source of the "robe" here.

[35] A gematria may be involved here: *dodi* = 24. See *Note* 33.

the Mishnah,[36] and the radiance of the glory of whose face shines like fire[ss] on account of the greatness of the wisdom and reasoning[tt] with which He discloses new meanings[uu] all day long;[vv] and He will publish these to His people on the great day.[ww37] And His banner [waves] over ten thousand times ten thousand angels who serve before Him."[38]

11. Hebrew Text:

His head is finest gold,
His locks are [in] heaps,
Black as a raven.[39]

Apparatus, Chapter 5

[ss] The syntax is slightly awkward. The translation assumes that *zhyryn* is plural by attraction to the preceding *ʾnpwy,* but is to be construed with *zyw.* The alternative translation would be "the radiance of the glory, wherewith his face shines, [is] like fire."

[tt] "Reasoning" = *sbrʾ* (Jast. 952b).

[uu] = *shmwʿwwn,* apparently used in the sense of the Hebrew *shamuaʿ* ("meaning": Jast. 1592a) rather than of *shamuʿah* ("tradition, traditional decision": Jast. 1593a). By definition one cannot disclose new *traditions* in Torah, especially not by *sebaraʾ.* Miq.Ged. actually reads here *shmwʿyn,* but seemingly without ms. warrant.

[vv] = *bkl ywmʾ. Shenei Luḥot ha-Berit* records a reading *ywmʾ wywmʾ,* "day by day."

[ww] "The great day" here = the Messianic Age, not Yom Kippur.

Notes, Chapter 5

[36] There is a distant echo here of the injunction to Israel to study the Torah "day and night" (Josh 1:8; cf. Ps 1:2). It is standard in Rabbinic tradition to see the day as appropriate for the study of the Written Torah and the night for the Oral Torah. Cf. Tg. Lam. 2:19, "Arise, O Congregation of Israel, who dwells in captivity; give heed to the study of the Mishnah in the night, since the majesty of the Lord dwells before you, and to the words of the Torah at the beginning of the morning watch"; Pirqei de R. El. 46: "Rabbi Joshua b. Qorḥa said: Forty days was Moses on the mountain, reading the Written Torah by day and studying the Mishnah by night." See also Midrash Ps. 19.7 (*Note* 33 above). The Mishnah stands for the whole of the Oral Torah.

[37] There is an allusion here to the heavenly Law Court or heavenly Yeshibah in which God sits and teaches every day like a great Torah sage (b. Sanh. 38b; Exod.R. 30.18; Lev.R. 24.2), and like a great Torah sage "He discloses new traditions every day"; cf. Gen.R. 49.2: "R. Berekhiah, R. Ḥiyya, and the Rabbis of that country [Babylon] said in the name of R. Judah: Not a day passes in which the Holy One, blessed be He, does not teach a new law in the Law Court above (*ʾein yom we-yom sheʾein ha-qadosh barukh huʾ meḥaddesh be-beit din shel maʿalah).* What is the proof? *Hear attentively the sound of His voice, and the meditation that goes forth from His mouth* (Job 37:2). Now *meditation* here refers only to Torah, as in the verse, *But you shall meditate therein day and night* (Josh 1:8)." See further Gen.R. 64.4; Num.R. 19.4.

It is standard in Rabbinic theology to regard the Torah as containing inexhaustible depths of meaning, but Tg., following faithfully the principle that "Torah is not in heaven" (*loʾ ba-shamayim hiʾ*: Deut 30:12; cf. b. Mak. 23b), is careful not to allow the jurisdiction of the heavenly court to intrude on that of the earthly courts. The discoveries and the decisions of the heavenly court will only be published at the end of history "on the great day," i.e., in the Messianic Age. Tg. to 8:1 depicts the exiles going up with the Messiah to Jerusalem to study the Torah. Thus, although strictly speaking a completely new Torah will not be promulgated in the Messianic Age, new and unheard-of depths will be revealed in the old Torah. Cf. Yalqut Shimʿoni, Isaiah §429 (to 26:2): "The Holy One, blessed be He, will sit in the Garden of Eden and will teach, and all the righteous will sit before Him . . . And the Holy One, blessed be He, will sit and expound new Torah which He will give by the hand of the Messiah."

[38] Cf. Dan 7:9-10 (*Note* 32).

[39] God's "head" *(roʾsh)* = the Torah. The equation could be derived from Prov 8:22; cf. Cant. R. 5:11 §1: "*His head* is the Torah, as it says, *The Lord made me as the beginning (reʾshit) of His way* (Prov 8:22)." See further Gen.R. 1.1. The equation would be reinforced by "finest gold" *(ketem paz),* which recalled Ps 19:11; cf. Cant.R. 5:11 §1: "*Finest gold:* this refers to the words of the Torah, of which it says, *More to be desired are they than gold, yea than much fine gold (paz)* (Ps 19:11)."

"His locks are [in] heaps" *(qewuṣṣotayw taltallim)*: the "locks," which belong to the head, represent the interpretations of the Torah. *Qewuṣṣot* ("locks") are taken as an allusion to the jots and tittles of the letters of the Torah (sometimes called *qoṣim,* lit. "thorns"), from which heaps *(tillim)* of halakhot can be deduced. Cf. Cant.R. 5:11 §1: "R. Azariah says: Even matters which seem nothing but strokes [*qoṣim* = the *tagim* or jots and tittles on the letters] are thorns upon thorns [*qoṣei qoṣim,* i.e., raise all

Targum:

"His head is His Torah,[xx] which is more desirable than fine gold,[40] and the interpretation of the words which are in it [involves] heaps upon heaps of reasonings[yy] and precepts.[41] To those who keep them they are white as snow, but to those who do not keep them they are black as the wings of the raven."[zz]

12. Hebrew Text:

His eyes are like doves
[Looking] upon springs of water,
Washed in milk,
Sitting in fullness.[42]

Apparatus, Chapter 5

[xx] Emending to *ryshyh ʾwrytyh* (cf. J K L M N)—a rather midrashic formula, but required by the syntax (note *ḏhyʾ*, not *hyʾ*). A and other Western mss. omit *ryshyh* through haplography of *rʾshw* in the lemma. Cf. Cant.R. 5:11 §1, "*His head* is the Torah."

[yy] Adding *tʿmyn* with the majority of the mss. *Tʿmyn* are legal reasons or arguments advanced to justify a decision (Jast. 543b). The word should probably be taken closely with the following *pyqwdyn:* cf. Hebrew *taʿamei ha-miṣwot*.

[zz] E I J K L M N: "like the face/appearance of [*kʾnpy* for *kʾgpy*] of the raven." Cf. Cant.R. 5:11 §3: "Were all the inhabitants of the world to come together and try to turn one wing of a raven white, they would not succeed."

Notes, Chapter 5

manner of thorny problems]. R. Eliezer and R. Joshua said: Heaps upon heaps [*tillei tillim*, sc. of halakhot]." For similar language see Cant.R. 5:11 §2; Lev.R. 19.1 [*qoṣei ha-ʾotiyyot*]; b. ʿErub. 21b; b. Menaḥ. 29b (". . . to expound upon every single *qoṣ* heaps upon heaps [*tillei tillim;* v. l. *tillim tillim*] of rules"); y. Ned. I, 36d; b. Ned. 9b.

"Black" normally has negative connotations in Rabbinic literature: see Tg. to 1:5, and further Cant.R. 5:11 §5: "*His locks are . . . black as the raven*: these are the scholars who look repulsive and black in this world . . . This refers to those texts of the Torah which seem on the surface to be too repulsive and black to be recited in public . . . ." This reading would have been reinforced by the negative image of the "raven" in the Rabbinic bestiary: "Altogether the raven is an unattractive animal. He is unkind toward his own young so long as their bodies are not covered with black feathers . . . until their feathers turn black and their parents recognize them as their offspring and care for them" (Ginzberg, *Legends* 1:38–39, 163–64; 5:56, nn. 178-83; 5:185, n. 46). Obviously the words of the Torah can be repulsive or unpleasing only to "those who do not keep them." To the righteous they are "white as snow." Tg., somewhat curiously, does not exploit the image of the white dove, the raven's opposite in the Rabbinic bestiary, but "white as snow" picks up the same phrase in the previous verse. Note, however, the reference to the milk-white dove in the following verse.

[40] "Which is more desirable than fine gold" *(dehiʾ regigaʾ middehab tab)* is virtually a quotation of Ps 19:11; cf. Tg. *ad loc.: drgygyn mdhbʾ wmn ʾwbryzyn* [Gk. *obryzon* = pure gold] *sgy.*

[41] Tg. stresses the polyvalency of the Torah, as in the preceding verse.

[42] "Eyes" are taken in a double sense: (a) as = God's eyes watching protectively over Jerusalem, and (b) by gematria (*ʿayin* = 70: see Tg. to 4:1, *Note* 2) as = the seventy members of the Sanhedrin, the "eyes" of the body politic of Israel. This leads to a double interpretation of the "doves beside the springs of water": (a) as a simile for God looking favorably on Jerusalem, just as doves delight to look on pools of water; and (b) as an image of the Sanhedrin engaged in the study and enforcement of the Torah = "springs of water." Cf. Tg. to 4:15, ". . . the words of the Torah, which are likened to a well of living waters" (*Note* 58 *ad loc.*). Further Cant.R. 5:12 §1: "*Beside springs of water (ʾafiqei mayim)*: because they [the Sanhedrin] have been put in charge *(ʾafiqim)* of the waters of the Torah [Jast. 104a]. For Ḥama b. ʿUqba said: Words of Torah invigorate those who study them devotedly."

The two interpretations are connected, for it is the work of the Sanhedrin and the Torah-study of the scholars that call forth God's complacency. The merits of the scholars are one of the major themes of the Tg.: see *Intro.* 4.3.

"Washed in milk": Tg. takes the clarity and smoothness of milk as symbolic of the fairness of the Sanhedrin's judgments. Cf. Cant.R. 5:12 §1: "*Washed in milk*: This refers to the *halakhot* which as it were they wash with their teeth [i.e., pronounce repeatedly] till they make them clear [lit. clean] like milk."

Targum:

"His eyes gaze constantly on Jerusalem (like doves that stand gazing at a spring[aaa] of water), in order to do her good and to bless her from the beginning of the year to its end,[bbb][43] on account of the merit of the members of the Sanhedrin, who engage in [the study of] the Torah and make justice shine[ccc] so that it is smooth like milk, and [who,] sitting in the House of Study, are deliberate in judgment[44] till they reach a decision for acquittal or condemnation."

13. Hebrew Text:

His cheeks are like a spice-bed,
Producing perfumes;
His lips are lilies,
Dripping with liquid myrrh.[45]

Apparatus, Chapter 5

[aaa] The tradition takes *mpqnwt* as a singular despite the Hebrew *ʾappiqei,* which Tg. clearly derived from the √*npq*.

[bbb] B D E F: "to the end of the year," a reading supported by Deut 11:12.

[ccc] "Shine" = *mnhryn* (paʿel or ʾafʿel: Jast. 882b). But it is possible that Tg. intended a denominative verb from *nehar,* "river, stream": hence "making justice stream, so as to be smooth[-flowing] like milk"; cf. Amos 5:24 and Cant.R. 4:15 §1.

Notes, Chapter 5

"Sitting in fullness" is taken as indicating the care with which the scholars deliberate—how fully they weigh the arguments—before pronouncing judgment. Cf. Cant.R. 5:12 §2: "R. Tanḥuma said: *In fullness (milleʾt)*: one contributes *(memalleʾ)* something to the argument and another contributes something to the argument until the *halakhah* issues like the Lebanon; for R. Tanḥuma said: One adduces one idea, and another adduces another until the *halakhah* issues like well-jointed beams." See also Cant.R. 4:15 §1.

[43] Cf. Deut 11:12, ". . . a land which the Lord your God cares for; the eyes of the Lord your God are always upon it, from the beginning of the year to the end of the year"; 1 Kgs 8:29, ". . . that Your eyes may be open toward this house night and day, even toward the place whereof You have said: My name shall be there."

[44] Cf. m. ʾAbot 1:1, "Be deliberate in judgment" *(hewu metunim baddin)*—one of the fundamental principles of the Men of the Great Assembly.

[45] "His cheeks" *(leḥayayw)* = the Two Tables of stone *(luḥei ʾabnin)*. Cf. Exod 31:8, "And He gave to Moses . . . the two tables of the testimony, tables of stone . . . "; 34:4, "and he hewed two tables of stone like the first . . . ." The spice-bed, with its neat rows of spices, is taken as a symbol of the rows of writing on the Two Tables of the Law (*Note* 46 below).

MT has "towers of perfumes" *(migdelot merḥaqim),* but Tg. has vocalized *megaddelot merqaḥim,* "producing perfumes." So LXX. "The *piʿel* or factitive stem of *gdl* is used of growing plants and children, Ps 144:12, and hair, Num 6:5" (Pope, 540). The "perfumes" are the multifarious meanings of the Torah. For God's words filling the earth with sweet scents see b. Shabb. 30b; 88b; b. Pesaḥ. 117a.

"His lips" = the lips of the Sages, who act as God's mouthpiece and pronounce his word. "Lilies" *(shoshannim)* by wordplay is taken to mean "those who study" *(she-shonim)*. "Dripping liquid myrrh" suggests both the abundance and the sweetness of the scholars' legal reasonings. Cant.R. 5:13 §1 partly agrees, partly differs: "*His lips are lilies (shoshannim)*: this is the scholar who is fluent in his Mishnah. *Dropping liquid myrrh (mor ʿober)*: this is the scholar who is not fluent in his Mishnah, so that his lips drop myrrh [i.e., he makes mistakes: *mor* ("myrrh") = *mar* ("bitter")]; all the same he revises *(ʿober)* and repeats what he has learned and masters it."

Targum:

"The Two Tables of stone which He gave to His people, written in ten rows, are like the rows in a spice garden,[46] [and] they produce[ddd] [legal] niceties[eee] as abundantly as the garden produces spices.[47] And the lips of His Sages who engage in [the study of] the Torah drip with [legal] reasonings on every side, and the utterance of their mouths is like choice myrrh."

14. Hebrew Text:

His hands are rods of gold,
Set with tarshish;[48]
His trunk is a column of ivory,
Overlaid with sapphires.[49]

Apparatus, Chapter 5

[ddd] The asyndetic participles *ktybn* ("written") . . . *dmyyn* ("resembling/like") . . . *mrbyyn* ("producing in abundance") are hard to construe, but *dmyyn* should probably be taken as the main clause following the structure of the underlying Hebrew.

[eee] A adds "and [legal] reasonings" *(wtʿmyn),* but this spoils the balance between *mrbyyn dqdwqyn* ("producing [legal] niceties in abundance") and *zlhyn tʿmyn* ("dripping [legal] reasonings"). *Tʿmyn* probably came in by vertical dittography from the line below. J K L M N omit.

Notes, Chapter 5

[46] The Midrash speculates as to how the Ten Commandments were arranged on the Two Tables. Note Cant. R. 5:14 §1: "How were they [the Two Tables] inscribed? Five commandments on one table and five on the other, as it says, *His hands are rods of gold* (Cant 5:14) [i.e., two hands = two tables; five fingers per hand = five lines per table]. . . . The Rabbis say there were ten on each stone table . . . R. Simeon b. Yoḥai said: There were twenty on each table . . . R. Simoi said: There were forty on each stone . . . ." Cf. y. Sheqal. VI, 49d; Exod.R. 47.6. Further Tg. to 1:11, *Note* 86.

[47] Tg. implies that the Decalogue contains the fundamental principles (the *kelalim*) of the whole Torah. Cf. Cant.R. 5:14 §2: "Ḥananiah the son of the brother of R. Joshua said: Between every two commandments [on the Two Tables] were written the sections and the minutiae of the Torah. When R. Joḥanan in the course of studying Scripture came to this verse, *Set in tarshish* (Cant 5:14), he used to say: I have to thank the son of the brother of R. Joshua for teaching me this: just as in the sea between every two large waves there are small waves, so between every commandment and the next one [on the Two Tables] the sections and minutiae of the Torah were written."

[48] Tg. sees in this verse an allusion to Israel. In the context of the description of the "body" of God this suggests that the nation of Israel, when her moral values shine forth, represents God: Israel is God "incarnate." Cant.R. 5:14 §§1-3 sees an allusion to Torah, God's other representative on earth.

"His hands" = the Twelve Tribes of Israel: perhaps two hands + ten fingers = twelve. In Tg. to 5:5 "hands" = the priests.

"Gold" suggested to Tg. the "gold plate" attached to the turban of the high priest. But he has made a curious mistake here in supposing that the names of the twelve tribes were inscribed on the plate: see *Note* 50 below. He interpreted Hebrew *gelilei zahab* as "*engravings* of gold." See *Apparatus fff.*

"Tarshish" is a particular kind of precious stone, but Tg. saw in it an allusion to twelve gems (*terei shesh* = 2 [x] 6) on which the names of the twelve tribes were engraved. According to Scripture the twelve gems inscribed with the names of Israel were attached to the high priest's breastplate. Tg. has them attached to the gold plate on his turban. "Tarshish" may also have been secondarily exegeted by Tg. as a reference to the twelve constellations.

[49] "His trunk" seems to correspond to "the constellations," but the link is obscure.

"Column" (Heb. *ʿeshet*) has been related by Tg. to *ʿshshyt* = "lamp" or "reflector of a lamp." "Lamp," "ivory," and "sapphires" are taken atomistically as symbols of Israel's moral virtues.

Targum:

"The twelve tribes of His servant Jacob are displayed[fff] on the gold plate of the holy crown,[ggg] engraved upon twelve gems.[hhh][50]

Yem.:[iii]

Along with the three fathers, Abraham, Isaac, and Jacob,[51] Reuben is engraved upon *ʾodem*; Simeon is engraved upon *pitedah*; Levi is engraved upon *barqan*; Judah is engraved upon *nofekh*; Dan is engraved upon *sappir*; Issachar is engraved upon *yahalom*; Gad is engraved upon *leshem*; Asher is engraved upon *shebo*; Naphthali is engraved upon *ʾaḥlamah*; Zebulun is engraved upon *tarshish*; Joseph is engraved upon *shoham;* Benjamin is engraved upon *yashefeh*.

West.:[iii]

Along with the three fathers of the world, Abraham, Isaac, and Jacob, Reuben is engraved upon *ʾaḥmar*; Simeon is engraved upon *ʿaqiq*; Levi is engraved upon *barqan zaʿafaran*; Judah is engraved upon *nofekh koḥali*; Issachar is engraved upon *ʾizmargad*; Zebulun is engraved upon *guhar*; Dan is engraved upon *birelaʾ*; Naphthali is engraved upon

Apparatus, Chapter 5

fff "Displayed" = *glyln*, here, unusually, in the sense of "unrolled, unfolded," hence "visible," rather than "rolled up" (Jast. 249b). There is an obvious play on the Hebrew *gelilei zahab* ("rods of gold"). J N read "engraved" *(glyp[y]n)*, but the repetition *glyp(y)n . . . glypn . . . glyp* is rather inelegant and contrary to the Tg.'s style. K L M omit "are displayed on the gold plate of the holy crown" by parablepsis.

ggg Reading *ṣyṣ klylʾ dqwdshʾ ddhbʾ* with J N for A's *ṣyṣ klyln ddhbʾ dqwdshʾ*. It is the *ṣyṣ* ("the plate") that is made of gold, not the *klylʾ* (the crown"). See *Note* 50.

hhh = *mrglyytʾ*, used here not specifically for "pearl" but generically for "gem, jewel, or precious stone"; cf. Ps-J Exod. 28:17.

iii The original Yemeni and Western forms of the list have been reconstructed. The mss. contain numerous variants and cross-contaminations. In the translation above the spelling of the gem names in Yem. follows the MT (the Yem. mss. themselves occasionally vocalize differently). The vocalization offered for the Western gem names is based partly on tradition and partly on presumed etymology. For a discussion see Appendix B.

Notes, Chapter 5

[50] The *ṣiṣ* was a gold plate fastened by blue lace to the front of the high priest's "turban" *[miṣnefet]* or "holy crown" *[nezer ha-qodesh]* (Exod 28:36; 39:30; Lev 8:9). Tg. verbally echoes Exod 39:30, "They made the plate of the holy crown of pure gold [*wa-yaʿasu ʾet ṣiṣ nezer ha-qodesh zahab tahor*; Onq., *wʿbdw yt ṣyṣ klylʾ dqwdshʾ ddhb dky*]." But Tg. seems to have made a serious mistake. The *ṣiṣ* was engraved with the inscription, "Holy to the Lord" (Exod 28:36; 39:30). (According to Josephus, *Ant*. 3.178; *BJ* 5.235; Aristeas 98, and Philo, *De Vita Mosis* 2.114, only the Tetragrammaton was inscribed on the *ṣiṣ*, in archaic Hebrew characters. This may represent distinctive Second Temple period practice or it may actually indicate the correct interpretation of the biblical text: "holy/holiness to the Lord" was not what was inscribed, but the "holiness of the Lord," i.e., his most holy name, the Tetragrammaton.) The twelve precious stones inscribed with the names of the twelve tribes were on the "breastplate" *[ḥoshen mishpat]* (see Exod 28:15-21). Tg. makes the same mistake again at Cant 7:2, as do several other medieval Jewish writers (perhaps misled by Tg.).

[51] It is unclear where the names of the "three fathers of the world" are engraved. According to Exod.R. 38.9 and Leqaḥ Tob to Exod. 28 (ed. Buber, 2:188) they were engraved, along with the name of Reuben, on the first stone. Hence the translation adopted above. Cf. b. Yoma 75b.

ʾaspor; Gad is engraved upon *tabʾag*; Asher is engraved upon *piruzag*; Joseph is engraved upon *meribag*; Benjamin is engraved upon *ʾappantor*.[52]

They resemble[jjj] the twelve constellations,[53] shining[kkk] like a lantern, resplendent in their deeds as elephant-ivory, and glittering like sapphires."[54]

15. Hebrew Text:

His legs are pillars of marble,
Set upon sockets of fine gold;[55]
His appearance is like the Lebanon,
A young man like the cedars.[56]

Targum:

"His righteous ones[lll] are the pillars of the world, set upon sockets of fine gold, that is, [upon] the words of the Torah, which they study, admonishing the people of the House of Israel to do His will. He is[mmm] filled with mercy toward them, like an elder, and He makes the

Apparatus, Chapter 5

[jjj] The syntax of *dmyyn* is awkward. It is possible that the list (i.e., everything from "Along with the three fathers of the world" down to *yashefeh/ʾappantor*) is a secondary insertion. See Appendix B.

[kkk] "Shining" = *bhyrn;* D E F: *nhyryn,* with the same sense; B J K L M N: *bḥyr(y)n,* "chosen, choice."

[lll] D E F J K L M N: "the righteous ones," but the pronominal suffix reflects the Hebrew "His legs."

[mmm] J K L M N have wrongly divided *wʾyhw* ("He is") into *yʾy hwʾ* ("He is comely").

Notes, Chapter 5

[52] For the textual history of this passage and the gems mentioned in it, see Appendix B.

[53] Strictly speaking Tg. merely says that Israel *resembles* the twelve constellations, but there is a late tradition that each tribe corresponds to a particular sign of the zodiac: see b. Ber. 32b; Yalqut Shimʿoni, Num. §418. Note also Exod.R. 15.6, "Just as the heavens cannot endure without the twelve constellations in the sky, so the world cannot exist without the twelve tribes."

[54] Cf. Dan 12:3, "And they that are wise shall shine as the brightness of the firmament; and they that turn the many to righteousness as the stars for ever and ever"—a verse applied to Israel in the world to come in Num.R. 2.13.

[55] "Pillars of marble *[shesh]*," suggested to Tg. a reference to the pillars of the world, which was created in six days *[sheshet yamim]*. But "pillars of the world" in turn recalled the idea of righteousness as the foundation of the world, and of the merit of the righteous as sustaining the world—a key idea in Tg. Cant (see *Intro.* 4.3). Hence "His legs" = the righteous. In context it is clear that by "the righteous" here Tg. is thinking primarily of the scholars. Cf. Midrash Ps. 136.5: "The world stands upon a single column which is called *ṣaddiq* (a righteous one), as it is written, *And a righteous one is the foundation of the world* (Prov 10:25)." Cant.R. 5:15 §1 (cf. Num.R. 10.1; Lev.R. 15.8) has a slightly different interpretation: "*His legs.* This refers to the world. *Pillars of marble.* [This refers to] the world being established in six *[shishah]* days, as it is written, *For in six days the Lord made heaven and earth* (Exod 20:11)."

"Fine gold" once again suggests Torah to Tg. (see 1:11, *Note* 82; 3:10; 5:16, *Note* 60). Cf. Cant.R. 5:15 §1: "*Set upon sockets of fine gold.* These are the sections of the Torah, which are interpreted in connection with what follows and what precedes them." See also Num.R. 10.1 and Lev.R. 25.8. The righteous may be the pillars that uphold the world, but they in turn rest upon the Torah which is the ultimate sustaining principle of creation (cf. Gen.R. 1.1).

[56] Tg. relates "Lebanon" to *laban,* "white," and interprets in a double sense: (1) God is like a gracious, white-haired "elder"; and (2) God "makes white" (i.e., forgives) the sins of Israel. The image of the white-haired elder recalls the Ancient of Days of Dan 7:9, whose raiment was "white as snow" and whose hair was pure "like wool." There, however, the context is one of judgment, here of mercy. Cf. Tg. to 4:3 (*Note* 17); the lips of the high priest on Yom Kippur "make white" the sins of Israel, with allusion to Isa 1:18. Lebanon = the Temple in 3:6 (*Note* 25); 3:9 (*Note* 48); and 4:15.

sins of the House of Israel as white as snow. And in the future He will wage victorious war on the nations[57] that transgress against His Word, like a young man, strong and sturdy as cedars."

16. Hebrew Text:

His palate is most sweet;
He is altogether desirable.
This is my Beloved, and this is my friend,
O daughters of Jerusalem.[58]

Targum:

"The words of His palate are as sweet as honey,[59] and all His precepts are more desirable to His Sages than gold[nnn] and silver.[ooo][60] This is the praise of God, my Beloved; this is the strength of the might of[ppp] my dear Master, O you prophets who prophesy in Jerusalem."

Apparatus, Chapter 5

[nnn] B: "than fine gold" *(mdhb tb)*.
[ooo] J K L M omit "and silver."
[ppp] Reading *ḥwsnyh* with the majority of mss. for A's *ḥwsny.*

Notes, Chapter 5

"A young man" = Hebrew *baḥur*: cf. Symmachus, *neaniskos*; NRSV "choice." Tg. works a piquant contrast between God as the gracious elder toward Israel and as a young man vengeful toward the nations. Note also the implicit contrast between this age and the age to come. For "elder" as signifying the attribute of mercy and "youth" the attribute of judgment see Mek. de R. Ishmael, *Shirta* 4: "*The Lord is a man of war, the Lord is His name* (Exod 15:3). . . . At the sea He appeared to them as a hero *[gibbor]* doing battle . . . At Sinai He appeared to them as an old man *[zaqen]* full of mercy."

[57] Cf. Isa 42:13, "The Lord goes forth like a mighty man, like a man of war . . . He shows himself mighty." Tg. seems to emphasize divine agency in the defeat of Israel's enemies at the eschaton: see 8:4 (*Note* 16).

[58] "His palate" = the words of his mouth = Torah. Cant.R. 5:16 §1 applies the words to the individual sweet utterances of Scripture: "*His palate is most sweet*. It is written, *For thus says the Lord to the House of Israel: Seek Me and live* (Amos 5:4). Could any dainty be sweeter to the palate than this? . . . "

"Desirable" *[maḥamaddim]* is taken as an allusion to the *miṣwot*: cf. Ps 19:10 (Heb. 11), "More to be desired *[ha-neḥmadim]* are they than gold, yea than much fine gold." See further *Note* 60 below.

"Daughters of Jerusalem" = the prophets. See 5:8 (*Note* 30).

[59] Cf. Ps 19:11, " . . . sweeter also than honey and the honeycomb"; Ps 119:103, "How sweet are Your words to my palate! Yea, sweeter than honey in my mouth!"

[60] Cf. Ps 19:10 (quoted above, *Note* 58); Ps 119:127, "Therefore I love Your commandments above gold, yea above fine gold." For gold and silver as a symbol of Torah see Tg. to v. 15 (*Note* 55).

CHAPTER 6

1. Hebrew Text:

Why has your Beloved gone,
O fairest among women?
Whither has your Beloved turned away,
That we may seek Him with you?[1]

Targum:

When they heard the praise of the Lord from the mouth of the Assembly of Israel,[2] the prophets replied and thus said:[a] "For what sin did the Shekhinah of the Lord depart from among you, you who are fairer in your deeds than all the nations? To what place did your Beloved turn away when He departed[b] from your Temple?"[3] The Assembly of Israel said: "For the sins of rebellion and sedition[c] that were found in me."[d4] The prophets said: "Return now in repentance, and let us rise up, you and we, and let us pray before Him, and we, with you, shall beseech [Him] for mercy."

Apparatus, Chapter 6

[a] The actual order of the clauses in Aramaic is "The prophets replied and thus said, when they heard the praise of the Lord from the Assembly of Israel," but it is odd that "thus said" does not stand directly before the speech. The "when" clause may be a secondary marginal gloss. D E F have made a half-hearted attempt to improve the situation: "The prophets replied when they heard, and thus said the praise of the Lord from the mouth of the Assembly of Israel"!

[b] N: "when His Glory departed."

[c] Lit. "for the sins and rebellion and sedition."

[d] J K L M N omit "in me," but the words are necessary for the sense.

Notes, Chapter 6

[1] Tg. detects here the voice of the prophets who admonished Israel in exile (cf. Tg. to 5:2). In keeping with the Midrashic view that Scripture is never redundant, the repeated Hebrew *ʾanah* is taken in a double sense: (1) "for what reason," and (2) "to what place." The latter is the normal sense; the former is hard to justify. The first question is answered, on the basis of Ezra 4:15-19 (see *Note* 4); the second is not (but see *Note* 3). The nations are compared to women, among whom Israel is the fairest. The "seeking" is naturally seen as a reference to prayer and petition (*baqqashah*).

[2] In Cant 5:10-16.

[3] The question is not answered, perhaps because the answer was regarded as obvious. Cf. the well-known Midrash on the ascent and descent of the Shekhinah through the heavens in response to human sin (Cant.R. 5:1 §1; Ginzberg, *Legends* 5:395, n. 31).

[4] An echo of Ezra 4:15, 19: "So you shall find in the book of records and know that this city is a rebellious city *(qiryaʾ maradaʾ)* . . . and that they have moved sedition *(ʾeshtaddur)* within it of old time . . . and it has been found that this city of old time has made insurrection against kings and that rebellion and sedition *(merad we-ʾeshtaddur)* have been made therein." Tg. seems to have taken the "rebellion and sedition" here as being against God, not against earthly kings: Israel rebelled against both earthly and heavenly authority.

2. Hebrew Text:

My Beloved went down into His garden,
[He went down] to the beds of spices,
To pasture [His flock] in the gardens,
And to gather roses.[5]

Targum:

The Sovereign of the World received their prayer with favor. He went down to Babylon, to the Sanhedrin of the Sages, and He gave respite[e] to His people, and, at the hand of Cyrus, Ezra, Nehemiah, Zerubbabel,[f] and the elders of the Jews,[g] He brought them out[h] from their exile.[i6] They rebuilt His sanctuary and appointed the Priests to take care of His offering,[j] and the Levites to have charge of the Holy Word.[k7] He sent fire from heaven and received with favor the offering and the incense of spices.[8] And as a man who sustains his beloved son with delicacies,[l] so He indulged them.[9] And as a man who collects roses from the plains, so He gathered them in[m] from Babylon.

Apparatus, Chapter 6

[e] Reading "respite" with the majority of the mss. A omits.
[f] D E F: "Zerubbabel son of Shealtiel."
[g] B C H I K L: "of Judah."
[h] D E F: "brought them up."
[i] B C G I J K M N: "from their exiles." Variation between singular "exile" and plural "exiles" is common in the mss. of Tg. Cant. Though Rabbinic tradition recognizes numerous exiles *(galuyyot)*, it is hard to see the point of the plural here. Hebrew *qibbuṣ galuyyot* really means "ingathering of exiled *people*."
[j] C D F J K L M N: "the offerings"; E: "the offering"; H: "their offering."
[k] = *wmny'w . . . lyw'y ʿl mtrt mymr' dqwdsh'*. Cf. Num 3:6-7: "Bring the tribe of Levi near, and set them before Aaron the priest, that they may minister unto him. And they shall keep his charge" *(we-shameru 'et mishmarto* = Onq. *wytrwn yt mtrtyh)*. The third person pronouns here were probably taken as referring to God, not Aaron. "Holy Word" *(mymr' dqwdsh')* = Torah.
[l] "Delicacies" = *tpnwqyn*. Tanḥuma, *Mishpatim* 10 (ed. Buber, 43b) interestingly sees *tafnuqim* as more appropriate to daughters than to sons: "Just as a father is obliged to provide delicacies for his daughter, so I brought down for you rain (Exod 16:14)."
[m] Reading *knyshynwn* with D F J K L M N for A's *knwshynwn*.

Notes, Chapter 6

[5] In response to Israel's prayer God restores to her the sense of his sustaining presence both in the Land of Israel and in exile. God's "garden" is the Sanhedrin in Babylonia (see *Note* 19 below); the "gardens" are probably, by analogy, the other houses of study in the Diaspora (*Note* 9). By way of contrast, "the beds of spices" are taken as an allusion to the (restored) Temple in Jerusalem where the incense of spices was offered up, and the gathering of the roses (from among the thorns) as a simile for the ingathering of the exiles from among the nations (contrast Cant.R. 6:2 §1, Gen.R. 62.2, and y. Ber. II, 5b-c, where the gathering of roses is interpreted as God taking the righteous at the opportune moment in death). The parallelism between the Sanhedrin/House of Study and the Temple as loci of the Shekhinah is noteworthy (*Intro.* 4.4).

[6] Cf. Ezra 1:1–2:2, " . . . The Lord stirred up the spirit of Cyrus, king of Persia, so that he made proclamation throughout all his kingdom . . . 'Whoever is among you of all his people let him go up to Jerusalem . . . and rebuild the House of the Lord . . . .' Then rose up the heads of the fathers' houses of Judah and Benjamin, and the Priests and the Levites, everyone whose spirit God had stirred to go up to rebuild the House of the Lord which is in Jerusalem . . . They came with Zerubbabel, Jeshua, Nehemiah, Seraiah, Reelaiah, Mordechai, Bilshan, Mispar, Bigvai, Rehum, and Baanah."

[7] For the teaching role of the Levites see Neh 8:7-9 and Tg. Cant. 3:3.

[8] The return of the Shekhinah is symbolized by the descent of fire to consume the sacrifices. The descent of the heavenly fire is recorded in Scripture with regard to the first Temple (2 Chr 7:1) and the Tabernacle (Lev 9:24; cf. 2 Macc 2:10-11), but not in the case of the Second Temple. 2 Macc 1:19-22, however, tells of the rediscovery of the holy fire in the Second Temple (in the form of "thick water"). Cf. for a similar tradition Yosippon 7:24-38 (ed. Flusser, 1:44–45).

[9] "And as a man who sustains his beloved son with delicacies, so he indulged them" is Tg.'s interpretation of "to pasture [His flock] in the gardens" (cf. Tg. of the next verse), the Hebrew *lirʿot* being taken to mean not "to feed" (intransitive) but "to

3. Hebrew Text:

I am my Beloved's,
And my Beloved is mine,
Who pastures [His flock] among the roses.[10]

Targum:

"And on that day I worshiped the Sovereign of the World,[n] my Beloved, and my Beloved[o] caused His holy Shekhinah to dwell in my midst, and He fed[p] me with delicacies."

4. Hebrew Text:

You are [as] comely, My Love, as an acceptable sacrifice,[11]
[As] beautiful as [was] Jerusalem,[12]
[As] frightening as [were] the camps with their standards.[13]

Apparatus, Chapter 6

[n] Reading *mry ʿlmʾ* with D E F. A and other mss. have *mry,* "my Sovereign."

[o] = *rḥymy wrḥymy.* J M: *rḥymy wḥbyby;* K L N: *ḥbyby wrḥymy.* The variation at first sight conforms with Tg. Cant.'s style, but note the repetition of *dodi* in the Hebrew.

[p] B: "which fed" (*dzn* for *wzn*). The idea of the Shekhinah feeding the people is found in the Aggadah and the Heikhalot texts, but the gender of the verb is wrong.

Notes, Chapter 6

pasture [a flock]." Israel is God's flock (cf. Jer 31:10; Isa 40:11). The interpretation is rather vague: it is unclear what are the "delicacies" and how Tg. has understood "gardens" in the Hebrew. Cant.R. 6:2 §1 takes "gardens" as signifying "synagogues and houses of study," which makes good sense if "garden" = the Sanhedrin, as above (though this is not Cant.R.'s view). Rashi picks up the idea and interprets that God's sustaining presence is felt not only in the Land of Israel but also in the exile, through prayer and study. The "delicacies," then, are probably not material but spiritual sustenance, such as choice interpretations of the Torah.

[10] Tg. contextualizes straightforwardly to a perceived period of good relations between God and Israel after the return from exile. "I am my Beloved's" = I worship God, my Beloved; "my Beloved is mine" = God causes his presence to dwell with me. On "who pastures [His flock] among the roses" see Tg. to previous verse (*Note* 9 above). The parallel in Cant 2:16 is interpreted differently.

[11] God praises Israel in a series of flashbacks. Israel is now restored to her former glories: the rebuilt Temple is comparable to Solomon's, and Israel's military prowess is as great as it was in the Wilderness. But the picture is idealized: contrast Hag 2:3, "Who is left among you who saw this house in its former glory? And how do you see it now? Is it not as nothing in your eyes?" (cf. Zech 4:10). "An acceptable sacrifice" = Hebrew *tirṣah*: Tg. takes this not as a proper name (= the old capital of the northern kingdom, 1 Kgs 6:8, 15, 24, as Jerusalem, mentioned in the next line, was capital of the southern), but as a noun or a verb from √*rṣh,* "be pleased, desire, accept," frequently in the context of sacrifice (cf. LXX *hōs eudokia*). So Cant.R. 6:4 §§1-2: "*You are comely, My Love, as Tirṣah*: These are the sacrifices, since through the sacrifices you become acceptable *(mitraṣṣim)* to God, as it says, *It shall be accepted (nirṣah) for him to make atonement for him* (Lev 1:4) . . . Another interpretation: *You are comely, My Love, as Tirṣah:* when you desire *(roṣah)* . . . "

[12] In the time of Solomon, the chief beauty of the city then being its Temple. Cf. Cant.R. 6:4 §1, "*Beautiful as Jerusalem:* this refers to the holy things [sacrifices] in Jerusalem."

[13] Tg. sees in the Hebrew *nidgalot* (only here and Cant 6:10: see *Note* 34 below) an allusion to the camps of Israel in the wilderness, with their standards *(degalim).* Cf. Vulgate *castrorum acies ordinata.* The biblical basis is Num 2:3, 10, 18, 25, "Now those that pitch on the east side toward the sunrise shall be of the standard of the camp of Judah . . . On the south side shall be the standard of the camp of Reuben . . . On the west side shall be the standard of the camp of Ephraim . . . On the north side shall be the standard of the camp of Dan . . . " Cf. Num 10:14, 18, 22, 25. Further Ginzberg, *Legends* 3:230–36. Contrast Cant.R. 6:10 §1, which interprets the phrase (in Cant 6:10) as an allusion to the hosts of heaven, though according to Num.R. 2.3 there is a link, the camps in the wilderness being organized "under standards, like the ministering angels." Tg. then takes "frightening" as a reference to the fear *(ʾeimah)* that Israel in the wilderness inspired in other nations: see further *Note* 14.

Targum:

The Lord said through His Word: "How comely are you, My Love, at the time when[q] your desire is to do My will! The Temple which you have built for Me is as beautiful as the former sanctuary which king Solomon built for Me in Jerusalem,[r] and the fear of you is on all the nations as in the day when[q] your four camps marched through the Wilderness."[14]

5. Hebrew Text:

Cause your "eyes" to sit round before Me,[15]
For they did homage to Me.[16]
Your hair is like the "flock of goats"
That made a memorial on Gilead.[17]

Apparatus, Chapter 6

[q] *bzmn d- . . . kywm' d- :* characteristic stylistic variation.

[r] Reading "in Jerusalem" with D E F. A and other mss. have "of Jerusalem" ("Solomon king of Jerusalem"). J K L M N read simply "which Solomon built for Me," omitting "king of/in Jerusalem," but some reference to Jerusalem is appropriate in view of the Hebrew.

Notes, Chapter 6

[14] Joshua 2:9, "The fear of you *('eimatekhem)* has fallen upon us, and all the inhabitants of the land melt away before you"; Ps 68:7-8, "O God, when You went forth before Your people, when You marched through the Wilderness, the earth trembled." Cf. Tg. Cant. 1:3, "At the news of Your miracles and mighty acts which You performed for Your people, the House of Israel, all the peoples trembled."

[15] Tg. records the reconstitution of the Sanhedrin/Great Assembly in the Land after the return, but much of it also celebrates Israel's faithfulness to God outside the Land, in exile in Babylonia, expressed in establishing schools for the study of the Torah and in acknowledging to the Gentiles the justice of God's punishment.

Hebrew *hasebbi 'einayikh minnegdi* is normally taken to mean "turn away your eyes from Me," but this is hardly appropriate in an address of God to Israel, so Tg. interprets "cause your 'eyes' to sit in a circle over against Me," "eyes" being identified with the Sages of the Great Assembly = the Sanhedrin of the Sages in v. 2 (see further *Note* 18 below). For "eyes" = Sanhedrin see Tg. to 4:1 (*Note* 6) and 7:5; contrast Tg. to 1:15 (*Note* 119). The reference is to the tradition that the Sanhedrin sat in a semicircle in the presence of the Shekhinah: "The Sanhedrin sat like the half of a round threshing-floor, and they sat in the Chamber of Hewn Stone close to the Shekhinah" (Maimonides, *Hilkhot Beit Ha-Beḥirah* 5:3, on the basis of m. Sanh. 4:3; 11:2; cf. Tg. to 7:3, *Note* 14).

[16] Hebrew *she-hem hirhibuni* is usually translated "for they disturb me" (Murphy, 175), but this is even less appropriate in the context of the Tg.'s reading of the verse than is the normal rendering of the preceding line. Tg. links *hirhibuni* with the MH sense of √*rhb,* "to acknowledge the authority of, submit to"; *hif'il,* "to declare great, do homage to," though only in exegetical contexts. See Jast. 1453b, quoting Exod.R. 27.9, "*Go humble yourself* (Prov 6:3) in the dust of the feet of princes and those greater than you, and make them kings over you *[we-hamlikhem]*, as it is written, *And acknowledge the authority of [u-rehab] your neighbor* (Prov 6:3): the word *rhb* always indicates royalty, as it says, *I will make mention of Rahab* (Ps 87:4)"; and Cant.R. 6:5 §1, "*She-hem hirhibuni*: they declared me king *[himlikhuni]* over them and said, *The Lord shall reign forever and ever* (Exod 15:18) . . . *She-hem hirhibuni*: they accepted My kingship *[hem qibbelu malkhuti 'aleihem]* at Sinai and said, *All that the Lord has said we will do, and obey* (Exod 24:7); and it is written, *I will make mention of Rahab and Babylon among them that know me* (Ps 87:4)."

[17] The parallel in Cant 4:1 is treated in the same way by Tg. See *Notes* 3 and 8 *ad loc.*

Targum:

"Cause your teachers, the Sages of the Great Assembly,[s18] to sit round in a circle before Me,[t] for they acknowledged My kingship[u] in exile, and instituted the school[v] for the teaching of My Torah.[w19] And the rest of your students and the people of the land[20] proclaimed Me as just through the word of their mouth, like the sons of Jacob, who gathered stones and raised a monument on Mount Gilead."[21]

6. Hebrew Text:

Your teeth are like a flock [of ewes] that are shorn,
Which have come up from the washing,
All of which bear twins,
And there is none bereaved among them.[22]

Targum:

"The Priests and the Levites,[x] who eat your offerings, the holy tithe and the heave-offering, are pure from any violence or robbery,[y] just as Jacob's flock[z] of sheep were pure

Apparatus, Chapter 6

[s] N omits "the Sages of the Great Assembly."

[t] Reading *lqbly* with the majority of the mss. for A's *lqybly.*

[u] "Acknowledged My kingship" = *ʾmlkwny,* not "consulted Me" (Gollancz). For this latter sense of the verb see Tg. to 6:12. For the sense here see *Note* 16, and further Tg. to 7:6.

[v] = *mdrshʾ.* E: *by mdrshʾ.* Midrash = "school" (= Beit Midrash) is both early and late usage. Note Arabic *madrasa,* but also Qumranic "midrash." See further Tg. to 7:14.

[w] N: "the Torah."

[x] B: "your Priests and your Levites." This makes the connection with "your teeth" even more obvious, but the rest of the mss. read simply "the Priests and the Levites," and see 4:2.

[y] The reading *ʾkly* ("eaters of [your offerings]" = Heb. "teeth") indicates that *dkyyn* introduces the main clause and is to be construed with *khnyʾ wlywʾy.* However the alternative, "the Priests and the Levites eat your offerings . . . which are pure from any violence or robbery," cannot be completely discounted. It has support from 4:2: see *Apparatus f ad loc.* The fact that no mss. reads here *ddkyyn* is not decisive. Tg. Cant. is fond of "hanging" participles.

[z] C G H J: "flocks." The fact that *dkyyn* is plural is immaterial since "flock" is a collective noun and could take a plural verb *ad sensum.*

Notes, Chapter 6

[18] Otherwise known as the Men of the Great Assembly/Synagogue, defined in Tg. to 7:3 as comprising Ezra the Priest, Zerubabbel, Jeshua, Nehemiah, and Mordechai Bilshan (cf. Ezra 2:2). The institution of the Great Assembly plays an important role in Rabbinic historiography of the Persian period, and various enactments are attributed to it (m. ʾAbot 1:1; further Ginzberg, *Legends* 6:447–49; Nadich, *Jewish Legends* 161–82), but its historicity is in considerable doubt. Tg. seems to hold, with Seder ʾEliyyahu Rabba 27, that the Great Assembly functioned in Babylon *during* the exile (cf. v. 2 and *Note* 19 below). What is probably envisaged here is its transfer to the Land of Israel.

[19] Some of the Babylonian academies claimed to go back to the exilic period—a claim usually made in a polemical context to stress their antiquity as against the Palestinian schools (Goodblatt, *Rabbinic Instruction* 13–16). Behind this may lie an interpretation of "the little sanctuary" in Ezek 11:16. On the possible light this may throw on the origins of Tg.Cant. see *Intro.* 8.2.

[20] "People of the land" (*ʿammaʾ deʾarʿaʾ* = Heb. *ʿam haʾareṣ*), the rest of the people who are not scholars, the non-rabbinically trained, apparently with no pejorative overtones.

[21] In Tg. to 4:1 the sons of Jacob are seen as examples of righteousness; here they appear to exemplify the justification of God (*ṣidduq haddin*)—an idea that is hardly prominent in Gen 31:46-54. However, the play may be on the name Gilead = *Gal ʿEd,* "Heap of Witness": just as Jacob and his sons gathered stones and built a structure to act as a witness, so the schools built by the Babylonian exiles were testimonies among the nations to God's truth.

[22] The parallel in 4:2 is treated almost identically by Tg., though there it is related to the Solomonic period of Israel's history. Here we are in the post-exilic era. See *Notes* to 4:2.

when they came up from the brook Jabbok, among which were none gained by violence or robbery.[aa] All of them were alike one to another, and bearing twins every time, and none of them was barren or miscarried."

7. Hebrew Text:

Your brow is like a slice of pomegranate
Behind your veil.[23]

Targum:

"As for the royal house of the Hasmoneans,[bb] they are all as full of precepts[cc] as a pomegranate, not to mention[dd] Mattathias the High Priest[24] and his sons, who are more righteous than them all,[ee][25] and [who] observe the precepts[ff] and the words of the Torah with zeal."[gg][26]

Apparatus, Chapter 6

[aa] F omits "just as Jacob's flock . . . robbery" by parablepsis.

[bb] "As for the royal house of the Hasmoneans" = *wmlkwt byt ḥshmwn'y.* The meaning of the phrase is unclear and the syntax awkward. Alternative translation: "In the kingdom of the house of the Hasmoneans [everyone is . . .]."

[cc] C adds "and words of the Torah" by vertical dittography from the line below.

[dd] "Not to mention" = *br mn*: see 4:3, *Apparatus i.*

[ee] Adding "than them all" with D E. A and the majority of mss. omit, probably by vertical haplography with the line above. The addition seems to be demanded by *br mn.*

[ff] F omits "as a pomegranate . . . the precepts" by parablepsis.

[gg] Reading *bṣḥwt'* with C G H I for A's *bṣḥwt'*. Lit. "with thirst": see *Note* 26. B, "with mildness" *(bnḥwt')*, does not seem appropriate in context.

Notes, Chapter 6

[23] Tg.'s interpretation here is broadly the same as in the parallel in 4:3: the pomegranate with its tightly-packed seeds is taken in both places as an image of the pious person, full of commandments. In both places two sets of people are detected, represented by the "brow" and "(those) behind the veil." In 4:3 the "brow" = the king; here it is the royal house; in 4:3 "(those) behind the veil" are the king's counselors; here they are Mattathias and his sons, though the distinction is rather forced since Mattathias and his sons are effectively the same as the "royal house" (see further *Notes* to 4:3).

Tg. uses the parallelism between 6:7 and 4:3 to suggest the idea that the Hasmonean state represented a return to the glories of the Solomonic era. The parallelism is a fact that requires explanation by the exegete, as Pope (*Song of Songs,* 566) notes: "The reason for the repetition of much of 4:1-3 here has been variously surmised . . . Joüon saw here a development in the thought of the author who describes now the return from Exile and repeats on purpose in order to stress the analogy of this event with the Exodus from Egypt and to show that the divine love towards Israel is as strong now as then." Given the generally negative attitude toward the Hasmoneans in the classic Rabbinic texts, the positive evaluation of the Hasmoneans in Tg.Cant. 6:7-12 is remarkable. See further *Intro.* 8.1.

[24] Strictly speaking the Hasmoneans were not a "royal house" (since they were not of Davidic descent), nor was Mattathias entitled to be "High Priest" (since he was not of the House of Zadoq): both the kingship and the high priesthood were usurped. However, Tg., in keeping with late Jewish historiographical tradition on the Second Temple period, regards the Hasmoneans as both kings and high priests: see, e.g., Ibn Daud, *Sefer ha-Qabbalah* 2:35–38 (ed. Cohen, 13): "In the 212th year after the building of the Second Temple, corresponding to the year 3621, Mattathias b. Joḥanan the High Priest, called Hasmonean, rebelled against Antiochus king of Greece. He and his sons rose up against the viceroy of the king of Greece, then ruling over Jerusalem, and killed him and all his army. The Hasmonean ruled *(malakh)* one year and died." See further Cohen, *Sefer ha-Qabbalah by Ibn Daud,* 113, n. 53.

[25] The referent of the pronoun is not clear: it is either the rest of the members of the "royal house of the Hasmoneans" or, more vaguely, the rest of the people.

[26] The correct reading is *bṣḥwt',* lit. "with thirst" (see *Apparatus gg*), clearly a secondary interpretation of Hebrew *ṣammah,* relating it to √*ṣm',* "to be thirsty." Thirst for the living waters of the Torah is an image of the Hasmoneans' zeal for the Law: cf. m. 'Abot 1:4, "Let your house be a meeting-house for the Sages and sit in the dust at their feet and drink in their words with thirst *(be-ṣama')*."

8. Hebrew Text:

Sixty queens [were] they,
And eighty concubines,
And maidens without number![27]

Targum:

Then the Greeks arose and gathered together sixty kings from the sons of Esau, clad in chain-mail and mounted[hh] on horses, and cavalry,[ii] and eighty commanders[jj] from the sons of Ishmael, riding on elephants, not to mention the rest of the nations, peoples and tongues that were without number, and they appointed the wicked Alexander[kk28] as head[ll] over them, and they came[mm] to wage war against Jerusalem.[nn]

Apparatus, Chapter 6

[hh] Reading *rkbyn* with C J K M for A's *rkby.*
[ii] "Cavalry" = *prshyn.* If a precise military distinction between these and the "kings mounted on horses" is intended, then the former are probably mailed knights (like the Parthian *clibanarius*) and the latter *light* cavalry.
[jj] = *dwkwsyn* = *duces.*
[kk] D F: "king Alexander" instead of "the wicked Alexander"; E: "King Antiochus" see *Note* 27.
[ll] E J K L M N omit "as head."
[mm] Reading "and they came" with the majority of mss. for A's "and he came."
[nn] = *byrwshlm* (lit. "in Jerusalem"); C J K L M N: *ʿl yrwshlm* ("against Jerusalem"); D F G I: *lyrwshlm* ("to Jerusalem").

Notes, Chapter 6

[27] Tg. takes the "queens," "concubines," and "maidens" as referring to the Gentile nations: cf. Cant.R. 6:8 §1: "*Sixty queens and eighty concubines*: Rabbi Ḥiyya of Sepphoris and Rabbi Levi referred this verse to the nations of the world. Rabbi Ḥiyya said: Sixty and eighty make a hundred and forty. Forty of them have a language of their own but no script; forty have no language of their own but they have a script. *And maidens without number*: This refers to the rest of them who have neither language nor script of their own." The text here is not clear, and may be corrupt. One would expect the "queens," as hierarchically the highest of the classes, to have *both* language *and* script, followed by the "concubines" whose script, so to speak, serves a language that is not their own. Then come the "maidens" who are totally subordinate to other cultures and use both a foreign language and script, unless the implication is that Israel is unique, and alone has her own language and script. Clearly the classification is cultural. In Tg., however, it is geographical and political. Writing from the standpoint of his own time, Tg. presents the picture of the whole world ranged against Israel: the descendants of Esau = the Greeks and Romans of the (Christian) west (= the "queens"); Ishmael = the Arabs in the (Muslim) east (= the "concubines"); and the rest of the nations (= the "maidens"). The picture has eschatological overtones, and recalls the massing of the Gentiles against Israel at the end of history. Alexander the Great in the next verse plays the role of Armillus in the battle of Armageddon. He is not generally seen as "wicked" in early Rabbinic tradition (see *Note* 28). Tg. may be reflecting the more negative evaluation of him in Islamic tradition, which was in turn influenced in part by Persian attitudes. Such an allusion here is in keeping with Tg.'s view of the repetitiveness of history. The bases of Tg.'s equivalents are not clear (though Tg. often takes the "daughters" and other women's choruses in Canticles as alluding to the Gentiles: see *Note* 30 below and Tg.Cant. 2:2, *Note* 5). However, *pilagshim* may have been taken in the sense of "descendants of the concubine Hagar (Gen 16:1-3)," hence "Ishmaelites."

[28] Tg.'s picture is historically confused. He has conflated the tradition of Alexander the Great's peaceful visit to Jerusalem with the attack of the forces of Antiochus on Jerusalem at the time of the Maccabean revolt. For the former see Josephus, *Ant.* 11.329–39; b. Yoma 69a; Scholion to Megillat Taʿanit (ed. Lichtenstein, 339–40); Yosippon 10 (ed. Flusser, 54ff.); Ibn Daud, *Sefer ha-Qabbalah* 2:1–14 (ed. Cohen, 11). Further Nadich, *Jewish Legends* 37–44. For the latter see 1 Macc 6:28-35: "The king was angry and gathered together all his friends who were leaders of his host, and those that were over the horse. And there came to him from other kingdoms, and from the isles of the sea, bands of mercenaries. And the number of his forces was 100,000 infantry, and 20,000 cavalry, and thirty-two elephants trained for war . . . And they set by each elephant 1,000 men armed with coats of mail, and helmets of brass on their heads." Megillat Antiochus 46: "He sent letters to every province of his kingdom that the mighty men should come, and not one of them should be left, and that elephants clad in armor should be with them." Cf. Yosippon 23 (ed. Flusser, 100ff.).

9. Hebrew Text:

My faultless dove is one;
She is one to her mother;
She is pure to her that bore her.[29]
The daughters saw her;
The queens and concubines called her happy,
And they praised her.[30]

Targum:

At that time the Assembly of Israel, which is likened to the perfect dove, was worshiping the Sovereign of the World[oo] with one heart,[pp][31] and [was] devoted[qq] to the Torah, and

Apparatus, Chapter 6

[oo] Reading *lmryh dʿlmʾ* with J K L M. A has *mrh,* which presumably means "her Sovereign" (cf. D *lmrhʾ*).

[pp] Reading *blb hd . . . blbb shlym,* following D E F H J K L M N. A has *blb shlym . . . blbb shlym,* but the variation is typical of Tg. Cant.'s style. See *Note* 31.

[qq] D E F's *ʾḥydʾ* is marginally preferable to A's *yḥydʾ*. The sense is more or less the same with either reading.

Notes, Chapter 6

29 The speaker would appear to be God, who praises Israel's fidelity in the face of the threat from the nations, but Tg. casts this as a third-person report.

The dove is a common image of Israel, usually stressing her innocence and purity, but sometimes her vulnerability: see Tg.Cant. 5:2, "Assembly of Israel, who are compared to the dove in the perfection of your deeds" (*Note* 9 *ad loc.*); Tg. Cant. 2:14, "the Congregation of Israel resembled a dove shut up in the clefts of the rock, with a serpent threatening her from within, and a hawk threatening her from without" (*Note* 87 *ad loc.*). Cf. Cant.R. 6:9 §5: "*My faultless dove is one*. This is the Community of Israel, as it says, *And who is like Your people, like Israel, a nation one in the earth* (2 Sam 7:23)"; Exod.R. 21.5: "Rabbi Joḥanan said: God addressed Israel as *O My dove* (Cant 2:14), for see what it says, *And Ephraim has become like a simple dove, without understanding* (Hos 7:11). The Holy One, blessed be He, said: With Me they are like a simple dove, for they obey and do all that I decree upon them; but against idolaters they are stubborn as beasts, for it says, *Judah is a lion's whelp . . . Benjamin is a wolf that ravens . . . Dan shall be a serpent in the way* (Gen 49:9, 17, 27)."

"Mother" has been taken as a symbol of Torah: cf. Num.R. 10.4: "*The words of king Lemuel; the burden wherewith his mother corrected him* (Prov 31:1). *His mother* alludes to the Torah which corrected Solomon, and which is called the mother of those who study it, as you read, *Call understanding Mother* (Prov 2:3)," reading *ʾem* for *ʾim*; b. Ber. 57a: dreaming of intercourse with one's mother signifies intercourse with the Torah (Wisdom). See further Tg. to 8:1, *Note* 1.

The repeated "one" (Heb. *ʾaḥat*) is interpreted as indicating Israel's single-mindedness in her devotion to God ("with one heart . . . with a perfect heart": see *Note* 31 below). Additionally, the second *ʾaḥat* has generated the translation *ʾaḥidaʾ*, "devoted to (God)" = MH *yaḥid* (Jast. 574a).

Tg. saw in Israel's birth an allusion to the Exodus. "Her who bore her" may be God, Israel being seen as his "children." Or Tg. construed Hebrew *yoladtah* as a noun, with the preposition *l-* indicating time (BDB 516b [6]): "pure is she (as) at the time of her birth." Following prophetic tradition, Tg. regards the Wilderness wanderings as a period when Israel was particularly close to God.

30 "Daughters," "queens," and "concubines" are taken as references to the Gentiles, as in v. 8 (*Note* 27 above). Cf. Cant.R. 6:9 §5: "*The daughters saw her, and called her happy.* As it says, *And all nations shall call you happy* (Mal 3:12). *The queens and the concubines, and they praised her.* As it says, *And kings shall be your foster-fathers* (Isa 49:23)." The same interpretation is found in Num.R. 9.14; 14.10.

31 "With one heart . . . with a perfect heart" *(be-leb ḥad . . . be-leb shalim).* The Midrash stresses how Israel accepted the Torah at Sinai "with one heart": Mek. de R. Ishmael, *Baḥodesh* 2, "*And all the people answered together [yaḥdaw]* (Exod 19:8). They did not give this answer with hypocrisy, nor did they get it from one another, but all of them decided with one heart and said, *All that the Lord has spoken we will do*"; *Baḥodesh* 5: "Then He said to them, 'Am I to be your king?' And they said

engaging in [the study of] the words of the Torah with a perfect heart.[pp][31] And all her merits were as pure as on the day when she went forth from Egypt. So[rr] when the sons of the Hasmoneans and Mattathias and all the people of Israel went out and waged war against them, the Lord delivered them into their hands.[ss][32] When the inhabitants of the districts saw [this], the kingdoms of the earth and the rulers called them happy and praised them.[tt]

10. Hebrew Text:

Who is she that looks like the dawn,
Beautiful as the moon,
Bright as the sun,[33]
Frightening as [were] the camps with their standards?[34]

Apparatus, Chapter 6

[rr] "So" = *h' bkyn*. The purpose of the conjunction is surely to indicate that piety was rewarded by victory in battle.

[ss] Adding "into their hands" with the majority of the mss. A omits.

[tt] J K L N: "and killed them" *(wqtlw lhwn)*—a Freudian slip for "and praised them" *(wqlsw lhwn)*! It seems clear that Tg. divided the Hebrew, "The daughters saw her, and the queens and the concubines called her happy and praised her." The Masoretic accents, however, suggest the division: "The daughters saw her, and called her happy; the queens and the concubines [saw her], and they praised her."

Notes, Chapter 6

to Him: 'Yes, yes!' Rabbi says: This proclaims the excellence of Israel. For when they all stood before Mount Sinai to receive the Torah they all decided with one heart to accept the reign of God joyfully." The phrase "with one heart" occurs twice in the Bible (1 Chr 12:39, *bi-lebab shalem . . . leb 'eḥad*; 2 Chr 30:12), but in neither case in reference to Sinai. The faithfulness to Torah in the Hasmonean era recalled Israel's faithfulness at Sinai. For the phrase "with a perfect heart" see Ps-J Gen. 22:8, "And they went both of them together, with a perfect heart" (= Heb. *yaḥdaw*).

[32] If there is an allusion here to a specific battle, it is likely to be Judas' victory over Nicanor (1 Macc 7:39-50; Yosippon 24:59-71 [ed. Flusser, 1:103–104]), which was celebrated on 13th Adar (Megillat Ta'anit 12, ed. Neubauer, 19).

[33] The nations praise Israel. The splendor of the dawn is seen as a metaphor for the splendor of Israel's deeds, probably in context a reference to military rather than moral prowess. The beauty of the moon denotes the beauty of the "young men," in context probably the young warriors rather than students (cf. 1 Maccabees' references to Judas's "young men," picked up in Yosippon's *baḥurayw*). But in the light of Tg. to v. 9 (where Heb. *barah* = moral excellence, "her merits were as pure as on the day when she went out from Egypt"), "merits" should be taken in a moral sense.

It is unlikely that Tg. missed the eschatological potential of the "sun/moon" language here. Elsewhere in the Midrash the sun and the moon symbolize the splendor of the righteous *in the world to come*—a radiance that, according to some traditions, will actually make the celestial luminaries redundant. See Lev.R. 30.2: "*In Your presence is fullness (soba') of joy* (Ps 16:11) applies to the seven *(sheba')* companies of righteous men who will in the future welcome the presence of the Shekhinah, and whose faces will be like the sun and the moon . . . Whence do we know that they will be like the sun? From the fact that it says, *Bright as the sun* (Cant 6:10). Whence that they will be like the moon? From the fact that it says, *Beautiful as the moon* (Cant 6:10)." Cf. the traditions collected in Yalqut Shim'oni to Ps 72:5-7 (§806), *They shall fear You while the sun endures, and so long as the moon, throughout all generations . . .* , especially v. 7, *In his days shall the righteous flourish; and abundance of peace till the moon be no more*: "Just as the sun and the moon give light to [this] world, so the righteous will give light to the world [to come], as it is written, *And the nations shall walk by your light* (Isa 60:3)." And note the play on the sun and moon in an eschatological context in Gen.R. 6.3. Tg. goes out of his way to stress that the Hasmonean period matched in every respect the other great peaks in Israel's sacred history—the Exodus (so vv. 4, 9, 10), the period of Solomon (so v. 4), and the days of the Messiah (so vv. 8, 10).

[34] As in 6:4 Tg. takes this as a flashback to the wilderness wanderings, when Israel's military array inspired fear in the nations (see *Notes* 13 and 14 above). Cant.R. 6:10 §1 relates the *nidgalot* to the bannered hosts of heaven, but then links these to the camps in the wilderness: "Rabbi Joshua of Sikhnin said: The Community of Israel said: The Holy One, blessed be He, has

Targum:

The nations said: "How splendid are the deeds of this people—like the dawn![uu] Her young men[vv] are as beautiful as the moon, her merits are as bright as the sun, and the fear of her is on all the inhabitants of the land as in the day when her four camps[ww] marched through the wilderness."

11. Hebrew Text:

I went down into the nut-garden,
To look at the green plants of the valley,[35]
To see whether the vine had budded,[36]
And the pomegranates were in blossom.[37]

Apparatus, Chapter 6

[uu] J K L M N: "The nations said: 'The deeds of this nation are like the dawn.'" This avoids the awkward mixed construction in A: (a) "How splendid are the deeds of this people," and (b) "The deeds of this people are as splendid as the dawn," but it is the weaker reading. Note again the careful stylistic variation: *zywwtnyn . . . shpyryn . . . bryrn.*

[vv] B F H: "her young girls," perhaps because the description "beautiful as the moon" seemed more appropriate for females.

[ww] Reading "four camps" with the majority of mss. A: "camps."

Notes, Chapter 6

brought me to His wine-cellar, namely Sinai. And there was Michael and his host; there too was Gabriel and his host. They said: Would that we might march like these celestial ranks! Thereupon the Holy One, blessed be He, said: Because my sons have desired to be like the heavenly hosts, let them encamp under standards, as it says, *The Children of Israel shall pitch by their fathers' houses; every man with his own standard, according to the ensigns* (Num 2:1)." Cf. Num.R. 2.3, which also states that the camps in the wilderness were organized "under standards, like the ministering angels." Further Midrash Ps. 22.1. Cant.R. 6:11 §1 sees in the "nut-garden" of the following verse an allusion to the four camps: "*I went down into the nut-garden. . . .* Rabbi Berekhiah said: Just as a nut has four quarters and a court [vacant space] in the center, so Israel were encamped in the wilderness, four standards, four camps, and the Tent of Assembly in the middle, as it is written, *Then the Tent of Meeting . . . shall set forward in the midst of the camps* (Num 2:17)."

[35] Tg. detects here the voice of God explaining how he descended (in his Shekhinah) into the Second Temple to test whether Israel was performing the commandments and studying the Torah. Verse 12 gives the answer in the affirmative.

Tg. treats the "nut-garden" as a symbol of the Temple. The image of the "garden" in Canticles is taken by Tg. as representing sometimes Paradise, sometimes the Temple, and sometimes the Sanhedrin/House of Study, these three being seen as subtly linked to each other (see 4:12, 15-16; 5:1; 6:2; 8:13; further *Note* 40 below). Nothing seems to be made specifically of the image of the nut. For an attempt to do so see Cant.R. 6:11 §1 (quoted in *Note* 34). See also b. Ḥag. 13a, and further Abrams, *Sexual Symbolism and Mystical Speculation* 60–73 on the mystical interpretation of this verse.

The "green plants of the valley" are compared to the burgeoning good deeds of the people.

[36] The vine is a symbol of Israel (Ps 80:9; Isa 5:1; Tg. Cant. 2:15 and 7:13; Lev.R. 36.2); its "buds" are its grapes = the Sages. Cf. the well-known Rabbinic metaphor in which Israel, the vine, is divided into its grape-clusters (*ʾeshkolot* = the scholars) and its leaves (*ʿalim* = the uneducated, the *ʿammei ha-ʾareṣ*). Cant.R. 1:14 §2: "What is meant by *ʾeshkol*? A man in whom is everything *(ʾish she-hakol bo)*—Scripture, Mishnah, Talmud, Toseftas, and Haggadot"; b.Ḥul. 92a. In some texts the term is used specifically for the succession of great scholars that ended in the Hasmonean period: m. Soṭah 9:9, "When Yosei b. Yoʿezer of Zeredah and Yosei b. Joḥanan of Jerusalem [cf. m. ʾAbot 1:4] died, the 'grape-clusters' ceased"; t. B. Qam. 8:13; y. Tem. IX, 24a; b. Tem. 15b. Cant.R. 6:11 §1 identifies the buds of the vine with "the synagogues and houses of study." Tg. to 7:8, 9 identifies the grape-clusters with Israel.

[37] The "blossom" is equated with the offspring of the Sages, the young scholars. Cf. Cant.R. 6:11 §1: "*And the pomegranates are in blossom.* These are the children who are busy learning Torah and sit in rows like pomegranate seeds." "Blossom," "bud," "sapling," "shoot" are all natural metaphors for the young: so "blossoms of the priesthood" *(pirḥei kehunah)* = the

Targum:

The Sovereign of the World said: "I caused my Shekhinah to reside in the Second Temple,[38] which had been built at the hands of Cyrus,[39] to see the good deeds of My people, and to see whether the Sages, who are compared to the vine, would be fruitful and multiply,[xx40] and [whether] their blossoms[yy] would be full of good deeds like pomegranates."

12. Hebrew Text:

I did not know . . . My soul counseled me . . .
In chariots . . . My people [is] noble.[41]

Targum:

And when it was revealed before the Lord that they were righteous and were engaging in [the study of] the Torah, the Lord said through His Word: "I will not again crush them,[zz]

Apparatus, Chapter 6

[xx] = *pshn wsgn*; cf. Gen 1:22, 28, *peru urebu* = Onq. *pwshw wsgw.*

[yy] "Their blossoms" = *lblwbyhwn*; J K L M N: "their hearts" *(lb[y]hwn).*

[zz] The form of the infinitive with suffix is somewhat anomalous *(lmkwkynwn)*: √*mkk* either in the sense of "humiliate, bring low" (cf. Tg. Ps. 146:6; Heb. *mashpil*), or in the sense of "to crush" (cf. Tg. Lam. 3:34; Heb. *ledakke'*).

Notes, Chapter 6

young priests (m. Midd. 1:8) and "saplings" *(neti'ot)* = the young scholars (b. Ḥag. 14b, according to one interpretation; Jast. 1407b). As in 4:3 (*Note* 15) and 6:7, Tg. takes the "pomegranates" as an image of a plenitude of *miṣwot*. Tg. treats the parallel in 7:13 rather differently.

[38] In contrast to some traditions, Tg. insists that the Shekhinah did take up residence in the Second Temple, as in the First and as in the Tabernacle.

[39] Cf. Ezra 1:2, "The God of heaven . . . has charged me to build Him a house in Jerusalem."

[40] The allusion to Gen 1:22, 28 is suggestive and picks up echoes of Paradise in the image of the garden used earlier in the verse. See further *Note* 35 above.

[41] "This verse is generally conceded to be the most difficult in the Canticle" (Pope, 584). "This is a famous *crux interpretum*; the proper reading has never been successfully discovered" (Murphy, 176). Tg. struggles and the link between his paraphrase and the Hebrew is not always clear. Generally he takes this verse as the answer to v. 11: God is satisfied that the people in the Second Temple period are obeying the Torah, and as a result promises to exalt their kingdom and never totally destroy them. Tg. seems to have interpreted the Hebrew atomistically, phrase by phrase (note the Masoretic accents), then joined the interpretations into a narrative. Cant.R. 6:12 §1 gives an entirely different reading of the verse, seeing it as describing an unexpected reversal of fortune, and applying it to Israel (at the Exodus), and to Joseph, David, Mordechai, and Justa the tailor of Sepphoris (!): "Just as you [the nations] are astonished at me [i.e., at my good fortune], so I am astonished at myself." Following this line it would be natural to identify Israel rather than God as the speaker.

"I did not know" *(lo' yada'ti)* = "I will not again crush them, or make a total end of them." Basis unclear.

"My soul counseled Me" *(nafshi samatni)* = "I will take counsel with Myself to do them good."

"In chariots" *(markebot)* = "to make them exalted in royal chariots." Tg. seems to echo Gen 41:43 (Pharaoh made Joseph ride in the second chariot), but the point of the allusion is unclear.

"My people [is] noble" *('ammi nadib)* = "for the sake of the merits of the righteous of this generation, who resemble Abraham their forefather in their deeds." In Rabbinic tradition Abraham is the Noble One, the Prince *(ha-nadib)*: Cant.R. 7:2 §3: "*O daughter of a prince [nadib]*. The daughter of Abraham who was called 'prince,' as it says, *The princes of the peoples [nedibei 'ammim] are gathered together, the people of the God of Abraham* (Ps 47:10)." Cf. b. Sukkah 49a; b. Ḥag. 3a. However, Tg. to 7:2 seems to interpret *nadib* there differently (though see *Note* 5 *ad loc.*).

nor shall I make a total end of them,*aaa*[42] but I will take counsel with Myself to do them good and make them exalted in royal chariots, for the sake of the merit*bbb* of the righteous[43] of this generation, who resemble Abraham their forefather in the beauty of their deeds."*ccc*

Apparatus, Chapter 6

aaa = *lʾ ʾʿbyd ʿymhwn gmyrʾ*; cf. Tg. Jer. 5:18, *lʾ ʾʿbyd ʿmkwn gmyrʾ* (lit. "I will not make a full end with you" = Heb. *loʾ ʾeʿeseh ʾittekhem*).

bbb B D F H J K L M N: "merits."

ccc The majority of mss. read simply "in their deeds."

Notes, Chapter 6

[42] Cf. Lev 26:44, "And yet for all that, when they are in the land of their enemies I will not reject them, to destroy them utterly *[lekallotam]*, and to break My covenant with them." Esth.R., Proem 4, relates *lekallotam* to the Greek period: "*I did not reject them*: in Babylon; *neither did I abhor them*: in Media; *to destroy them utterly*: when subject to Greece; *to break My covenant with them*: when subject to the kingdom of wickedness; *for I am the Lord their God*: in the Messianic era." Cf. Ps-J Lev. 26:44; b. Meg. 11a.

[43] Once again Tg. stresses the importance of the doctrine of merits. See *Intro*. 4.3.

CHAPTER 7

***1. Hebrew Text:**

Return, return, O Shulammite;
Return, return, that we may see visions about you![1]
What you see with regard to the Shulammite [is]
As the defiling of the two camps.[2]

Targum:

"Return to Me, Assembly of Israel, return to Jerusalem, return to the House of Instruction in the Torah,[a] return to receive prophecy[b] from the prophets who prophesy in the name of the Word of the Lord![3] What business have you,[c] false prophets, to lead astray the people of Jerusalem with your prophecies, which you speak in revolt against the Lord?[d4] [What business have you] to defile the camps of Israel and Judah?"

2. Hebrew Text:

How beautiful are your feet in sandals,
O daughter of a prince![5]

*7:1 in the Hebrew text = 6:13 in the English.

Apparatus, Chapter 7

[a] C: "in My Torah."
[b] J K L M N omit "prophecy."
[c] B G J K L M N: "and what [are] you" *(wmʾ/h ʾtwn* for *wmʾ tybkwn).*
[d] F: "against the Word of the Lord," but see Onq. Deut 13:6.

Notes, Chapter 7

[1] God homilizes Israel. Tg., in typical midrashic fashion, differentiates the four "returnings": (1) "return to Me" (in repentance); (2) "return to Jerusalem" (either from exile or, as in the next verse, to celebrate the pilgrim festivals); (3) "return to the House of Study"; (4) "return to receive prophecy." Cant.R. 7:1 §1 also differentiates the four returnings but relates them to the four empires that have subjected Israel and from which she has returned unscathed. The "Shulammite" generates both "Assembly of Israel" (cf. Cant.R. 7:1 §1, the nation to which God gives peace *[shalom]*), and "Jerusalem." Interpretation 4 depends on associating the verb *ḥazah* with prophecy (as in *ḥazon,* "[prophetic] vision," and *ḥozeh,* "seer": BDB 302a). Cf. b. B. Bat. 15a: "*That we may look on you* (Cant 7:1) . . . refers to prophecy, as it is written, *Vision [ḥazon] of Isaiah the son of Amos* (Isa 1:1)."

[2] The change to the second person plural signals a change of subject: Tg. detects a reference to false prophets by deriving Hebrew *meḥolah* not from *ḥwl* I, "to dance" (BDB 298a), but from *ḥll* III, "pollute, defile, profane" (BDB 320a). The "two camps" are identified as "Israel and Judah." *Maḥanaim* is associated with Jacob's vision in Gen 32:3, but there the "camps" are normally interpreted as hosts of angels (Gen.R. 74.17; Cant.R. 7:1 §2).

[3] Since Tg. is speaking about the Second Temple period, and has just mentioned the Hasmoneans, the reference to prophecy is significant. According to Rabbinic tradition prophecy ceased in the time of Ezra (Urbach, "When did prophecy cease?"; idem, *The Sages* 576–79). However, Tg. is logical: if the Hasmoneans marked a great high point in Israel's history (like the Exodus, the Solomonic period, and the days of the Messiah), it is inconceivable that prophecy should have been totally absent.

[4] Cf. Deut 13:6, "And that prophet, or that dreamer of dreams, shall be put to death, because he has spoken in revolt against the Lord" *(ki dibber sarah ʿal yhwh*; Onq. *ʾry mlyl styʾ ʿl yyy).*

[5] Tg. takes the physical charms of the bride in vv. 2-10 as a picture of the glories of Israel in the Second Temple period, exemplified by its Temple and Sanhedrin, which he regards as complementary institutions (see *Intro.* 4.4). The speaker is God, as v. 7 makes clear (cf. the rubric to v. 9). The rubrics to vv. 2 and 9 that identify Solomon as the speaker (v. 2, "through the

The curves of your thighs are like jewels,
The work of the hands of a craftsman.[6]

Targum:

King[e] Solomon said through the spirit of prophecy from before the Lord: "How beautiful are the feet of Israel when they go up to appear before the Lord three times a year in sandals of badger-skin,[f7] bringing votive and freewill offerings, and their sons, the issue of their loins, are as comely as the jewels[g] that are fixed[h] in the holy crown,[8] which Bezaleel the craftsman made for Aaron the [High] Priest."

Apparatus, Chapter 7

[e] Adding "king" with K L M N. A and other mss. omit.

[f] J K L M N omit "of badger-skin." The meaning of *ssgwn'* is in some doubt. It is the standard Onq. translation for *taḥash,* the skin used to form the covering of the Tabernacle (Exod 25:5; 26:14; 35:7, 23; 36:19; 39:34; Num 4:6, 8, 10-12, 14, 25); cf. b. Shabb. 28a, ". . . that is why we translate *taḥash* by *sasgona',* because it glistened with many colors" *(ss bgwwnyn hrbh)*; further b. Ḥag. 3a. For the interpretation that some sort of (? fabulous) animal skin is intended see *Note* 7. But. Jast. 1009a suggests that *ssgwn'* denotes here a color, "scarlet," comparing Syriac *sasgawna',* for which Payne Smith 2682 postulates a Persian derivation.

[g] "Jewels" = *ywhryn;* J K L M N: *zhryn,* presumably with the same meaning. Cf. Lam 4:7, "they were more ruddy in body than rubies *[peninim]*" = Tg., "their appearance was ruddier than jewels [*yhwryn/zhwryn*]." Lag. conjectures here *gwhryn,* "jewels" (cf. Arabic *jauhar,* "gem, precious stone"). *Gwhr* (A: *gyh'r*) is one of the precious stones mentioned in the Western recension of Tg. to 5:14. See Appendix B.

[h] B I: "held" *(nqyt[y]n),* for A's "fixed" *(qby'n).*

Notes, Chapter 7

spirit of prophecy" because he is foretelling events that are future to him) do not contradict this: Solomon is still the narrator even though he is recording God's words. Or possibly "Solomon" here = God, "the one to whom belongs peace" (see Tg. to 1:1, *Note* 2), but this does not fit v. 2.

The "feet" are the feet of the pilgrims coming up to Jerusalem for the three pilgrim festivals *(shalosh regalim)*—Pesaḥ, Shabu'ot and Sukkot (Exod 23:14; 34:23; Deut 16:16; 2 Chr 8:13). Cant.R. 7:2 §1 also sees a reference here to the pilgrim festivals. Cf. Gen.R. 43.9; b. Suk. 49b; b. Ḥag. 3a.

The "prince" *(nadib)* may have been taken as Abraham (as in 6:12, *Note* 41): hence "daughter of the prince" = Israel. So Cant.R. 7:2 §3: "*O daughter of a prince.* The daughter of Abraham, who was called 'prince.'" However, *nadib* has clearly generated the reference to the "freewill offerings" *(nedabot)* that the pilgrims bring up to the Temple.

[6] "Thighs" suggests loins, and loins, offspring. The Hebrew hapax *ḥala'im* possibly means "rings" (Murphy, 182; Cant.R. 7:2 §3 = "links of a chain . . . chaplet round a pillar . . . hollow of a pearl"; cf. MH *ḥulya',* "section of a column; vertebra of the spinal column": Jast. 434a). Tg. has taken it to mean "jewels" (see *Apparatus g*), which it identifies specifically with the jewels on the high-priestly crown (further *Note* 8 below). This leads naturally to identifying the "craftsman" with Bezaleel, the Daedalus of Jewish tradition (Exod 31:2; 35:30; 36:1-2; 37:1; 38:22; Ginzberg, *Legends* 3:154–56).

[7] "Sandals of badger-skin" is a learned allusion to Ezek 16:10, where, as a token of his love toward Israel, God says that he gave her sandals of *taḥash, taḥash* being the skin that was used to form the covering of the Tabernacle and is normally rendered by the Targumim *sasgona'* = (possibly) "badger skin" (see *Apparatus f*). The *taḥash* in the Aggadah is a fabulous beast, created for the express purpose of providing skin for the Tabernacle but disappearing once it had fulfilled its purpose. Sandals of *taḥash*-skin would therefore be a novelty, more characteristic of the days of the Messiah, like Leviathan meat (on the *taḥash* see Ginzberg, *Legends* 1:34; 5:53, n. 166; further Tg. to 8:2, *Note* 9).

[8] Once again Tg. mistakenly supposes that there were jewels in the high-priestly crown. See *Notes* to 5:14.

3. Hebrew Text:

Your navel is [like] the bowl of the moon,
Wherein mixed wine is not wanting;[9]
Your belly is a heap of wheat,
Fenced round by roses.[10]

Targum:

"The Head of your College, through whose merit all the world[i] is sustained,[11] just as the fetus is sustained through its navel[j] in the belly of its mother, shines with [a knowledge of] the Torah like the disc of the moon, when he comes to pronounce pure or impure,[k] innocent or guilty,[12] and the words of the Torah never fail [to flow] from his mouth, just as the waters of the great river which issues from Eden[13] never fail. Seventy Sages surround him, like a

Apparatus, Chapter 7

[i] Reading "world" with B C D E F G H I for A's "worlds"; J K L M N: "people"; G²: "peoples, nations, and languages."

[j] Or "its umbilical cord" (Jast. 1244b).

[k] B G H I omit "and impure."

Notes, Chapter 7

[9] It was a common Rabbinic view that the "navel" here alluded to the Sanhedrin, which was so called because it sustained Israel like an umbilical cord, because it sat in a circle (*Note* 14 below), and because it met in Jerusalem, the "navel" of the earth. See Cant.R. 7:3 §1: "*Your navel is like a round goblet. Your navel* indicates the Sanhedrin. Just as the fetus, so long as it is in its mother's womb, lives only from the navel, so Israel can do nothing without her Sanhedrin." b. Sanh. 37a: "*Your navel* is the Sanhedrin. Why is it called *your navel*? Because it sits at the navel of the earth." Cf. Num.R. 1.4; Pesiq. Rab. 10.2; b. Soṭah 45a; b. Nid. 30b; Tanḥuma, *Ki Tissa* 1 (ed. Buber, 52a). Tg. typically nuances the tradition. It notes that the biblical text speaks of both "navel" and "belly." It identifies the former with the "head" of the Sanhedrin, the latter with the body of the Sages who make up the Sanhedrin (though, through double interpretation, it applies to the Sanhedrin as a whole the roundness of the "navel"). Tg. has clearly understood Hebrew *ʾaggan ha-sahar* here as referring to the "disc of the moon" *(ʾugnaʾ de-siharaʾ),* but it probably also recognized *ʾaggan* in the sense of "goblet, bowl," which makes sense of the following reference to "mixed wine." The head of the college is both a "goblet" containing the "mixed wine" of Torah and a "moon" reflecting the light of Torah. The equation Torah = wine is both natural and common (e.g., Deut.R. 7.3, and "house of wine" = Sinai).

[10] The "belly" in contrast to the "navel" suggests the body of the scholars, but once again the image of the "bowl of the moon" is picked up and taken as alluding to the seating arrangements of the Sanhedrin (see *Note* 14 below).

"Heap of wheat" suggests the ingathering of the tithes to the "treasuries" *(ʾoṣarot)* mentioned in Neh 12:44-47 and 13:10-13. See further *Note* 14 below.

"Fenced round" *(sugah)* suggested the Rabbinic concept of a "fence" *(seyyag)* around the Torah (m. ʾAbot 1:1; 3:14). Since the "fence" was ordained by the scholars, it followed that they must be alluded to in the "roses."

[11] The role of the Head of the College as a world-sustaining *ṣaddiq* is noteworthy. The ancient Galilean Hasid Ḥaninah ben Dosa was seen as playing a similar role: b. Taʿan. 24b: "The whole world is sustained on account of Ḥaninah My son" (cf. b. Ber. 17b; b. Ḥul. 86a: Vermes, *Post-Biblical Jewish Studies* 201–202). See Tg. to 4:4 (*Note* 20) and 3:10 (*Note* 52).

[12] In Pesiq. Rab. 10.2 the role of the Sanhedrin is defined as pronouncing "what is prohibited and what is permitted, what is impure and what is pure."

[13] The equation of the house of study with Eden is pointed (cf. Tg. to 6:2, 11). The comparison of the pronouncements of the Head of the College with the waters of Eden is hardly exaggerated given his world-sustaining role. The "great river" alludes to Gen 2:10, "And a river went out from Eden to water the garden; and from there it parted and became four heads." Tg. to 4:12 speaks of "the spring of living water that gushes out from beneath the roots of the Tree of Life and that divides into four heads of rivers" (see *Notes ad loc.*) Cf. Ben Sira 24:23-27, ". . . the Law that Moses commanded us . . . overflows like the Pishon with wisdom, and like the Tigris at the time of first-fruits. It runs over, like the Euphrates, with understanding . . . it pours forth instruction like the Nile, like Gihon at the time of vintage"—a text that could have been known to Tg.

round threshing-floor,[14] and their treasuries are full of[l] the holy tithes, votive and freewill offerings,[15] which Ezra the priest, Zerubbabel, Jeshua, Nehemiah, and Mordechai Bilshan,[16] the Men of the Great Assembly,[17] who are compared to roses, ordained for their benefit,[m] so that they might be enabled[n] to engage in the study of the Torah day and night."[18]

4. Hebrew Text:

Your two breasts are like two fawns,
Twins of a gazelle.[19]

Targum:

"Your two deliverers, who will deliver you, the Messiah son of David and the Messiah son of Ephraim, are like Moses and Aaron, the sons of Jochebed, who are compared to two fawns, twins of a gazelle."

5. Hebrew Text:

Your neck is like a tower of ivory;[20]
Your eyes are [like] the pools of Heshbon,

Apparatus, Chapter 7

[l] Reading *mlyyn mn* with the majority of mss. for A's *mlyyn*. The preposition may have dropped out of A before the following *m'sr*.

[m] Or "reserved for them" = *syygw lhwn*. The verb echoes m. ʾAbot 3:14, "tithes are a fence [*seyag*] for wealth, vows are a fence for abstinence." Perhaps translate here: "ordained as a 'fence'"; then, since the "fence" relates to the donor rather than the recipient, take *lhwn* as a *dativus commodi*, "for their benefit." B: "increased/multiplied for them" (*sgyʾw lhwm;* cf. K L: *sgyn*), but the Hebrew *sugah* supports *syygw.*

[n] Lit. "so that they might have the strength."

Notes, Chapter 7

[14] m. Sanh. 1:6, "The greater Sanhedrin was made up of seventy-one" = the seventy Sages plus the President (Exod 24:1; Num 11:16, 24). m. Sanh. 4:3, "The Sanhedrin was arranged like the half of a round threshing-floor"; b. Sanh. 36b; Lev.R. 11.8. Cf. Tg. to 6:5 (*Note* 15).

[15] Neh 12:44-47 and 13:10-13 gave rise to the tradition that the Men of the Great Synagogue "ordained that the tithes and the Terumah should be given, though according to the biblical law these obligations ceased when the Jews were exiled. They drew up a document to the effect that they had taken anew upon themselves these duties, and left it in the Temple overnight. In the morning they found the heavenly seal placed under the names attached to the document" (Ginzberg, *Legends* 6:448). Here, however, the tithes are meant to support the Sages rather than the priests.

[16] "Bilshan" was regarded as an epithet of Mordechai = *baʿal lashon,* "master of languages." "Being a member of the great Sanhedrin he understood all the seventy languages spoken in the world" (Ginzberg, *Legends* 6:458 n. 62; cf. b. Menaḥ. 65a). The list of members of the Great Assembly here is based on the names of the leaders of the returnees in Ezra 2:2 and Neh 7:7.

[17] For the Men of the Great Assembly see Tg. to 6:5 (*Note* 18).

[18] Cf. Josh 1:8, "This book of the law shall not depart out of your mouth, but you shall meditate therein day and night." Though ostensibly speaking of the Sanhedrin in the Second Temple period, Tg. has clearly in mind the great Rabbinic schools of his own day, which were supported by voluntary contributions from the community. See further Tg. to 8:9 (*Note* 43). For the possible historical background see *Intro.* 8.2.

[19] See parallel in 4:5, which Tg. renders in the same way. These repetitions in Canticles are important for Tg.'s interpretation since they support his cyclical view of the *Heilsgeschichte.*

[20] Tg. continues his idealized picture of the Sanhedrin, momentarily interrupted by v. 4.

The "neck" is identified with Father of the Court *(ʾAb Beit Din),* who supports the "Head" of the College and is second in authority only to him. His functions are given as adjudicating cases, binding, and scourging. "Binding" suggests that Tg. linked

By the gate of Bat-Rabbim;[21]
Your nose is like the tower of Lebanon,
Which looks toward Damascus.[22]

Targum:

"The Father of the Law Court[o] who judges your cases, having power over the people to bind and to scourge[23] whoever is condemned to scourging by the court, is like king Solomon, who made the tower of ivory, and subdued[24] the people of the House of Israel,[p] and brought them back to the Sovereign of the World. Your scribes are as full of wisdom as pools of water, and they know how to make the calculations for intercalation, and they

Apparatus, Chapter 7

[o] "Father of the Law Court" = *ʾAb Beit Din*. See *Intro.* 8.2.

[p] Adding "of the House of Israel" with the majority of the mss.

Notes, Chapter 7

Hebrew *ṣawwar,* "neck" with Hebrew/Aramaic √*ṣwr,* "bind, tie" (Jast. 1270a). In 4:4, however, the "neck" is identified with the Head of the College.

"Tower of Ivory" probably = the Temple (see Rashi *ad loc.*), but the phrase is not attested elsewhere. The comparison of the *ʾAb Beit Din* with Solomon is apposite because of the latter's fabled wisdom in judgment (1 Kgs 3:16-28).

[21] "Eyes" = scribes, here specifically functionaries of the Great Sanhedrin. Cant.R. 7:5 §2: "*Your eyes* are the Sanhedrin, who are the eyes of the congregation, as it says, *And it shall come to pass, if it be hidden from the eyes of the congregation* (Num 15:24). There are two hundred and forty-eight limbs in a man's body and all follow the eyes; and similarly Israel can do nothing without their Sanhedrin."

"Pools": once again water suggests knowledge, wisdom, Torah. *Ḥeshbon* has been etymologized as "calculation," specifically the calculations required for setting the calendar and fixing the dates of the festivals (Jast. 441a). Cant.R. 7:5 §2 gives a similar etymology but applies it differently: "*Pools of Ḥeshbon.* Decisions which depend on counting *(ḥushban),* as when thirty-six declare innocent and thirty-five guilty." Tg. 1 Chr 12:32 is close to Tg. Cant. here: MT, "And of the children of Issachar, men that had understanding of the times, to know what Israel ought to do; the heads of them . . . "; Tg. "And the children of Issachar, experts in the knowledge of the times, wise in fixing the beginnings of months and the beginnings of years, at intercalating the months and the years, clever calculators [*sophistin* = Gk *sophistai*] of the beginnings of the new moon, to fix the festivals in their times, competent in the solstices, astrologers [versed in the science] of the planets and the stars, to know that which the House of Israel must do, their masters, chiefs of Sanhedrins . . . ." Cf. Gen. R. 72.5 for a similar interpretation of 1 Chr 12:32.

"Bat Rabbim" has been taken by *ʾal tiqrei* as "Beit Rabbim" = House of the Many/Majority, i.e., the Sanhedrin, which decided cases strictly by majority vote. Cf. Cant.R. 7:5 §2: "*The gate of Bat Rabbim.* This refers to the *halakhah* which issues from the gate [of the Chamber of Hewn Stone where the Sanhedrin sat] and spreads to the public *[rabbim].* Rabbi Judah b. Rabbi said: It refers to the precept *Incline [i.e., pass judgment] in accordance with the majority [rabbim]* (Exod 23:2)." Cf. the use of "The Many" *(Ha-Rabbim)* as a title for a plenary session of the Qumran community (1QS 6.1, 8 and frequently).

[22] "Nose" = chief of the family of the House of Judah. See *Note* 26 below.

"Tower of Lebanon" is curiously not identified with the Temple (so Cant.R. 7:5 §3; for Lebanon = Temple see Tg. to 3:6, *Note* 25), perhaps because this is already seen as alluded to in the Tower of Ivory, but with the citadel of Zion. Cf. 2 Sam 5:7-11, "David took the citadel of Zion *[meṣudat Ṣiyyon]* . . . And David dwelt in the citadel . . . And Hiram king of Tyre sent messengers, and cedar trees . . . and they built David a house."

Tg. takes "which looks toward Damascus" to mean that the tower is so tall that from its top one can see Damascus (cf. Rashi *ad loc.*). Cant.R. 7:5 §3 detects an eschatological reference here: "*Which looks toward Damascus.* Rabbi Joḥanan said: Jerusalem in the time to come will extend as far as the gates of Damascus."

[23] "Binding" has the sense either of putting in the stocks or in prison (Jast. 662b–663a). Scourging was a common form of Rabbinic punishment: those who were scourged were first bound (m.Mak. 3:12). However, "binding" and "scourging" are probably only used *exempli gratia,* to illustrate the *ʾAb Beit Din's* general powers of physical coercion and of executing punishment.

[24] Cf. 1 Chr 22:17-18, "David commanded all the princes of Israel to help Solomon his son, saying, . . . [T]he Lord . . . has delivered the inhabitants of the land into my hand; and the land is subdued *[nikhbeshah]* before the Lord."

intercalate years, and fix the beginnings of years and the beginnings of months[25] in the gate of the house of the Great Sanhedrin. The chief of the family of the House of Judah[26] is like king David who built the citadel of Zion which is called the tower of Lebanon; anyone who stands upon it is able to count all the towers that are in Damascus."

6. Hebrew Text:

The head upon you is like Carmel,[27]
And the hair on your head is like purple;
A king is bound in the tresses.[28]

Targum:

"The king, who is appointed as head over you, is as righteous as Elijah the prophet, who was very zealous[q] for the Lord of Heaven, and killed the false prophets on Mount Carmel,[29]

Apparatus, Chapter 7

[q] = *qny qyn'yt'*. The cognate accusative expresses intensity; cf. 1 Kgs 19:10, 14, "I have been very zealous [Heb. *qanno' qinne'ti* = Tg. *qn'h qnyty*] for the Lord, the God of hosts"; Num 25:11, "He was very zealous for my sake" [Heb. *beqan'o 'et qin'ati* = Onq. *bdqny yt qn'ty*].

Notes, Chapter 7

[25] The calculation of the calendar was an important function and disputes over it broke out from time to time between the Babylonian and Palestinian Schools. Knowledge of the "secret of intercalation" *(sod ha-ʿibbur)*, i.e., how to reconcile the lunar and the solar years, was jealously guarded by the scholars (*EJ* 5:48–50).

[26] The chief of the family of the House of Judah must refer to either the Patriarch or the Exilarch. Implied here is a claim to be of Davidic descent. See further *Intro.* 8.2(2). Gen.R. 98.8 claims Davidic descent for the House of Hillel.

[27] Tg. continues its description of the ideal polity of the Hasmonean period by introducing the king and the commoners.

"Head" = king. "Carmel" suggested a reference to Elijah's contest with the prophets of Baal on Mount Carmel (1 Kgs 18:20-40). Just as Elijah showed his zeal by killing the false prophets, so the ideal king should show his zeal by putting false prophets to death. Cant.R. 7:6 §1 also sees an allusion to Elijah: "The Holy One, blessed be He, said to Israel, *Your head [ro'shekh] is upon you like Carmel.* The poor *(rashim)* among you are as dear to me as Elijah who went up to Mount Carmel, as it says, *And Elijah went up to the top of Carmel . . . and put his face between his knees* (1 Kgs 18:42)." However, Tg. links the "poor" to "hair" and not to "head" (see *Note* 28 below). Cf. Lev.R. 31. 4.

[28] Tg. linked Hebrew *dallat* ("hair") with *dallim*, "poor," hence commoners in contrast to the king. "Purple" suggested the elevation of the poor, just as Daniel (Dan 5:29) and Mordechai (Esth 8:15) were elevated and donned the purple. Cant. R. 7:6 §1: "The Holy One, blessed be He, said: The poor *[dallim]* and the needy in Israel are as dear to Me as David . . . Some say, as Daniel, of whom it is written, *They clothed Daniel in purple* (Dan 5:29)." Note how Tg. adds, appositely, Mordechai. "Head" suggested the bowed head of the socially inferior.

"A king is bound in the tresses": Tg. atomized the Hebrew and discovered allusions to meritorious acts in the lives of Abraham, Isaac, and Jacob. "King" = God (Cant.R. 7:6 §1: "The *king* is the supreme King of kings, the Holy One, blessed be He"). This suggested to Tg. the crucial moment in Abraham's life when he abandoned idols and "acknowledged the Lord of the World as king"—a story not found in the Bible but lovingly embellished in the Midrash (Ginzberg, *Legends* 1:189–203).

The "binding" suggested the binding of Isaac. Cf. Gen 22:10 and the Targumim *ad loc.* The "tresses" *(rehatim)* recalled the "watering troughs" *(rehatim)* of Gen 30:38—though it is hard to see how the incident recorded there (see *Note* 31 below) constituted a pious act (but see Zetterholm, *Portrait of a Villain*)! Cf. Lev.R. 31.4: "*The King is bound in the tresses.* This signifies that the Holy One, blessed be He, bound himself by an oath that He would cause His Shekhinah to dwell under the rafters *[rehitin]* of Jacob. By reason of whose merit? Rabbi Abba b. Kahana said: By reason of the merit of our father Abraham, of whom it is written, *And Abraham ran [Heb. raṣ = Tg. rehat] unto the herd* (Gen 18:7). Rabbi Levi said: It is by reason of the merit of Jacob, of whom it is written, *And he set the rods which he had peeled over against the flocks in the watering-troughs [rehatim]* (Gen 30:38)." See also the parallel in Cant.R. 7:6 §1.

[29] If Tg. is thinking of the Hasmoneans, the references to zeal for the Law and to prophecy are noteworthy. Cf. Tg. to 6:7 and 7:1. Note the echo of 1 Kgs 18:39, "And Elijah brought down the prophets of Baal to the brook Kishon and slew them there."

and brought back the people of the House of Israel to the fear of the Lord his God.[30] And the poor of the people, who go about with bowed head, because they are despised, will don purple, as did Daniel in the city of Babylon, and Mordechai in Shushan, on account of the merit[r] of Abraham, who long before had acknowledged the Lord of the World[s] as king,[t] and through the righteousness[r] of Isaac, whose father bound him to offer him up,[u] and through the piety[r] of Jacob who peeled the rods at the watering-troughs."[31]

7. Hebrew Text:

How fair and how pleasant are you,
Love, in delights![32]

Targum:

King Solomon said: "How fair are you, Assembly of Israel, at the time[v] you take[w] upon yourselves the yoke[x] of My kingdom,[33] when[v] I reprove you with chastisements for your sins, and you accept them with love, and they seem in your eyes like delights."[34]

8. Hebrew Text:

This, your body, resembles a palm-tree,
And your breasts clusters [of grapes].[35]

Apparatus, Chapter 7

[r] J K L M N: "merits." *Zkwtʾ . . . ṣdqtʾ . . . ḥsydwtʾ*: typical stylistic variation. The reference is uniformly to the *zekhut ʾabot*.

[s] B H G I: "Lord of Heaven," as earlier in the verse.

[t] = *ʾmlyk*. For this sense of the verb see Tg. to 6:5, *Apparatus u*.

[u] J M: "to burn him" *(lmyqdyh)*; J[2]: *lmʿqdyh*, presumably intended in the general sense of "to sacrifice him," to avoid tautology with the preceding *kptyh*. For *kpt* = Hebrew *ʿqd* see the Targumim to Gen 22:10. C: "to offer him up for a burnt offering"; G[2]: "to offer him up for a burnt offering before the Lord."

[v] *bzmn d- . . . bʿydn d-* : stylistic variation.

[w] For "take" Tg. uses *sbl* instead of the normal √*qbl* for stylistic reasons, to avoid repeating √*qbl*, which occurs later in the verse.

[x] "Yoke" = *nyr*; J K L M have the synonym *ʿwl*—a Hebraism.

Notes, Chapter 7

30 Cf. Tg. to v. 5: "King Solomon who . . . brought the people of the House of Israel back to the Lord of the World."

31 Cf. Gen 30:37, 38: "Jacob took rods . . . and peeled white streaks in them . . . and he set the rods which he had peeled . . . in the watering-troughs."

32 The incipit of the Tg. suggests a change of voice, but in fact it clearly regards the words as addressed by God to Israel. Israel's beauty consists of her patient submission to divine punishment: she accepts it with "love" as "delights." Cant.R. 7:7 §1 takes the more obvious midrashic line by seeing Israel's beauty as expressed in her performance of the commandments. Tg., as usual, is subtly different and finds a reference to the sufferings of love (see further *Note* 34 below). Midrash Shir ha-Shirim (ed. Grünhut, 45a) sees Israel's beauty here as alluding to Herod's Temple. Tg. interestingly does not take this line, though it would have fitted well with its chronology. (Grünhut refers to b. B. Bat. 4a and b. Suk. 51b.)

33 Cf. Tg. to 1:10, "How comely is their neck to bear the yoke of my precepts, so that it should be upon them like a yoke upon the ox which plows the field and supports itself and its master" (*Note* 78 *ad loc.*).

34 Cf. b. Ber. 5a: "If a person is visited by suffering, let him examine his actions. Should he find them blameless, let him attribute it to neglect of the study of Torah. If he still finds no cause, let him accept that they are the chastenings of love, as it is said, *For whom the Lord loves He chastens* (Ps 94:12)." Note also Ps 119:71. See further Urbach, *The Sages* 444–48.

35 The "body" = the priests, specifically when they pronounce the Priestly Blessing (Num 6:22-27). Standing lined up before the congregation with their arms raised and fingers spread, they recall to Tg.'s mind a row of stately date palms. Cf. Ben

Targum:

"And when your priests spread their hands in prayer[y] and bless their brethren, the House of Israel,[36] the parted fingers of their hands resemble the branches of the date-palm[z][37] and their bodies are like the palm.[aa] And your assemblies,[bb] positioned facing the priests,[cc] with their faces bowed to the ground,[38] are like bunches of grapes."

9. Hebrew Text:

I said: I will go up into the palm-tree;
I will take hold of its branches;[39]

Apparatus, Chapter 7

[y] J K L M N omit "in prayer."

[z] Emending to *dmyyn ʾṣbʿt ydyhwn mtprsn klwlby dtmr.* The syntax is awkward. J K L M read: "the fingers of their hands are parted like the branches of the date-palm." This is easier, but *dmyyn* is supported by the Hebrew *dametah.* D E F have *ʾrbʿt yd(y)hwn,* "their four hands," for *ʾṣbʿt ydyhwn,* but this does not make sense. *ʾrbʿt* is probably a corruption of *ʾdbʿt,* a dialectal variant of *ʾṣbʿt,* "finger" (cf. A).

[aa] *tmr . . . dyqlʾ*: stylistic variation.

[bb] The reference is to the assemblies at festivals.

[cc] Lit. "standing face-to-face with the priests," but "standing" is too literal in view of the following, "with their faces bowed to the ground."

Notes, Chapter 7

Sira 50:12, "When he [Simon son of Onias, the High Priest] received the portions from the hands of the priests, as he stood by the hearth of the altar with a garland of brothers around him, he was like a young cedar on Lebanon, surrounded by the trunks of palm trees."

The "breasts" = the ordinary people. The tightly-packed mass of worshipers, prostrate during the pronouncement of the Priestly Blessing, resemble a bunch of grapes. For "grape-clusters" = the scholars see Tg. to 6:11 (*Note* 36). "Breasts" are interpreted differently at 4:5 and 7:4 (= the two Messiahs), and at 8:10 (= sons).

[36] Cf. m. Taʿan. 4:1, "Three times in the year the priests lift up their hands four times during the day (at Morning Prayer *[Shaḥarit],* at the Additional Prayer *[Musaf],* at the Afternoon Prayer *[Minḥah],* and at the Closing of the Gates *[Neʿilah]*): namely, on the days of fasting, at the *Maʿamads,* and on the Day of Atonement."

[37] The raising of the hands with the fingers splayed in the well-known fashion (*nesiʾat kappayim;* note the use of *kaf* in the sense of date-frond: Jast. 657a) was part of the ritual of the Priestly Blessing: "In the provinces the priests raised their hands as high as their shoulders, but in the Temple above their heads, excepting the High Priest, who raised his hands only as high as the frontlet. Rabbi Judah says: The High Priest also raised his hand above the frontlet, for it is written, *And Aaron lifted up his hands toward the people and blessed them* (Lev 9:22)" (m. Tamid 7:2; cf. m. Soṭah 7:6).

[38] It was (and is) customary for the congregation to avert its gaze from the priests when they pronounce the blessing. Here they appear to be prostrate with their foreheads on the ground (though see *Apparatus cc*). On the Priestly Blessing see Maimonides, *Yad: Hilkhot Tefillah* XIV 7; *EJ* 13, cols. 1060-63; Elbogen, *Jewish Liturgy* 62–66.

[39] Tg. applies vv. 9-10 to the testing of Daniel and the Three Hebrew Children. This is traditional: see Cant. R. 7:8§1-10§1; Num.R. 3.1; Sifra to Lev. 18:15 (§194); b. Sanh. 93a. The traditional interpretation, however, applied v. 8 also to Daniel and the Three Children (Tg. is different: see above), and in fact v. 8 was the nub of the exegesis, which is well summarized by Rashi *ad loc.*: "*This, your body, resembles a palm tree.* We witnessed the beauty of your stature in the days of Nebuchadnezzar, for all the nations prostrated themselves and fell down before the image, but you remained standing upright like the palm tree. *And your breasts clusters [of grapes].* This refers to Daniel, Hananiah, Mishael, and Azariah, who were like breasts from which you could draw [spiritual] nourishment. Just as the grape-cluster gives abundant drink, so they gave abundant nourishment by teaching everyone that there was no fear like their fear of God" (cf. especially Sifra). But the chronology is rather awkward for Tg., which is here dealing with the Second Temple period. In Rabbinic historiography the chronologies of the exilic and post-exilic periods are hopelessly confused: note how in the book of Daniel events take place both under the Babylonian Nebuchadnezzar (the Three Children in the fiery furnace: Daniel 3) and under the Persian Darius (Daniel in the lions' den: Daniel 6–7). Within Tg.'s schema the flashback to the Babylonian exile explains why the glories of the Second Temple period, which Tg. has just described, were possible: they came about through the merit of four righteous men who were faithful to God in exile. The theme of faithfulness in exile resonates in Tg. Cant. (*Intro.* 4.1). The flash forward to the eschatological resurrection of the dead in v. 10 is also important. Such anticipations of the eschaton are a feature of Tg. Cant.

And let your breasts be as clusters of the vine,
And the scent of your nose like apples.[40]

Targum:

The Lord said through His Word: "I will go up and test Daniel, and I will see if he is able to withstand this testing,[dd] as Abraham his forefather,[ee] who resembles a palm-tree,[ff] withstood ten trials.[dd][41] And I will also prove[gg] Hananiah, Mishael, and Azariah, and if they are able to withstand their tests,[42] I will, on account of their merit,[hh][43] redeem the people of the House of Israel, who are compared to bunches of grapes. And the names of Daniel, Hananiah, Mishael, and Azariah will be heard throughout all the world,[ii] and their scent will spread like the scent of the apples of the Garden of Eden."[44]

Apparatus, Chapter 7

[dd] *nsywn᾽ . . . nsyn:* stylistic variations; for *nes* = *nissayon* see Jast. 915a.
[ee] D E F L omit "his forefather."
[ff] "Palm-tree" = *lwlb᾽;* cf. *tmr* and *dyql᾽* in the preceding verse (Heb. *tamar* in both places).
[gg] "And I will also prove" = *wbḥyn ᾽n᾽ ᾽wp*. J K L M O: *wbkyn (᾽n᾽) ᾽nsynwn,* "then I will test them [Hananiah, Mishael, and Azariah]." But the variation *᾽nsy . . . bḥyn ᾽n᾽* is typical of Tg. Cant.'s style. *Bḥyn,* participle = *futurum instans.*
[hh] B C G H I J K L M O: "merits."
[ii] B D E F G H I J K L M O: "all the land."

Notes, Chapter 7

The "palm tree" = Daniel/Abraham, possibly via the palm as the image of the righteous man: cf. Ps 92:13, "the righteous shall flourish as the palm tree," with Num.R. 3.1's comments *ad loc*. The "branches" = Hananiah, Mishael, and Azariah: cf. Num.R. 3.1: "As the palm tree never bears less than three new shoots, so Israel never lacks three righteous men in the world—like Abraham, Isaac, and Jacob, or Hananiah, Mishael, and Azariah"; b. Sanh. 93a: "R. Samuel b. Naḥmani said in R. Jonathan's name: What is meant by, *I said: I will go up to the palm tree; I will take hold of its branches* (Cant 7:9)? *I said: I will go up to the palm tree*: this refers to Israel; but now I grasped but the one bough of Hananiah, Mishael, and Azariah." Cant.R. 7:9 §1 is parallel, but not so clear.

40 "Breasts" are taken as a symbol of redemption: cf. Tg. to 4:5 and 7:4 where "two breasts" symbolize Israel's two redeemers at the eschaton. "Clusters of the vine" = Israel: see Tg. to 6:11 (*Note* 36). "Scent" = fame: see Tg. to 1:3 (*Note* 20), 1:12 (*Note* 91), and 4:10 (*Note* 41).

41 According to the Midrash, Abraham successfully withstood ten trials, of which the first was the fiery furnace ("*Ur* of the Chaldeans" [Gen 16:31] = the *fire* of the Chaldeans, the furnace into which Nimrod cast Abraham for rejecting idolatry [Ginzberg, *Legends* 1:195–203]; cf. the story of the Three Hebrew Children), and the last the binding of Isaac (Genesis 22). See m. ᾽Abot 5:3; ARN A.33; Gen.R. 55.1; 56.11; Exod.R. 15.27; 30.16; 44.4; Num.R. 15.12; 18.21; Pirqei de R. El. 26-31; Midrash Ps. 18.25. The tradition is pre-Rabbinic: see Jub. 17:17 and 19:8, with Charles, *Jubilees*, notes *ad loc*. Further Ginzberg, *Legends* 1:217; 5:218, n. 52.

42 The fiery furnace in Daniel 3 (the Three Children) and the lions' den in Daniel 6–7 (Daniel).

43 Once again the stress on the merits of the righteous is noteworthy. The merits of Daniel and the Three Children are reckoned equal to those of Abraham! Each phase of the *Heilsgeschichte* has its righteous men whose merit covers the sins of the people. Cf. Cant.R. 7:8 §1: "This is the source of the popular oath, 'By Him who established the earth on three pillars.' Some say these are Abraham, Isaac, and Jacob; some say they are Hananiah, Mishael, and Azariah." Midrash Ps. 114.5 expresses the curious idea that the Exodus from Egypt took place through the merits of the Three Children—an idea possibly alluded to enigmatically in Cant.R. 7:10 §1. The redemption here, however, is the return under Cyrus seen as a new Exodus. Tg. constantly discovers cyclicality in the *Heilsgeschichte*.

44 The "apple of the Garden of Eden" is the ethrog (Zohary, *Plants of the Bible* 123), not the common apple, the normal sense of *tappuaḥ* in biblical Hebrew (KB 1773b). Cf. b. Shabb. 88a. Ethrogs are more pungent than apples. Implicit here is the identification of the forbidden fruit of Gen 2:17 with the ethrog. Cf. Ginzberg, *Legends* 5:97, n. 70.

10. Hebrew Text:

Your palate is like the wine of the Good One,[45]
Going smoothly for my Beloved,[46]
Causing the lips of those who sleep to speak.[47]

Targum:

Daniel and his companions said: "We shall surely take[jj] upon ourselves the decree of the Word of the Lord, as Abraham our forefather, who is compared to old wine,[kk] took [it] upon himself. And we shall walk in the paths that are right before Him, as Elijah and Elisha went, the prophets by whose merit the dead, who resemble[ll] a man asleep,[48] arose, and like Ezekiel the son of Buzi, the priest, by the prophecy of whose mouth those who slept the sleep of death[mm] in the Plain of Dura awakened."[49]

Apparatus, Chapter 7

[jj] "We shall surely take" = *qbl' nqbl,* a Hebraism.

[kk] L: "wine new and old"; O: "new wine." See further Tg. to 8:2, *Apparatus h.*

[ll] Reading *ddmy(y)n* with B C D E F J K L M for A's *wdmyyn.*

[mm] Reading *dmyky mwt'* ("those who slept the sleep of death") with B G H I for A's *dmyky.* J K L M O read simply "the dead" *(myty').*

Notes, Chapter 7

[45] Daniel and his companions (Dan 1:19) express their submission to the divine testing and their determination to come through it successfully. Though there were two separate tests (the furnace and the lions' den), under two different kings (Nebuchadnezzar and Darius), the Midrash represents Daniel and the Three Children as acting in concert. According to Cant.R. 7:8 §1, the Three Children consulted their "master" Daniel.

"Palate" = God's decree, probably through a semantic link (palate > speech > decree), though a pun on *ḥekh* (palate) and *ḥoq* (decree) is not impossible. "Decree" may allude here specifically to God's declaration that he would not stand by the Three Children if they defied the king. According to the Aggadah God told Ezekiel, whom the Three Children approached to intercede for them, that he would not stand by them if they defied the king—yet they still refused to bow down! God later reveals himself to Ezekiel and says, "Ezekiel, did you imagine that I would not stand by them? I will certainly stand by them . . . But let them go all unsuspecting [lit., in their uprightness, *mehallekhin be-tomam*], as it says, *He who walks uprightly [holekh ba-tom] walks securely* (Prov 10:9)" (Cant.R. 7:8 §1; further Ginzberg, *Legends* 4:331; 6:470, n. 420).

"Wine of the Good One": Tg. follows the Masoretic vocalization (*ke-yein ha-tob* rather than *ka-yayin ha-tob,* "like good wine") and identifies "the Good One" with Abraham.

[46] Tg. took Hebrew *le-mesharim* in an ethical sense, "in uprightness, equity" (BDB 449a) and may have heard in the phrase *holekh . . . le-mesharim* an echo of *holekh ba-tom* in Prov 10:9, which Cant.R. 7:8 §1 applied to the Three Children (see *Note* 45 above).

[47] "Those who sleep" = the dead; "causing those who sleep to speak" (thus, implicitly, Tg. understands the problematic *dobeb*: cf. b. Sanh. 90b) indicates resurrection: see *Note* 49 below.

[48] Cf. Dan 12:2, "And many that sleep in the dust of the earth [*yeshenei 'admat 'afar*] shall awake, some to everlasting life, and some to reproaches." Here, however, the reference is not to the eschatological resurrection but to a temporary anticipation of it. See *Note* 49 below.

[49] Daniel and the Three Children are compared in merit to Elijah, Elisha, and Ezekiel, all of whom are associated with the resurrection of the dead: Elijah in 1 Kgs 17:17-24; Elisha in 2 Kgs 4:23-37; Ezekiel in Ezek 37:1-10, the Valley of the Dry Bones. Indeed, the Midrash implies that it was through the merit of the Three Children that the dead were raised by Ezekiel, the "valley" where Ezekiel performed the feat being identified with the Plain of Dura where Nebuchadnezzar set up his image, and the resurrection occurring on the very day of the Hebrews' defiance. Cf. b. Sanh. 92b, "Our Rabbis taught: When the wicked Nebuchadnezzar threw Hananiah, Mishael, and Azariah into the fiery furnace, the Holy One, blessed be He, said to Ezekiel: *Go resurrect the dead in the plain of Dura.*" Further Cant.R. 7:9 §1; Ginzberg, *Legends* 4:332–33; 6:422, n. 95; Goodenough, *Jewish Symbols* 10:180–84, 194–96. The reference is not to the final, eschatological resurrection, but to a temporary anticipation of it: note the past tenses. According to b. Sanh. 92b "the dead whom Ezekiel resurrected stood up, uttered a song, and [immediately]

11. Hebrew Text:

If I am my Beloved's,
Then His desire is toward me.[50]

Targum:

Jerusalem[nn] says: "So long as I walk in the ways[oo] of the Lord of the World, He causes His Shekhinah to dwell among me, and His desire is toward me. But when I deviate from His ways[oo] He removes His Shekhinah from me, and makes me wander among the nations, and they rule over me as a husband rules over his wife."[pp]

12. Hebrew Text:

Go, my Beloved,
Let us go forth into the field;
Let us lodge in the villages.[51]

Apparatus, Chapter 7

[nn] K L: "the Assembly of Israel." "Jerusalem" is clearly *lectio difficilior,* but why suddenly Jerusalem?

[oo] A inconsistently reads "way . . . ways." Read the plural in both places *(ʾwrḥtyh . . . ʾwrḥtyh)* with the majority of the mss.

[pp] Lit. "like a husband whose rule is over his wife" *(kgbr dy shwltnyh bʾynttyh).* D E F have the simpler *kgbr dshlyt bʾynttyh/bʾnttʾ* ("like a husband who rules over his wife"), but stylistic variation is in favor of the A reading.

Notes, Chapter 7

died," hence "causing the lips of those who sleep to speak." The anticipation of the eschaton is important to Tg. "It may be stated as a general principle that all the miracles which take place in the 'time to come' have been performed 'in miniature' during the present order. . . . Ezekiel is not the only man who made the dead come to life; in the world to come the righteous will perform the miracle of the resurrection of the dead" (Ginzberg, *Legends* 6:422, with references).

[50] Cf. the partial parallels in 2:16 and 6:3. Verse 11 forms a fitting coda to the description of the glories of the Second Temple period. Somewhat unusually it is put in the mouth of "Jerusalem" (though see *Apparatus nn*). Tg. has read it as conditional: "If I am my Beloved's, then His desire is toward me," but conversely, "If I am not my Beloved's, then His desire is not toward me." The Hebrew *we-ʿalai teshuqato* = either "His desire is toward me" or "desire for Him is upon me." Tg. probably takes the former option, though the Aramaic is as ambiguous as the Hebrew, and Gen 3:16 suggests that the "desire" is that of the woman toward the man. *Teshuqah* here clearly recalled the use of the word in Gen 3:16, "To the woman he said: . . . Your desire shall be to your husband, and he shall rule over you" (cf. Cant.R. 7:11 §1). Tg. saw the woman's "desire" as evidence of her submissiveness ("as a husband rules over his wife"). The implication is that if Israel is not "married" to God she is "married" to the nations, and they have the right to dominate her (cf. Hos 2:1-23). Tg. also faintly echoes the interpretation of *wkbshh* in Gen 1:28 as "subdue *her*": see Rashi *ad loc.*: "The *waw* is missing, thereby teaching you that the male dominates the female, so that she should not become a gadabout; and also teaching you that the commandment to be fruitful and multiply was given to the man, whose nature is to dominate, and not to the woman."

[51] Tg. detects here the voice of Israel praying to God, asking for his presence with her in the "field" and the "villages," i.e., in exile. A new exile is somewhat casually introduced, starting with the destruction of the Second Temple by the Romans (which, curiously, is not explicitly mentioned). Thus we enter the final period of the *Heilsgeschichte* stretching from the destruction of the Temple to the coming of the Messiah. This is Tg.'s own era and he treats it very sketchily (effectively only in this and following verse), preferring to concentrate on the Messianic Age (7:14–8:10). See further *Intro.* 3.2.

The "field" recalled to the Tg. "the field of Edom" in Gen 32:4 (English 32:3), "And Jacob sent messengers . . . to Esau in the land of Seir, the field of Edom." Edom in turn was taken as a reference to Rome, an identification common in Rabbinic literature from the Bar Kokhba period onwards. Later Edom = Christendom (see Ego, *Targum Scheni* 40–42, with bibliography cited there). Though Tg. probably lived under Islamic rule (see *Intro* 8.1), the reference here only to Edom is historically correct, since Rome was the agent of the exile. Moreover, according to one tradition Edom would remain the eschatological foe *par excellence,* despite the emergence of Islam: see Tg. to 8:4 (*Note* 15).

Targum:

When the people of the House of Israel sinned,[qq] the Lord exiled them in the land of Seir,[rr] the field of Edom.[ss] The Assembly of Israel said: "I beseech you, Master of all the World,[tt] receive my prayer, that I am praying before You in the cities of the exile[uu] and the provinces of the nations."

13. Hebrew Text:

Let us go early to the vineyards;
Let us see whether the vine has budded,
Whether the vine-blossom is open[52]
And the pomegranates are in blossom.
There I will give You my love.[53]

Apparatus, Chapter 7

[qq] O: "when the people of the House of Israel returned and rebelled [or: rebelled again]." This unique reading probably reflects the scribe's perception that a new section begins here and a stronger transition is needed.

[rr] J K L M N: "to the land of Seir." Gen 32:4 Heb. (*Note* 51) has "in the land of Seir," but note Onq. *ad loc.*, "to the land of Seir."

[ss] D E F G: "fields of Edom." Gen 32:4 Heb. has "field of Edom" and note singular "field" in the Hebrew here. However, Onq. Gen. 32:4 has "fields of Edom" (v. l.: field).

[tt] J M O: "Master of all the Worlds."

[uu] G: "exiles."

Notes, Chapter 7

"Villages" = cities of the exile and the provinces of the nations. Cant.R. 7:13 §1 also detects here a reference to exile: "*Come, my Beloved, let us go forth into the field.* The holy spirit cries aloud: 'Let us take a walk through the public places [*dymwsyn*] of the world. *Let us lodge in the villages* [*kefarim*], among those who deny Him [*koferim*].' These are the cities of the nations of the world, who deny the Holy One, blessed be He. Rabbi Abba bar Kahana said: However, it is only for a time." *Koferim* suggests Christendom, but note that this interpretation seems to apply *dodi* to Israel!

This verse is echoed in the famous Sabbath hymn of the sixteenth-century Safed Qabbalist Solomon Alkabetz, *Lekhah Dodi* (Singer, *ADPB* 229–34; Fine, *Safed Spirituality* 35–36, 38–40), and it influenced the Sabbath-eve rituals of the Safed community (Scholem, *On the Kabbalah and its Symbolism* 139–44). Such highly-charged mystical interpretations could not be farther from the Tg.'s reading: see further *Intro.* 6.2.

52 Tg. detects the voice of Israel in exile in his own days (note the present tense, "the Children of Israel *say* . . ."), exhorting one another to inquire whether the redemption is at hand.

"Vineyard" is a common image of Israel: so Cant.R. 7:13 §1, quoting Isa 5:7, "The vineyard of the Lord of Hosts is the House of Israel" (cf. Tg. to 2:15). Tg. typically nuances by taking "vineyards" as = synagogues and houses of study, and "vine" in the following line as = Israel (see Ps 80:8; Jer 2:21; Ezek 17:6; further Tg. to 7:8, *Note* 35; 6:11, *Note* 36; 8:11, *Note* 50). Vineyard = House of Study is appropriate, since it is the place where Israel the vine is nurtured.

The "budding" of the vine is taken as a symbol of the redemption, perhaps precisely the "beginning of the redemption" *(ʾatḥalta' di-geʾulta')*, in contrast to the "opening" of the vine-flower in the following line = the fullness of the redemption. Cf. Isa 27:6, "In days to come Jacob shall take root; Israel shall blossom and bud: and they shall fill the face of the earth with fruit"; and note the use of "Branch of David" *(Ṣemaḥ David)* as a title of the Messiah (Isa 4:2; Jer 23:5; 33:15; Zech 3:8; 6:12). Tg. treats the rare *semadar* rather differently in 2:13, 15.

53 "Pomegranates" = the righteous who are as full of *miṣwot* as a pomegranate is full of seeds (see Tg. to 4:3, *Note* 15). The "blossoming" of the pomegranates is interpreted as God taking cognizance of the merits of the righteous. Contrast Tg.'s treatment of the parallel in 6:11 ("to see whether the vine had budded, and the pomegranates were in blossom"). "There" = Jerusalem; "giving of love" = offering of sacrifice.

Cant.R. 7:13 §1 interprets rather differently: "*Let us see whether the vine has budded.* This refers to the recital of the *Shemaʿ*. *Whether the vine-blossom is open.* This refers to the synagogues and houses of study. *And the pomegranates are in flower.* This refers to the children busily learning the Torah. *There I will give You my love.* There I produce righteous men and women, the prophets and prophetesses who have arisen from me."

Targum:

The Children of Israel[vv] say to one another: "Let us rise early in the morning[54] and let us go to the synagogues and the houses of study.[ww] Let us search in the scrolls of the Torah[xx] and see whether the time for the redemption of the people of the House of Israel (who are compared to the vine) has come,[55] when they will be redeemed[yy] from their exiles.[zz] Let us ask the Sages whether the merit[aaa] of the righteous, who are as full of precepts as pomegranates,[bbb] is revealed before the Lord, and whether the term[ccc] has come to go up to Jerusalem,[56] there to give praise to the God of Heaven, and to offer burnt offerings and holy sacrifices."[57]

14. Hebrew Text:

The balsam has given forth scent;[58]
At our doors are all manner of precious fruits

Apparatus, Chapter 7

[vv] J K L M N O: "House of Israel"—the more usual expression in Tg. Cant., but note "Children of Israel" again at 8:1, 6.

[ww] Some mss. (D E F J K L M N O) read "synagogue and house of study," some (B G H I) inconsistently "synagogue and houses of study."

[xx] D E F I: "scroll of the Torah." O points "scribes *(saferei)* of the Torah," but this does not sit easily with the verb *nbqr*.

[yy] The syntax of the infinitive *l'ytprq'* is awkward. It should be construed as epexegetical of *zmn*: "the time for [Israel] to be redeemed." The intrusion of *pwrqn'* does not alter this relationship or turn the infinitive into a consecutive clause ("so that they are redeemed").

[zz] B D E F G H I K L: "from their exile."

[aaa] C G H K L N: "merit."

[bbb] B G I J M N O: "who are as full as pomegranates"; K L: "who are compared to pomegranates."

[ccc] "Term" = *qyṣ'*, used here not simply as a stylistic variant of *zmn*, but in the technical sense of "the time of redemption" (Jast. 1403b); cf. Dan 9:26; 12:3; b. Meg. 3a; b. Sanh. 92b; 97b; *Note* 55.

Notes, Chapter 7

[54] Hebrew *nashkimah*: "When the temporal phrase 'in the morning' is absent, the verb *hshkm* means 'to get busy'. . . . Although the phrase 'in the morning' is absent here, there is implicit reference to night in the antecedent verb *l(w/y)n* which suggests that the subsequent action is to take place the following morning" (Pope, 646).

[55] There appears to be a reference here to calculating the end from Scripture, a practice frowned upon by many Rabbinic authorities but nonetheless widespread. Cf. b. Meg. 3a (the Hagiographa contain intimations about the Messianic term); b. Sanh. 97b; Maimonides' *Thirteen Principles*, no. 12, Alexander, *Textual Sources* 115. Tg. elsewhere warns against forcing the redemption, and stresses that the Messiah will come in God's good time (see 2:7, *Note* 49, and 3:5; further 7:14, *Note* 58).

[56] It is not clear why one should inquire of the Sages specifically about this, or how they would know. There appears to be a contrast between searching the Scriptures for the date of the Messiah's coming and inquiring of the Sages whether the merits of the righteous have availed to bring the end. But the contrast may be somewhat forced: the intention is to control popular Messianic enthusiasm by putting the decision on this matter at the discretion of the Sages. Through their closeness to God *they* can best decide when the time is right.

[57] There are distant echoes of the ʿAmidah. Note also Tg. to 8:14.

[58] Tg. detects here the voice of God addressing the Messiah, his "Beloved" *(dodi!)*, and telling him that the merits of the righteous and the studies of the scholars have created the right conditions for bringing about the redemption.

There may be an element of self-correction here: Tg. wishes to avoid any misunderstanding of his allusions to calculating the end in v. 13 (*Note* 55 *ad loc.*). The coming of the end is contingent on Israel's merits, but it is up to "the good pleasure of the Lord" alone to decide when they are righteous enough: it is, therefore, effectively incalculable. Cf. b. Sanh. 97b: the dates of the redemption, calculated from Scripture, have passed, and everything now depends on repentance. Further b. Sanh. 98a: "Jerusalem will be redeemed only by virtue of righteousness/charity *(ṣedaqah)*"; b. B. Bat. 10a: "Great is righteousness/charity *(ṣedaqah)* because it brings nearer the redemption"; b. Yoma 86b: "Great is repentance *(teshubah)* because it brings about the redemption." See further *Notes* 59 and 61 below.

Hebrew *duda'im* is normally rendered "mandrakes" (KB 215b); Tg. clearly identifies it with "balsam." "Balsam" = the righteous, and the "scent" of the righteous = their good deeds. Cant.R. 7:14 §1 does not see any Messianic reference in the verse, and interprets very differently.

—both new and old.[59]
My Beloved, I have laid [it] up for you.[60]

Targum:

When it shall be the good pleasure of the Lord to redeem His people from exile, He will say[ddd] to the King Messiah: "The term of the exile is already completed,[eee] and the merit[fff] of the righteous has become as fragrant before Me as the scent of balsam.[ggg] The Sages of the generation[hhh] are fixed at the doors of the schools,[iii] diligently studying the words of the Scribes and the words of the Torah.[jjj][61] Arise now,[kkk] and receive the kingdom[lll] that I have stored up[mmm] for you."[62]

Apparatus, Chapter 7

[ddd] Miq. Ged. (= Lag.): "it will be said"—more reverential: note the extremely reverential language of the preceding clause (lit. "when there shall be good pleasure from before the Lord"). Mss. "He will say" is more dramatic.

[eee] F omits "He will say to the King Messiah: 'The term of exile is already completed'" by parablepsis.

[fff] Reading "merit" with C G H I J K L M N for A's "merits." The following verb *(ʾytbsm)* is singular.

[ggg] J K L M N O: "scent of spices."

[hhh] Reading "Sages of the generation" with B C E G K L O, for A's "generations"; cf. the Hebrew expression *gedolei ha-dor.*

[iii] = *mdrshy*ʾ rather than *bty mdrsh*ʾ; see Tg. to 6:5, *Apparatus v.*

[jjj] There must be a contrast here between Oral Torah and Written Torah. Since *ʾwrytʾ* refers to the latter, *spryʾ* must refer to the former. If *spryʾ* is to be vocalized as *sifrayyaʾ* (cf. D N) then the books cannot be Sifrei Torah or the twenty-four books of Tanakh (Jast. 1018a), but must be Sifrei deBei Rab (b. Sanh. 86a; b. Yoma 74a)—a usage that dates from a time when written texts were common in the schools. However, the absolute use of "books" for the Oral Torah is awkward. Hence vocalize *saferayyaʾ,* "the Scribes" (with J K L M N O) = the Sages; cf. 7:5; 8:9; and "Moses the Great Scribe" (1:2; 2:4; 3:3).

[kkk] J M O have "like giants" for "arise, now" by faulty word-division: *kʿnqym/n* instead of *kʿn qy/wm!*

[lll] J M vocalizes "the kingdoms"; G: "your kingdom."

[mmm] "That I have stored up" = *dgnzyt*; K L: *dgnʾt*, for which Levey, *Messiah* 161 n. 58, proposes the translation "which has been lying dormant," but this is forced.

Notes, Chapter 7

[59] The "doors" are the doors of the schools; the "precious fruits" are the products of the Sages' studies; "new" alludes to the Oral Torah ("the words of the Scribes": see *Apparatus jjj*), "old" to the Written Torah. Cf. b. ʿErub. 21b: "*Both new and old*: the latter are the commandments derived from the words of Torah [= *old*], while the former are those derived from the words of the Sages [= *new*]." For a similar view that the studies of the scholars hasten the redemption see b. Sanh. 99b; see also Tg. to 6:1-2, where it is implied that the return from exile in Babylon came about because of repentance and study.

[60] Following the Masoretic accents, Tg. treats this as an independent clause. "The Beloved" is here the Messiah, and the implied object of the verb is the kingdom. See further *Note* 62.

[61] That the Messiah will only come when Israel is particularly faithful and righteous is the standard Rabbinic view, used to reinforce the study of the Torah and the performance of the *miṣwot.* An alternative scenario, which stresses more divine grace, sees the Messiah as coming when Israel is particularly wicked and unfaithful: cf. 3 Enoch 48A:5-6, "But when the Holy One, blessed be He, shall see that there is none righteous in that generation, none pious on the earth, no righteousness in men's hands, no one like Moses, no intercessor like Samuel, who could entreat the Omnipresent One for salvation, for redemption, for His kingdom to be manifested in the whole world, for His great right hand to be set before Him once again, so that He might effect with it a great deliverance for Israel; then the Holy One, blessed be He, will at once remember His own righteousness, merit, mercy, and grace, and, for His own sake, will deliver His great arm, and His own righteousness will support Him" (cf. Cant.R. 2:13 §4; further Alexander in Charlesworth, *OTP* 1:301, note k). Certain later mystical circles pushed this line of thought to extreme antinomianism by proclaiming that the redemption could be hastened through *sinning* (see Scholem, "Redemption Through Sin")! Nothing could be farther from Tg.'s mind.

[62] "Arise" recalls the frequent use of *qum* in the Psalms for God rising up to judge the enemies of Israel (e.g., Ps 68:2, "Let God arise and let his enemies be scattered"; cf. Pss 9:20; 44:27; 74:22; 82:8). There may be an echo of Ps 2:7-9, but this psalm, perhaps for polemical reasons, is not interpreted messianically either in the Targum *ad loc.* or elsewhere in Rabbinic literature (Levey, *The Messiah* 105). The concreteness of "stored up" suggests the common apocalyptic image of the Messiah, the New Jerusalem *(Yerushalayim shel maʿalah),* and the eschatological Temple already existing in the heavens, simply awaiting the time when they shall descend to earth. Cf. 1 Enoch 90:28-29; 2 Bar 4:2-7; 4 Ezra 7:26; Gal 4:26; Rev 21:2; b. Taʿan. 5a; b. Ḥag. 12b; (further Strack-Billerbeck 3:796, and Alexander in Charlesworth, *OTP* 1:300, note h to 3 Enoch 48A:3).

CHAPTER 8

1. Hebrew Text:

Would that you were as a brother to me,
Sucking the breasts of my mother![1]
[When] I find you outside [and] kiss you,
Even they do not despise me.[2]

Targum:

And at that time the King Messiah will be revealed[a3] to the Assembly of Israel, and the Children of Israel[b] shall say to him:[c] "Come, be a brother to us, and let us go up to Jerusalem and suck out with you the reasons for the Torah,[d4] just as an infant sucks at the breast of its mother. For all the time that I was wandering outside my land, when I was mindful of the

Apparatus, Chapter 8

[a] A and the majority of the mss. read the present participle *mtgly* ("is revealed"), perhaps to indicate the speed with which the divine command to the Messiah at the end of 7:14 is fulfilled. E: *ytgly* ("will be revealed"); D F: *ʾtgly* ("has been revealed").

[b] J K L M N: "House of Israel," but the expression "Children of Israel" is appropriate here in the context of the new Exodus. For the variant see 7:13 *Apparatus vv.*

[c] Adding "to him" with D F G H. A omits.

[d] "Reasons for the Torah" = *tʿmy ʾwrytʾ*; cf. Tg. to 5:11 (*Apparatus yy*) and 5:13.

Notes, Chapter 8

[1] The voice is the voice of Israel, but Tg. detects two addressees: (1) the Messiah (lines 1-2); and (2) God (lines 3-4).

"Mother" = Torah; cf. b. Ber. 57a (Tg. to 6:9, *Note* 29). The image is apt: just as the mother nourishes the child, so the Torah nourishes Israel. The "milk" extracted is the "reasons" for the Torah (see *Note* 4). "Milk" = spiritual sustenance is a common simile in both early Jewish and early Christian literature. See, e.g., Cant.R. 1:2 §3; 1 Pet 2:2 (with Selwyn's note *ad loc.*); Odes of Solomon 8:17 ("I [God] fashioned their members. My own breasts I prepared for them that they might drink My holy milk thereby"); b. ʿErub. 54b ("*Her breasts will satisfy you at all times* [Prov 5:19]. Why are the words of the Torah compared to a breast? As with a breast, however often the child sucks it, so often does it find milk in it. So it is with the words of the Torah: as often as a man studies them, so often does he find relish in them").

[2] "Outside" = outside the Land of Israel, in exile. "Kissing" is taken as a mark of homage and worship (see m. Sanh. 7:6, which refers to kissing an idol, and Schäfer, *Synopse* §259, "Wretch, perhaps you are of the seed of those who kissed the [Golden] Calf!"; cf. §408; Cant.R. 7:9 §1). The affirmation of God "outside" the Land leads to martyrdom *(qiddush ha-shem)*. Tg. posits a causal connection between martyrdom and going up to the Land: the former earns the right to the latter. Cf. Tg. to 7:9-10, where the merit acquired by Daniel and the Three Hebrew Children through sanctifying God's name "outside the Land" brought about the return from Babylon.

"They" = the Gentiles. See further *Note* 6.

[3] The Messiah is not "born," but "revealed," either from heaven or from where he has been living incognito (see b. Sanh. 98a; Sefer Zerubbabel, ed. Lévi, 134; *Intro.* 4.5). Tg. recognizes two Messiahs—the Messiah son of David and the Messiah son of Ephraim (see 4:5, *Note* 23). The reference here is to the former. The Messiah's role is notably unmilitaristic: he will be a scholar and will teach Israel Torah, which Tg. would see as a surer defense for Israel than any weapon of war. Cf. Tg. to v. 2, and see further *Note* 4.

[4] Inquiring into the "reasons for the commandments" *(taʿamei ha-miṣwot)* was one of the tasks of the advanced Rabbinic scholar (see *EJ* 5:783–92). Both Israel and the Messiah will study Torah, which will disclose new and hidden depths in the Messianic Age. Tg. pointedly avoids Messianic antinomianism: there will be no new Torah in the Messianic Age; rather the old Torah will yield up new secrets that will suffice for the new era. Contrast "The Holy One, blessed be He, is destined to sit in the

Name of the Great God and gave up my life for His divinity,[5] even the nations of the earth did not despise me."[6]

2. Hebrew Text:

I will lead you, and bring you
Into the house of my mother;
You shall teach me;[7]
I will cause you to drink from spiced wine,
From juice of pomegranates.[8]

Targum:

"I will lead you, O King Messiah,[e] I will bring you up into my Temple,[f] and you will teach me to fear the Lord, and to walk in His ways.[g] There we will partake of the feast of Leviathan[9] and we will drink [from] old wine which has been preserved in its grapes from

Apparatus, Chapter 8

[e] J K L M N: "O Messiah."
[f] B E G H I: "the Temple," but "*my* Temple" picks up the Hebrew "house of *my* mother."
[g] K L N O: "His way."

Notes, Chapter 8

Garden of Eden and to expound. All the righteous will sit before Him with the whole household of heaven standing on their feet . . . The Holy One, blessed be He, will expound to them the reasons behind the new Torah *(ta'amei Torah ḥadashah)* which He is destined to give them at the hands of the Messiah" (Even-Shmuel, *MG* 347 = Alphabet of Rabbi 'Aqiba, Wertheimer, *BM* 2:367–68). "The Messiah is destined to sit in the college [= the heavenly Beit Midrash], and all those about to come into the world will come and sit before him to hear the new Torah, and the new commandments and the deep insights which he teaches to Israel" (Even-Shmuel, *MG* 349). The idea that there will be a new Torah—a second Sinai, so to speak—in the Messianic Age is rare in classic Rabbinic literature for obvious polemical reasons, but is not uncommon in the medieval Qabbalah. See Davies, *Torah in the Messianic Age*; Tishby, *Wisdom of the Zohar* 3:1079–1112, especially 1104–1105.

[5] Tg. may be thinking particularly of the martyrdom of 'Aqiba, who died proclaiming the unity of God (b. Ber. 61b). Cf. Tg. to 1:4 (*Note* 33) and 8:6 (*Note* 29).

[6] For the idea that Israel's steadfast sanctification of the name of God earns the respect of the Gentiles, cf. the case of Nebuchadnezzar (Dan 3:28-30).

[7] "House of my mother" = the Temple, the restored Temple which Tg. may envisage as descending to earth from heaven: note the lack of reference to the building of the Temple in the Messianic Age. Cf. *Midrash Wayyosha':* "Then the Holy One, blessed be He, will bring down the Temple from heaven . . . And Israel shall dwell there two thousand years and eat Leviathan" (Eisenstein, *OM* 1:156a).

"You shall teach me": Tg. sees a continuation of the theme of Messianic study from the previous verse. There, however, Israel and the Messiah study together; here the Messiah teaches Israel. Note how Tg. sees the Temple as a locus of study. The Temple and the Beit Midrash functionally overlap in his thinking (*Intro.* 4.4).

[8] "I will cause you to drink" recalls to Tg. the Messianic banquet. "Spiced" wine suggested "old wine," "juice" *('asis)*, new wine: see *Apparatus h*, and further *Note* 10. The Hebrew mentions only beverages, but no Messianic menu would be complete without a serving of Leviathan. See *Note* 9.

[9] The idea of the Messianic feast is old (see, e.g., 1QSa [Messianic Rule] 2.11-22; Matt 26:29; m. ʾAbot 4:6; b. Shabb. 153a; b. Ḥag. 14b; b. B. Bat. 74a), but later Jewish apocalyptic and folklore offered ever more fantastic elaborations of the theme, perhaps trying to trump the sensually explicit depictions of the joys of Paradise in Islam. Three types of meat will be served, drawn from three fabulous beasts—fish (from Leviathan), flesh (from Behemoth), and fowl (from Ziz, a mythical bird discovered in Ps 50:11). See *Secrets of Rashbi*: "And Israel shall dwell securely for two thousand years and eat Behemoth, Leviathan, and Ziz, slaughtering Behemoth [themselves], whereas Ziz will rend Leviathan with its claws. Then Moses will come and

the day that the world was created, and from pomegranates[h] and fruits[i] which are prepared for the righteous in the Garden of Eden."[10]

3. Hebrew Text:

His left hand is under my head,
And His right hand embraces me.[11]

Targum:

The Assembly of Israel says: "I am chosen out of all the people, because I bind *tefillin* on my left hand and on my head, and I fix the *mezuzah* on the right hand side of the door

Apparatus, Chapter 8

[h] = *mrwmny.* The *me-* corresponds to the Hebrew *me-*, but what is the syntax in the Aramaic? The phrase must go (by zeugma) with the verb *nyshty,* and the reference must be to a beverage made from pomegranates. Tg. probably intended to contrast the "old wine" stored up from creation with the "new wine" (= Heb. *ʿasis*) made from the fruits of the Garden of Eden (which is here not the historical Garden, but the abode of the righteous in the east of the world). Curiously, Tg. does not translate *ʿasis,* but the expression "old wine" may harbor a "ghost" of *ʿasis* in the sense of "new wine." Perhaps his intended translation was: "we will drink old wine . . . and [new wine] from pomegranates and fruits . . . ." For "old wine" see Tg. to 7:10, *Apparatus kk.* MT's *ʿasis rimmoni* is vocalized to mean "the juice of my pomegranate" or "my pomegranate juice" (note *ʿasis* is in the construct) rather than "pomegranate juice" (*rimmoni* as an adjective). This suggests the possibility of reading Tg.'s *rwmny* as "my pomegranate" (*rummani:* cf. K L M N O). However, the majority Tg. tradition vocalizes *rummanei* = Hebrew *rimmonim,* which is read by some MT mss. (Pope, 659–60).

[i] D E F: "fruits," presumably to be construed in apposition to *rwmny* = "(from pomegranates), fruits (which have been prepared . . .)."

Notes, Chapter 8

slaughter Ziz Sadai" (Jellinek, *BHM* 3:80). Tg., somewhat restrained, mentions only Leviathan. According to tradition Leviathan was created on the fifth day: originally, like all other animals, it was created male and female, but the Holy One realized that together they would multiply and destroy the earth, so he killed the female and salted her to preserve her for the Messianic feast. The male too will finally be killed (his eschatological slaughter recalls Ancient Near Eastern myths about battles with the chaos monster), and both will be served to the righteous in the world to come (see 4 Ezra 6:49-52; 2 Bar 29:4; b. B. Bat. 74a-75a; Pirqei de R. El. 9 and 10; Ps-J Gen. 1:21; Midrash Ps. 18.25; *Banquet of Leviathan*, Jellinek, *BHM* 6:150–51; further Ginzberg, *Legends* 1:26–31; 5:41–49).

[10] For wine at the Messianic banquet cf. Matt 26:29, "I tell you I shall not drink again of this fruit of the vine until the day when I drink it new with you in my father's kingdom" (par. Mark 14:25; Luke 22:18), and note the reference to the "new wine" *(tirosh)* in 1QSa 2.18. The "special Messianic elixir, wine preserved in its grapes since Creation" (Levey, *Messiah* 131), is mentioned also in b. Ber. 34b; b. Sanh. 99a; Yalqut Shimʿoni, Gen. §20 (to Gen 2:8). There may be an allusion to the idea that the rewards of the righteous and their means of redemption were already prepared by God at creation (cf. the ram of the ʿAqedah: Ps-J Gen. 22:13); or else the thought may be that the sinful world was simply not worthy of the blessing of such a splendid wine (Exod.R. 35.1). The *Chapters of the Messiah* also mention pomegranate wine at the Messianic banquet, possibly in dependence on Tg.: "Then the Holy One, blessed be He, will prepare tables and slaughter Behemoth and Leviathan and Ziz Sadai, and He will make a great banquet for the righteous, and He will seat everyone according to his rank. The Holy One, blessed be He, will say to them, 'Do you wish to drink apple-wine, or pomegranate-wine, or grape-wine?' And the righteous will say, 'You have the power to do whatever You wish.' And the Holy One, blessed be He, will bring them wine preserved in its grapes from the six days of creation, as it is written, *I will cause you to drink from spiced wine* (Cant 8:2)" (Jellinek, *BHM* 3:76).

[11] Tg. takes the parallel in 2:6 as also expressing God's protection of Israel, but the detail is worked out differently. Here he sees an allusion to the *tefillin* ("left hand" and "head" = *tefillin shel yad* and *tefillin shel roʾsh*) and the *mezuzah* ("right hand" = right-hand doorpost). The implication in context is that Israel will be redeemed from her present exile only if she observes the commandments of the *tefillin* and *mezuzot.* There may be an echo of Mek. de R. Ishmael, *Beshallaḥ* 7: "*But the*

frame [in] the third toward the lintel,[j][12] so that the Destroyer[k] should not have permission to harm me."[13]

4. Hebrew Text:

I adjure you, O daughters of Jerusalem,
Not to stir up, nor awaken love,
Till it please.[14]

Apparatus, Chapter 8

[j] Reading *(k)lqb(y)l t(y)ky* with D F G H J M N O for A's *kl qbl*. The grammar is awkward and the terms obscure, but Tg. appears to take the view that the *mezuzah* should be placed in the top third of the right-hand door post as one enters (*Note* 12). The noun *tyqy/tqy,* only here and in Ps-J Deut. 6:9; 11:20, seems to be derived from Greek *thēkē,* apparently in the (? late or vulgar) sense of "lintel." Onq. Exod 12:23 uses *shqp'*.

[k] Reading "Destroyer" with D F J M; A and other mss. read the plural, "destroyers" (= demons): see *Note* 13.

Notes, Chapter 8

children of Israel walked on dry land in the midst of the sea, [the waters being a wall to them on their right hand and on their left] (Exod 14:29) . . . Do not read *ḥomah* (wall), but *ḥemah* (anger). And what helped them escape? *On their right hand and on their left. On their right hand* suggests the merit of the Torah which they were destined to receive, as it is said, *At his right hand was a fiery law unto them* (Deut 33:2). *And on their left* suggests prayer. Another interpretation: *On their right hand* suggests the *mezuzah,* and *on their left hand* suggests the *tefillin*." Cf. Mek. de R. Ishmael, *Beshallaḥ* 6; Cant.R. 1:9 §4; 2:6 §1. There are clear allusions in Tg. to the going out from Egypt (see *Note* 13): just as the Exodus from Egypt was achieved through the merit of the *mezuzot* and the *tefillin,* so also will be the Messianic Exodus.

[12] Cf. b. Menaḥ. 33a: "R. Zera said in the name of R. Mattena who said in the name of Samuel. The proper performance of the precept [of the *mezuzah*] is to fix it at the beginning of the upper third of the door post"; but the text goes on to cite an alternative opinion that anywhere on the door post above a handbreadth from the ground to a handbreadth from the lintel is valid. Massekhet Mezuzah 9 gives as Rabbi Meir's opinion the middle of the door-post, or any part above it. Tg. here is close to Ps-J Deut. 6:9, which should probably be translated: "You shall fix them in the third towards the lintel *(tyqy)* upon the door posts of your houses and on your gates, on the right as you enter" (cf. also Ps-J Deut. 11:20).

[13] Tg. regards both the *tefillin* and the *mezuzah* as amulets that protect Israel from demonic attack. Maimonides and other rationalists opposed this view (*Yad: Tefillin* 5:4), but it was old and widespread. Note the Greek translation of *tefillin* as "phylacteries" (Arndt and Gingrich, 876a). Charms and amulets were often placed at the door of a house (e.g., beneath the threshold): the door, marking the transition between two domains, was seen as a place of danger and a locus of magic (cf. b. 'Abod. Zar. 11a; Gen.R. 35.3). The "Destroyer" recalls the *Mashḥit* of Exod 12:13, 23 (see S. A. Meier, *DDD* 456–63). The word Tg. Cant. uses *(maziqa')* occurs in the plural in 3:8 (*Note* 45) and 4:6 (*Note* 31), and often elsewhere, as a designation for demons. The echoes of the sprinkling of the blood on the lintel and doorposts at the time of the first Passover, to protect the Israelites from the Angel of Death, are appropriate in the context here of the new Exodus of the Messianic Age. Cf. Mek. de R. Ishmael, *Pisḥa* 7: "*And the Lord will pass over the door.* Behold, by using the method of *qal waḥomer* we can reason as follows. With respect to the performance of the rite with the blood of the paschal sacrifice in Egypt, the less important *[qal],* since it was only for that time, was not to be observed both by day and by night, and was not to be observed in subsequent generations, it is said: *And he will not let the Destroyer come in.* The *mezuzah,* the more important *[ḥomer],* since it contains the name of God ten times and is prescribed for both the day and the night and for all generations, should all the more be the cause of God preventing the Destroyer from entering our homes."

[14] The King Messiah warns Israel not to stir up Messianic fervor to such a pitch that it provokes rebellion against the Gentiles and encourages attempts to force the redemption. Tg. interprets the parallels in 2:7 and 3:5 as warnings by Moses to the generation of the wilderness not to enter the land prematurely.

"I adjure you, O daughters of Jerusalem" = "I adjure you, O people of the House of Israel." "Not to stir up . . . love" = "not to be stirred up against/attack the nations of the world, so as to go out from exile." "Nor awaken love" = "nor to rebel against the hosts of Gog and Magog." In both cases *'ahabah* = *'ahabat ṣiyyon* (love or longing for Zion). "Till it pleases" = (literally) "till . . . there is a will from before the Lord of the World to redeem you."

Targum:

The King Messiah will say: "I adjure you, O my people[l] of the House of Israel, not to be stirred up against the nations of the world, in order to escape from exile,[m] nor to rebel against the hosts of Gog and Magog.[15] Wait yet[n] a little till the nations that have come up to wage war against Jerusalem[o] are destroyed,[16] and after that the Lord of the World will remember for your sake the love of the righteous,[p] and it shall be the Lord's good pleasure to redeem you."[q][17]

Apparatus, Chapter 8

[l] J K L M N: "O people."

[m] Reading *lmypq mn glwtʾ* for A's *lmypq mn yrwshlm* ("to go out from Jerusalem"), *mn glwtʾ* with D E F. J K L M O: *lmysq mn yrwshlm,* "to go up from (!) Jerusalem." It is tempting to emend to *lmysq mn glwtʾ,* "to go up [to the Land] from exile," but √*npq* may have been chosen deliberately to express the idea of a new Exodus. "Jerusalem" may have displaced "exile" by vertical dittography from the line below.

[n] The syntax of the particle *pwn* (Jast. 1143a) is unclear. It could be construed with the preceding verb, "would that you would wait" (Levey, *Messiah*), or with the following adverb, "yet a little" (as above).

[o] G adds "the city of the Lord."

[p] I.e., the love of the righteous for God, perhaps as shown specifically in their willingness to sanctify God's name in martyrdom.

[q] N: "to visit them [in judgment]": *lmpqdhwn* for *lmprqkwn.*

Notes, Chapter 8

[15] The parallelism indicates that Gog and Magog are the "nations of the world" who are currently oppressing Israel. They are not, therefore, to be identified with the wild tribes beyond the Caspian gates of Christian tradition (Anderson, *Gog and Magog*; Bøe, *Gog and Magog*; Strack-Billerbeck 3:831–40). They are the same as Edom in 7:12 (*Note* 51). Even after the rise of Islam, Jewish apocalyptists still anticipated that the final battle would be against Edom. The tradition, dating probably from no earlier than the seventh century, that the Antichrist who will lead the Gentiles against Jerusalem will be Armillus (= Romulus *redivivus*), king of Rome, persisted well into the Islamic period (see Sefer Zerubbabel, Prayer of Rabbi Shimʿon bar Yoḥai and Saʿadya [*Book of Beliefs and Opinions* VIII; Treatise on Armillus, Even-Shmuel, *MG* 117–28]; further Dan, "Armillus," and for the identification of Edom with Gog and Magog, see Hai Gaon, *The Matter of Salvation* (Even-Shmuel, *MG* 137). Some held that Edom would conquer Ishmael and capture Jerusalem, only to be defeated in the last great battle (though this precise tradition may reflect the Crusades: see Judah Halevi, Shirman 2:477; Buchanan, *Revelation and Redemption* 285–86; 582). On Gog see further *Note* 36.

[16] The Messiah's role in the defeat of the nations in Tg. Cant. is muted, perhaps because the Messiah here is the Messiah ben David, whereas the Messiah anointed for war was Messiah ben Joseph (mentioned in Tg. to 4:5 [*Note* 23], though noticeably absent here). But Tg. may have taken the view that God himself would fight against Gog and Magog (with pestilence and other disasters reminiscent of the plagues of Egypt: cf. Tg. to 5:15, "God will wage victorious war on the nations"; Saʿadya, *Book of Beliefs and Opinions* VIII; Hai Gaon, *The Matter of Salvation*, Even-Shmuel, *MG* 137). According to Ps-J Num. 11:26, God will destroy Gog and Magog "with a scorching breath and a burning flame that will come from beneath the Throne of Glory" (cf. Rev 20:7-10). The Messiah ben David is a scholar who fights primarily with spiritual weapons (see Tg. to 8:1-2). This pacifist line was probably close to the views of the Rabbinic establishment: see b. Ketub. 110b-11a, quoting Jer 27:22; further *Intro.* 4.6. "Verse 8:4 sounds a Messianic note that remains influential in some quarters to this day. Deliverance must be a divine act, not human, and even the Messiah is only a symbol. The Jewish people is not to strive for victory and vindication of itself, but to wait for divine intervention. An extreme Orthodox wing of Judaism to this day is opposed to the modern Zionist ideal on these grounds" (Levey, *Messiah* 132). Other sources, however, depict the Jews themselves, led by their general the Messiah ben David, as triumphing over their enemies in bloody battle (Neof. and FT to Num. 11:26: the King Messiah will defeat Gog and Magog. This idea is old: see the *War Scroll* from Qumran and 4Q285 [Sefer ha-Milḥamah]; contrast Ps-J to the same verse, as quoted above; further Ginzberg, *Legends* 6:88, n. 482).

[17] The ingathering of the exiles here does not take place until after the defeat of Gog and Magog. This view, held also by Saʿadya, *Book of Beliefs and Opinions* VIII, and by Hai Gaon, *The Matter of Salvation*, Even-Shmuel, *MG* 138, is found as early as 1 Enoch 56–57 and 4 Ezra 13:12. Note once again how the merit of the righteous brings the redemption: see further *Intro.* 4.3.

5. Hebrew Text:

Who is this coming up from the Wilderness,
Leaning on her Beloved?[18]
[Who says to her:]
"Under the apple tree I wakened you.
There your mother was in travail with you;
There she who bore you was in travail."[19]

Targum:

Solomon the prophet said: When the dead revive,[20] the Mount of Anointing[r] will split apart and all the dead of Israel will issue from beneath it, and even the righteous who have died in exile will come by way of tunnels[s] below the ground and issue from beneath the Mount of Anointing.[21] And the wicked who have died and been buried in the Land of Israel

Apparatus, Chapter 8

[r] *twwr myshḥ'* = Hebrew *har ha-mishḥah,* either a designation for the Mount of Olives (m. Rosh Hash. 2:4), or more specifically for the southern portion of the mountain where the village of Silwan stands. According to tradition (Vilnay, *Legends of Jerusalem* 295–96), the mountain was so called because it produced excellent olives that were used to prepare the anointing oil for kings and priests. When Solomon built on it places of idolatry its name was deformed into "Mountain of Destruction" *(har ha-mashḥit):* see 2 Kgs 23:13 (Tg. *drwm ltwr zyty'* = "the south of the Mount of Olives").

[s] "Tunnel" = *kwky'*. Strictly speaking a *kukh* is a "cavity, cave, or burial chamber" (Jast. 619a), but here some sort of tunnel linking the Mount of Olives with the lands of exile is indicated. There are many subterranean *kukhim* in the vicinity of Jerusalem. Perhaps the Tg. knew some of them and regarded them as the exits of the tunnels through which the righteous dead would reach the land of Israel (Vilnay, *Legends of Jerusalem* 293). J K L M N: "will come gently/with ease *[bnyḥ]* beneath the ground."

Notes, Chapter 8

[18] As in 3:6 and 6:10, Tg. identifies the voice as that of the Gentiles, the referent as Israel. Here the nations express surprise when they see the resurrection of the righteous dead and their ingathering into the Land of Israel. Lines 3-5, however, are easiest taken as addressed by God, the Beloved, to Israel as she comes up out of exile. Tg. probably construed them as a quotation within the speech of the nations (see *Note* 19 below). "Wilderness" = metaphorically the wilderness of exile, but with an allusion to the Wilderness of the Exodus from Egypt. "Leaning on her Beloved" = "that delights in the love of her Lord."

[19] "Under the apple tree I wakened you" = "as on the day when she appeared beneath Mount Sinai to receive the Torah." Mount Sinai = "the apple tree." Cf. Cant.R. 8:5 §1: "*Under the apple tree I wakened you.* Paltion, a man of Rome, said in a discourse: The mountain of Sinai was uprooted and stood in the height of heaven, and Israel were placed under it, as it says, *And you came near and stood under the mountain* (Deut 4:11) [see further *Note* 24 below]. Another explanation: *Under the apple tree I wakened you.* This refers to Sinai. Why is it compared to an apple tree? Because just as an apple tree produces its fruit in Sivan, so the Torah was given in Sivan." The resurrection not only replicates the Exodus from Egypt but Sinai as well. The devotion to God of the newly resurrected righteous recalls Israel's devotion at Sinai. It reminds God of when Israel was first "wakened" and "born" as a covenant people. In the context of the resurrection the "travail" is the travail of Zion ("your mother") and Jerusalem ("she who bore you"), with echoes of the idea of "the birth-pangs" of the Messianic Age (*Note* 25): the righteous dead emerge from the Mount of Anointing as from her womb.

[20] The resurrection of the righteous dead follows the ingathering of the righteous living. It can only take place in the Land of Israel, the "land of the living" (Ps 116:9, with Pesiq. Rab. 1.4).

[21] The "Mount of Anointing" = the Mount of Olives (see *Apparatus r*) is the only point at which the dead will emerge from the earth, even those who died outside the land. First those who died in the Land will be resurrected (Tg. may have been aware of Jewish burials on the Mount of Olives), then those who died outside. Cf. Gen.R. 96.5: "Our teachers said . . . in R. Ḥelbo's name: Why did the Patriarchs long for burial in the Land of Israel? Because the dead of the Land of Israel will be the first to be resurrected in the days of the Messiah and enjoy the years of the Messiah."

will be cast out[t] as a man casts a stone from a sling.[u22] Then all the inhabitants of the earth will say: "What is the merit[v] of this people, that comes up from the earth in myriads upon myriads, as on the day when she came up from the Wilderness to the land of Israel,[23] and [that] delights in the love of her Lord,[w] as on the day when she appeared beneath Mount Sinai to receive the Torah?"[24] At that hour Zion, which is the mother of Israel,[x] will give birth to her sons, and Jerusalem will receive her exiles.[y25]

Apparatus, Chapter 8

[t] Reading *(lmyhwwyhwn) rmy(y)n* with B D E F G K L for A's *(lmyhwwyhwn) dmyyn.* The circumlocution for the itpe. infinitive *(le-ʾitremaʾah)* is clumsy: "the wicked are made ready for their being thrown."

[u] Reading *bqlʿ(ʾ)* with B N for *bʾlʾ,* the reading of A and the majority of mss. An *ʾalaʾ* (Heb. *ʾallah*) is a club, mace, or knobkerry: m. Shabb. 6:4; m. Kelim 16:8; b. Pesaḥ 57a; b. B. Bat. 73a. Bertinoro to m. Kelim 16:8 describes it as "an iron rod with its head rounded like a ball from which protrude studs like almonds." But "as a man casts a stone with a club" is hardly good sense (unless there is an allusion to some early form of baseball!). *Qelaʿ/Qilʿa,* "sling" (Jast. 1381a) is clearly better, though it is so poorly attested in the mss. that one might suspect a (probably correct) scribal emendation. It is possible that there is an allusion to the *kaf ha-qelaʿ,* one of the tortures of the damned (b. Shabb. 152b).

[v] Reading "merit" with B C D E F G H I J M N O for A's "merits." The agreeing verb is singular.

[w] J K L M N O omit "as on the day when she came up . . . her Lord" by parablepsis.

[x] Reading "which is the mother of Israel" with B D E F G H I J K L M N O for A's "which is their mother."

[y] Reading "her exiles" with J for A and majority of mss. "the sons of the exile(s)."

Notes, Chapter 8

The splitting of the Mount of Olives goes back to Zech 14:3-4, "Then the Lord shall go forth, and fight against those nations, as when He fights in the day of battle. And His feet shall stand in that day on the Mount of Olives, which is before Jerusalem in the east, and the Mount of Olives shall be split apart . . . ." In Zechariah this event is associated with the last battle (so also in late Hebrew apocalyptic: Buchanan, *Revelation and Redemption* 373, 402, 424). Here the splitting is linked with the resurrection and is meant to facilitate it: cf. Pesiq. Rab. 31.10 quoted below.

For the "tunnels" cf. Gen.R. 96.5: "What does God do? He makes cavities like tunnels for them [those buried outside the Land], and they roll along in them until they reach the Land of Israel, where the Holy One, blessed be He, will infuse into them a spirit of life and they will arise." Pesiq. Rab. 31.10: "As for those swallowed up [in the exile], God will make passageway after passageway for them, and they will find their way underground through them until they arrive under the Mount of Olives . . . and after it is split for the exiles, they will come out of it (Zech 14:4 and Isa 49:21)."

On the resurrection of the dead see also: y. Kil. IX, 32c; y. Ketub. XII, 35b; b. Ketub. 11a; b. Sanh. 90b; Eccl.R. 1:4 §2; further Vilnay, *Legends of Jerusalem* 285–87, 293–95; Ginzberg, *Legends* 6:408; Sysling, *Teḥiyyat ha-Metim.*

[22] Cf. Pirqei de R. El. 34: "Rab Huna said: As for all Israel who die outside the Land, their souls are gathered into the Land, as it is said, *Yet the soul of my lord shall be bound in the bundle of the living* (1 Sam 25:29). All the heathens who die in the Land of Israel have their souls cast out outside the Land, as it is said, *And the souls of your enemies shall He sling out, as from the hollow of a sling* (1 Sam 25:29), [even] beyond the Land." What is implied here is not the resurrection of the wicked or of the Gentiles, but the expelling of the polluting corpses of idolaters from the Land.

[23] The comparison of the ingathering of the exiles in the Messianic Age with the Exodus from Egypt, fundamental to Tg.'s thought, is already found in the Bible: e.g., Jer 23:7-8; Isa 52:12.

[24] The idea is that Sinai was raised in the air and the Israelites literally stood under it: see Cant.R. 8:5 §1 (*Note* 19 above); b. Shabb. 88a; b. ʿAbod. Zar. 2b; Mek. de R. Ishmael *Baḥodesh* 3; further Ginzberg, *Legends* 6:36, n. 202.

[25] The ingathering of the exiles is seen as Zion/Jerusalem travailing and giving birth. There is an allusion here to the idea of the "birthpangs of the Messiah" (Schürer, *History* 2:514–15; Buchanan, *Revelation and Redemption* 533ff.). There may be an echo of Isa 54:1, "Sing, O barren, who does not bear, break forth into singing, and cry aloud, you who did not travail; for more are the children of the desolate than the children of the married wife, says the Lord." Note also the use of similar imagery in Rom 8:22-23, "We know that the whole creation has been groaning in travail together till now, and not only the creation, but we ourselves who have the first fruits of the Spirit groan inwardly as we wait for the adoption of sons, the redemption of our bodies" (Strack-Billerbeck 1:950; 4:977–78).

6. Hebrew Text:

Set me as a signet upon Your heart,
As a signet upon Your arm;[26]
For love is as strong as death,
Jealousy as harsh as Sheol.[27]
Its flashes are flashes of fire,
The flame of the Lord.[28]

Targum:

The Children of Israel[z] will say on that day to their Lord: "We beseech You, set us like the engraving of a signet ring[aa] upon Your heart, and like the engraving of a signet ring[aa] upon Your arm, so that we shall never be exiled again, for the love of your divinity is as strong as death,[29] and the jealousy which the nations bear us is as harsh as Gehinnom, and the enmity which they harbor against us is like the blazing coals of Gehinnom, which the Lord created on the second day of the creation of the world to burn therein idolaters."[bb][30]

Apparatus, Chapter 8

[z] K L: "House of Israel."
[aa] "Like the engraving of a signet ring" = *kglwp dʿyzqʾ;* for the phrase see Onq. Exod. 28:11 and Tg. Jer. 22:24; Hag 2:23; *Note* 26. Strictly speaking the *gelof* is not the "impress" made by the signet ring, but the engraving on the ring that makes the impress.
[bb] Lit. "worshipers of strange worship" = Hebrew *ʿobedei ʿabodah zarah.*

Notes, Chapter 8

[26] Israel, restored to the Land, will plead with God to protect her and save her from ever suffering again the bitterness of exile.

Lines 1-2 reminded Tg. of Hag 2:23, where the image of the signet or seal suggests divine favor and protection: "In that day, says the Lord of Hosts, will I take you, O Zerubbabel, My servant, son of Shealtiel, and will set you as a signet *[we-samtikha kaḥotam];* for I have chosen you, says the Lord of Hosts." In Jer 22:24 plucking off the signet suggests loss of divine favor and protection: "As I live, says the Lord, though Coniah the son of Jehoiakim, king of Judah, were the signet upon My right hand, yet would I pluck you thence." Cf. Cant.R. 8:6 §2, which explicitly links Cant 8:6 with these two verses.

[27] Tg. takes the "love" as Israel's love of God, which is strong enough even to endure death to sanctify his name (see *Note* 29 below). Cf. Cant.R. 8:6 §4: "*For love is strong as death.* The love which the generation of the destruction [of the Second Temple] bore to the Holy One, blessed be He, as it is said, *Nay, but for Your sake are we killed all the day* (Ps 44:23)." The "jealousy" *(qinʾah)* is taken as the implacable zeal with which the nations persecute Israel, and the harsh decrees *(gezerot qashot)* that they issue against her: cf. b. Meg. 7a: "You will rouse the jealousy of the nations against us." It could equally have suggested Israel's zeal for God (Jast. 1388a; Hengel, *Zealots* 146–228), or God's "jealousy" for Israel (so Cant.R. 8:6 §4: "*Jealousy is cruel as the grave.* For God will one day be greatly jealous for Zion, as it says, *Thus says the Lord: I am jealous for Zion with a great jealousy* [Zech 1:14])."

"Sheol" = Gehinnom: see *Note* 30.

[28] Tg. understands the difficult "flashes of fire" *[rishpei ʾesh]* as "blazing coals" (lit. "coals of fire"). Rabbinic tradition was uncertain how to understand *reshafim,* taking it sometimes as demons, sometimes as burning pains, sometimes as flames, and sometimes as a bird of prey (Jast. 1502a; further P. Xella, *DDD* 1324–30). The unusual *shalhebetyah* has been read as meaning "the fire of God" (the ending of the word being construed, following the Masoretic pointing, as the divine name *Yah:* see Murphy, 191–92) = Gehinnom, the hell-fire God has prepared especially for idolaters (see *Note* 30 below).

[29] The phrase "love of God's divinity" here is effectively the equivalent of *qiddush ha-shem*: see Tg. to 1:4 (*Note* 33) and 8:1 (*Note* 5).

[30] For the creation of Gehinnom on the second day of creation see Gen.R. 4.4: "Why is *that it was good* not written in connection with the second day? . . . Because Gehinnom was created on it, [as it was written,] *For Topheth is ordered from yesterday* (Isa 30:33), which signifies a day to which there was a yesterday but not a day before yesterday." Further Gen.R. 9.9;

7. Hebrew Text:

Many waters cannot quench love,
Nor can rivers sweep it away.[31]
If a man should give all the wealth of his house for love,
A double portion of plunder will be assigned to him.[32]

Targum:

The Lord of the World said to His people, the House of Israel:[cc] "Even if all the nations, which are likened to the waters of the sea,[33] which are many,[dd] should gather

Apparatus, Chapter 8

[cc] B E G H I J K L M N: "the people of the house of Israel," the normal expression in Tg. Cant.

[dd] Reading *d'(y)nwn sgy'yn* with B E F G I for A's *sgy'yn*. J K L M N: "for, behold, they are many."

Notes, Chapter 8

Exod.R. 15.22; Pirqei de R. El. 4; Tanḥuma, *Ḥayyei Sarah* 3 (ed. Buber, 59a); b. Pesaḥ. 54a. Just as the rewards for the righteous have been prepared from creation (see Tg. to 8:2, *Note* 10), so have the punishments of the wicked. There is a hint of *middah ke-neged middah*: the fires of martyrdom (as in the martyrdom of ʿAqiba) will be punished by God with the fires of Gehinnom. For idolatry as one of the sins supremely worthy of hell-fire, see Rev 21:8, "But as for . . . idolaters . . . their lot shall be in the lake that burns with fire and brimstone." On the fires of Gehinnom see *The Tractate on Gehinnom* (Jellinek, *BHM* 1:147–49), and similar works; further Himmelfarb, *Tours of Hell;* Bauckham, *The Fate of the Dead*.

[31] Tg. detects here the voice of God responding to Israel's eschatological prayer in v. 6 with assurances of love and protection, and with promises of reward to those who study Torah. But the narration is from the perspective of this age: note "the Lord of the world *said*," and the reference to "the world to come." Tg. may have heard in the biblical verse a distant echo of Ps 46:1-3.

"Waters" = "the nations"; "rivers" = "the kings" of the nations. So, generally, Cant.R. 8:7 §1, but note yet again how Tg. finesses the midrash: "*Many waters*. These are the nations of the world, as it says, *Ah, the uproar of many peoples, that roar like the roaring of the seas* (Isa 17:12) . . . *Nor can rivers sweep it away*. These rivers are the other nations, as it says, *In that day shall the Lord shave with a razor that is hired in the parts beyond the River . . . Now, therefore, behold, the Lord brings upon them the waters of the River* (Isa 7:20; 8:7)." Num.R. 2.16 is closer to Tg., but it interprets the latter part of the verse differently (see below, *Note* 32): "*Many waters cannot quench love* . . . R. Samuel, son of R. Naḥman, said: This verse speaks of two loves. The beginning speaks of the [mutual] love of Israel [and God]. If all the nations of the world should assemble in an endeavor to steal away the love existing between Him and Israel they would not succeed, as it is said, *Many waters cannot quench love: Many waters* alludes to the nations of the world; as it is said, *Ah, the uproar of many peoples . . . The nations shall rush like the rushing of many waters* (Isa 17:12). *Nor can rivers sweep it away* alludes to their kings and princes, as it is said: *Now, therefore, behold, the Lord brings upon them the waters of a mighty River, mighty and many, even the king of Assyria and all his glory [= princes]* (Isa 8:7)." See also Exod.R. 49.1; Midrash Ps. 15.4.

The "love" is God's love for Israel: cf. Cant.R. 8:7 §1: "*Cannot quench love*: the love which the Holy One, blessed be He, bears for Israel, as it says, *I have loved you, says the Lord* (Mal 1:2)." Further Num.R. 2.16 quoted above.

[32] "Love" here = love of the Torah (see *Note* 35 below). "A double portion of plunder shall be assigned to him": literally, "Plundering shall they plunder for him." Tg. derives *boz yabuzu* from √*bzz*, "to plunder" rather than from √*bwz*, "to despise" (Murphy, "he would be thoroughly despised"). The repetition of the verbal root indicates a doubling. Tg. sees an allusion to the despoiling of the hosts of Gog after the last battle (see *Note* 37 below). Cf. Cant.R. 8:7 §1: "R. Joḥanan was once going on foot from Tiberias to Sepphoris accompanied by R. Ḥiyya bar Abba. As they passed a certain field R. Joḥanan said: 'This field used to belong to me, and I sold it so that I could devote myself to the study of Torah' . . . When R. Joḥanan was laid to rest, his generation applied to him the verse, *If a man should give all the wealth of his house for love*—for the love which R. Joḥanan bore to the Torah—*plundering shall they plunder for him*." Contrast Num.R. 2.16, which seems to derive *boz yabuzu* from √*bwz:* "If all the idolatrous nations of the world should assemble and say, 'We shall sell all our possessions and observe the Torah and the commandments,' the Holy One, blessed be He, will still say to them: 'Even if you sell all your possessions in order to acquire the Torah, you will still be contemptible.'"

[33] The equation "waters/sea" = nations is already in the symbolic lexicon of Bible: see Isa 17:12 (cf. 22:5-7) quoted above (*Note* 31), and further Ps 144:7 where "foreigners" stands in apposition to "great waters." Note also Ps 46:5, "There is a river,

together,[34] they would not be able to quench My love for you.[ee] And if all the kings of the earth,[ff] who are likened to the waters of a river that flow strongly, should assemble,[gg] they would not be able to blot you out from the world. And if a man should give all the wealth of his house to acquire wisdom[35] in exile, I shall return to him double in the world to come, and all the spoil which shall be plundered from the camp[hh] of Gog[ii][36] shall be his."[37]

8. Hebrew Text:

We have a sister [who is] little,
And she has no breasts.[38]

Apparatus, Chapter 8

[ee] Lit. "My love *from* you." The syntax is slightly awkward and raises the possibility of the alternative translation, "love of Me from you." But the context argues against this: God here, in response to Israel's prayer in v. 6, assures her of his unchanging love and protection. B G: "His love from you."

[ff] K L: "kings of the nations of the earth."

[gg] Reading *mtknpyn* with C F for A and the majority of mss. *myknshyn*. Tg. Cant.'s penchant for stylistic variation supports *mtknpyn.*

[hh] B E J K L: "camps."

[ii] Lit. "which they shall plunder from the camp of Gog," third plural active verb = passive; but J K L M N have "which the camp(s) of Gog shall plunder."

Notes, Chapter 8

the streams whereof make glad the city of God"; Tg., "The peoples are like rivers and their streams come and make glad the city of God, and they pray in the Temple of the Lord."

[34] As the reference to Gog later in the verse shows, this alludes to the eschatological gathering of the nations against Israel in the Valley of Decision. The motif of the final battle ("Armageddon"), ubiquitous in both early and late Jewish apocalyptic, draws on Ezekiel 38–39, Isaiah 22, and Joel 3:9-21. For a late treatment of the theme see, e.g., Pirqei Heikahlot Rabbati 37 (Wertheimer, *BM* 1:125–27).

[35] "Wisdom" = Torah, a standard equation in Rabbinic literature: see, e.g., Gen.R. 1.1 where it is simply assumed that Wisdom in Proverbs 8 = Torah. Tg. may have detected in the Canticles verse an echo of Prov 4:7, "Wisdom is the principal thing; therefore get wisdom: yea, with all that you have acquired get understanding." The reference here is either to acquiring wisdom personally, or vicariously through supporting the schools with financial contributions. See further Tg. to v. 9 (*Note* 43 below).

[36] In v. 4 Tg. speaks of "Gog and Magog" (*Note* 15); here and in v. 8 only of "Gog." Jewish sources treat "Gog and Magog" in a variety of ways: according to some, they are two names for one and the same nation; according to others they are two different eschatological enemies of Israel who combine against her (e.g., "Gog" = Christendom, and "Magog" = Islam). A third view took "Gog" as the name of the king (cf. Ezek 38:2) and "Magog" as the name of his people. See Buchanan, *Revelation and Redemption* 582–83. Tg. probably reflects the third view.

[37] The Torah scholars will have the pick of the booty. Ezek 39:9-10 graphically describes the spoil after the defeat of Gog: "Then those who dwell in the cities of Israel will go forth and make fires of the weapons and burn them, shields and bucklers, bows and arrows, handpikes and spears, and they will make fires of them for seven years; so that they will not need to take wood out of the field or cut down any out of the forest, for they will make their fires with the weapons; they will despoil those who despoiled them, and plunder those who plundered them, says the Lord." The spoil after the last battle is mentioned also in 4Q285 (Sefer ha-Milḥamah) Frg. 10 (ed. Alexander and Vermes), but there, as in Ezekiel (the spoil is *burned!*) and in the Achan story in Joshua (Josh 7:10-26), the booty is *ḥerem*: note how in 4Q285 it must be collected by those who despise gain, and who will not, therefore, like Achan, be tempted to hold on to any of it. Here, however, the plunder is kept. There is a double "measure for measure": those who despoiled Israel will be despoiled; those who give away their wealth for Torah will be requited with wealth. Cf. Ben Sira 51:28; Mark 10:29-30; Luke 18:29-30; m. ʾAbot 2:19. The paradigm in view may be the Israelites' despoiling of the Egyptians at the Exodus (Exod 12:35-36), rather than the despoiling of the hosts of Gog in Ezekiel.

[38] Tg. contextualizes to the heavenly law court: the angels look down and observe the unfolding drama of the eschaton. Gog and his host are encamped against Jerusalem, but as yet neither the Messiah ben Joseph nor the Messiah ben David has appeared. Behind Tg. lies the idea that each nation on earth has its celestial representative, and that events on earth are mirrored in heaven: see Dan 10:20-21; 3 Enoch 30:2 (with Alexander's note *ad loc.*, in Charlesworth, *OTP* 1:285, note e).

What shall we do for our sister,
On the day when she shall be spoken against?[39]

Targum:

At that time the angels in heaven[jj] will say one to another: "We have one nation on earth, whose merits are few, and who has no kings or rulers to go out and wage war against the camps[kk] of Gog. What shall we do for our sister on the day when the nations speak of going up against her to war?"

9. Hebrew Text:

If she is a wall,
We will build against her a rampart of silver;[40]
And if she is a door,
We will enclose her with a tablet of cedar.[41]

Apparatus, Chapter 8

[jj] B G I J K L M N: "the angels."

[kk] C H J K L M N: "camp."

Notes, Chapter 8

"We have a sister [who is] little": note the precise syntax of the Hebrew: *ʾaḥot lanu qetannah,* not *ʾaḥot qetannah lanu.* The "sister" is Israel, who is "little" in merits. The scenario may imply the apostasy of Israel before the final redemption, but see the development of the thought in the next verse (*Note* 45).

"Breasts" = kings or rulers, specifically the Messiah ben Joseph and the Messiah ben David. See Tg. to 4:5 (*Note* 23).

[39] "On the day when she shall be spoken against": "The expression *ledabber be-* has different meanings according to context. It may denote disapproval and hostility, 'to speak against,' as in Num 12:1; 21:5, 7; Ps 50:20" (Pope, 678).

Cf. Cant.R. 8:8 §1: "*We have a little sister.* This is Israel. R. Azariah said in the name of R. Simon: In the time to come all the [celestial] princes of the nations of the world will come and accuse Israel before the Holy One, blessed be He, saying: Sovereign of the Universe, these worshiped idols and those worshiped idols; these acted lewdly and those acted lewdly; these shed blood and those shed blood. Why do these go down to Gehinnom, while those do not? The Holy One, blessed be He, will say to them: *We have a little sister.* Just as a child, whatever he does, is not reproved, because he is but a child, so however much Israel may be defiled by their iniquities throughout the year, the Day of Atonement atones for them, as it says, *For on this day shall atonement be made for you* (Lev 16:30)." But note the differences: in Cant.R. the angels of the nations play the role of Satan, the Accuser. In the Tg. they speak in a spirit of concern and helpfulness: God's celestial *familia* act as groomsmen in his eschatological "marriage" with Israel.

[40] Tg. continues contextualizing in the heavenly law-court: Michael, Israel's celestial representative, says that if Israel continues to support the schools, then the celestial *familia* (the angels) and the terrestrial *familia* (the Sages) will combine to form a protective rampart around her. And even if Israel does not observe the *miṣwot* they will intercede for God's mercy and grace on her behalf. The basic idea is that even in the Messianic Age Israel's safety still depends on the study of the Torah.

The "wall" calls to Tg.'s mind the picture of Israel in the Messianic Age standing firm among the nations in her profession of the unity of God, and rejecting the "Ways of the Amorites."

The "rampart of silver" suggested a defensive wall that repels the attack of the nations as easily as silver repels the attack of the moth or the worm. But, again following the principle of "measure for measure," Tg. also detects an allusion to the "silver" paid out by Israel to support the schools (*Note* 43 below): just as in v. 7 the man who lays out wealth in this world to acquire wisdom will be rewarded with wealth in the world to come, so the silver Israel pays to support the study of Torah will be matched by the "silver rampart" of angelic protection. Cf. b.Yoma 9b.

[41] "Door" *(delet)* is linked with *dal,* "poor," and "poor" is in turn taken as "poor in the performance of the *miṣwot.*" Cf. how Lev.R. 34.4 interprets "poor" *(√mwk)* in Lev 25:25 as meaning "poor in the knowledge of the Torah." Cant.R. 8:9 §1, applying the text to Abraham, finds a double reference in *delet:* "*And if she is a door . . .* If he [Abraham] is poor [*dal*] in pious acts, and swings to and fro in his conduct like a door . . . " Cf. Gen.R. 39.3.

Targum:

Michael, the Prince of Israel,[42] will say: "If she stands firm like a wall[ll] among the nations, and gives her silver to buy the unity of the name of the Lord of the World,[43] then we, you and I, along with their Scribes,[mm][44] will surround her like ramparts[nn] of silver, so that the nations have no power to rule over her, just as[oo] the worm has no power[pp] to rule over silver. And even if she is poor in precepts, we will seek mercy for her before the Lord,[45] and He will remember for her the merit[qq] of the Torah which the children study,[46] which is written on the tablet of the[ir] heart[s], and [which] stands like a cedar against the nations."

Apparatus, Chapter 8

[ll] "Wall" = *ʾwshʾ*, but this is an anomalous rendering of the Hebrew *ḥomah* ("wall"). Aramaic *ʾushaʾ*, strictly = "foundation" (Ezra 4:12; 5:16; 6:3), is used in Tg. 1 Kgs 6:16, 7:7 to translate Hebrew *qarqaʿ*, and in Tg. Micah 1:6 to translate Hebrew *yesod*. Here *ʾwshʾ* is apparently equivalent to *ʾshytʾ/ʾwshytʾ* = "frame-wall, wall of a house" (Jast. 128a). Since there are no variants in the mss., the confusion of *ʾwshʾ* and *ʾwshytʾ* probably goes back to the Tg. himself. Cf. Ps 11:3, where the opposite mistake is made, the Hebrew *shatot* ("foundations") being rendered *ʾshytʾ/ʾwshyytʾ* ("walls"), instead of *ʾwshyyʾ* ("foundations"). The normal Targumic equivalent of Hebrew *ḥomah* is *shur* (see, e.g., Onq. Lev. 25:29, 30, 31, and above all Tg. Cant. 8:10). It is puzzling why the Tg. did not choose this or some other such word here. Can he possibly have intended a pun on the name Usha, the seat of the Sanhedrin during the Hadrianic persecutions? For Usha used in Talmudic literature to stand for "the rabbinical synods and enactments during and after the Hadrianic persecutions" see Jast. 35b.

[mm] "*Their* scribes" is slightly awkward in context; C: "the scribes"; H: "their books."

[nn] H: "with ramparts."

[oo] J K L M omit "the nations have no power to rule over her, just as" by parablepsis.

[pp] F I omit "to rule over her, just as the worm has no power" by parablepsis.

[qq] Reading "merit" with C E F G H I J K L M for A's "merits."

Notes, Chapter 8

The "cedar" = the Torah. The "tablet" *(luḥaʾ)* then recalls the "slate" on which the Torah was written in primary school to teach small children how to read. So Silber, quoting b. Giṭ. 60a and Deut.R. 8.3; see further Blau, *Buchwesen* 67. Silber then argues that "of the heart" is intrusive and should be removed. But the phrase "tablet of the heart" is found in all the mss. and, although it overloads the exegesis, echoes Prov 3:3; 6:20-21; 7:2-3, where it is used in the context of instructing a son, appropriately, since the heart of an innocent child can easily be regarded as a *tabula rasa*. Moreover, writing the Torah on the heart is an eschatological motif: see Jer 31:33. "We will enclose her with the tablet of the Torah" thus = "we will protect her (through prayer) by invoking the merit of the schoolchildren who study Torah from the *luaḥ*."

[42] For Michael as the guardian angel of Israel see Dan 10:13, 21; 12:1 ("Michael, the great prince, who has charge of your people").

[43] The phrase "to buy the unity of the name of the Lord of the World" is unusual (cf. Tg. Lam. 3:28). It has been taken as denoting the payments made by Israel to the nations to allow her to profess her religion freely (Jast. 573b). Loewe ("Apologetic Motifs," 167) suggests there is a specific reference to the *jizya*. (*EI*[2] 2:559–67, sub *d̲jizya*). But Tg. contextualizes v. 9 to the Messianic Age, when Israel is gathered back to her land. Continued payment of taxes to the nations is thus unthinkable. The phrase should probably be interpreted here as referring to giving contributions to the schools that promote the unity of God in the world. Note the reference to the study of the Torah later in the verse (*Note* 46 below), and the parallelism between "giving silver to buy the unity of God" and "giving property to buy wisdom" in v. 7, where the reference is to studying Torah (see *Note* 35 above). And for payments to the schools see Tg. to 7:3 (*Note* 18), and further *Intro.* 8.1(6).

[44] "Scribes" = Sages, a common usage in Tg. Cant. (7:5, 14); cf. Moses as "the Great Scribe" (Tg. to 1:2; 2:4; 3:3). For the idea of the Sages as the true "guardians of the city" *(netorei qartaʾ)* see y. Ḥag. I, 76c.

[45] Tg. reflects the inconsistency of Rabbinic theology over the relationship between "works" and "grace." Israel will be rewarded and protected if she keeps the Torah. However, even if she does not, God's mercy may still be invoked, though his grace here is not entirely unearned: it is granted on the basis of the merit of the schoolchildren who study the Torah—a striking variation on one of the central themes of Tg. Cant., viz., that the merits of the patriarchs and of the righteous of every generation atone for Israel. See *Intro.* 4.3, and further Alexander, "Tora and Salvation," and Avemarie, *Tora und Leben*.

[46] Children were supposed to start school at the age of five (m. ʾAbot 5:21). The aim of the school was to teach them to read the Torah in Hebrew (see Safrai, "Education and the Study of the Torah"). The stress on teaching Torah to the next generation is

10. Hebrew Text:

I am a wall,
And my breasts are like towers.[47]
Then I was in His eyes
As one that found peace.[48]

Targum:

The Assembly of Israel answers and says: "I am strong as a wall through the words of the Torah, and my sons are sturdy as towers."[rr] And at that time the Assembly of Israel will find mercy in the eyes of her Lord, and all the inhabitants of the earth will seek [to promote] her peace.[ss49]

11. Hebrew Text:

Solomon had a vineyard in Baal Hermon;
He gave it over to guardians.[50]

Apparatus, Chapter 8

[rr] E F J K L M: "as a tower," but note the plural in the Hebrew.

[ss] Reading "her peace" with C G J K L M; B E F: "peace." A's *shlmh* is unclear.

Notes, Chapter 8

already in Scripture: see Sifrei Deut. §46: "*And you shall teach them to your children [beneikhem]* (Deut 11:19). Your sons and not your daughters, so taught R. Yosei ben ʿAqiba. Hence the Sages have said: Once an infant begins to talk, his father should converse with him in the holy tongue and should teach him Torah, for if he fails to do so, it is the same as if he had buried him alive." For the "merit" of schoolchildren, cf. the saying that "the world is sustained only by the breath of schoolchildren" (b.Shabb. 119b).

[47] Israel in the days of the Messiah confidently affirms her steadfastness in Torah in response to Michael's declaration in v. 9. "At that time" = at the eschaton.

"Wall" and "towers" are symbols of strength; "breasts" = those who suck the breast, children. Israel and her sons are strong in the study and performance of the words of the Torah. Cf. Cant.R. 8:9 §2: "*I am a wall.* Israel said before the Holy One, blessed be He: Sovereign of the Universe, we are a wall and we will be firm in religious observance and good deeds like a wall. *And my breasts are like towers.* Because we are destined to raise up numbers of righteous descendants like ourselves in Your world." Gen.R. 39.3, taking a similar line, identifies the sons as Hananiah, Mishael, and Azariah. But b.Pesaḥ. 67a, "wall" = Torah, and "breasts" = scholars, and b. B. Bat. 7b-8a, "wall" = Israel, and "breasts" = synagogues and houses of study. Cf. Pesiq. Rab. 35.1.

[48] Though first-person speech continues in the Hebrew, Tg. reports in the third person in the voice of the narrator.

Tg. has taken the Hebrew as if it read: "Then I was as one who found peace in His eyes," "to find peace" being equated with the common Hebrew phrase "to find favor" or "mercy" (cf. Onq.'s rendering of the phrase in Gen 6:8). "Peace" is also secondarily exegeted as the peaceful relations that will exist between Israel and the nations in the last days (see *Note* 49). Tg.'s exegesis does not seem to be paralleled precisely elsewhere in the Midrash.

[49] There is an echo of Ps 122:6, "Seek after the peace of Jerusalem" (note the wording of Tg. *ad loc.*). Tg. presumably envisages more than the nations saying "Shalom" to Israel: rather, they will actively promote her welfare.

[50] The chronology is awkward. The text leaves little option but to flash back to the time of King Solomon, but this does not fit easily in a context that is speaking of the Messianic Age. However, a reference to the division of the kingdom is not entirely inappropriate in a section devoted to the restoration of the Davidic kingdom and the final realization, under the Messiah, of the divine purpose frustrated ever since its division.

"Solomon" has been taken in a double sense: (1) as the historical king Solomon, and (2) as a title for God, "the king to whom belongs peace." So Cant.R. 8:11 §1: "*Solomon* is the king to whom belongs peace" [*la-melekh she-shalom shello*]. Cf. Num.R. 11.3.

"Vineyard," as frequently, = Israel. So Cant.R. 8:11 §1: "*Solomon had a vineyard.* This refers to Israel, as it says, *For the vineyard of the Lord of Hosts is the house of David* (Isa 5:7)." See further Tg. to 7:13 (*Note* 52).

"Baal-hamon" = Jerusalem: cf. Rashi: "*In Baal-hamon.* That is in Jerusalem, which is great with people and a numerous population." See also Midrash Leqaḥ Tob quoted below (*Note* 51).

The "guardians" are the kings of the house of David. God is the landlord; they are only "tenant farmers."

A man came for its fruit—
A thousand [pieces] of silver.[51]

Targum:

One nation, which is likened to[tt] a vineyard, fell to the lot of the Lord of the World,[uu] with whom is peace. He caused her to dwell in Jerusalem and gave her[vv] into the hand of the kings of the house of David, so that they should guard her, as a tenant farmer[ww] guards his vineyard. But after[xx] Solomon the king of Israel[yy] died, she was left in the hands of Rehoboam his son. Jeroboam, the son of Nebat, came and divided with him the kingdom,[zz] and took from his hands ten tribes, in accordance with the word spoken by Ahijah from Shiloh, who was a great man.[52]

Apparatus, Chapter 8

[tt] Reading *lkrmʾ* with C E F I J K L M for A's *bkrmʾ*.
[uu] There is an echo here of Deut 32:9, "For the portion of the Lord is His people, Jacob the lot of His inheritance" (see Onq. and Neof. *ad loc.*); further Lev 16:10 with Neof. *ad loc.*
[vv] J M omit "in Jerusalem and gave her" by parablepsis.
[ww] For *ʾrysʾ* = "tenant farmer" see Jast. 120a; Sokoloff 74b.
[xx] Reading *wbtr* with J K L M for A's *btr.*
[yy] E omits "king of Israel."
[zz] K L omit "the kingdom," but the resultant text "and divided with him" is clearly unsatisfactory. J M attempt to improve by changing *ʿmyh* ("with him") to *ʿlyh* ("against him"): "divided against him" = (?) "rebelled against him."

Notes, Chapter 8

[51] Tg.'s exegesis is convoluted and hard to follow. Tg. may have exploited the defective spelling in MT to read *ʾish yaboʾ* (rather than *ʾish yabiʾ*), which he then linked to 1 Kgs 12:3 [*qerei*] and 12:12, "And Jeroboam came [*wa-yabo Yorobʿam*] . . . to Rehoboam." The tense of the verb is future, which is correct from the narrative's supposed perspective in the time of Solomon. The events alluded to still lay in the future. Tg. may have read Hebrew *be-piryo* as "against his [Solomon's] fruit" = the fruit of his loins, i.e., his son Rehoboam. The "thousand [pieces]" represents the ten tribes (10 x 100) taken by Jeroboam, just as the "two hundred" in v. 12 represent the two tribes retained by Rehoboam (2 x 100). "Silver" may = Ahijah. However explained, Tg.'s method here appears to be atomistic. Rashi, ingeniously, saw a reference to the exorbitant taxes levied by the kings of Israel and Judah.

Midrash Leqaḥ Tob to Cant 8:11-12 depends on the Tg. and offers an interesting reading of it (see Liebreich, "Midrash Leqaḥ Tob"): "*Solomon had a vineyard.* Israel is the vineyard which belonged to the Lord. *In Baal-hamon.* As it is written, *A throng [hamon] keeping holiday* (Ps 42:5), for the Temple is the place of the thronging of Israel. *He gave the vineyard to guardians.* He gave his people to kings who were guarding them as a man guards a vineyard. *A man brought for its fruit a thousand [pieces] of silver.* This is Jeroboam the son of Nebat, as it is written, *And the man Jeroboam was a mighty man of valor* (1 Kgs 11:28). *Brought for its fruit.* He brought into his kingdom *a thousand [pieces] of silver,* that is to say ten hundreds, ten tribes . . . Another interpretation: The *man* is Ahijah the Shilonite, the man of God . . . When he heard the prophecy of Ahijah Solomon sought to kill Jeroboam but *Jeroboam arose and fled to Egypt* (1 Kgs 11:40) . . . The Lord says to Solomon: *My vineyard, which is Mine, is before Me.* This is Israel who are in My power to make king over them whoever I wish. *The thousand are yours, Solomon.* The ten tribes, which are ten hundreds, are yours, Solomon son of David, and I will not take them from your authority all your days, but after your death I will take them from you and will give them to Jeroboam, and the *two hundred,* the two tribes of Judah and Benjamin will belong to Rehoboam, for they are *keeping its fruit.*"

[52] Cf. 1 Kgs 12:15, "So the king hearkened not to the people; for it was a thing brought about by the Lord, that he might establish His word, which the Lord spoke by the hand of Ahijah the Shilonite to Jeroboam the son of Nebat." According to the Midrash Jeroboam was a disciple of Ahijah, who was regarded as a great prophet: "The prophet Ahijah, of the tribe of Levi, was venerable, not only by reason of his hoary age—his birth occurred at least sixty years before the exodus from Egypt—but because his piety was so profound that a saint of the exalted standing of Simon ben Yoḥai associated Ahijah with himself. Simon once exclaimed: 'My merits and Ahijah's together suffice to atone for the iniquity of all sinners from the time of Abraham until the advent of the Messiah'" (Ginzberg, *Legends* 4:180; 6:305, nn. 3-5).

12. Hebrew Text:

My vineyard, which is Mine, is before Me;
You, Solomon, shall have the thousand,
And those who guard its fruit two hundred.[53]

Targum:

When Solomon the king of Israel heard the prophecy of Ahijah from Shiloh he sought to kill him. But Ahijah fled[aaa] from Solomon and went to Egypt.[54] At that hour it was told through prophecy to Solomon the king[bbb] that he would rule over ten tribes all his days, but after his death Jeroboam the son of Nebat would rule over them; and [as for] the two tribes of Judah and Benjamin,[ccc] Rehoboam the son of Solomon would rule over them.[ddd]

13. Hebrew Text:

You who dwell in gardens,
The companions are listening to your voice.
Cause Me to hear [your words].[55]

Apparatus, Chapter 8

[aaa] E: "to kill Jeroboam. But Jeroboam fled." The variant is textually very poorly supported and probably represents a scribal correction. See *Note* 54.

[bbb] Silber suggests that *lshlmh mlk'* should be taken in the sense of *'l shlmh mlk'* ("concerning Solomon the king"), since 1 Kgs 11:29 seems to imply that the prophecy was not spoken to Solomon, but only to Jeroboam. But this is a quibble. 1 Kgs 11:40 ("Solomon sought to kill Jeroboam") surely implies that Solomon knew the prophecy.

[ccc] K L omit "Jeroboam the son of Nebat would rule over them; and [as for] the two tribes of Judah and Benjamin" by parablepsis.

[ddd] Tg. is muddled. Surely what he intended to say was: "Solomon the king would rule over twelve tribes all his days, but after his death Jeroboam the son of Nebat would rule over ten of them; and [as for] the two tribes of Judah and Benjamin, Rehoboam the son of Solomon would rule over them."

Notes, Chapter 8

[53] Tg. implicitly takes the voice here as God's, but reports it in the third person in the voice of the narrator. God asserts his ownership of the vineyard of Israel and his right to assign authority over it to whom he pleases. The verse is a cryptic summary of the prophecy of Ahijah.

"My vineyard, which is Mine, is before Me" is not directly translated: presumably it was felt that, after v. 11, its meaning is obvious. For the "thousand" = the ten tribes, and the "two hundred" = the two tribes see v. 11 (*Note* 51). "Those who guard its fruit" = the kings of the house of David (as in v. 11), and especially Rehoboam, Solomon's son. There may also be the implication that, in contrast to the house of Jeroboam, the house of David remained (on the whole) faithful to God.

[54] Tg. appears to state that Solomon tried to kill Ahijah and as a result Ahijah fled to Egypt. But this is in contradiction to 1 Kgs 11:40, which says that it was Jeroboam whom Solomon tried to kill, and who fled to Egypt. Tg. is unparalleled. See further *Apparatus aaa*.

[55] Verses 13-14 form a coda to the whole Tg.: God exhorts Israel, yet again, to attend the House of Study (v. 13); Israel, yet again, prays for the redemption (v. 14). The phrase "at the end of days" (v. 13) cannot refer to the Messianic Age since it is picked up in v. 14 by "at that hour," and v. 14 makes it clear that the "land" is still polluted and the redemption has not yet come. "End of days," therefore, means "the latter days" and denotes Tg.'s own time, which he believes is the era of the "ninth song," on the *eve* of the Messianic redemption (see Tg. to 1:1). See further *Note* 56 below.

"Gardens" is given a double reading: (1) Garden = a nation: Israel is a "little garden" among the "gardens" of the world (cf. 4:12); (2) Garden = Sanhedrin/House of Study. Cf. Rashi: "You who are dispersed in exile, pasturing in the gardens of others, and who dwell in the synagogues and houses of study." The Hebrew *ḥaber* was crucial to Tg.'s reading and naturally suggested to him a "scholar" or "student" (further *Note* 57). Israel's "voice" is the voice of the Head of the College.

Targum:

Solomon the prophet[eee] said at the end of his prophecy: The Lord of the World will say to the Assembly of Israel at the end of days:[56] "You, Assembly of Israel,[fff] who are likened to a little garden among the nations, and [who] sit in the House of Study[ggg] with the members of the Sanhedrin,[57] and [with] the rest of the people,[hhh] who listen to the voice of the Head of the College, and learn from his mouth the teachings of the Torah,[58] cause Me to hear the sound of your words,[iii][59] when you sit to acquit and to condemn, and I will approve all that you do."[60]

14. Hebrew Text:

Flee, my Beloved,[61]

Apparatus, Chapter 8

[eee] F omits "the prophet."

[fff] J K L M omit "at the end of days: You, Assembly of Israel" by parablepsis.

[ggg] Reading "House of Study" with B C E F G H I J K L M for A's *by mdrshy'*, which is presumably intended as a plural.

[hhh] Reading "people" with B E F G H I J K L M for A's "peoples."

[iii] F: "and learn from his mouth his teachings, cause Me to hear the Torah, the sound of your words" (= Lag.).

Notes, Chapter 8

"Cause Me to hear [your words]" alludes to the scholars functioning as a Beit Din. See further *Note* 60.

Cf. Cant.R. 8:13 §2, which gives a similar reading but with different nuances: "When Israel go into their synagogues and recite the *Shemaʿ* with devotion, with one voice and with one mind and thought, the Holy One, blessed be He, says to them: *You who dwell in the gardens,* when you call out, *the Companions,* I and My household, *are listening to your voice* [saying] *'Cause Me to hear [it].'*"

[56] "End of days" *(sof yomayyaʾ)* is not found in the Hebrew Bible, though note *qeṣ ha-yamin* in Dan 12:13. It denotes here the days *preceding* the advent of the Messiah, a usage found also in early Christian texts (see 2 Pet 3:3; Barn. 16:5 [with a free allusion to 1 Enoch 89:55-56]). Like *ʾaḥarit ha-yamim,* the phrase *sof ha-yamim* was probably ambiguous, and could denote either the latter days or the Messianic Age itself. See further *Note* 55 above.

[57] *Ḥaber* = "scholar/student," "less than a *ḥakkim* or *zaken*" (see b. Qidd. 33b; b. Sanh. 8b; b. B. Bat. 75a: Jast. 421b; Sokoloff 185b). Here, however, *ḥaber* appears to be the title for a member of the college—a late usage (Gil, *History of Palestine* 656).

[58] Melamed, "Targum Canticles" 215, sees here an allusion to the *pirqaʾ,* and thus locates the Tg. in Babylon, but the reference is far from certain. See *Intro.* 8.2(2).

[59] The variant, "Cause Me to hear the Torah, the sound of your words" (see *Apparatus iii*) is striking: God learns Torah from the Sages! Cf. b. Shabb. 63a, "When two Sages hear a law one from the other, the Holy One, blessed be He, listens to their voice, as it is written, *Cause Me to hear [your words]* (Cant 8:13)."

[60] The celestial Beit Din will approve the decisions of the terrestrial Beit Din! Cf. Midrash Ps. 4.4, "R. Hoshaia said: Is there another nation like this nation to whose decrees God himself conforms [*she-maskim ʾelohim ʿimmah*]? Conforms in what way? When the elders of Israel meet to decree a leap year, the Holy One, blessed be He, conforms to their decision . . . It is the way of the world that when a mortal king enacts a decree his counselors cannot annul it, even if they wish to do so. They must carry out the decrees of the king, whether they are acceptable to them or not. But the king, if he wishes to carry out his decree, he carries it out, and if he wishes to annul it, he annuls it. On the other hand, the Holy One, blessed be He, carries out whatever decree the Sanhedrin on earth enacts [*ʾabal mah she-sanhedrin shel mattah gozerin huʾ meqayyem*]." Cf. Matt 16:19, "Whatsoever you bind on earth shall be bound in heaven" (see Strack-Billerbeck 1:741–47). The relationship of the celestial and terrestrial Batei Din was a matter of considerable moment for Rabbinic theology: see the famous story in b. Ber. 19a about the oven of Akhnai and note the conclusion: "The Holy One, blessed be He, laughed and said, 'My sons have defeated me, my sons have defeated me!'" (Alexander, "Sixtieth Part of Prophecy").

[61] Israel replies to God: the "time" of this and the preceding verse is the real time of Tg. and his readers, the exile of Edom, specifically the period just before the advent of the Messiah (see *Note* 55 above). Tg. concludes with a prayer for continuing divine protection and for the final redemption. "Like the Christian Apocalypse, the Midrash on the Song of Songs [Cant.R. 8:14 §1]

And be like a gazelle or young hart
Upon the mountains of spices.[62]

Targum:

Then the elders of the Assembly of Israel[jjj] will say: "Flee away, my Beloved, Lord of the World, from this polluted land,[63] and cause your Shekhinah to dwell in the highest heavens,[64] but at the time of our distress,[kkk] when we pray before You, be like a gazelle, which, when it sleeps, [has] one eye shut and one eye open,[lll] or like the young of the hart, which, when it flees, looks behind it.[65] So watch over us[mmm] and observe our trouble and affliction from the highest heavens, till such time as You are pleased with us and redeem us and bring us up to the mountains[nnn] of Jerusalem, where the priests will offer up before You incense of spices."

Apparatus, Chapter 8

[jjj] H J K L M: "elders of Israel."

[kkk] B C G I: "time of distress."

[lll] The sentence "one eye shut and one eye open" has no verb. Miq. Ged. (= Lag.; cf. F) adds *yhy:* "one eye shut and one eye *is* open," but this is surely secondary. The Aramaic of this verse is particularly awkward.

[mmm] *kn ʾnt mshgh bn,* "so You will be watching over us," a polite imperative.

[nnn] Reading "mountains" with B G H I J M, in accordance with the Hebrew; A has "mountain."

Notes, Chapter 8

ends with a prayer: 'So may it be God's will speedily in our days, Amen'" (Pope, 701). God's "fleeing" is interpreted as the removal of his presence from sinful earth to the highest heavens. "Highest heavens" may involve a secondary exegesis of *besamim* by *ʾal tiqrei* as *ba-shamayim* ("in the heavens"). Cf. Cant.R. 8:14 §1: "*Upon the mountains of spices [besamim].* In the very highest heavens [*bishemei shamayim ha-ʿelyonim*]." For the primary reading of the phrase see *Note* 62.

[62] Tg. treats the partial parallel in 2:17 quite differently. Here the "gazelle" and the "hart," following some sort of ancient bestiary (*Note* 65), are taken as symbols of watchfulness: God, though removed from earth, is not indifferent to what happens upon it, especially the sufferings of Israel. Cf. Cant.R. 8:14 §1, with slightly different nuances: "*And be like a gazelle.* Just as the gazelle sleeps with one eye open and one eye closed, so when Israel act according to the desire of the Holy One, blessed be He, He looks upon them with both eyes, as it is written, *The eyes of the Lord are toward the righteous* (Ps 34:16). But when they do not act according to His desire, He looks upon them with one eye, as it says, *Behold the eye of the Lord is toward those that fear him* (Ps 33:18)."

The "mountains of spices" = the mountains of Jerusalem, particularly Mount Moriah (the Temple Mount), where the priests offered up spices in the past and will again offer them in the restored Temple in the Messianic Age. See Tg. to 7:13 (*Note* 57). Cf. Rashi: "*Upon the mountains of spices.* That is Mount Moriah and the Temple, may it be rebuilt speedily in our days!"

[63] *ʿarʿaʾ* = either "earth" or "land." There is no reason why the phrase "polluted land" should not refer to the Land of Israel (contra Melamed, "Targum Canticles" 215, who takes it as evidence that the Tg. was written in Babylonia; see Heinemann, "Targum Canticles" 126; Loewe, "Apologetic Motifs" 163, n. 23; cf. p. 183). The fact that Eretz Israel is "holy" makes it all the more susceptible to impurity. In the prophets idolatry is the particular cause of impurity to the land (e.g., Jer 7:30, "The children of Judah . . . have set their abominations in the house which is called by my name to defile it [Heb. *letammeʾo*; Tg. *lsʾbwtyh*]), and may be in Tg.'s mind here. Tg. Cant. is much exercised by the theme of "idolatry": see *Intro.* 4.2.

[64] For idolatry driving the Shekhinah back to "highest heaven" see 3 Enoch 5:1-14; cf. Gen.R. 9.7; Lam.R., Proem 24; Pesiq. Rab Kah. 1.1.

[65] There must surely be an allusion here to a bestiary tradition. In general for Rabbinic interest in bestiaries see b. ʿErub. 100b; "If the Torah had not been given we would have learned modesty from the cat, aversion to robbery from the ant, chastity from the dove and sexual mores from the rooster." On the western Christian bestiary see Baxter, *Bestiaries and their Users.*

APPENDIX A

The Midrash of the Ten Songs (Tg. Cant. 1:1)

The Tg. to Cant 1:1 contains a version of a Midrash—the Midrash of the Ten Songs—that is attested elsewhere in Rabbinic literature. Major sources for it are as follows:

(1) Mekhilta de-Rabbi Ishmael, *Shirta* 1 (ed. Lauterbach, 1:2–7);[1]
(2) Mekhilta de-Rabbi Shimʿon b. Yoḥai (ed. Epstein and Melamed, 71–72);[2]
(3) Midrash ha-Gadol to Exod 15:1 (ed. Margulies, 285–86);[3]
(4) Midrash Leqaḥ Tob to Exod 15:1 (ed. Buber, 91–92);[4]
(5) Yalqut ha-Makhiri to Ps 18:1 (ed. Buber, 103);[5]
(6) Yalqut Shimʿoni, Exod. §242;[6]
(7) Yalqut Shimʿoni, Josh. §20;
(8) Aggadat Shir ha-Shirim (ed. Schechter, 10; ed. Buber, 9);[7]
(9) Saʿadya, Commentary to *Wayyoshaʿ*.[8]

From Table 1 it will become clear that these texts cite in total sixteen biblical songs, though each individual Midrash presents only ten in its definitive list. Within the tradition the Mekhiltas, Midrash ha-Gadol, Leqaḥ Tob, and the Yalquts (1–7 above) form a closely related group, though they differ slightly as to what constitutes the "Song of Solomon." The source here is probably the Mekhilta de-Rabbi Ishmael. The remaining texts all show significant differences from this Mekhilta recension and from each other. Tg. Cant. agrees quite

[1] Jacob Z. Lauterbach, ed., *Mekilta de-Rabbi Ishmael; a critical edition on the basis of the manuscripts and early editions with an English translation, introduction and notes*. 3 vols. (Philadelphia: Jewish Publication Society, 1933–1935). See further Judah Goldin, *The Song at the Sea* (New Haven: Yale University Press, 1971) 68–75.

[2] Jacob N. H. Epstein and Ezra Melamed, eds., *Mekhilta de-Rabi Shimʿon ben Yoḥai* (Jerusalem: Mekitse nirdamim, 1955).

[3] Mordechai Margulies, ed., *Midrash ha-gadol ʿal ḥamishah ḥumshei Torah: Sefer Shemot* (Jerusalem: Mosad ha-Rav Kuk, 1966 or 1967).

[4] Solomon Buber, ed., *Midrash Lekaḥ Tob, ha-mekhuneh Pasikta Zutarta ʿal Ḥamishah Ḥumshei Torah*. 4 vols. (Vilna: Rom, 1880–1884).

[5] Solomon Buber, ed., *Yalkut ha-Makiri* (Berdyczew, 1899). Cf. Judah Z. Spira, ed., *Yalkut ha-Makhiri ʿal Yeshaʿyahu* (Berlin, 1894; repr. Jerusalem, 1964) 37, to Isa 48:20, where the list is presented in the name of *Haggadat Shir ha-Shirim*.

[6] Numerous editions, e.g., Abraham Abele, ed., *Yalkut Shimʿoni: Midrash ʿal Torah, Neviʾim, u-Khetuvim* (New York: Title Publishing, 1944).

[7] Solomon Schechter, ed., *Agadath Shir haShirim* (Cambridge: D. Bell, 1896); Solomon Buber, ed., *Midrash Zuta ʿal Shir ha-Shirim, Rut, Eikhah ve-Kohelet* (Berlin, H. Itzkowski, 1894).

[8] See the text printed by Haggai Ben-Shammai on p. 320 of his article, "New Findings in a Forgotten Manuscript: Samuel b. Hofni's Commentary on *Haʾazinu* and Saʿadya's 'Commentary on the Ten Songs,'" *Qiryat Sefer* 61 (1986–87) 313–32, which is the most important recent discussion of the Midrash of the Ten Songs. Ben-Shammai draws attention to an earlier study by Abraham Epstein, "The Song of Abraham our Father," which first appeared in the periodical *Mimmizraḥ umimmaʿarab* 1 (Vienna, 1894) 85–89 (reprinted in Abraham M. Habermann, ed., *Kitbei Rabbi A. Epstein* [Jerusalem, 1957] 1:251–54 [Hebrew]). See further: Judah Goldin, "This Song," in idem, *Studies in Midrash and Related Literature*, ed. Barry L. Eichler and Jeffrey H. Tigay (Philadelphia: Jewish Publication Society, 1988) 151–61; Menahem M. Kasher, *Torah Shelemah* (Jerusalem: Beit Torah Shelemah, 1927–) 14:289–90; Ginzberg, *Legends* 6:11, n. 59. The list of sources given above is by no means exhaustive: see, e.g., *Midrash We-Hizhir* (Israel M. Freimann, ed., *Ve-hizhir: yesodo hefeṣ ʾaluf* . . . 2 vols. [Leipzig, 1873–80]) 20a-b. Albert E. Harkavy, *Teshubot ha-Geonim* (New York: Menorah, 1959) no. 66 (pp. 30–31) prints a responsum of Hai Gaon in which he was asked what Saʿadya meant by "the Song of Abraham" in his list of the Ten Songs.

closely with Aggadat Shir Ha-Shirim. However, it does not have the problematic "Song of Abraham," replacing it with the "Song of Hannah," which is not found in any other source. And it disagrees with Aggadat Shir ha-Shirim as to what constitutes the "Song of the World to Come." It proposes Isa 30:29, whereas Aggadat Shir ha-Shirim has Isa 42:10. Saᶜadya's version is the most idiosyncratic of all, in that it has two songs, the "Song of Isaiah" and the "Song of Hezekiah," that are not attested anywhere else.

It does not seem possible to draw up a satisfactory tradition history of the variant versions of the Midrash of the Ten Songs. It is probable, however, that the Midrash sometimes circulated in a form that only *named* the songs. In most cases this did not cause problems since the song intended was obvious (e.g., the Song at the Sea, or the Song at the Well). But in some cases (e.g., the Song of David, the Song of Solomon, the Song of the World to Come) the title was ambiguous and was identified by different *darshanim* with different passages of Scripture. In general, external considerations suggest that the versions in Tg. Cant., Aggadat Shir ha-Shirim, and Saᶜadya are late, and that the Mekhilta tradition is earlier. There is abundant evidence to suggest that the Targumist of Canticles knew the Mekhilta de-Rabbi Ishmael (see the *Notes* passim). It is all the more puzzling, therefore, why he changed the Mekhilta's list. This runs from the Song of the First Passover to the Song of the World to Come and would have fitted in very well with the Tg.'s historical schema, which starts with the Exodus from Egypt and ends with the Exodus of the returning exiles in the Messianic Age. It is true that the Targumist manages to work in the Song of the First Passover obliquely by making Isa 30:29 the Song of the World to Come, but it is still puzzling why he chooses to jump chronologically backwards to the creation by beginning with the Song of Adam—a move that appears to have forced him to introduce the anomalous "Song of Hannah."

The tradition of the Ten Songs can be traced back within Rabbinic literature at least to the late fourth or early fifth century, the earliest plausible date for the compilation of the Mekhilta de-Rabbi Ishmael. Origen's *Commentary on Canticles* suggests it originated even earlier. Origen (d. ca. 254) has a list of seven songs, the final one of which is Canticles, which he takes as the marriage-hymn of Christ, the Bridegroom, when he was about to take the Church, his Bride, to himself. The other six songs were sung by the Law and the Prophets to the Bride, "while she was still a little child and had not yet attained maturity."[9] Five of these six songs agree with the Midrash of the Ten Songs (see Table 1). The one anomaly is the Song of Asaph, which is not attested in any version of the Midrash of the Ten Songs. This agreement can hardly be coincidental. There are numerous "songs" in the Bible that could have been chosen: that Origen and the Midrash hit on the same six out of seven by chance is surely implausible. It is more likely that Origen knew a version of the Midrash of the Ten Songs and adapted it for his own Christian purposes. He may have reduced the ten to seven basically for numerological reasons, preferring to stress the idea of perfection (one of the numerological associations of seven) rather than completeness (one of the numerological associations of ten).

[9] Origen, *Commentary on Canticles*, Prologue 4. Translated and edited by Luc Brésard and Henri Crouzel, with the collaboration of Maurice Borret. SC 375-376 (Paris: Cerf, 1991–92) 1:146–57. English translation by R. P. Lawson, *Origen: The Song of Songs, Commentary and Homilies*. Ancient Christian Writers 26. (Westminster, Md.: Newman, 1957) 46–52.

Table 1: The Midrash of the Ten Songs

	Tg. Cant.	MRI	MRashbi	MHG	LTov	YM Ps 18	YS Exod.	YS Josh.	Ag.Shir	Sa'adya	Origen
(1) Song of Adam	(1) Ps 92:1								(1) [Ps 92:1]		
(2) Song of Abraham									(2) [Gen 14:22]	(1) Gen 14:22	
(3) Song of the First Passover		(1) Isa 30:29	(1) Isa 30:29	(1) Isa 30:29	(1) Isa 30:29	(1) Isa 30:29	(1) Isa 30:29	(1) Isa 30:29			
(4) Song at the Sea	(2) Exod 15:1	(2) Exod 15:1	(2) Exod 15:1	(2) Exod 15:2	(2) Exod 15:1	(2) Exod 15:1	(2) Exod 15:1	(2) Exod 15:1	(3) [Exod 15:1]	(2) Exod 15:1	(1) Exod 15:1
(5) Song at the Well	(3) Num 21:17	(3) Num 21:17	(3) Num 21:17	(3) Num 21:17	(3) Num 21:17	(3) Num 21:17	(3) Num 21:17	(3) Num 21:17	(4) [Num 21:17]	(3) [Num 21:17]	(2) Num 21:17
(6) Song of Moses	(4) Deut 32:1	(4) Deut 31:24	(4) Deut 31:30	(4) Deut 31:30	(4) Deut 32:1	(4) Deut 31:24	(4) Deut 31:24	(4) Deut 31:24	(5) Deut 32:1	(4) Deut 32:1	(3) Deut 32:1
(7) Song of Joshua	(5) Josh 10:12	(5) Josh 10:12	(5) Josh 10:12	(5) Josh 10:12	(5) Josh 10:12	(5) Josh 10:12	(5) Josh 10:12	(5) Josh 10:12	(6) [Josh 10:12]		
(8) Song of Deborah and Barak	(6) Judg 5:1	(6) Judg 5:1	(6) Judg 5:1	(6) Judg 5:1	(6) Judg 5:1	(6) Judg 5:1	(6) Judg 5:1	(6) Judg 5:1	(7) [Judg 5:1]	(5) Judg 5:1	(4) Judg 5:1
(9) Song of Hannah	(7) 1 Sam 2:1										
(10) Song of David	(8) 2 Sam 22:1	(7) 2 Sam 22:1	(7) 2 Sam 22:1	(7) 2 Sam 22:1	(7) 2 Sam 22:1	(7) Ps 18:1 = 2 Sam 22:1	(7) Ps 18:1 = 2 Sam 22:1	(8) 2 Sam 22:1	(8) [2 Sam 22:1]	(6) 2 Sam 22:1	(5) 2 Sam 22:1

Table 1: The Midrash of the Ten Songs

(11) Song of Asaph											(6) 1 Chr 16:1 = Ps 105:1ff
(12) Song of Solomon	(9) Canticles	(8) Ps 30:1	(8) Ps 30:1	(8) Ps 30:1 Or: Canticles	(8) Ps 30:1	(8) Ps 30:1	(8) 1 Kgs 8:12/ 2 Chr 6:1	(8) 1 Kgs 8:12/ 2 Chr 6:1	(9) Canticles	(7) Canticles	(7) Canticles
(13) Song of Jehoshaphat		(9) 2 Chr 20:21	(9) 2 Chr 20:21	(9) 2 Chr 20:21	(9) 2 Chr 20:21	(9) 2 Chr 20:21	(9) 2 Chr 20:21	(9) 2 Chr 20 :21			
(14) Song of Isaiah										(8) Isa 5:1	
(15) Song of Hezekiah										(9) Isa 38:9	
(16) Song of the World to Come	(10) Isa 30:29 (= 3 above)	(10) Isa 42:10 + Ps 149:1	(10) Isa 42:10 + Ps 149:1	(10) Isa 42:10 + Ps 149:1	(10) Isa 42:10	(10) Isa 42:10 + Isa 48:20	(10) Isa 42:10 + Ps 149:1	(10) Ps 149:1	(10) Isa 42:10	(10) Isa 26:1	

Key:
Tg. Cant = Targum Canticles
MRI = Mekhilta de-Rabbi Ishmael
MRashbi = Mekhilta de-Rabbi Shimʿon b. Yoḥai
MHG = Midrash ha-Gadol
LTov = Leqaḥ Tob
YM = Yalqut ha-Makhiri
YS = Yalqut Shimʿoni
Ag.Shir = Aggadat Shir ha-Shirim
Saʿadya = Saʿadya's Commentary on *Wayyoshaʿ*
Origen = Origen's Commentary on Canticles
[ ] indicates that the source uses only a name for the song (e.g., Song of David) but does not identify the song precisely by a quotation.

APPENDIX B

The Tribes of Israel: Their Precious Stones and Star Signs (Tg. Cant. 5:14)

Tg. 5:14, which contains a list of twelve gemstones inscribed with the names of the twelve tribes of Israel, presents the most complex textual problem in the whole of Tg. Cant. This list is clearly derived from Exod 28:15-21, though there the gems are located on the high priest's "breastplate" *(ḥoshen mishpat),* whereas here, oddly, they are on the plate *(ṣiṣ)* fastened to his turban or "holy crown" (Tg. to 5:14, *Note* 50).

The list, which in the light of Exod.R. 38.9 and Leqaḥ Tob to Exodus 28[1] should be taken as running from "Along with the three fathers of the world" to "*yashefeh*/*ʾappantor,*" appears to be a secondary insertion. The Tg. originally read: "The twelve tribes of His servant Jacob, displayed on the gold plate of the holy crown, engraved upon twelve gems, resemble the twelve constellations, shining like a lantern, resplendent in their deeds as elephant-ivory, and glittering like sapphires." The list of the inscribed gems was then inserted after "upon twelve gems," with the result that *dmyyn* was left awkwardly hanging in the air, far removed from its antecedent "the twelve tribes." When the list was inserted *dmyyn* should, for the sake of clarity, have been modified to *wʾynwn dmyyn.*

The mss. of Tg. Cant. offer basically two recensions of the list—one found in Yemenite mss. (= Yem.), and the other in mss. of Western provenance (= West.). These recensions differ both in the names they offer for the gemstones and in the order in which they list the tribes.

The Yemenite recension originally contained a list of stones identical (with the slight exception of *barqan* for *bareqet*) to that found in the Hebrew text of Exod 28:17-20. This list has suffered contamination from Western readings, resulting sometimes in the displacement of the original Yem. reading (e.g., *ʾḥmr* for *ʾwdm*), sometimes in conflated readings, and sometimes in the insertion of the West. readings in the margins and between the lines (see Fontela's and Melamed's *Apparatus*).[2] The West. recension has a list of contemporary names, i.e., contemporary with the author. Most of the names seem to be Arabic in origin or in form. This list implicitly contains a set of identifications for the stones on the high priest's breastplate in Exod 28:17-20. It can be compared with other such lists: e.g., Onq., FT, Ps-J, Neof., Samaritan Tg., Peshitta, Saʿadya, Leqaḥ Tob and LXX to Exod 28:17-20; Josephus, *Ant.* 3.168; *BJ* 5.234; Tg. Jon. and LXX to Ezek 28:13; Exod.R. 38.8; and Rev 21:19-20. The West. equivalents do not agree with any other set of identifications, save for that in Leqaḥ Tob, which is almost certainly based on Tg. Cant.

The names of the tribes in both recensions follow the patronymic listing of the tribes (cf. Gen 29-30; 35:23-26; 46:8-25; 49:3-27; Exod 1:2-4; Deut 27:12-14; Ezek 48:31-35; 1 Chr 2:2), rather than the geographic, which drops Levi as having no tribal territory but brings the number back up to twelve by replacing Joseph by his two sons Ephraim and

[1] Solomon Buber, ed., *Midrash Lekaḥ Tob, ha-mekhuneh Pasikta Zutarta ʿal Ḥamishah Ḥumshei Torah.* 4 vols. (Vilna: Rom, [1880–84]) 188.

[2] Carlos Alonso Fontela, *El Targum al Cantar de los Cantares (Edición Crítica)* Madrid: Editorial de la Universidad Complutense de Madrid, 1987; Raphael H. Melamed, *The Targum to Canticles according to six Yemen MSS, compared with the "Textus Receptus" (Ed. de Lagarde).* (Philadelphia: Dropsie College, 1921).

Manasseh (cf. Num 1:5-15; 2:3-31; 7:12-83; 13:4-15; 26:5-51; Joshua 13–19; 21:4-7, 9-39). However, the way in which the two recensions list the names is quite different. Yem. puts them in the chronological order of their birth, as implied by the narrative in Genesis 29–30 (save that Issachar and Naphtali have, probably accidentally, changed places): Reuben, Simeon, Levi, Judah, Dan, Issachar, Gad, Asher, Naphtali, Zebulun, Joseph, Benjamin. This agrees with Ps-J to Exod 28:17-20 and 39:10-13, though Ps-J has Issachar and Naphtali in their correct places. This arrangement was known to Josephus, who states that the names of the tribes were listed on the high priest's breastplate "according to the order in which each of them was born" (*Ant.* 3.169), though he himself knows also a different principle of ordering the tribes, viz., by mothers (*Ant.* 1.344; 2.177-83). West., by way of contrast, classifies by mothers in the order: (a) sons of Leah (Reuben, Simeon, Levi, Judah, Issachar, Zebulun); (b) sons of Bilhah, Rachel's handmaid (Dan, Naphtali); (c) sons of Zilpah, Leah's handmaid (Gad, Asher); (d) sons of Rachel (Joseph, Benjamin). This follows precisely the order in Jub. 34:20; LAB 26:10-11 (cf. 8:11-14); Testaments of the Twelve Patriarchs; Neof. and FT to Exod 28:17-20; Neof. to Exod 39:10-13; Exod.R. 38.8-9; Num.R. 2.7 (though Gad and Naphtali are reversed). This listing is not found anywhere in the biblical text, though it is very close to the order of the names in Exod 1:1-5, save that, perhaps more logi-cally, it puts Benjamin at the end (as the youngest and as Joseph's full brother), rather than eighth, as in the biblical text. Grouping by mothers is attested already in the Bible (e.g., Gen 35:22-26) and seems to have been standard in post-biblical tradition. However, the order in which the mothers were listed varies: the normative list has the rather surprising chiastic arrangement wife—handmaid—handmaid—wife. Other arrangements list the two wives before the two handmaids, or wife + her handmaid, wife + her handmaid (cf. Jub. 32:22; 11QT 24.10-16; Josephus, *Ant.* 2.177-83; LAB 8:6; 25:4; 25:9-13; Rev 7:5-8).

See further Christopher R. Smith, "The Portrayal of the Church as the New Israel in the Names and Order of the Tribes in Revelation 7.5-8," *JSNT* 39 (1990) 111–18; Richard Bauckham, "The List of the Tribes in Revelation Again," *JSNT* 42 (1991) 99–115.

It seems to follow from this analysis that three stages in the evolution of the text of Tg. Cant. to 5:14 can be distinguished. Stage one is represented by the current text minus the list of gems. Into this text was inserted at stage two a preexisting list of the stones on the high priest's breastplate. This list was then replaced for some obscure reason at stage three by an alternative list that gave different names for the gems and ordered their corresponding tribes according to a different principle of arrangement. As Saul Lieberman points out, there was considerable interest in the identification of the gems on the high priest's breastplate. "Translations of the names of the stones, both oral and written, existed among the Jews until late mediaeval times. Many glossaries containing such translations were discovered in various countries."[3] An interesting list of Greek equivalents, which is independent of the LXX (but may represent the lost Aquila), has been preserved in Exod.R. 38.8. It should be noted that ms. J of our Targum has a series of interlinear glosses that offer six alternative identifications not found in any other Yem. or West. mss.[4] These glosses, some of which also seem to be Arabic in form, constitute, in effect, a third recension of the list of gemstones. It is a

[3] *Greek in Jewish Palestine: Studies in the Life and Manners of Jewish Palestine in the II–IV Centuries C. E.* (New York: Jewish Theological Seminary, 1942) 56.

[4] See Fontela, *El Targum al Cantar de los Cantares* 28, and his *Apparatus*.

moot point whether Yem. or West. represents stage two. It is at first sight tempting to suppose that the Yem. recension, which has the biblical gem names, is older at this point and that the West. recension involves a later attempt to identify the stones by supplying contemporary equivalents. But it is just as possible that the development went the other way: Yem. is a "biblicizing" of the West. text. Certainly the West. text is in general older than the Yem.

The identification of the precious stones has been a matter of fierce debate. The NRSV (Exod 28:17-20) suggests the following equivalents for the biblical names: (1) *ʾodem* = carnelian, (2) *pitedah* = chrysolite, (3) *barqan* = MT *bareqet* = emerald, (4) *nofekh* = turquoise, (5) *sappir* = sapphire, (6) *yahalom* = moonstone, (7) *leshem* = jacinth, (8) *shebo* = agate, (9) *ʾaḥlamah* = amethyst, (10) *tarshish* = beryl, (11) *shoham* = onyx, (12) *yashefeh* = jasper. The gem names on the West. list are mostly Arabic in origin or in form (see Melamed 395, and Fontela 28). The following are possible equivalents: (1) *ʾaḥmar*: obviously a red stone (cf. Heb. *ʾodem*), possibly "ruby"; (2) *ʿaqiq* = carnelian; see *EI*² 1:336a sub *ʿakik*; (3) *barqan zaʿafaran*: the second element here is obviously equivalent to the Arabic *zaʿfaran*, "saffron." If *barqan* denotes some sort of emerald, then we may have a reference to *chrysoberyl*, "beryl with a tinge of gold color" (*LSJ* 2010a); (4) *nofekh koḥali*: the second element here is clearly adjectival, "like *koḥl*." *Kuḥli* is used in Arabic to denote a dark blue color. This would fit *nofekh* as turquoise; hence "dark turquoise" (see *EI*² 5:356a, sub *al-Kuḥl*); (5) *ʾizmargad* (v. l. *ʾizmurad*): clearly ultimately derived from the Greek *smaragdos, zmaragdos,* which denotes "several green stones, including the *emerald*" (*LSJ* 1619a); Jast. 38a; cf. Arabic *zumurrud,* "emerald"; (6) *guhar*: clearly related to Arabic *jauhar.* This, however, is normally used generically for a "jewel" or "gem," whereas *guhar* here must be a specific type of gem, perhaps "pearl," or "diamond" (cf. *EI*² *Supplement*, 250–62, sub *d̲jawhar*); (7) *birelaʾ* (v. l. *bilʾar*) = Greek *berullos,* "beryl"; Arabic *billaur* (= "rock crystal": *EI*² 1:1220b, sub *billawr*); (8) *ʾaspor* (v. l. *ʾaspir*) = sapphire; related to Hebrew *sappir*; Greek *sappheiros*; Arabic *asfar;* (9) *tabʾag* = Greek *topazos,* "topaz" or "chrysolite"; cf. Arabic *taufaj/taubaj*; (10) *piruzag* = turquoise; Arabic *firuzaj* (*EI*² 2:927a, sub *firuzad̲j*); (11) *meribag*: the identification is completely uncertain; there are several alternative spellings in the mss. *(mdb'g*; *mrysg*; *myrwsg)*; (12) *ʾappantor* (read *ʾappantir*): a variant spelling of *pantiri* (Jast. 1191a). This is obviously derived from the Greek *panther* (which could, it seems, be used for a number of different big cats), and presumably denotes a spotted or striped stone of some sort; cf. the Latin *pantherinus* (Pliny, *NH* 35, 138). Possibly this is some form of jasper: note it stands against *yashefeh* = jasper in the Hebrew list.

See further Wilhelm Bacher, "Une ancienne liste des noms grecs des pierres précieuses relatées dans Exode XXVIII, 17-20," *REJ* 29 (1894) 79–90; Maurice Simon, "On Josephus, *Wars*, V,5,7," *JQR* 13 (1901) 547–48; George St. Clair, "Israel in Camp: A Study," *JTS* 8 (1907) 185–217; Max Bauer, *Edelsteinkunde* (3rd ed. Leipzig: Tauchnitz, 1932); Saul Lieberman, *Greek in Jewish Palestine* 56–59; S. von Gliszczynski, "Versuch einer Identifizierung der Edelsteine im Amtsschild des jüdischen Hohenpriesters auf Grund kritischer und ästhetischer Vergleichsmomente," *Forschungen und Fortschritte* (Berlin) 21–23 (1947) 234–38; Heinrich Quiring, "Die Edelsteine im Schild des jüdischen Hohenpriesters," *Sudhoffs Archiv für Geschichte der Medizin und Naturwissenschaft* 38 (1954) 198–213; J. S. Harris, "The Stones of the High Priest's Breastplate," *Annual of the Leeds University Oriental Society* 5 (1963–65) 40–58 (see also 59–62, J. McDonald on the Samaritan traditions); Walther Zimmerli, *Ezechiel.* Biblischer Kommentar Altes Testament (Neukirchen-Vluyn: Neukirchner Verlag, 1969) 673–74; Una Jart, "The Precious Stones in the Revelation of St. John xxi.18-21," *Studia Theo-*

logica 24 (1970) 150-81; Thomas F. Glasson, "The Order of the Jewels in Rev xxi.19-20: A Theory Eliminated," *JTS* 26 (1975) 95–100; Reynold A. Higgins, *Greek and Roman Jewellery* (2nd ed. Berkeley and Los Angeles: University of California Press, 1980), especially 35–39; William J. Reader, "The Twelve Stones of Revelation 21:19-20," *JBL* 100 (1981) 433–47; Roland Bergmeier, "Jerusalem, die hochgebaute Stadt," *ZNW* 75 (1984) 86–106; Jonathan A. Draper, "The Twelve Apostles as Foundation Stones of the Heavenly Jerusalem and the Foundation of the Qumran Community," *Neotestamentica* 22 (1988) 41–64; Ludwig Koehler and Walter Baumgartner, *The Hebrew and Aramaic Lexicon of the Old Testament*. Translated and edited by M. E. J. Richardson, 5 vols. (Leiden: Brill, 1994–2000) under the individual words.

Tg. states that the twelve tribes "resemble the twelve constellations, shining like a lantern, resplendent in their deeds as elephant-ivory, and glittering like sapphires." The wording is notably careful: the primary thought is that the tribes through their good deeds shine like the stars. But there is probably also another idea being hinted at, viz., that each tribe corresponds to one of the signs of the zodiac. However, unlike the case of the twelve gemstones, Tg. has not attempted to spell out the correlations between the tribes and star signs. There are several such lists extant in Jewish tradition: e.g., Yalqut Shimʿoni Exod. §418, speaking of the Israelite camp in the wilderness, locates Judah, Issachar, and Zebulun on the east side and correlates them respectively with Aries, Taurus, and Gemini; Reuben, Simeon, and Gad on the south side are correlated with Cancer, Leo, and Virgo; Ephraim, Manasseh, and Benjamin on the west side are correlated with Libra, Scorpio, and Saggitarius; Dan, Asher, and Naphtali on the north side are correlated with Capricorn, Aquarius, and Pisces. This will not map precisely onto the Tg.'s list of tribes, since it omits Levi and replaces Joseph by Ephraim and Manasseh, but it is probable that Tg. knew such a list. It is hard to say how old this idea is. It may be hinted at in b. Ber. 32b, and could possibly lie behind the representation of the zodiac in synagogue floor mosaics (Beth Alpha and Hammath Tiberias). But the extant literary attestations of it are late.

On Rabbinic interest in astrology see Kocku von Stuckrad, *Das Ringen um die Astrologie* (Berlin and New York: Walter de Gruyter, 2000).

INDEX OF SCRIPTURAL AND RABBINIC PASSAGES

HEBREW BIBLE

INDEX OF MODERN AUTHORS

Shirman, Ch., 193
Silber, E., 147, 200
Simon, M., 35, 212
Singer, S., 94, 78, 129, 186
Smith, C. R., 211
Smolar, L., 20, 38
Sperber, A., 4, 29
Stec, D. M., 2, 3
Stemberger, G., 35, 36
Stuckrad, K. von, 213
Sysling, H., 195

Tal, A., 8, 11
Tishby, I., 190
Tournay, R., 51

Ulmer, R., 101
Ulrich, E., 35
Urbach, E. E., 21, 38, 115, 175, 181

Van der Heide, A., 2, 4
Vermes, G., 23, 55, 122, 135, 177, 198
Vilnay, Z., 127, 194, 195

Walfish, B. D., 45
Walton, B., 3
Weitzman, M. P., 11
Wither, G., 50
Witte, J., 49

Xella, P., 196

Zetterholm, K., 132, 180
Zimmerli, W., 212
Zohary, M., 183

GENERAL INDEX